Images of Ambiente

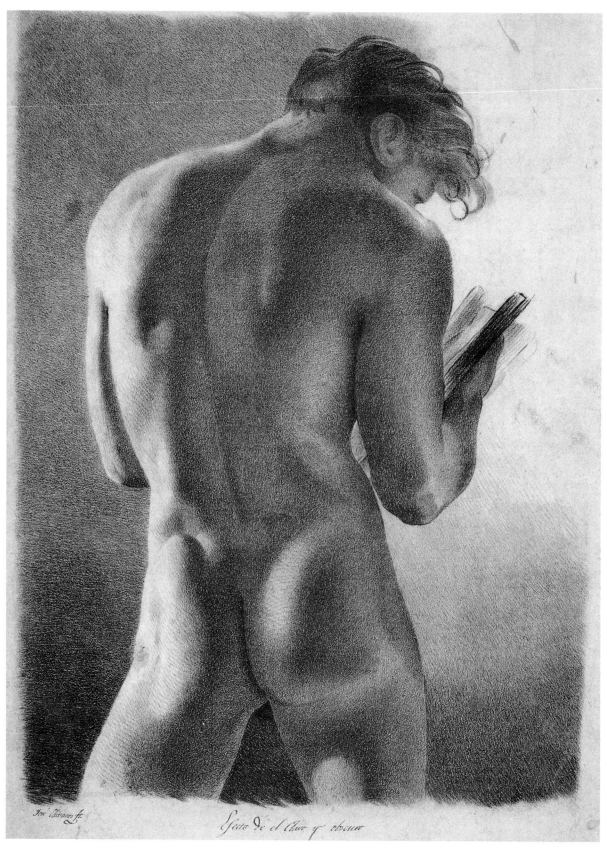

Efecto de el Claro y obscuro

José Olivares, *Estudio de claro y obscuro* (1831)

Images of Ambiente

Homotextuality and Latin American Art, 1810–Today

Rudi C. Bleys

CONTINUUM
London and New York

à Jacques, c/c . . .

Continuum
Wellington House, 125 Strand, London WC2R 0BB
370 Lexington Avenue, New York, NY 10017–6503

First published 2000
© Rudi C. Bleys 2000

British Library Cataloguing-in-Publication Data
A catalogue record for this book is available from the British Library.

ISBN   0-8264-4722-8 (hardback)
            0-8264-4723-6 (paperback)

Library of Congress Cataloging-in-Publication Data
Bleys, Rudi C.
      Images of ambiente: homotextuality [sic] and Latin American art, 1810–today / Rudi C. Bleys.
         p. cm.
      Includes bibliographical references and index.
      ISBN 0-8264-4722-8 (hb) — ISBN 0-8264-4723-6 (pbk)
         1. Homosexuality in art. 2. Lesbianism in art. 3. Art, Latin American. 4. Art, modern—19th century—Latin America. 5. Art, modern—20th century—Latin America. I. Title.

   N8217.H67 B58 2000
   704'.0664'098—dc21

                                                                    99-086252

Designed by Ben Cracknell Studios

Printed and bound in Great Britain

Contents

Figures

Plates

Acknowledgements

The preparation and research for *Images of Ambiente* has been a complex and, at times, even difficult endeavour. Only very few publications on the topic exist, so I had to gather most information at first hand. At times, artists, curators and museum staff were reluctant to help when I informed them about the focus of my book being homosexuality. In a few instances, artists refused to cooperate or objected to the risk of ghettoization. Obtaining permission to include illustrations of their work even proved impossible in one or two cases.

But writing this book has proved to be a redeeming and challenging experience as well. Many artists or artists' estates welcomed me with open arms and I would like to thank them in the first place: Laura Aguilar, Ben-Hur Baz Viaud, José Luis Cortés, Federico Correa, Ismael Costa Dias, Tony de Carlo, Daniel Fernández (Jaime Bellechasse), Frank Franca, Susana Herrero Kunhardt, Andy Glasgow (Alberto Valderrama), Maria Elena González, Max Carlos Martínez, Linda Matalón, Marcia Ochoa, Maria de Mater O'Neill, Reyes Meléndez, Néstor Millán, Paul Polubinskas (Teddy Sandoval), Mario Patiño, René Peña, Geraldo Porto, Ernesto Pujol, Enrique Renta, Miguel Angel Reyes, Abnel Rodriguez, Paulo Sayeg, Adir Sodré, Miguel Ventura and Edilson Viriato.

Informants in the USA have shared most valuable information with me: in New York Visual Aids, Héctor Santiago and Clara Morera, both exiled Cubans, and Sandra Levinson (Center for Cuban Studies); in Washington DC José Quiroga; in San Francisco Luis de la Garza (Mexican Museum), Yvonne Yarbro-Bejarano (Stanford University) and Biron.

In Los Angeles, precious data were provided by James Green and Linda Vallejo (Las Americas Gallery). Walter Williams and Jim Kepner welcomed me at the University of Southern California Center for Scholars in Residence, Los Angeles, while John O'Brien and Mischa Schutt assisted me at the International Gay and Lesbian Archives. Thanks also to Durk Dehner and Valentine Hooven II, for providing valuable information at the Tom of Finland Foundation.

Many thanks to the numerous galleries and auction houses that provided me with useful information, photographs and/or slides: Andrea Rosen Gallery, Art in General, Elga Wimmer Gallery, Jack Shainman Gallery, Mary-Ann Martin Gallery, Nancy Hoffman Gallery, Robert Miller Gallery, Sotheby's, and Throckmorton Fine Art, all in New York. In San Francisco, I would like to thank Paule Anglim Gallery, as well as Polanco Gallery.

In Puerto Rico, I owe gratitude to the Museo de Arte e Historia in San Juan and the Museo de Historia, Antropologia y Arte de Puerto Rico, Universidad de Puerto Rico, Rio Piedras.

In Cuba, valuable assistance was given to me by the Fundación Ludwig in Havana, while I obtained valuable information from Sylvia Blanca of the Cuban Embassy in Belgium.

In Mexico, expressions of thanks must go also to the Museo Nacional de Arte, the Instituto Nacional de Bellas Artes, and the Instituto Nacional de Antropología e Historia, the Museo de Arte Moderno, Galería Arvíl, Galería OMR, and Galería Praxis, all located in Mexico City. I especially would like to thank Cecilia Gutiérrez of the Instituto de Investigaciones Estéticas (UNAM), as well as Alan Stark Dickinson, Margareth Hudak, Claudia Irán Jasso Apango and Kátia Romero Llanes of the Centro Nacional de las Artes. Many thanks also to Juan Molina.

In São Paulo, Brazil, I was given useful information and assistance by the Museu de Arte Moderna, the MAC/USP, Gustavo Marx of the Instituto de Estudos Brasileiros (USP), and Ricardo Resende of the Projeto Leonilson, while I owe gratitude also to Pedro Xexéo of the Museu Nacional de Belas Artes in Rio de Janeiro. Additional information was given to me by the Museu de Arte Contemporânea José Pancetti in Campinas. Many thanks also to Roberto Teixeira Leite and to the photographers Raúl Lima and Romulo Fialdini.

Every effort has been made to trace all copyright holders and obtain permissions. The editor and publishers sincerely apologize for any inadvertent errors or omissions and will be happy to correct them in any future editions.

Back in Europe, I want to thank my patient and considerate editors at Cassell/Continuum, then Cherry Smyth and Christie's Images, all in London. Thanks also to the Stedelijk Museum in Amsterdam, and the Center for the Arts Witte de With in Rotterdam. Many thanks, finally, to Galerie Xavier Hufkens in Brussels and Galerie Geukens and De Vil in Knokke.

On the homefront, I would like to express my gratitude to my family, as well as to Zach, Joshua, Daniel, Paul and Mark. My part-time colleagues of the Aidsteam in Antwerp have been most understanding when I was finishing the manuscript.

Three dear friends deserve special mention, finally. In New York, honours go to Mauricio Laffitte-Soler, who not only was my guide and mediator, but proved equally devoted to this project himself. I would like to dedicate Chapter 6 especially to him as an acknowledgement of both his expertise regarding Puerto Rican, Cuban, Cuban American and *Nuyorican* art and his assistance and genuine friendship.

In Mexico, I was offered not only hospitality but inspiring friendship by Gabriel Gálvez Prado, who made me love his country even more than I already did.

I have most dearly appreciated the support, finally, of my friend Jacques, to whom I dedicate this book for reasons only he can fully understand.

Abbreviations

Note on conventions used in this text: English translations appear as notes in the margin.

CHAPTER ONE

Introduction

*Aún cuando la sensualidad esté un poco prohibida en
la historia del arte mexicana, el cuerpo tiene todos esos
códigos sin llegar a ser muy reiterativo.**
  Roberto Cortázar

Da adversidade vivemos . . .[†]
  Hélio Oiticica

A positive outcome of today's debate, in the wake of 'queer' theory and politics, on multiculturalism within the gay and lesbian community is its stimulating effect on new historical and anthropological studies of 'gay' experience through time and across the world. The debate between social constructionists and essentialists within the field of gay and lesbian studies has given rise to an awareness of both change and continuity, universality and idiosyncrasy when comparing (homo)sexual experience through time and across the globe.

The mapping-out of the social and cultural diversity of homosexual experience can profit from a critical 'reading' of its *artistic* representations also, and this *beyond* the geographic boundaries of the northern hemisphere. New, comparative studies are to be written, accordingly, about homoeroticism, 'gay sensibility' – and, as its mirror image, homophobia – in literature, paintings, sculpture, photography, film and video in the past and present of other continents of the world. Central to such an approach is the question if and to what extent different social and cultural contexts provoke divergent and alternative expressions of sexual and gender difference in the arts. We must ask also how such artworks can be deconstructed by means of historical reconstruction and biographical contextualization, by hermeneutic reading or semiotic analysis.

*'Although sensuality is somewhat taboo in the history of Mexican art, the body does carry all of its codes without being very faithful.'

[†]'Opposition is our life.'

I conceive of this study as an interpretation of 'homotextuality' in nineteenth- and twentieth-century Latin American art. This concept is more comprehensive than 'homosexuality', 'gay/lesbian identity' or 'homoeroticism' and allows us to trace the slow genealogy of a modern-style 'gay' and 'lesbian' identity, alongside postmodern 'queer' discursivity in Latin American society. Being both 'Western' and 'non-Western' at the same time, the hybrid culture of Latin America provides an exciting framework not only for studying the interaction between social realities and artistic creativity, but also for analysing the perennial quest for a 'Latin American' identity between the dialectical poles of cultural idiosyncrasy and modernization, between the mimesis of European and North American examples and the emphasis of 'Latino/a' alterity. How this is reflected in a search for homosexual expression in the visual arts and how the Latin American context defines the artists' images of a gay *ambiente* is central to the focus of this book. It may contribute, I hope, not only to the historical and cross-cultural study of gay and lesbian experience, but also to some wider issues of Latin American social and cultural history.

Socio-cultural context: negotiating Latin American 'otherness'

The interpretation of homoeroticism and gay sensibility in Latin American art calls for a heuristic framework acknowledging the continent's social and cultural complexity. The mere insertion of Anglo-American or European vocabulary would be inadequate because of the coexistence of various registers of sexual ontology, of more than one definition of gender variety and orthodoxy. The 'modernization' of homosexual identity may well have become visible in Latin America and a gay *ambiente* can nowadays be seen in the metropolises across the continent. But underneath this evolution one can detect more traditional or alternative sex/gender systems that are different from and often persist in a dialectical relationship with a modern, Western one.

Studying 'gay art' in Latin America, therefore, is an even more complex endeavour than it already is elsewhere. Nelly Richard's comment on the risks of 'disinsertion' and 'fetishization' applies equally to the definition and location of a trope of homotextuality in the art of Latin Americans. Disinsertion, or the decontextualized transplant of Eurocentric categories and concepts, of an Anglo-European vocabulary of sexual roles and identities to Latin America, would violate the continent's permanent stagings of simultaneous and partially overlapping sexual cultures, practices and identities. Fetishization, similarly, would imply unsound adoption of those Anglo-European categories at the cost of adequate understanding of the individual artist's creative universe.[1]

Along with a strategy that recognizes the idiosyncrasy of Latin American sexual culture goes a more wide-reaching perspective on the alterity or 'otherness' of Latin American art in general, yet without falling into the traps of exoticism and stereotypical projection that characterized historiography and criticism of Latin American art for many decades. Rather than focusing on the static, immanent and folkloric, art history ought to take into account the multiplicity and changeability of Latin America's artistic production, and presumed timeless narratives of mystery, magic realism, colourfulness and sensuality must be replaced by more precise, multifaceted descriptions of the continent's divergent aesthetic languages and vocabularies. If Latin America runs the risk of becoming a token for decentralizing, 'multicultural' discourses in the art world's centre, then it should be clear also that this results partly from the continent's actual postmodern outlook, from the synchronicity of 'tradition' and 'modernity' along with discursive reflection on many levels about this very phenomenon. Nestor Canclini calls this 'multitemporal heterogeneity' and emphasizes how this in itself must not become a signifier of Latin American alterity. Social and cultural studies of Latin America should not only lay bare the richness of 'incomplete modernization', but should encourage scholars and critics of cultures elsewhere to question *le gran récit* of linear modernization as such.[2]

The *Gleichzeitigkeit des Ungleichzeitige* – the simultaneous coexistence of distinct historically rooted aesthetics – already made Latin American art postmodern *avant la lettre* and calls for a close look not only at recent artistic production, but also at its antecedents from, roughly, the era of newly gained political independence (the years from 1810 until 1830). 'Negotiation', in fact, between cultural models from the centre and alternative ones from the periphery has been a dynamic of innovation and creativity ever since the decolonization of the continent. The art of the Latin American élites showed greater affinity with that of their European cultural mentors than with the 'folkloric' expressions of the New World's popular classes. Modernity in the arts, as initiated by the founding of national academies, was a mere 'simulacrum of an élite' that 'acted as if [it was] creating national cultures, while in fact [it was] creating élite cultures'.[3]

Art became a vehicle predominantly for *social distinction* (a term used by the sociologist Pierre Bourdieu) and was largely based on the copying of European models. But, whereas this has long prompted art historians to discard it as largely 'mimetic', it is important to reveal the hidden codes of appropriation that made Latin American art distinct, at the same time, from the exemplary Old World. Was there not already a moment of rebellion in favouring France, rather than Spain or Portugal, as the inspiring cultural signifier for most newly independent nations of Latin America? And didn't the adoption of French and Italian art education reveal an incipient *bricolage* from the earliest stages of independence, despite most of the continent's Iberian heritage? Harbouring influences from across the world, Latin America became a distinctly eclectic territory, especially towards the end of the nineteenth century and the early twentieth century, when not only France but other countries too were explored for new visual languages and a proliferation of styles was reinforced by the collective effort of new waves of immigrants.

Art history's closet redefined

Latin American art history has addressed issues of national and cultural identity largely at the cost of other themes. New and valuable studies are being published nowadays on class, gender and also sexuality. Yet, the question of homoeroticism, gay identity and gay sensibility strangely lags behind. The gap reflects a more general situation within the disciplines of art history and criticism everywhere, which are largely homophobic in their disproportionate focus on the artwork's formal qualities.[4] Or, as Catherine Lord puts it, 'the luxury of believing that the art is always more important than the artist'.[5] The gradual inclusion of questions regarding sexual identity is the outcome of a slow process towards 'contextualization' on the level of both artistic production and criticism. 'Social' issues have been addressed since the 1960s, when the formal innovations of Modernism resulted in a new politics of the arts. Sexuality and gender gained prominence as themes of artistic production and topics of aesthetic debate. Art history came closer to visual studies and cultural studies, focusing on 'the complex relations of cultural artifacts to ideology, reception, and to political, cultural and psychosexual formations'.[6]

Yet, the issue of 'gay art' remained underexposed even in the 1970s, when some artists profiled themselves as such in the wake of Gay Liberation. The realm of Body and Performance Art also remained predominantly straight, particularly in press coverage and academic studies commonly neglecting its gay and lesbian expressions.[7] Even today's publications on 'erotic art' remain silent on gay and lesbian imagery, while nevertheless including fetishism or S/M. Their focus frequently remains fixed on female nudity, orgasmic pleasure and the consolidation of a straight male gaze.[8]

Only recently have art historians paid more attention to the sexual and gender politics of art, or, as it was phrased by the curators of 'Féminin/Masculin' (Centre Georges Pompidou, Paris, 1995), 'le sexe de l'art' (the gender of art). Such an investigation targets how twentieth-century art destabilizes the biological, anatomical and cultural fates traditionally attached to sexuality.[9] In this way, an opening has been made towards a more comprehensive study of the interaction between artistic and symbolic production and the social and cultural construction of sexuality and gender.

Still, art history's efforts remain uneven, as homosexuality is often addressed only reluctantly, as if the connection would be an improbable one. 'The homoerotic content', says Dynes, '[while] obscured by generations of prudery and obfuscation, still eludes recognition'.[10] The disclosure of gay content or biography, suggests a critic, lags behind not least because 'art history, in its heterosexual drag, does its best to marginalize gay and lesbian experience'.[11] Critics often conspire with artists in maintaining the closet by abstracting from personal biography or by strategic considerations. The disclosure of an artist's sexual identity may threaten his or her career, pigeonhole the work, diminish its market potential and value.

A more legitimate position is taken by artists who refuse to adopt presumably static categorizations of sexual identity, as well as by critics and historians who rightly claim that the concept of 'gay' or 'queer identity' cannot be applied indiscriminately to artists in societies that are structured differently on the level of sexual roles and identities. The position remains valid even when their biographies show or showed evidence of homosexual tendencies. Claiming that an artist's oeuvre must be labelled 'gay' or 'queer' merely on the basis of biographical fact is fairly irrelevant to this book when the artist has in no way addressed sexual identity, gender politics or homoeroticism.

Let there be no misunderstanding, as I myself plea for openness and honesty regarding one's own identity. In fact, I subscribe to the position of Lawrence Mass, who claims 'that it is important to be affirmative rather than defensive about one's minority status with regard to one's art. Why', he wonders, 'should the affirmation of an artist's minority status imply compromise of artistic integrity?'[12] Drawing from music history, Mass condemns not only how critics consider sexual identity as a merely irrelevant detail in view of a composer's universal and timeless achievements, but also how artists themselves surrender to the closet's tyranny. He attacks 'those legions of men and women, gay and non gay, whose sense of privacy, decorum, and good taste (i.e. whose careers) seem to be more important than the truth'.[13]

But the position of Mass and others[14] is not necessarily workable as a heuristic device for historical or cross-cultural research – unless one would like to impose Euro-American concepts on altogether distinct social realities or apply them anachronistically to a more remote past. Perhaps the polarized terms of debate can be somewhat softened if proponents of 'disclosure' and 'outing' acknowledge the need for cross-cultural and historical accuracy, while conservative critics, historians and artists realize that the obfuscation of sexual identity contributes *actively* to the perpetuation of homophobia. The politics of the closet certainly aren't likely to change the social and cultural climate, nor do they allow for a more genuine understanding of artistic production beyond a mere iconographic and formal analysis. Needed to solve the issue is a joint effort of artists, critics and historians to turn the existing discourse upside down (politics of difference) without falling into the traps of provincialism and mutual indifference (neotribalism).

Much can be learned here from feminist and post-feminist art critique and praxis, as it insists on sexual difference in order 'to *strategically* rupture the power systems that operate upon this explicit, sometimes latent, use of gender as an axis of hierarchy and power'.[15] Applied to the issue of art and homosexuality, a similar tactical emphasis is required to question not only masculine bias but its heterosexist structure in order to reach a level where the artist's sexual identity can be acknowledged more objectively. Such a vision would be based on the interpretation of artistic practice as 'a signifying productivity whose resources are the subject – defined as subjectivity-on-trial, a constantly unstable intersection between individual and social histories, individually inflected and socially circulated signs'.[16] Rather than dividing art into gay versus straight art, it aims at 'reading' the complex and changing dynamic between desire, identity and artistic expression. It highlights a homoerotic heritage, diachronically and cross-culturally, instead of identifying and inventorizing 'gay' and 'lesbian' artists in a timeless, static manner. The artists' modes of disclosure are not *a priori* catalogued as 'politically correct' or 'incorrect', but instead should be the very object of historical research.

The effects of feminist criticism, moreover, are manifold, whether on a simple, straightforward level, as a renewed critical and historical attention to the male as opposed to the female body,[17] or, more elaborately, as the subversion of (straight) male representational politics. 'A Feminist interpretation', claims Richard, 'addresses the relationship between biographical authorship (the sexual determinant of being a woman artist) and gender representation (the cultural symbolic records of the feminine that articulate and disarticulate the language of the work)' – which then proceeds by calling into question the hegemonic male-dominated culture 'that skillfully hides the mechanisms of signification by which the absolute masculine is made equivalent to the universal-transcendent'.[18] Or, put differently, 'seeking to speak in the name of women, Feminist analysis perpetually deconstructs the very term around which it is politically organized'.[19] Critical focus, accordingly, on the gender of women's art is indispensable as a means to 'deconstruct' how it relates to gender relations, both politically and symbolically, that already exist or are in the making, and secondly, to create an alternative circuit of 'perception' that upsets the politics of the male gaze.[20]

Along with the subversion of the male gaze goes a critique of its straight equivalent, male or female. For not only is the marginalization of the artistic expression of homosexual eros and identity comprised within the sexual politics of patriarchy. Feminist discourse itself has contributed to the invisibility of lesbian expressions of the self in art. This resulted partially from a reaction against lesbian prominence in early feminist politics, but often lesbian artists avoided issues of gender and sexuality in order to be taken seriously as 'female' artists. They simply abstained from emphasizing their own sexual identity.[21]

The problem of retrieving the gay dimension of part of the world's art production is complicated by analytical and theoretical issues aside from those raised by feminist criticism. A 'metacritical' framework is needed that encompasses cultural and diachronic diversity and embraces a narrative of cross-cultural continuity and temporal change. It must reveal the common, 'gay' dimension underneath the differences and idiosyncrasies of so many artists, certainly *beyond* the confines of a Euro-American 'gay community', yet it ought to highlight also how artistic expression of homotextuality is embedded in culture and society, in this instance in the distinct and hybrid culture of Latin American society.

Art history's closet is not as untransparent as is suggested, somewhat simplistically, by a bipolarity of gay versus straight, closeted versus out. Its agenda goes further than a mere inventory of 'out' 'gay' and 'lesbian' artists, even when such is an as yet unfinished task. Also it goes beyond a rather controversial 'outing' of artists past and present, as if our rather static categories of sexual identity can be applied unproblematically to divergent social and cultural contexts historically or cross-culturally. Like feminist art and criticism, its gay and lesbian counterpart calls for a deconstruction of the very notion of gay and lesbian identity, around which it is politically organized. Queer theory and feminist criticism join efforts to clarify how gender and sexual identity are to a high degree constructed socially and culturally, which obviously has far-reaching implications for a study of the art produced by women, lesbians or gay men. In a historical and critical study of gay and lesbian art, one must be aware of cultural and temporal context. Queer readings of homoerotic heritage indeed intend to highlight this, rather than apply a notion of reified identity. 'S'il n'y a pas d'essence féminine ou homosexuelle, de la même manière il ne saurait y avoir . . . d'art qui se qualifierait catégoriquement comme tel'* – declared the curators of 'Féminin/Masculin', who claim that the increased visibility of feminist, 'gay' or 'lesbian art' is needed to restore a balance in the first place: 'S'il existe en cette fin de siècle la perspective d'un art qui, de façon militante, se revendique comme féministe ou homosexuel avec tant de vigeur, on peut dire que c'est "de bonne guerre". Car il s'agit bien de se situer au-delà des clivages masculin/féminin, hétérosexuel/ homosexuel, de conquérir – ou de reconquérir – une position par une réévaluation de l'opposition jusqu'ici dévalué.'†22

A 'deconstructive' approach allows for inclusion of artworks that were produced by 'closeted' gay or lesbian artists, as well as works by heterosexual or bisexual artists, to the degree that they provide imagery relevant to a critical study of homoeroticism, community life or (anti-)homosexual politics in the arts. Crucial here is an analysis of how individual artistic expression occurs within a wider context of social and cultural discourses that are publicly available, rather than an illegitimate extension of Western categories into an altogether distinct context.[23]

But a problem arises as studies of gay art have focused too exclusively, until recently, on Europe and North America. Mostly, they are Eurocentric, in fact if not by intention, and reflect the lack of research on homosexuality in the arts of other continents. Only two non-European gay and one bisexual woman artists are included in Cooper's *The Sexual Perspective*, all of whom were or are living in exile in Europe (Guevara, Caballero, Fini).[24] Lucie-Smith includes only Caballero and Cinalli.[25] Gay and lesbian art shows similarly focus on North American and European artists. Only Jerome Caja was included

*'If there is no feminine or homosexual essence, then there can be no art either, that could be categorized as such.'

†'If, at the end of this century, there is an art that militantly and vehemently presents itself as feminist or homosexual, one may well say that it is "a good war". What it aims at is to place itself beyond the boundaries of masculine and feminine, of heterosexual versus homosexual, and to finally conquer "or reconquer" a position by re-evaluating the very opposition itself.'

in 'In a Different Light' (Berkeley, California, 1995), while 'Gender Fucked' (Seattle, 1996) showed work by Maria Elena González almost as the token Latina. Work by Goulart, Guimarães and Viriato was included in 'Le monde du SIDA' (Geneva, 1998).

Sexual identity remains unaddressed in most review shows on Latin American art, while only some careful references to an artist's gay or lesbian identity can be found in reference works.[26] The show 'Latin American Women Artists, 1915–1995' avoided the controversial issue of sexual identity and chose a rather safe curatorial approach.[27] Galán's and Zenil's sexuality are briefly discussed in one recent publication on Mexican art, while in another issues of homosexuality are altogether avoided. The censorship story, for example, behind Roberto Montenegro's mural *El arból de la ciencia* (1921–23) remains unaddressed in the catalogue of *Art d'Amérique latine, 1911–1968*.[28]

Signs of change can be detected, however. As early as 1983 Hayden Herrera described the intimate, female friendships of Frida Kahlo, while the sexual identity of artists like Michel, Galán, Zenil, Sánchez, Alfonzo, Oiticica, Leonilson, Davila, Caballero, or Pittman is addressed in monographs or catalogues.[29] The lesbian identity of Laura Aguilar is openly discussed by Yarbro-Bejarano.[30] Blas Galindo published a first analysis of contemporary 'gay art' in Mexico,[31] while careful beginnings have been made of a more open interpretation of some academic and turn-of-the-century art in Mexico and Brazil.[32] Bibliographical research on Latino gay art has been done by Luis de la Garza[33] and myself,[34] and 'gay art shows' have been organized in Mexico (since 1982), Argentina and Cuba.[35] The Mexican show 'Ex Profeso' (1989) was brought to San Francisco in 1990, and shows of Chicano gay art were organized yearly at the San Francisco Mission Cultural Center. 'Queer Raza' was installed in 1995 at the same city's Galería de la Raza.[36] No more systematic attempt has been made, however, to comprehensively inventorize expressions of homoeroticism or 'gay identities' in modern and contemporary Latin American art.

Method: revealing the tropes of 'homotextual' expression

To at least partially fill the gaps, I have set out to offer, however tentative and incomplete, an inventory of what I call images of *ambiente* – a metaphor for visual imagery not only of homoeroticism, but also of the social and cultural realities of homosexual life, of men and women who are 'in the life', part of an at first hardly visible, then later more visible gay community in Latin America. I deliberately chose the term *ambiente*, as it better captures the diversity of (homo)sexual life, the simultaneous coexistence of various patterns of sexual behaviour and identity. Its somewhat vague, implicit character also allows for describing the changing outlook of Latin American homosexual life through time.

The persistence, especially, of a bisexual praxis to this very day and beyond the small community of men and women defining themselves as such, calls for caution when trying to locate 'gay' and 'lesbian' experience in Latin America. Not only is the development of gay and lesbian identity a recent, urban and middle-class affair, but the antecedent 'homosexual' networks were hardly inclusive of all gay, lesbian and bisexual experience. A pre-industrial discourse on 'sodomy' persists that emphasizes the active versus passive sexual act, rather than identity. No legal barriers existed, as sodomy had been lifted from most national penal codes, which left room for the active partner to uphold and even confirm his masculinity while having male-to-male sex.[37] Especially among the working classes, this pattern of role-defined sexual identities remains valid through to today.

Tradition was accompanied by modernity from the early twentieth century onwards, when physicians and legalists started copying the vocabularies of mostly European sexologists and imported the modern construction of 'homosexual identity'. The modern concept was based on object choice rather than sexual role, and conflicted with the still persistent, so-called 'traditional' pattern. It spread more easily among the middle classes, yet too little historical research has been done in order to grasp how this 'modern' homosexual minority defined itself in terms of sexual roles. There are numerous indications that modern homosexual identity did not only include those who exclusively or predominantly assumed a passive ('female') role, and this despite the physicians' disproportionate attention to homosexuals whose behaviour crossed the boundaries of gender. Portrayals by physicians, sexologists and criminologists were somewhat misleading also in making us believe that their feminine gender behaviour was always accompanied by passive, sexual behaviour.[38]

The image of a male, bisexual population having active sexual intercourse with both men and women accordingly needs to be modified. Some, in fact, proved to be quite versatile in their relations with other men, often homosexuals, even when maintaining a 'masculine' image towards the outside world. A man's married status not only fails to guarantee his presumed heterosexual identity, but also his active role-playing during sexual intercourse with other men. The fact remains that both traditional and modern sex/gender systems inform homosexual life in Latin America simultaneously, giving rise to complex, fluid networks of sexual socialization.

Simply tracing 'gay' and 'lesbian' art, therefore, would fail to grasp the complexity of Latin American sexual culture, or even the complexity of the sexual culture of Europe and North America. Strictly speaking, one can talk accurately only of gay and lesbian artists for the period from approximately 1970 until 1990 whose artistic output was part of Gay Liberation, taking off during the late 1960s and facing criticism from the late 1980s onwards. Not only was the modern concept of gay and lesbian identity unknown before, but it is questioned today from a 'queer' angle that at least modifies the concept's familiar bearing and content. 'Gay', so it goes, is tied up too exclusively to a generation of predominantly male, white middle-class Americans and Europeans, from which many others feel alienated and even excluded. Lesbians emphasize their autonomous agenda, criticizing their suppression by gay male chauvinism and misogyny. Gay and lesbian people of colour, either within or outside the Euro-American world, stress issues more or less alien to a class of privileged gays: poverty, *machismo*, strict gender roles, high HIV-prevalence, lack of family support, and so on. Transgender people criticize the phallocracy of Castro-clonism.[39] Bisexual people oppose the either/or dichotomy of earlier gay militancy. Younger generations define their own queer existence differently from their elderly colleagues, partly in view of a different experience of the AIDS crisis, partly as the spokespeople of alternative economic, social and cultural values.

This book will make clear that in Latin America, too, the realm of gay and lesbian culture styled after the West is as yet limited. The rather late and limited dissemination in the 1980s of an Anglo-European model of sexual identity may very well reveal the presence in Latin America of a postmodern, 'queer' approach *avant la lettre* on the level of sexual praxis especially that questions the essentialism of static sexual identities and unveils a more fluid, nomadic libidinous practice traditionally embedded within Latin American society. Representations of same-sex desire and homosexual identity reflect the continent's social and cultural construction of sexuality, and are embedded in its culturally idiosyncratic narratives or actually aim at challenging these. This book accordingly reflects the often hybrid and diversified reality of (homo)sexual life in both Latin America and the Latino communities abroad, and interprets the production of images of *ambiente* as reflecting the complex and dynamic relationships between sexual identity, gender politics and artistic expression.

As such, the book subscribes to a new, 'queer' tradition of art historical and critical scholarship, as it 'deconstructs' sexual identity as such. Definitions are often too static, too reifying, and sexual behaviour cannot always be classified in a series of well-defined groups. The search, accordingly, for images of a Latin American *ambiente* leads beyond the boundaries of a Westernized 'gay and lesbian' élite, while including artistic representations that nevertheless reveal a diachronic homosexual *imaginaire*.

A lesson can be learned, in this respect, from Nayland Blake and Lawrence Rinder, curators of the show 'In a Different Light'. They 'think of gay and lesbian culture less as tied to sexual behaviour and more as a mutable cultural phenomenon with issues that can be taken up by anyone'.[40] Perhaps their stance is too radical and their 'deconstructive' approach too far-reaching, but it surely is legitimate to push 'gay' and 'lesbian' art beyond the narrowly confined pool of art produced by 'lesbian' and 'gay' people, expressing immediate, gay and lesbian contents.

Thus, the criterion for selection of relevant works in this book is not simply 'art produced by gay male and lesbian artists'. Not only is one's self-definition as 'gay' or 'lesbian' a relatively new and culture-bound concept, less disseminated in a Latin American context of *machismo* and gender-defined sexual roles, but the nomadic outlook of sexual praxis, especially in Latin America, calls for caution when trying to pin down the realm of homoeroticism both within and outside the more or less visible world of 'homosexuals'. Not all art potentially interpreted by the audience as having a homoerotic or 'gay' content was/is actually made by artists who were/are or defined/define themselves as homosexual or even bisexual, while one's sexual inclination is not necessarily reflected in one's artistic production.

The expression of 'gay' content can be direct and intentional, through narrative disclosure or iconographic content. Often, however, it remains hidden underneath the artist's apparent adoption of publicly available representational tropes and can be revealed only after close scrutiny. Extrapolating from Foster's analysis of literature, one may say that in art, too, unequivocal references to homoeroticism occur, but that often 'a critical hermeneutics [must be applied] to [an artwork] not generally viewed as dealing with homosexuality'. Its relevance cannot be read directly from a mere observation of iconographic content, but has to be retrieved from underneath layers of codification and camouflage.[41]

I therefore adopt the concept of homotextuality as a heuristic catch-all term, which is diachronic instead of being tied to all-too-reifying notions of 'homosexual' or 'gay' identity. It allows for cross-cultural comparison and avoids the pitfalls of Eurocentric conceptualization. It is inclusive at once of artistic expressions of homoeroticism, as of their perceptions by various audiences. It embraces an image's potential reception as a site of homotextual meaning, even when not intended so by the artist him/herself. It also includes 'documentary' images that, while neutral on a primary semantic level, reveal something of a hidden, codified homosexual content when properly contextualized and that appear as visualizations of an *ambiente*, clearly recognizable by an informed eye.

An inventory will be made, first, of artworks that reveal homotextual meaning directly visible or readable from iconographic narrative. Often, however, a 'gay' intention was executed in a codified and latent way only. Homotextuality was often legitimized by pictorial narratives of anatomical study, mythology, religious tradition, or history painting. An inventory, for example, of the numerous images of Saint Sebastian may well exemplify how 'the study of the nude's erotic implications were carefully directed' in Latin America as well as in Europe.[42]

It should be clear, finally, that the erotic dimension may have come into being *a posteriori* only and ought to be accredited to the artwork's reception itself. In that case, homotextual meaning was not intended – as some icons of European and American 'gay art' have become so only over time and as the outcome merely of 'gay' reception and discursivity. Perhaps the most famous illustration of this is Hyppolyte Flandrin's *Figure d'étude* of 1835.[43] This merely reflects the fact that, as observed by Mieke Bal and Norman

Bryson, 'once launched, the work of art is subject to all of the vicissitudes of reception'.[44] One must be aware, next, of how a work's homotextual dimension may have been eclipsed from largely homophobic art historical studies or critical reception. The complex issue of how to 'read' a painting, sculpture or photograph should make us aware that its homoerotic dimension may not necessarily have been or be the artist's intention or responsibility, while revealing, at the same time, that it is not entirely wrong either to recognize a certain 'gay' content merely by virtue of contextualization within a secular trope of homotextual expression even when no such artist's intention can be documented through archival evidence.

As yet, very little archival information is currently available and my book accordingly is often speculative. I predominantly rely on critical evaluation of the existing literature as well as on formal and semiotic analysis. My interpretations must be verified, ideally, by extensive research of archival documents or in-depth interviews with the artist when still alive, but at this point, I merely want to outline how the field can be further explored. I follow the guidelines of current art historical research, as it has moved beyond a mere formal and historical analysis. Contextualization now is enriched by both semiotics and the so-called 'aesthetics of reception'. This has not only laid bare the multi-interpretability of a visual image, but acknowledges the weight of audience reception, of the 'mobilization' of visual inventory through space and time, in sum, of the relative autonomy of the image.

Relevant here, no doubt, is Gloria Anzaldúa's notion of a 'queer *facultad*', allowing one 'to "see into" and "see through" unconscious falsifying disguises by penetrating the surface and reading underneath the words and between the lines'.[45] Whereas Anzaldúa focuses on literature, a similar approach obviously can be applied to the study of the visual arts. For here, too, one must take into account 'not only the actual text [read: image, RB], but also, and in equal measure, the actions involved in responding to that text [image]'.[46] One may speak indeed of a triangular structure, artists–artwork–audience, that encompasses both the textual poetics of artistic production *and* the poetics of 'audience reception'. All three instances must be included in order to retrieve the at times highly codified homographesis in the visual arts.[47]

Lesbian (in)visibility

Whereas Latin American gay male art has been studied only scantily, it is even harder to obtain a picture of lesbian art on this continent. Women's art generally remains underexposed despite efforts to lessen the gap. But very little attention has been paid, as yet, to expressions of lesbian identity and eroticism. Female artists, at the earliest times of Independence, were few in numbers and their contribution to academic art was marginalized in an overwhelmingly male art world. Lesbian sensibility remained virtually intangible during the first half of the twentieth century. Frida Kahlo's current iconic status as a 'bisexual' artist clashes with the silence of Mexican art historians during previous decades, and it is clear also that her story is rather like the exception to the unwritten rule that women's art must not violate gender orthodoxy.[48]

Female homoeroticism in the arts remains problematic even today and is expressed far more rarely than its male counterpart. The situation in Latin America is actually not much different from the presumably more sexually 'enlightened' countries of Europe and North America. Homotextuality often remains more obliquely present, first of all, which calls for even more careful interpretation than already is the case in some work by male gay artists. The scarcity of outspoken lesbian art itself is due to both external homophobia and reticence among lesbian artists themselves. Some repress depiction of lesbian content merely to remain in tune with a rather orthodox interpretation of feminism, opposing male objectification, or in order to present a less controversial image of female sexuality. Such self-censorship can be compared to recurrent gay male intolerance of effeminate queens as a topic of representation. Other artists, defining themselves explicitly as 'queer', tend to find the notion of a reified 'lesbian art' oppressive and break through the very barriers of fixed sexual identities, thus making it hard for the viewer to 'locate' homotextuality. Only some artists take on a pragmatic view and express lesbian identity and sexuality in an open, straightforward way. 'Significantly', says Cherry Smyth, 'they are no longer allowing their own sexual subjectivities to be limited by fear of male objectification or a self-loathing erotophobia. They are more willing, and able to negotiate the dilemma of being exhibited in a heterosexist, homophobic art world.'[49]

Still, the peculiar situation of lesbian art production will inevitably lead to a somewhat unbalanced picture in this book. A joint study of both male gay and lesbian art together seems appropriate to me for two reasons, however: first, the rise of a younger generation of 'out' lesbian Latina artists, who themselves may also welcome information about their predecessors; second, the impact of feminist and lesbian art criticism on the production of both female and male gay art. An understanding especially of today's 'queer' art requires consideration of the wider debate on art and feminism, sexuality and gender.

The core material of this study is composed of drawings, engravings, lithos, paintings, sculptures, murals, photographs, performances, videos and mixed-media installations. For practical purposes, I am limiting myself to four countries: Brazil, Mexico, Cuba and Puerto Rico. Together, they provide a representative sample of as diverse a political and cultural continuum as 'Latin America'. I also include a chapter on art produced by gay Latino/a artists in the USA – and, marginally, Europe – in view of the increasing artificiality of the border between 'North' and 'South', as a looking-glass also of the peculiar dialectic existing between 'Western' and 'alternative' models of gay/lesbian identity as expressed in artistic imagery.

The selection of only four countries leads to an incomplete picture, and to the omission of important artists, bisexual, homosexual, gay or otherwise relevant as visual commentators on sexual politics and gender roles in their countries. I am aware that my focus remains predominantly Hispano-American and that the Dutch-, French- and English-speaking territories, largely in and around the Caribbean Sea, are excluded. Most Andean countries also remain outside the focus of this book. Obviously, more research needs to be done before a more complete and balanced picture can be drawn.

Notes

1 N. Richard, 'Chile, women and difference', in G. Mosquera (ed.), *Beyond the Fantastic* (London and Cambridge, MA, 1996), pp. 138–9. Also, see S. O. Murray (ed.), *Latin American Male Homosexualities* (Albuquerque, 1995), pp. 49–70.

2 N. García Canclini, 'Los estudios culturales de los ochenta a los noventa: perspectivas antropológicas y sociológicas', in N. García Canclini (ed.), *Cultura y pospolítica* (Mexico, 1991), pp. 35–8.

3 See N. García Canclini, 'Modernity after postmodernity', in Mosquera, *Beyond the Fantastic*, pp. 20–1. For a critical study of this issue in a wider context, see O. Baddeley and V. Fraser, *Drawing the Line: Art and Cultural Identity in Contemporary Latin America* (London and New York, 1989).

4 See, in this context, M. C. Ramírez, 'Beyond the fantastic: framing identity in US exhibitions of Latin American art', in Mosquera, *Beyond the Fantastic*, pp. 231–2. Her criticism of decontextualized readings of Latin American modernism can be applied equally to formal interpretations of art, produced by artists, whose homosexuality is considered irrelevant.

5 C. Lord, *Pervert* (Irvine, CA, 1995), p. 9.

6 A. Solomon-Godeau, *Male Trouble: A Crisis in Representation* (London and New York, 1997), p. 8.

7 Remarkably little if any evidence can be found of 'gay art' in the pre-1980s studies on 'erotic art': see for example E. Fuchs, *Illustrierte Sittengeschichte vom Mittelalter bis zur Gegenwart* (Munich, 1909–12), 3 vols; K. Clark, *The Nude: A Study in Ideal Form* (Princeton, 1956); T. Bowie and C. V. Cristenson (eds), *Studies in Erotic Art* (New York and London, 1970); P. Cabanne, *Psychologie de l'art érotique* (Paris, 1971); V. Kahman, *Eroticism in Contemporary Art* (London, 1972); E. Lucie-Smith, *Eroticism in Western Art* (London, 1972) (Chapter 15 of the 1991 re-edition was changed to include new feminist and gay artworks and perspectives); F. Carr, *European Erotic Art* (London, 1972); R. Melville, *Erotic Art of the West* (New York, 1973).

8 'Lesbian' art, evidently, is distinct from lesbian sexual scenes in much straight male art (and pornography). Examples of more recent straight male-based surveys of 'erotic art' are P. Webb, *The Erotic Arts* (New York, 1983); P. and E. Kronhausen (eds), *The Complete Book of Erotic Art: A Survey of Erotic Fact and Fancy in the Fine Arts* (New York, 1987); C. Hill and W. Wallace, *Erotica II: An Illustrated Anthology of Sexual Art and Literature* (New York, 1993);

and P. Weiermair (ed.), *Erotic Art from the 17th to the 20th Century* (Munich, 1995). An exception is E. Lucie-Smith's new *Ars Erotica: An Arousing History of Erotic Art* (London, 1997).

9 M.-L. Bernadac and B. Marcadé, 'Ouverture', in *Féminin/masculin: Le sexe de l'art* (Paris, 1995), p. 11.

10 W. R. Dynes, 'Introduction', in W. R. Dynes and S. Donaldson (eds), *Homosexuality and Homosexuals in the Arts* (New York and London, 1992), p. viii.

11 K. Killian, 'The secret histories. Interview with Nayland Blake and Lawrence Rinder', *Artforum* (February 1995), p. 23.

12 L. Mass, 'Musical closets. A personal and selective documentary history of outing and coming out in the music world', in M. Bronski (ed.), *Taking Liberties* (New York, 1996), p. 418.

13 *Ibid.*, p. 397.

14 See M. Bronski, 'Outing: the power of the closet', *GCN*, 6 March 1990, p. 11, and M. Signorile, *Queer in America* (New York, 1993).

15 G. Pollock, 'Inscriptions in the feminine', in M. C. de Zegher (ed.), *Inside the Visible: An Elliptical Traverse of 20th Century Art in, of, and from the Feminine* (Boston and Kortrijk, 1996), p. 70.

16 *Ibid.*, p. 81.

17 See M. Walters, *The Nude Male: A New Perspective* (New York and London, 1978), and G. Saunders, *The Nude: A New Perspective* (London, 1989).

18 N. Richard, 'Women's art practices and the critique of signs', in Mosquera, *Beyond the Fantastic*, p. 145.

19 W. Chadwick, *Women, Art and Society* (London and New York, 1996), p. 11.

20 E. Ann Kaplan, 'Is the gaze male?', in A. Snitow (ed.), *Powers of Desire* (New York, 1983), pp. 309–27.

21 See J. Fernandes, 'Sex into sexuality. A feminist agenda for the '90s', *Art Journal*, 50, 2 (Summer 1991), p. 36, and E. Lucie-Smith, *Artoday* (London, 1995), pp. 461–79. The curators of the lesbian art show 'Gender, Fucked' criticized the 'heterosexualization of feminist art histories' while simultaneously claiming the feminist dimension of much lesbian art. See H. Hammond and C. Lord, *Gender, Fucked* (Seattle, 1996), p. 1.

22 B. Marcadé, 'Le devenir-femme de l'art', in Bernadac and Marcadé, *Féminin/masculin*, pp. 45–6.

23 See, in this context, L. Manzor-Coats, 'Introduction', in D. W. Foster (ed.), *Latin American Writers on Gay and Lesbian Themes* (Westport, CT, and London, 1994), p. xvi: 'imagination becomes a social practice based on negotiation between sites of agency (individuals) and globally defined fields of possibility'. The author quotes from Appandurai's theory on fractal culture (A. Appandurai, 'Disjuncture and difference in the global cultural economy', *Public Culture*, 2, 2 (Spring 1990), pp. 1–24), yet I claim that negotiation takes place on a smaller scale also, i.e. within the boundaries of a particular culture or society.

24 See C. Beurdeley, *L'amour bleu* (New York, 1978); R. Biederbeck and B. Kalusche, *Motivmann: Der männliche Körper in der Modernen Kunst* (Giesen, 1987); E. Cooper, *The Sexual Perspective: Homosexuality and Art in the Last One Hundred Years in the West* (London, 1994) (2nd, rev. edn); E. Cooper, *Fully Exposed: The Male Nude in Photography* (London, 1995) (2nd, rev. edn); A. Ellenzweig, *The Homoerotic Photograph: Male Images from Durien/Delacroix to Mapplethorpe* (New York, 1992); D. Fernandez, *Le rapt de Ganymède* (Paris, 1989); A. Foster, *Behold the Man: The Male Nude in Photography* (Edinburgh, 1988); D. Leddick, *The Male Nude* (Cologne, 1998); E. Lucie-Smith, *The Male Nude* (New York, 1979); E. Lucie-Smith, *Race, Sex and Gender in Contemporary Art* (New York, 1994); E. Lucie-Smith and S. Boyd, *Life Class: The Academic Male Nude, 1820–1920* (London, 1988); C. Smyth, *Damn Fine Art by New Lesbian Artists* (New York and London, 1996); Walters, *The Nude Male*; P. Weiermair, *Geschichte des*

männlichen Akts in der Photographie des 19. und 20. Jahrhunderts (Vienna, 1987); P. Weiermair (ed.), *Il nudo masschile nella fotografia del XIX e del XX sec.* (Ravenna, 1984); J. Weinberg, *Speaking for Vice: Homosexuality in the Art of Charles Demuth, Marsden Hartley and the First American Avant-garde* (New Haven, 1993).

25 Lucie-Smith, *Race, Sex and Gender in Contemporary Art*, p. 126. *The Male Nude: A Modern View*, edited by F. de Louville and E. Lucie-Smith (New York, 1985), includes work only of the Chilean Andres Monreal and the Argentinian Manuel Cancel, both having lived mostly in exile in Europe.

26 For example E. J. Sullivan (ed.), *Latin American Art of the Twentieth Century* (London, 1996), p. 10 on Ernesto Pujol and Juan González. Also, see references on pages 127 and 135 of *Artistas latinoamericanos del siglo XX* (Sevilla, 1992), as well as in the English edition (New York, 1993). Juan Davila's homoerotic imagery is addressed scantily in G. Brett (ed.), *Transcontinental* (London and New York, 1990), pp. 106–7.

27 *Latin American Women Artists, 1915–1995* (Milwaukee, 1996).

28 Compare *Nuevos momentos del arte mexicano/New Moments in Mexican Art* (Mexico and New York, 1990), pp. 27–9, 50; and *Bilder und Visionen: Mexikanische Kunst zwischen Avantgarde und Aktualität* (S.l.), 1996, pp. 154–9. Also, see *Art d'Amérique latine, 1911–1968* (Paris, 1992/3), pp. 194–5.

29 See O. Debroise, *Alfonso Michel* (Mexico, 1992); J. Poot, *Julio Galán* (Amsterdam, 1992); and J. Poot, 'The world and my world', in *Julio Galán* (Monterrey and Mexico, 1994), pp. 50–73; *Nahum B. Zenil: Witness to the Self/Testigo del ser* (San Francisco, 1996); E. García Gutiérrez, 'Eros y Zilia Sánchez', *El nuevo día*, 6 October 1991, pp. 12–15; and *Carlos Alfonzo* (Miami: Miami Art Museum, 1998). Also covering the gay dimension of artistic production are G. Brett, 'Hélio Oiticica. Rêverie and revolt', *Art in America*, 77, 1 (January 1989), pp. 163–5; L. Lagnado, *Leonilson: São tantos as verdades* (São Paulo, 1996); *Hysterical Tears: The Art of Juan Davila* (London, 1985); E. Lucie-Smith, *Luis Caballero: Paintings and Drawings* (London, 1992); C. Detrez, *Caballero ou l'irrésistible corps de l'homme dieu* (Colmar, 1980); H. N. Fox (ed.), *Lari Pittman* (Los Angeles, 1996).

30 Y. Yarbro-Bejarano, 'Laying it bare: the queer/colored body in photography by Laura Aguilar', in C. Trujillo (ed.), *Living Chicana Theory* (Berkeley, 1998), pp. 277–305.

31 C. Blas Galindo, 'Cultura artística y homosexualidad', in *Ex Profeso: Recuento de afinidades* (Mexico, 1989), pp. 16–21.

32 F. Ramírez, 'Notas para una nueva lectura de su obra', in *Saturnino Herrán: Pintor mexicano (1887–1987)* (Mexico, 1987), pp. 7–32, and *O desejo na Acadêmia: 1847–1916* (São Paulo, 1992).

33 L. de la Garza, 'Preliminary Chicano and Latino lesbian and gay bibliography' (1994).

34 R. C. Bleys, 'Homotextuality and gay identity in Latin American art, 1800–today: A preliminary bibliography' (unpublished manuscript, 1998).

35 For Mexico, see *Ex Profeso: Recuento de afinidades*. In Buenos Aires, a first show on gay art took place at the Centro Cultural Ricardo Rojas, directed by Jorge Gumier Maier. It was curated by the New Yorker Bill Arning and showed mainly North American artists. In Havana, a show was curated by Fidel Pérez at the Centro Cultural Yara.

36 See 'Recuento de afinidades/Inventory of affinities', *Out/Look*, 12 (Spring 1991), pp. 61–5, and *Queer Raza. El corazón me dio un salto* (San Francisco, 1995). 'Queer' Mexican art was also prominent at the 'Tendencies' exhibition, San Francisco Art Institute, 1995. Curators Ruben Gallo and Terence Gower had installed the show earlier in Mexico City.

37 See D. F. Greenberg, *The Construction of Homosexuality* (Chicago and London, 1988), p. 352.

38 See S. O. Murray, 'Introduction', in *Latin American Male Homosexualities*, pp. xi–xvi; J. Salessi, 'The Argentine dissemination of homosexuality, 1890–1914', *JHSex*, 4, 3 (1994), pp. 337–68; and C. A. Messeder Pereira, 'O direito de curar: homossexualidade e medicina legal no Brasil

dos anos 30', in M. M. Herschmann and C. A. Messeder Pereira (eds), *A invenção do Brasil moderno: medicina, educação en eghenaria nos anos 20–30* (Rio de Janeiro, 1994), pp. 88–129.

39 To avoid any misunderstanding: Castro-clonism refers to the 1980s adoption by gay men of a rather uniform, macho look, visible most prominently then in the Castro neighbourhood of San Francisco.

40 Killian, 'The secret histories', p. 23.

41 D.W. Foster, *Gay and Lesbian Themes in Latin American Writing* (Austin, 1991), p. 131.

42 For a reconstruction of this painting's reception history, see M. Camille, 'The abject gaze and the homosexual body: Flandrin's *Figure d'étude*', *JHom*, 27, 1/2 (1994), pp. 161–88.

43 Cooper, *The Sexual Perspective*, p. 24.

44 M. Bal and N. Bryson, 'Semiotics and art history: a discussion of context and senders', in D. Preziosi (ed.), *The Art of Art History: A Critical Anthology* (Oxford and New York, 1998), p. 251.

45 G. Anzaldúa, 'Del otro lado', in J. Ramos (ed.), *Compañeras: Latina Lesbians. An Anthology* (New York, 1987), p. 238.

46 W. Iser, quoted in Manzor-Coats, 'Introduction', in Foster, *Latin American Writers on Gay and Lesbian Themes*, p. xxxi.

47 The triangular structure artist–work–audience also shaped the exhibition 'Male Desire. Homoerotic Images in 20th-Century American Art', Mary Ryan Gallery, New York, 1995. The curator defined it as a field of 'confrontation between the male artist and the erotic male body, and the spectator's role in that relationship'. Also, see D. Borim, Jr. and R. Reis, 'The age of suspicion: mapping sexualities in Hispanic literary and cultural texts', in D. W. Foster and R. Reis (eds), *Bodies and Biases: Sexualities in Hispanic Cultures and Literature* (Minneapolis and London, 1996), p. xxiv. Also, see W. Davis, 'Introduction', *JHom*, 27, 1/2 (1994), pp. 1–10.

48 Frida's popularity only rose after feminist art historians started focusing on her work and a genuine 'Frida business' grew, catering largely to the North American and European market. See O. Baddeley, 'Her dress hangs there: de-frocking the Kahlo-cult', *Oxford Art Journal*, 14, 1 (1991), pp. 10–17.

49 Smyth, *Damn Fine Art by New Lesbian Artists*, p. 5.

CHAPTER TWO

Framing the homoerotic

(1 8 1 0 – 1 9 1 0)

Introduction

Throughout the first three-quarters of the nineteenth century, a distinct 'homosexual' identity was virtually unknown in Latin America. In fact, it didn't exist in Europe or North America either, even when there at least the social role of so-called 'sodomites' had given rise to urban subcultures and networks, catering to the satisfaction of their social and sexual needs. Research will have to demonstrate to what extent such sodomite subcultures existed in Latin American cities in that era as well.

The import of cultural goods and ideas from Europe accelerated towards the eve of the nineteenth century, leading to the dissemination, at least within the circles of the educated élites, of 'modern' sexology and new theories of 'homosexual identity'. In modernizing Mexico and Brazil, the discursive focus shifted from repressive legislation of the 'sodomitical act' to a medicalized understanding of 'homosexual personality disorder' and 'pathology'. Within the small circles of both countries' social and cultural élites, this gave rise to new understandings of sexual roles and identities, and to the discrete development of a 'homosexual discourse'.

The sexual economy at that time remained characterized by double standards, combining a cult of heterosexual marriage on the one hand and, on the other, illegitimate adventures or romances with either prostitutes and mistresses, or, at least for some, with boys or men. Sexual praxis remained embedded in a rather widespread pattern of implicit bisexuality, reconciling a public call to family consciousness and responsibility with covert and hidden exploration of sexual diversity.

The time was not yet ripe for the social organization and, *a fortiori*, institutionalization of homosexual life. Most educated men who were homosexually inclined regarded artistic discourse and visual language as the only medium for expression, allowing for an erudite, if codified cult of male-to-male affinity, for a literally framed, early iconography of homosexual eros. The visibility of a homosexual subculture thus remained limited to the realm of the arts and literature.

This was not a small achievement and even today, one is easily impressed by texts and images all too little known. My findings about the visual arts confirm what has become evident in studies of prose and poetry, namely that a relatively rich homotextual dimension can be located already at that time, at least in the most advanced countries of Latin America, such as Mexico and Brazil.

Careful historical interpretation is essential here, and it would be wrong to anachronistically apply a vocabulary that doesn't fit the mind and society of that time. Also, this discourse is remarkably male-centred. In fact, this entire chapter will reflect the absence of women artists in most of both countries' nineteenth-century artistic scene. It must be emphasized at once, however, that this is based primarily on a survey of existing literature. Far more research needs to be done before this picture can be confirmed. I assume, however, if only by extrapolating from European and North American evidence, that both the codified production and implicit perception of homotextuality in the visual arts did not occur among women-loving women in the same way as it did among men-loving men.

The relative unimportance at that time of an autonomous art production in both Cuba and Puerto Rico also makes this chapter somewhat off balance. Most art then found on both islands was bought and imported from Europe. The remaining works consist of landscapes, portraits and religious scenes which, after close inspection, hardly prove relevant for this book. Not so for Mexico and Brazil, where numerous works were created that lend themselves to a queer reading and actually disclose a more or less subterranean trope of 'framed' homotextuality. I will focus first on how this was achieved in academic art, then continue by describing how new developments specific to the turn-of-the-century Latin American context were advantageous for innovative presentations of male-to-male homoeroticism.

1810–1920: academic masculinities

Little, if any, evidence of outspoken homosexual desire can be derived from the artistic works produced within the context of Latin American academic art. Yet, it is obvious that the classical repertoire of images allowed for representations of the male nude, alongside the female one, either as an object of anatomic studies, or as the embodiment of protagonists in mythological or religious narratives. Often a potentially homoerotic dimension can be traced, but the question whether this was intended by the artist, or was merely a side-effect of narrative content, seems bound to remain unanswered. Lack of evidence generally prevents the historian from determining if so-called *académies* of male nudity were perceived as homoerotic, at least by that part of the public who shared such a sensibility.

Yet, when looking closely, one cannot but conclude that both the artistic messages and the viewers' perceptions may theoretically have been of a homoerotic kind. Latin American academic art reproduced a codified reality that could be perceived also in Europe or North America. Academic training had been a largely homosocial affair since the Renaissance, not only because art education was accessible only to men, but because the models too were men more often than women. Stockholm allowed for female models in 1839, but it took much longer in, for example, Naples (1870) and Berlin (1875). Many models were working-class men, soldiers, even policemen, eager to pose naked for extra cash. Peace was disturbed only when female students were allowed and the male models' nudity provoked reaction mostly from parents, concerned about the implied 'violation of maidenly delicacy'.[1] Female models in front of an exclusively male audience gave rise to feelings beyond the merely aesthetic, as was generally known – which should make it clear, at least hypothetically, that academic studios may have equally harboured a homoerotic gaze for some of their students.

Still, academic training focused on male models especially for reasons of decency in the first place. The high output of images of men is hardly an indication of the artists' sexual preference. Abigail Solomon-Godeau has convincingly explained how the academic tradition was characterized by its outspoken homosocial organization and how this was even reinforced in France by the Revolutionary and Jacobin ethic. Women were marginalized empathically, even from the range of representable objects, which allowed for representations instead of both virile and effeminate, androgynous male nudity. The prominence, in fact, of beautiful, androgynous ephebes was not so much a sign of relaxed attitudes towards homosexuality, as the outcome of Republican discourse, positioning sexual difference within the realm of masculinity and ascribing political and moral values to these effeminate young men. The situation changed from the 1830s onwards, however, when male nudity became problematic and was gradually eclipsed in favour of the eroticized, de-politicized female nude.[2]

Solomon-Godeau warns against overestimations of the 'homosexual' content in academic art. Homosexual identity being an invention of the late nineteenth century only, it would be inaccurate to project it into periods further removed in time. Much academic art, moreover, was the outcome of powerful iconographic traditions rather than the expression of the individual artist's intention. Iconographic deciphering calls for accurate understanding of the political, social and cultural context, because meanings are manifold and change through time.[3]

It is certainly true that the imagery of male nudity extended 'beyond identifiably gay artists and audiences', but this must not prevent the historian altogether from addressing the issue of homoerotic inspiration of *certe tendenze*, as it was put rather delicately by the critic Mario Praz.[4] The gradual evolution from depersonalizing, idealistic depiction of classical beauty to more realistic and personal portraiture may very well reflect how art implied some personal investment, empathy and, perhaps, attraction. It corresponded moreover with contemporary homoerotic imagination about men of lower social status, even when public acknowledgement of such desire had become increasingly difficult especially in view of the growing visibility of a 'homosexual' minority. The abandonment of 'life class' may thus illustrate how 'homosocial arrangements'[5] drew suspicion from wider social circles, just as the heterosocialization of twentieth-century life resulted, eventually, into a virtual eclipse of the male nude particularly in Modernist art.

In most Latin American countries, national academies were founded which copied European examples. They served predominantly to lend respectability to a bourgeois élite that lived by agro-export mainly, yet whose cultural profile was until then rather poor.[6] In Cuba, the Academia de San Alejandro had existed since 1818 and several countries witnessed the foundation of national Academies shortly before or after Independence:[7] Brazil 1816, Gran Colombia 1836, Mexico 1843, Chile and Ecuador 1849. Other countries had to wait until the late nineteenth or even early twentieth century, when Modernism was already reaching the continent: Costa Rica 1897, Argentina 1905, Uruguay 1905, El Salvador 1911, Peru 1919, Guatemala 1920. Nothing at all happened in Puerto Rico after Spanish rule was replaced by North American control in 1898.[8]

As in Europe, art training remained an equally exclusively male affair. Explicit recognition of the male body's desirability remained off limit, perhaps *a fortiori* in Latin America, where Mediterranean heritage had produced a Creole variety of *machismo*. A pattern of strict gender roles had been disseminated since early times and was reflected in a kind of castration, as in the Old World, of the male body in academic art. Yet, heterosexism did not eradicate a subtly homoerotic dynamic even in Latin America. With the adoption of European aesthetics, its implicitly homoerotic vocabulary was also imported. In fact, there was room, as I will indicate below, for artistic expression of an eroticized male body *if only* when this remained framed by the technical rationale of anatomical drawing or covered by the narrative codes of religion and mythology. The eroticized male body thus remained an acceptable object of representation longer than it did in Europe, partly due to the relatively late dissemination of European sexological discourse in Latin America. Eventually, it was accompanied by its female counterpart, yet this did not preclude the subterranean expression of homoerotically inspired images, nor did it stand in the way of homoerotic 'readings'.

The alibi of mythology

From the early era of Mexican independence initiated in 1810, the relationship between the centre and the periphery, between the newly founded republic of Mexico and the Old World, was still defined in a hardly contentious way. In fact, nothing was further from the mind of Mexico's newly independent Creole élite than an intention to affirm a cultural identity that was different from the Spanish motherland. Along with self-assured expressions of political independence went a much weaker cultural politics that imitated European heritage rather than rejecting it.

The Academia Nacional de San Carlos, founded in 1843[9] and imitating its European examples, proved to be the least probable environment for innovative artistic production. It was academic in its copying of Ancient Greek and Roman, to a lesser extent Renaissance and Mannerist, models, in its focus upon classical anatomy and in its neglect of the local and national context. The depiction of Mexico's *mestizo* population remained anathema, as did the incorporation of themes and motives of the vast land's flora and fauna, mountains and rivers, houses and towns.

What was left were themes from Greek and Roman mythology, from Christian iconography and, finally, the study of the male and female body, largely as part of craftsman training. The female body actually remained underrepresented, for decency's sake, says the Mexican art historian Justino Fernández, but partly also because there may not have been a sufficiently strong impulse to break the academic studio's homosocial atmosphere.[10]

A drawing is kept at the Academia today, of Castor and Pollux. Its author, Juan Fortí, may have merely obeyed the rules of contemporary art education and painted this mythological couple purely as an icon of classical beauty. But nothing excludes the possibility that the artist's pleasure may have been physical as well. Further archival research may offer some keys to a less speculative claim, but one must not expect too much from such a departure since traditional Mexican society was not very condoning of verbal expressions of homosexual desire, even when it did somewhat tolerate it at the margins, that is, within a particularly Latin American code of sexual roles.[11] This explains also why biographical evidence, such as an artist's marriage or passion for the opposite sex, does not necessarily refute any claim regarding his less or more passionate desire for men.

The same agnostic deontology ought to guide the art historian's interpretation of other academic works, if only to postulate the *theoretical* possibility that to some of them a homoerotic dimension may have been ascribed by either the artist or (part of) the audience, and to rectify art history's unjustified silence regarding the issue. This is not simply to put the identification of 'homosexual' artists on the agenda, but to attempt to understand the production of male imagery, much of which consists of male nudes, as the expression, jointly, of artistic craftsmanship and homosocial eros.

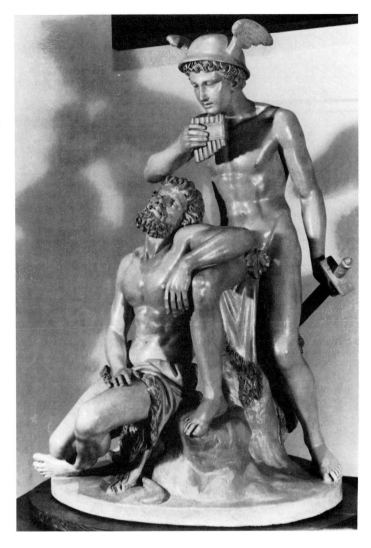

Figure 1 Felipe Sojo, *Mercúrio y Argos* (1854),
marble, 95 × 71 × 131 cm, Museo Nacional de Arte,
Mexico City, courtesy of Instituto de Investigaciones
Estéticas, Universidad Nacional Autonoma de México,
Mexico City.

Pedro Ocampo drew a sitting Mercury in a sensual style, not necessarily with an intention to create an object for the homosexual gaze, but undoubtedly aware of the physical attraction of the classical figure. Luis Coto's drawing of a dancing faun and Ramón Moctezuma's *Fragmento del fauno Barberini* are examples of a similar kind, using figures from a mythological past as a narrative context for the depiction of male nudes.

Felipe Sojo's *Mercúrio y Argos* (1854) eradiates a clearly homoerotic sensibility. It even reproduces a particularly pederastic ethic that is inherent to its Ancient Greek original and that was perhaps perceived as such in nineteenth-century Mexico. Other examples of subdued homoeroticism are *Gladiador Romano*, an anonymous work, and Ximeno's *Apolo egipcio*, illustrating how the more remote past of Ancient Egypt also inspired art that embraced male beauty.

The academic context somewhat neutralized and de-sexualized images that were undoubtedly physical originally and made them acceptable to the general audience. But

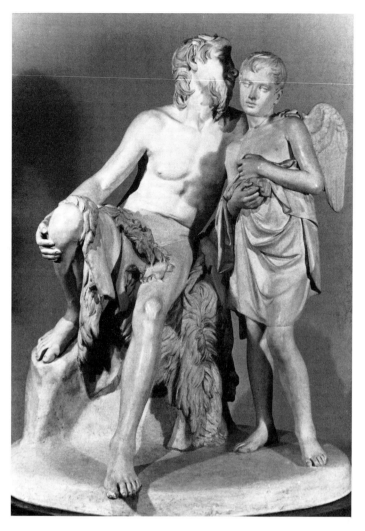

Figure 2 Miguel Noreña, *La lección* (1876), marble, 146 × 119 × 96 cm, Museo Nacional de Arte, Mexico City, courtesy of Instituto de Investigaciones Estéticas, Universidad Nacional Autonoma de México, Mexico City.

a certain ambiguity may have persisted among nineteenth-century viewers, especially towards works that seemingly pertain to the realm of pederasty. The depiction of adolescent or even prepubescent boys as objects of an erotic gaze was generally constrained, as can be seen in sculptures by Agustín Franco (*Un pescador*, 1858), Epitácio Calvo (*Ïsaac*, 1862) and Gabriel Guerra (*Un atarrayador*, 1875). Rodrigo Gutiérrez's painting *El pescador* (n.d.) and José Guadelupe's *El genio de la pintura* (1871) also seemingly embraced a pederastic eros, if only in a subtle, implicit way.

Less ambiguous, on the other hand, was Miguel Noreña's *La lección* (1876).[12] It shows an adult, satyr-like man, who whispers in the ear of a young boy. The lad's innocence is emphasized by the defensive position of his shoulders, whereas the man's joyous grimace suggests a mischievous intention. Such qualities lent a rather suspicious aura to the teacher/pupil relation suggested by the work's title. It is an altogether very ambiguous work, undoubtedly rooted in the European, neoclassical fashion of Anacreontism,[13] but contains elements also of an Ancient Greek sensibility, where satyr-like figures were said to be endowed with great sexual prowess as opposed to the male citizen, whose genitalia are traditionally represented as little and flaccid. The artist's compromise, so it seems, is laid within the veil that covers his (erect?) penis and attenuates the sculpture's apparent lascivious content.

In Brazil, too, academic art allowed for images of male nudity in the context of classical mythology. *Fauno*, for example, a drawing by Carlos Oswald, illustrates great reverence for the homoerotic undertones of Greek mythology.

Several of Vítor Meirelles de Lima's (1832–1903) male nudes reiterate themes from classical mythology as well, an example of which is *Fauno com Baco* (*c.* 1855), drawn by the artist during his studies at the Parisian atelier Cogniet. It is made after classical statues, of which plaster copies were available for instruction in Latin America at the time.

Often male nudity is represented alongside the more prominent naked female body,[14] but sometimes the artist's emphasis is divided equally between both. Male and female

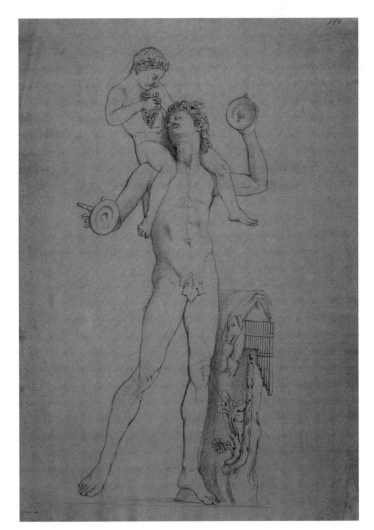

Figure 3 Vítor Meirelles de Lima, *Fauno com Baco* (*c.* 1855), graphite on paper, 39.3 × 28.8 cm, Museu Nacional de Belas Artes, Rio de Janeiro, photo: Raúl Lima.

nudity are both celebrated in *Fauno e Bacante* (n.d.) by Jean Leon Pallière Granjean Ferreira (1823–87), for example, while an infant, also naked, is looking into the viewer's eye. It seems to give its blessing to the viewer's voyeurism – which makes this painting into a precursor of *fin de siècle* sensuality.

Most remarkable is the almost explicit homotextual message to be detected in a drawing by Pedro Américo de Figueiredo e Mello (1843–1905). It is titled *Sócrates afastando Alcebiades do vício* (*c.* 1864) and represents the Greek philosopher, who leads Alcibiades away from a naked woman. Alcibiades leers back at the woman, which apparently supports a heterosexual narrative, yet this is supplemented simultaneously – and ironically – by the coded homosexual story of Socrates and Alcibiades.[15]

Prepubescent boys were a theme, among others, for Augusto Rodrigues Duarte (*Copia de um gesso*, 1875), João Batista da Costa (*Nu*, n.d., and *Nu*, 1889), and Eliseu d'Angelo Visconti (1866–1944) (*Estudo de nu*, 1893; *Sem título*, 1897, and *Academia masculina/criança*, *c.* 1898) without, however, attributing any exclusive value to such imagery. Nor can we establish for certain if any remotely erotic motive inspired the artists. Academic art actually allowed for representations of adolescent and infant nudity, whether male or female, and paid tribute, within a Brazilian context, to the Baroque angels of Aleijadinho

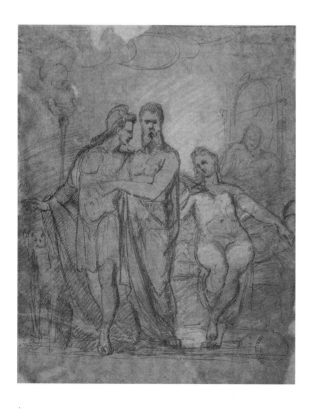
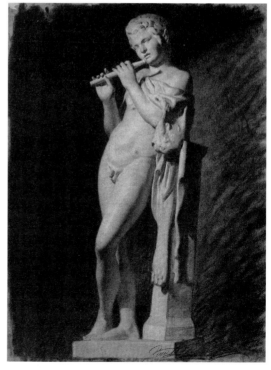

and Manoel da Costa Athaíde. But now they were portrayed differently as inhabitants of a secular, mythological universe, rather than of an otherwise sensuous iconography of Catholic devotion.

The focus on physicality was conventional at the time and presumably without any erotic connotation. Such an interpretation may well be more idealizing than justified, however, for, as with nudity, so too do a society's notions of sexual availability or, at least, of sexual attraction evolve and the boundaries between legitimate and illegitimate sex are subject to historical change. Intergenerational sex, though a major taboo today, was somewhat less frowned upon in more remote times of the past – which certainly explains the sensuality of Baroque imagery of naked angels, and also the continuous presence of prepubescent boys and girls until the end of the nineteenth century.

It seems more probable, however, that the ephebe or even infant remained popular precisely because its image precluded sexuality. Also, the child was a carrier of both feminine and masculine physical traits and embodied an androgynous ideal that had been disseminated by the art historical studies of Johann Joachim Winckelmann.[16] The adolescent's *Anmut* (grace) and *Weichigkeit* (*mollesse*, softness) were highly appreciated by artists and commentators in his wake, not only in Europe but in Latin America as well.

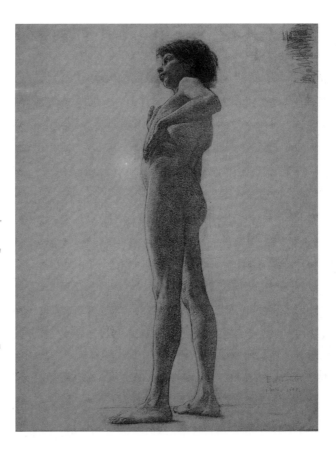

Figure 4 *(far left)* Pedro Américo de Figueiredo e Mello, *Sócrates afastando Alcebiades do vicio* (c. 1864), graphite and chalk on paper, 44.3 × 36 cm, Museu Nacional de Belas Artes, Rio de Janeiro, photo: Raúl Lima.

Figure 5 *(left)* Augusto Rodrigues Duarte, *Copia de um gesso* (1875), charcoal on paper, 63 × 47.7 cm, Museu Nacional de Belas Artes, Rio de Janeiro, photo: Raúl Lima.

Figure 6 *(right)* Eliseu d'Angelo Visconti, *Academia masculina (criança)* (c. 1898), charcoal on paper, 62 × 47.6 cm, Museu Nacional de Belas Artes, Rio de Janeiro, photo: Raúl Lima.

The sexes of Christian iconography

Christian narratives, aside from mythological ones, allowed for the representation of nudity or semi-nudity in ways that would otherwise be considered sexual or, at least, sensual. At times, religious imagery offered an implicit context also for the depiction of homoeroticism, if disguised, naturally, behind the pictorial storylines of Roman Catholic tradition. This can be seen, for example, in Santiago Rebull's painting *La muerte de Abel* (1851) or Gregorio Figeroa's *Adan y Abel* (1857), where the historic relationship between Biblical characters is accompanied by a more sensual one, detached from the idiosyncrasy of narrative representation. The story of Cain and Abel, of course, was copied from European examples (by de Champagne, Rosa, Guercino, Le Brun, Poussin, Fabre), many of which were very homoerotically tinged works as well.[17] Both Felipe Valero's sculpture *San Sebastian* (1857) and José Ibarrán y Ponce's *El mártir cristiano* (1877) are classic examples of hagiographic representation and homoerotic iconization combined, even when such may have occurred subconsciously or on the level of a *posteriori* reception only. Luis Monroy's painting *El hijo pródigo* (n.d.) (Plate 1), finally, portrays the prodigious son, staring dreamily at the sky, lost and forlorn. His limbs, long hair and sensuous eyes

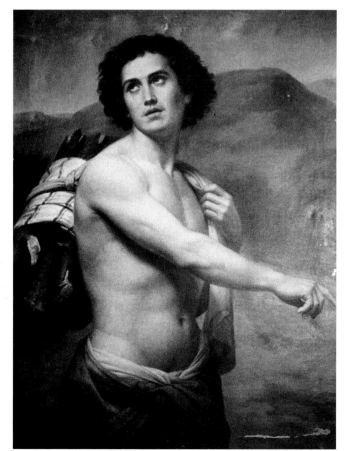

Figure 7 *(left)* Petronilo Monroy, *Isaac* (n.d.), oil on canvas, 112 × 90 cm, Museo Nacional de Arte, Mexico City, courtesy of Instituto de Investigaciones Estéticas, Universidad Nacional Autonoma de México, Mexico City.

Figure 8 *(right)* José Bernardelli, *Santo Estevão* (1879), bronze, 166 × 67 × 58 cm, Museu Nacional de Belas Artes, Rio de Janeiro, photo: Raúl Lima.

suggest androgyny, not unlike the Raphaelite portrait of Isaac (n.d.) by Petronilo Monroy.

Similar ambiguity permeates religious narrative in Brazilian academic art. Hagiography offered an apology for rather sensual representations in drawings, paintings and sculptures of male (semi-)nudity. The flesh is almost tangible in *São João Batista* (n.d.) by João Zeferino da Costa (1840–1915) or in *Santo Estevão* (1879) by José Bernardelli (1852–1931). The latter, in fact, reminds one of Jacques-Louis David's *Mort de Joseph Bara* (1794), a similar image of androgynous, if not sexless, youth, that carried within itself a reference to virtue, religious (Bernardelli) or otherwise (David), while radiating sensuality at the same time.

Crude physicality also radiates from drawings of the Crucifixion scene by Oswald, notwithstanding the dramatic religious content. The same is true for José Ferraz de Ameida Junior's (1850–99) *Cristo crucificado* (1889), clearly showing the muscular torso of Jesus Christ.

Vítor Meirelles de Lima's *Degolação de São João Batista* (1855) is another fine illustration of how religious imagery lent itself to devotional representations of male physical beauty. His *Flagelação de Cristo* (1856) reflects the physical tangibility of pain, so typical of Latin American representations of this theme, yet is at the same time ambiguous in its mixture of suffering and ecstasy.

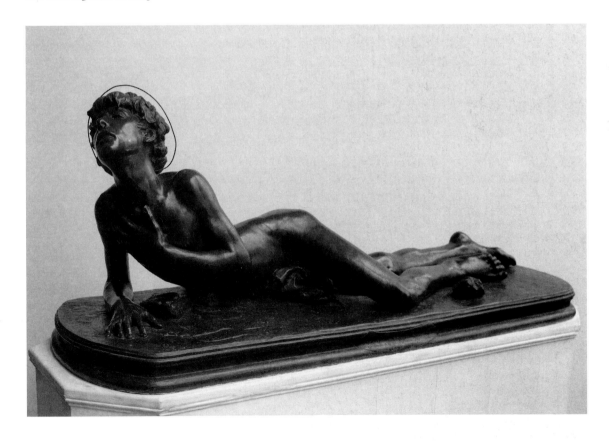

Anatomies of desire

The study of human anatomy probably provided the most direct and undisguised excuse for the visual representation of muscular, virile bodies, as can be seen in drawings by, among others, Rafael Calvo, Gonzalo Carrasco and Ruperto Gómez. Ponsiano Gunderrama's *Torso of a satyr* also reveals a passionate eye for the masculine physique. An unlikely 'modern' looking drawing is of an 1831 male nude, seen from behind as he is reading a book. It is titled *Estudio de claro y obscuro* and was submitted by José Olivares during the annual concourse of the Academia.

Initially, academic drawing was idealizing and aimed at the depiction of rather impersonal, classical beauty. Such was the legacy, clearly, of J. J. Winckelmann, who had claimed to find ideal beauty in the artistic values of classical antiquity and, as Academies were founded in Latin America, so too was this Eurocentric notion imposed upon an altogether very distinct and multicultural society.[18]

Occasionally, however, portraiture became more realistic, if not always as spontaneous and empathic as in the drawing by Olivares. The model's social characteristics became more visible, as did his facial expression of emotion or ideas. In Brazil, especially, some drawings and paintings were produced that combine the imperatives of academic portrayal with historical presence and allow for introspection, to some extent, into the model's soul. Vítor Meirelles de Lima's drawings of male nudes are typical of this close, psychological scrutiny, even when emphasis remains on the study of physical characteristics and anatomy. An *Academia masculina* of 1856 shows a man of mixed descent, whose protruding buttocks and lifted left arm lend a particularly erotic dimension to the work. Yet, the viewer is invited also to see the model's inner emotion as he turns away his face and looks down at the floor rather introspectively. In other studies, too, Meirelles de Lima focuses on the model's inner life as much as on his anatomy – which may reveal, in fact, that the technical enterprise of drawing was accompanied by empathy and communication (*Academia masculina*, n.d.).

In other instances, however, the artist remains faithful to a more classical academism, as can be seen in the splendid drawings of a classical bust (*Estudio de torso masculino*, n.d.) and of a man, seen from behind, who is lifting his arms up in the air (*Academia masculina*, 1854). The study of a Paraguayan soldier (*c.* 1872), anticipating his famous *Combate Naval de Riachuelo*, is a mere exercise in anatomy also, impregnated with a classical ideal of beauty and virility.

Anatomical precision is the main goal also of de Figueiredo e Mello's studies (1892/3) for *Tiradentes Esquartejado*, while classicism prevails in Rodrigues Duarte's *Academia masculina* of 1875. It shows a naked man who lifts his right arm in a rather imperial gesture.

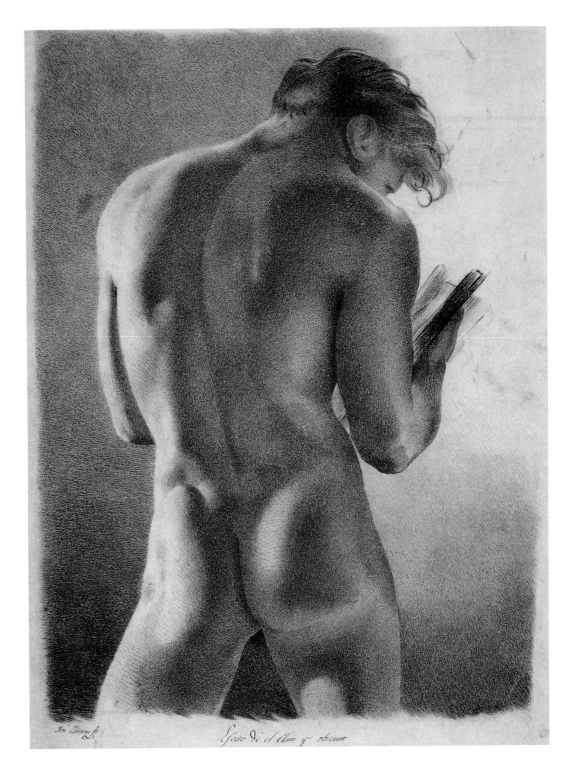

Figure 9 José Olivares, *Estudio de claro y obscuro* (1831), charcoal and pencil on paper, 44.5 × 31 cm, private collection, courtesy of the Consejo Nacional de la Cultura y las Artes and the Museo Nacional de Arte, Mexico City.

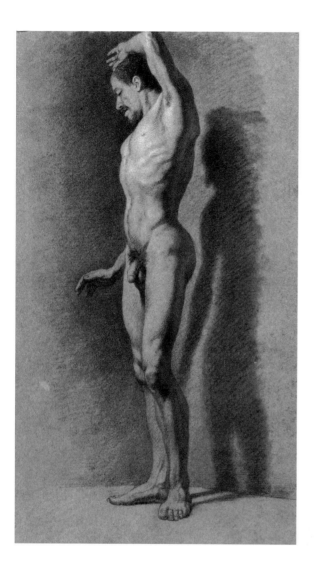

Figure 10 Vítor Meirelles de Lima, *Academia masculina* (1856), graphite on paper, 57.7 × 44.8 cm, Museu Nacional de Belas Artes, Rio de Janeiro, photo: Raúl Lima.

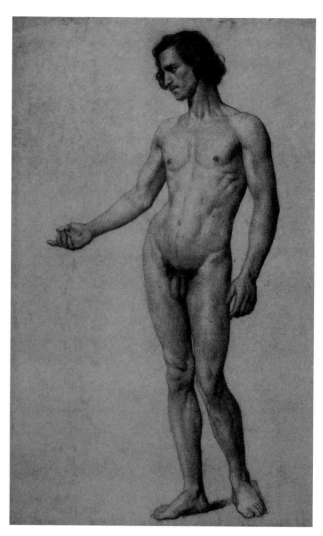

Figure 11 Vítor Meirelles de Lima, *Academia masculina* (n.d.), charcoal on paper, 61.5 × 46.7 cm, Museu Nacional de Belas Artes, Rio de Janeiro, photo: Raúl Lima.

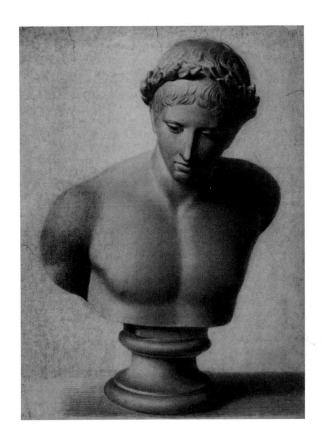

Figure 12 Vítor Meirelles de Lima, *Estudio de torso masculino* (n.d.), charcoal on paper, 72.2 × 54.3 cm, Museu Nacional de Belas Artes, Rio de Janeiro, photo: Raúl Lima.

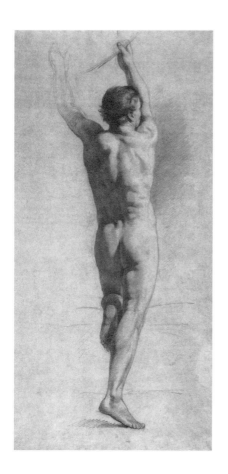

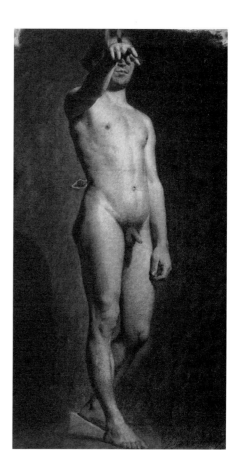

Figure 13 Vítor Meirelles de Lima,
Academia masculina (1854), charcoal on paper,
58.5 × 44.6 cm, Museu Nacional de Belas Artes,
Rio de Janeiro, photo: Raúl Lima.

Figure 14 Augusto Rodrigues Duarte,
Academia masculina (1875), charcoal on paper,
64 × 46 cm, Museu Nacional de Belas Artes, Rio de
Janeiro, photo: Raúl Lima.

Many drawings exist by the Chilean *émigré* Henrique Bernardelli (1858–1936), who, after studies in Rome, taught art in Rio de Janeiro. A drawing *Homem nu* (n.d.) is a rather sketchy image in ink where part of the male model's body seems to be submerged by its own shadow. Another drawing shows a man, lying asleep on his back in a rather languorous pose. His genitalia are sketchy – which may indicate, as did the shadow game elsewhere, that the artist felt somewhat reluctant to focus on the male sex. Another drawing by Bernardelli may reveal something like caution: a naked man is carrying a heavy book on his shoulders, which may be intended to lend a more cerebral, Platonic dimension to the image of male nudity. The recognition of male sensuality is often unmistakable, however, as can be seen in an untitled, undated drawing, showing a young man trying to lift a heavy rock. His tensed muscles, though a postulate of academic drawing, are a pleasure to the eye (*Sem título*, n.d.). Similarly endowed with sensuality is another study, this time of an adolescent, dressed in a tanga only, and gently leaning forward as if to make the curving lines of his lean, muscular thighs more prominent (*Sem título*, n.d.).

José Bernardelli produced images of women predominantly, yet some works fit the image of implicitly male homoerotic academism. An untitled, undated work shows a naked man – a javelin thrower? – whose musculature certainly illustrates how the artist has mastered the art of drawing. The portrayal is a very personal one of a man, whose look betrays the claustrophobia of a studio.

A painting by Rodolfo Amoêdo (1857–1941), *Tronco de homem* (1880), stands out by its spontaneity as well as by the artist's neglect of classical standards of beauty. The model seems real, as is shown both by his relatively underdeveloped body and by the relaxed positioning of his arms. The portrait of a young boy pupil, *Retrato do aluno Conceição* (*c.* 1891) by Antonio Rafael Pinto Bandeira illustrates the growing realism resulting from the influence of the new medium of photography. As with José Bernardelli and Vítor Meirelles de Lima, we are far removed in both these paintings from the idealized, heroic expression of purely classicist works – which may in fact reveal a somewhat more equivocal communication, a certain 'complicity' between the artist and his model.

A moment of homotextuality may be hidden indeed in the production process of academic art itself, as it implies a certain complicity between the artist and his model. This complicity is not necessarily of an erotic kind – in fact, no data seem available on whether any of these artists were homosexually inclined, nor is it probable that archive research will offer conclusive evidence. Yet, the homosocial context of academic art did allow for implicit expression, theoretically at least, of a Platonic sensibility. Audience perception, in addition, may have harboured a homosexual gaze even when this was 'framed' by the aesthetic language of the Academia and de-sexualized at least towards the outside world.

It is important to remember that the identification of homotextuality does not require that the artist actually pursued a homosexual or even bisexual lifestyle. Passion for members of one's own sex may have remained purely Platonic and intellectual instead. Latin American society, in this respect, was hardly different from the United States or Europe, where some works of artists like Géricault, Eakins, or Sargent have nevertheless become icons of 'gay art'.[19] The now familiar division between 'gay', 'straight' and even 'bisexual' was unknown to nineteenth-century Latin America, which makes the realm of homoeroticism at once less tangible and more ubiquitous. Recognition of the eroticized male body may have been a subtext of academic art, even when this cannot be empirically verified.

It is in this light, too, that drawings by other artists *may* – not *must* – be seen as carriers of homotextuality. Portrayals of men are actually accompanied, more often than not, by those of women, which may indicate that technical draftsmanship prevails, no matter what the object is; or that homosexual and heterosexual eros were in no way exclusive categories. Theoretically, it is possible also that an equilibrium was pursued by the artist merely to avoid the audience's curiosity regarding his libidinous inclinations, but such alertness seems to conflict with the actual pragmatics of nineteenth-century Latin American discourse on gender and sex.

Unmistakably homoerotic drawings or sculptures, detached from any wider context – classical mythology, Christian tradition, the teaching of human anatomy – remained within the realm, perhaps, of the very private. Not only were current beliefs regarding the artist's task at odds with such intentions. The social context prevented him from revealing such desires because they remained taboo, unspoken if pursued in secret. The social code regarding homosexuality made him reluctant, undoubtedly, to expose himself.

Yet, the limited visibility of unequivocal homotextuality was at odds with the wide dissemination of male nudity, originating, for different purposes, from what Abigail Solomon-Godeau has called a 'homosocial continuum'. This 'extends from relatively de-eroticized forms of male bonding to lifetime sexual unions and all variations between' and explains why aesthetic appreciation of male beauty was expressed equally by the ostensibly 'straight', the 'homosexual', the sexually ambiguous, the misogynist *célibataires* or even the sexual enigmas.[20] The context of homosociality remained pervasive indeed in Latin America also, where modern theories of 'homosexual identity' were, as yet, shared by only very few educated men. The imagery of ephebic youths especially remained unproblematic, just like androgynous men, because they could be accommodated within the *machisto* ethic underlying local sexual codes. The viewer's masculinity was not challenged by their gender ambiguity since the gender system, still noticeable in working-class circles today, was structured alongside the axis of 'active' versus 'passive'. And, if this became provocative, then it was relieved at once by the Latin American élite's mimetic attitude towards European, classical heritage, imported originally to lend respectability to the new nations' cultural identity. Thus a platform existed that allowed for inconspicuous representations of homosocial eros, framed within a legitimate narrative context.

1880–1910: *Indigenismo* and symbols of male affinity

Academic tradition was gradually exchanged for the new trends of history painting, *Indigenismo* and Symbolism, each limiting the representation of male nudity within the confines of new social and cultural narratives once more. Yet, even when contextualization provided the necessary excuse, it was during this period that some of Latin America's most explicitly homoerotic imagery was produced. In Mexico and Brazil some artists, subscribing to the new fashions of Symbolism and *Indigenismo*, reflect a new discourse on bodily culture and sexuality, as it accompanied newly imported aesthetic traditions.

Porfiriato Mexico

In 1876, Porfirio Díaz became president of Mexico and would remain in power until 1910. The era, known in historiography as the Porfiriato, was characterized by economic 'modernization', leading to wealth for a new, entrepreneurial class yet leaving the poor countryside underdeveloped and exploited as before. The social contrast actually opened the eyes of a small number of intellectuals, who paved the way not only for social criticism but also for a cultural movement, commonly known as *Indigenismo*. It was characterized by new representations, both in paintings and sculpture, of 'local' figures, characters and personae, of Indian heritage rather than of the 'Westernized' Creole élite.

Indigenism, moreover, is a label in the art history of Latin America that covers many meanings, and one ought to make a distinction, suggests Garrido, between 'la preocupación por los indios vivos, con sus problemas de explotación, miseria y abandono' and 'el interés en un pasado más o menos idealizado e intemporal, poblado por seres de rara belleza, en que las tendencias más decorativas del modernismo hallaron ocasión para desplegarse'.*[21] Social awareness became prominent only in the wake of the Revolution (1910–17).

Before that, the inspiration of Indigenist art was, on the contrary, mostly romanticist and frequently tied to a rhetoric of patriotism and heroism. 'Modern' readings of Pre-Columbian heritage represented Aztec and Mayan protagonists as the impersonators of a *mestizo* identity that was – and is – said to constitute the core of Mexican identity despite genocide and marginalization since Cortés.

*'the attention for living indigenous people, for their problems of exploitation, misery and marginalization' and 'the focus on a more or less idealized and timeless past, populated by beings of exceptional beauty, allowing for the most decorative tendencies of modernism to unfold themselves'

The rupture with the earlier academism was limited, moreover. Neoclassicism remained in vogue throughout the Porfiriato, renewed at times by similar trends in the Old World. Both French neoclassicism and the British Pre-Raphaelite school influenced the Veracruzan painter Alberto Fuster (1870–1922), who spent much time in Italy and especially France. He then returned to his city of birth, Tlacotalpan, after which he travelled to New York and committed suicide.

His neoclassical painting *Virgilio declamando* was highly derivative of Puvis de Chavannes. It depicts Virgil citing poetry in front of an audience of two men and five women. The latter are carefully draped in luxurious robes and so is one of the men. The other man, however, is virtually naked, which may indicate the painter's personal admiration for the male nude.

Other paintings by Fuster show both masculine and feminine nudity, but rarely do both sexes interact with one another. Beauty, admittedly, is portrayed as a female semi-nude in *Culto a la Belleza* (n.d.), which was inevitable, in fact, in the light of iconographic convention. But male nudes are prominent as well and these are fully nude, as opposed to the women in this painting. Some are represented in somewhat narcissistic poses, as if the painter wanted to suggest that male nudity is a legitimate subject in itself.

The grand painting *Apoteosis de la Paz* (1903) also portrays male and female nudity, but the equilibrium is once again surrendered to subtle, homoerotic suggestion. In the foreground, a young boy looks over the shoulder of a naked man, sitting in a Roman chair. The familiar pederastic theme is accompanied elsewhere by a group of naked soldiers, whose anatomy contrasts with the drapery of the female figures both to the right and to the left. Only one of the women is fully nude.

The painter's potentially homosexual inspiration, finally – one commentator speaks of 'sexual ambiguity'[22] – may be confirmed by *Luzbel* (n.d.) and *San Sebastián* (n.d.), both representations of male nudity that, again, reveal a careful and passionate perception of masculine anatomy.

The Academia's heritage, initially, weighed on history painting too, as it depicted men and women who, though 'indigenous', were attributed with a classical European physique. Similarly, some history painting, though Latin American, chose themes from the European past. An example of this, which is somewhat homoerotic in its focus on male nudity, is Santiago Rebull's *La muerte de Marat* (1875).

Many history painters remained far removed from a genuine acknowledgement of indigenous or *mestizo* beauty, as can be seen in Manuel Vilar's robust sculpture of *Tlahuicole, general Tlaxcalteca, en el acto de combatir en el sacrificio gladiatorio* (1851). It combines an Aztec hairstyle with a European facial physiognomy and thus compromises the work's indigenous content with an aesthetic that remains derivative of the European canon. Luis Monroy's *Últimos momentos de Atala* (1871), while representing a theme from Aztec history, remains inscribed within European iconography and shows a universalized,

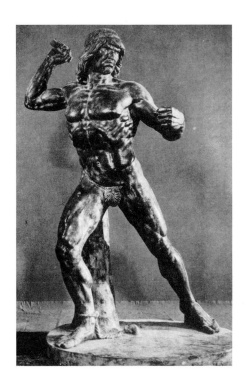

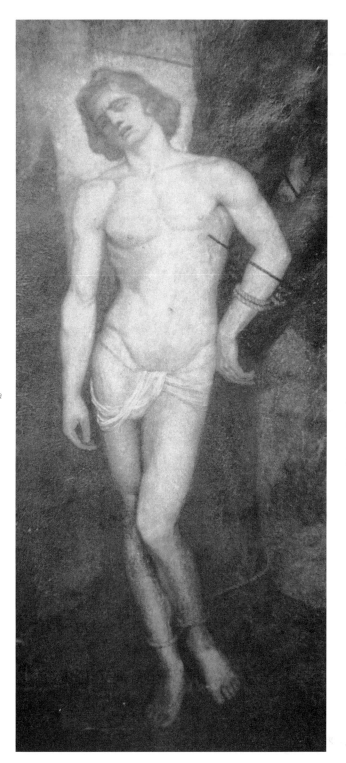

Figure 15 *(above)* Manuel Vilar, *Tlahuicole, general Tlaxcalteca* (1851), marble, 135 × 100 × 214 cm, Museo Nacional de Arte, Mexico City, courtesy of Instituto de Investigaciones Estéticas, Universidad Nacional Autonoma de México, Mexico City.

Figure 16 *(right)* Alberto Fuster, *San Sebastián* (n.d.), oil on canvas, 246 × 100 cm, Casa de la Cultura de Tlacotalpan, Mexico, courtesy of Instituto de Investigaciones Estéticas, Universidad Nacional Autonoma de México, Mexico City.

'white' anatomy. Chactas's earring and long, black hair are elements of Romanticism, adopted from René Chateaubriand's short novel (1802) rather than from direct, historical information about the story itself. The painting also imitates French examples, especially a painting by Anne-Louis Girodet-Trioson (1808).[23]

The famous paintings by Leandro Izaguirre, José Obregon and Felix Parra also make Indians look more European than they really are, but they clearly are a step closer to a Mexican redefinition of national beauty, rooted as it is in the history of widespread *mestizaje*. Two of Parra's huge canvases are perhaps interesting also within the context of this chapter, for they represent male nudity in a consistent way. Male nudity can be seen, both in *Fray Bartolomé de las Casas* (1875) and *Escenas de la Conquista* (1877), in the shape of dead bodies. Women, dressed in indigenous clothing, sit weeping and hold onto their children. Drawing any far-reaching conclusion would be unsound, yet one wonders if the artist took advantage of the theme of slain Indian men, stretched out on the pavement of Aztec temples, in order to expose their nudity.

Patriotic earnestness made history painting an altogether infertile soil for sensual portrayals and its rather austere outlook was gradually replaced by a new aesthetic at the turn of the century. This was influenced by European innovations and shared much of the Old World's *fin de siècle* taste for 'decadent' refinement and sensuality. *Indigenismo*, in this new context, would be redefined according to the guidelines of Art Nouveau and Liberty style, lending a far more physical dimension to the representation of the Indian or *mestizo* population.

Two painters ought to be reviewed here whose artistic oeuvre is typical not only of a turn-of-the-century sensualism and refinement, but also of how such an aesthetic context proved to be fertile soil for subtle artistic expression of homoeroticism. Subtle, because Mexico maintained traditional boundaries of sexual tolerance. Such had become clear in 1901, when the police raided a party of homosexual men. Forty-one were arrested, which led to the code word *un cuarenta y uno* for a homosexual man. A series of engravings by José Guadalupe Posada – '*Aquí están los maricones/muy chulos y coquetones*'* – contributed to the public notoriety of the incident. The next year, travesty on stage, though common since the mid-nineteenth century, led to new criticism by the press.[24] Neither incident led to successful resistance of homosexual women or men and the word remained with authors such as Eduardo Castrejón. His novel *Los cuarenta y uno. Novela crítico-social* (1906) merely reinforced existing stereotypes among the Mexican people of homosexuals as effeminate *maricones, jotos, putos*. Such a social climate would explain why either exile, as in the case of Ángel Zárraga, or romantic idealization, as with Saturnino Herrán, were indispensable strategies for making the expression of homoeroticism publicly acceptable.

The painter Ángel Zárraga Argüelles (1886–1946) remained within the shadows of Mexican art history until the late 1960s, when a one-man show was organized at

*'This is where the faggots are/very queer and frivolous.'

the Museo de Arte Moderno in Mexico City. His prolonged stay in Paris contributed to his relatively marginal status at home, yet, presumably, this resulted equally from his rather right-wing political views, clashing with the progressive and leftist climate created as a result especially of the cultural policy of José Vasconcelos. Zárraga's sensualism and religiosity proved incompatible with the upcoming movement of socialist *muralismo*.[25]

The stylistic changes of Zárraga's work were limited. His earliest work was Symbolist and reflected the artist's weakness for a mixture of spirituality and sensuality. His most beautiful painting, in fact, dates from this early period. It is titled *Ex-voto* (1910–12) (Plate 2) and shows Saint Sebastian in a slightly feminine pose, imbued as usual throughout the history of art with great sensuality. The saint's figure constitutes a major icon of homoerotic imagination in Mexico, despite the figure of a praying woman on the left-hand side. The painting's intimacy seems to be reinforced by the female figure, who enters the closed space of an *ex-voto* image as if she were the transgendered personification of the artist himself. Such an effect is neutralized at once, however, by the inscription at the lower right side: 'SEÑOR, no sé celebrarte en versos complicadas; pero acepta SEÑOR, esta obra áspera y humilde que he hecho con mis manos mortales. Angel *ZÁRRAGA*.'* It re-objectifies what may, in fact, have become too subjective, too involved.

Double edges can also be detected in *La adoración de los Reyes Magos* (1911) (Plate 3). Its composition is quite severe and contains both the newborn baby Jesus and the Three Kings within a geometrical grid of lines and diagonals. Somehow, it echoes the Napoleonic aesthetic of so-called *Egyptomanie* due to both its geometric outlook and the vestimentary details of especially the two younger kings. One is standing up in the middle, lifting up his arms and stretching them halfway, symmetrically and as if preparing for common prayer. The other is kneeling down, praying also but in a pose that makes one think more easily of a swimmer about to dive. Both kings are virtually naked, apart from luxurious loincloths and Egyptian headwear. Their bodies look athletic and, again, most sensual. Here, too, the artist seems to 'negotiate' between a sense of religiosity on the one hand, and erotic fascination on the other.

Zárraga reached his definitive, personal style after a brief interlude of Cubist experiments. Often described as post-Cubist, his most mature work is in fact closer to a geometrical Symbolism that attributed sharper edges to often languid, de-materialized figures. His human figures appear as almost immobile sculptures and radiate a certain spirituality. Much of his work, like *San Jorge* (1913), is religious, which is congruent with the artist's meditative mood.

Such is the case even in the many portraits of sportsmen, especially soccer players, that Zárraga painted. The thematic choice may be significant in itself. The painter may indeed have had a weakness for sportsmen and athletes. But more telling is the peculiar way of presenting the soccer players in static, mysterious portraits, which, again, radiate

*'SIR, I cannot honour you with complicated verse; but SIR do accept this rudimentary and modest work, which I made with my own mortal hands. Angel ZÁRRAGA.'

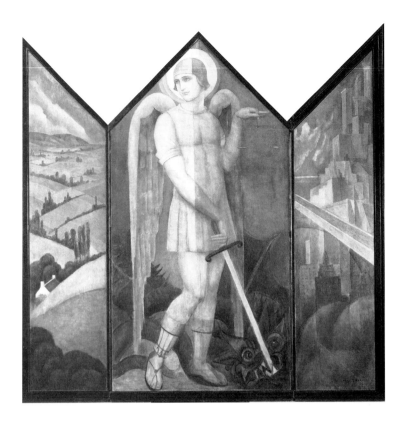

Figure 17 Ángel Zárraga, *San Jorge* (1913), oil on canvas, 142 × 142 cm, private collection, courtesy of Sotheby's, New York.

a controlled dimension of sensuality. This is visible in his portrait of Ramón Navarro, *Deportista* (1925), and, more clearly, in *Tres futbolistas con Boina* (n.d.). The position of each of the three soccer players is such that a certain intimacy between all three of them becomes inevitable. One holds a wooden pole, with his left arm downwards, while he rests his right hand on the shoulder of the man in the middle. The youngest one, to the left, holds a football together with the middle one, right in front of the latter's genitalia. The middle one holds his hand quite low, on the left one's hip. The one on the right looks at the one in the middle, who, in his turn, gazes away. The one on the left looks at the painter/viewer, curious as to what moves him. The careful composition suggests an intimacy that trespasses locker-room conviviality. It is somewhat similar, in this respect, to the image manipulations used to convey a hidden homotextuality by Andy Warhol. Warhol's *Double Elvis*, for example, displays a relation 'in which several erotic hierarchies are put into play: top and bottom, extension and recession, activity and passivity, dominance and submission'.[26]

Queer 'complicity' may be derived also from the unfinished mural, *La voluntad de construir* in the reading room of the Biblioteca de Mexico (1946). Its iconography is quite unusual. Centrally, a naked woman holds up a baby that in its turn embraces a huge stone cross. The crucifix, along with the Plumed Serpent, are represented as a double symbol of Mexico's *mestizo* identity. Surrounding the woman and child are numerous men. They are fully naked and either white, Indian, *mestizo* or black. They hold up stone pillars, holding onto them as if they were gigantic phallic symbols, or are occupied erecting one in a collective performance of virile strength.

The mural's artistic qualities are dubious: the composition is rather unbalanced, as if the painter himself was overwhelmed by the multitude of figures and forms, but here too an almost Dionysian homoeroticism can be detected. Perhaps its meaning would have become clearer within the wider narrative context of the full, completed mural, but the author's death prevented this.

What to think, finally, of the distant, uninterested look of the artist in the painting *Estudio del pintor Zárraga en Paris*, also titled *El pan y el agua* (1935/6). At the left, two women carry bread and water, but the artist, Zárraga, looks away from them, dreamy, unhappy. There may very well be something or someone to the right of him, but we are not allowed to see, nor can we penetrate his mind. The painter's self-portrait may express his sense of alienation from the female sex, despite the numerous paintings he devoted to them during his life.

Perhaps too much programmatic reading is implied by my decoding of Zárraga's works. I readily admit that my claims remain speculative. Still, both a 'close reading' of Zárraga's portrayals of men in the light of a wider understanding of homosexual *imaginaire* and biographical data – his bachelor's status, absence of documentary evidence about heterosexual relationships, his prolonged stay in Paris – may allow us to tentatively conclude that some of Zárraga's work can indeed be labelled as of a homoerotic nature. Eventually, documentary evidence will either corroborate or falsify such a claim.

Fascinating also is the oeuvre of Saturnino Herrán (1887–1918), much of which is clearly homoerotic – a fact, moreover, that cannot be dismissed by referring to his status as a married man and father of a son. His marriage with Rosario Aurellano in 1914 seems congruent, actually, with the social expectations even in a diligently modernizing Mexico. Even a man who was aware of his 'bisexual' or 'homosexual' inclination was likely to respond to the pressures of society – a decision that may have been facilitated by the silently accepted homosexual libido among Mexican men as long as certain codes of behaviour were maintained.

Little seems known about Herrán's sexual practices either within or outside marriage, so no clear statements regarding these can be made. Carlos Fuentes, who has known some of Herrán's contemporaries, suggests that he was like a *dandy finisecular*. His relationship with Rosario seems to have been characterized by her 'almost incestuous' affection for her *niño*, her *adorable chachito*, her eternal adolescent − qualifications that may indeed suggest that their marriage was a quite enlightened, if patronizing, one, where Rosario was sufficiently informed and accepting of her husband's sexual ambiguity.[27]

An analysis of his artistic oeuvre certainly identifies an outspoken erotic interest in young or adult men, even when, or perhaps just because, this was incorporated within a narrative context of Decadence or Naturalism, and subsequent *Indigenismo*. Herrán's strategies for representing the male nude were so manifold, in fact, that it becomes clear how 'mediation' between his inner personal impulses on the one hand and social and public expectations on the other hand must have been on his mind throughout his career.

Initially, Herrán's representations of the male nude were 'academic': an Adonis and a David alongside a classical column and a Greek amphora vase – icons, worldwide, of a homoerotic sensibility but no more than exercises, perhaps, consistent with the predictable agenda of art classes at the time.

Social uproar, eventually leading to the Revolution (1910–17), may have impelled the artist to execute his first great work, *Labor* (1908), a panel showing labouring men on one side, a resting family on the other side. Already, men are the majority here, some of them half-naked, virile, showing muscles strained by the hardship of physical efforts. In this work, there is a striking difference between his rather dull and sketchy portrayals of female nudes, and the fine, exquisite lineature of his representations of male nudes. The men, here and in his later works, are executed with more devotion and care.

Initially, Naturalism allowed Herrán to proceed from academic drawing and to exchange the timeless, classical imagery for depictions of contemporary society, including 'real-life' people in 'real-life' clothes. He shared in the artistic interest of his time for 'lo fantástico, lo lujoso, lo superfluo, la cosmopolita, lo criminal, lo miserable, lo decadente, . . . lo horrible'*[28] and painted blind, decaying men, artisans, or workers. Herrán's Naturalism is an ambiguous one, however, and he hardly ever escaped his sense of the aesthetic, which made even the margins of society look beautiful. *Labor*, mentioned earlier, is idealizing in its representation of athletic, muscular workers, and in its depiction of a working-class family in the foreground. A man watches as his wife breastfeeds their child. Garrido rightly emphasizes how Herrán's vision of work, family and happiness was somehow deceptive and closer to the official political discourse of the time than to reality.[29]

An idealization of family life is obvious also in *Forjadores* (1913) as well as in two panels, titled *Alegoria de la construcción* and *Alegoria del trabajo*. These panels were painted from 1910 to 1911 and are now located in the presidential residence of Los Pinos. Both traditional artisanry and modern industrial labour are represented, along with a woman and children, references to family life. The panels' tenor is optimistic and far removed

*'the fantastic, the luxurious, the superfluous, the cosmopolitan, the criminal, the miserable, the decadent, . . . the horrible'

from the *spléen* visible in Decadent paintings of the late nineteenth and early twentieth century in Mexico as well as Europe.

In fact, Herrán himself soon set out to make paintings and drawings that focused on the indigenous male and to adorn the latter with an almost Decadent sensuality. He somewhat reiterated the familiar narrative of Romantic *Indigenismo*, yet gave it a particularly *fin de siècle* touch by focusing on the male Indian's nudity and physicality. Examples are indeed manifold of his idealizing and sensual depictions of male Indians, whose ethnic identity remains vague beyond rather fantastic, imaginary constructions of Aztec (or Mayan) ancestors.

La raza dormida (1912) shows two semi-nude men sitting against a tree, asleep – icons of a dormant heritage, of the marginalization of indigenous people in Mexico, but a reminder at the same time of how indian ancestry co-defined Mexican national identity: 'la idea de una raza adormecida en un sueño de siglos, postrada en una tierra con la que se funde, rodeada por una atmosféra de hieratismo, heredera de un saber oculto y poderoso'.*[30] Such mystification of people, who, in reality, were hardly acknowledged any civil rights, was typical of an asocial, idealizing *Indigenismo* that Herrán subscribed to also in other works such as *Sátiro* (n.d.) or the almost Arcadian *La leyenda de los Volcanes* (1910). *The satyr* shows a man of Greek profile, simultaneously given indigenous features, which makes it quite ahistorical and aestheticizes its subject to a high degree. The same goes for an emblematic *Caballero Aguila* (1918), bought for 17 pesos by the publisher Porrúa when times were dire. A neo-Hellenic sensibility can also be found in *Indígena con vaso ceremonial* (1916) or, reminding the viewer of Praxiteles, in *Indio con niño* (n.d.). Another idealizing representation, at once stereotyping and sensual, is the drawing *El guerrero* (1917).

El quetzal (1917) presents a kneeling Indian seen from behind, exposing his naked back and buttocks. He is lifting up a quetzal, symbol of Indian-American identity. The quetzal is an outspoken masculine symbol, as opposed to flowers, fruits and fabrics, which are frequently depicted alongside women. Herrán maintains the rigid gender codes himself, as can be seen in portrayals of women like *Bugambilias*, *Desnudo de mujer con flores* and *La tehuana*.

The male symbols in yet another work, *El flechador* (1918) (Plate 4) are the bow and arrow, which fit the artist's clear-cut vision of both female and male social roles. But, whereas the artist reproduces gender roles in this work on one level, he simultaneously challenges these on another. *El flechador* in fact reflects yet another of Herrán's strategies for representing male nudes and for attributing a sexual dimension to an otherwise neutral imagery. The background to such manipulation of signifiers was the artist's incorporation of hermetic philosophy, of theosophic and Vedantic ideas, and finally, of introspective, Eastern religion in its widest sense. A double message is hidden, says Fausto Ramírez, in *El flechador*:'donde estaria implicado por la figura descendente del dios,

*'the idea of a race, sunk away in a dream of centuries, prostrated in the very soil that are its roots, surrounded by an atmosphere of hieratism, heir of an occult and powerful knowledge'

labraba en la lápida, y la sugerencia de un impulso ascendente en la flecha puesto en el arco. El indio que empuña el arma nos remite de nuevo al arquetipo del andrógino.'*[31]

Androgyny is visible also in the artist's illustration for an almanac of the Universidad Popular Mexicana of 1919, in *El flechador acuclillado* on a cover of the cultural journal *Pegaso*,[32] and even more clearly in the drawing *Exposición Herrán* (1914). Even Garrido, who reluctantly recognizes the homoerotic dimension in Herrán's work, admits that sexual ambiguity is unmistakable here: 'Un indio asexuado – que puede vincularse con otro de los arquetipos modernistas, el del andrógino, "con tus neutros encantos, tu faz de efebo,/tus senos *pectorales* . . .", en el conocido soneto de Amado Nervo – parece avancar hacia el frente con los ojos cerrados y los brazos cruzados sobre la frente, concentrado en la voz interior que lo guía y rodeado por una diadema de estrellas.'†[33] It is quite well known that androgyny was an ideal, cherished by homosexual men in particular even when it seemed to imply de-sexualization and sublimation of a most commonly ephebophile inclination.[34] To merely emphasize the intellectual inspiration of the cult of androgyny, as Garrido seems to maintain, is inadequate because it neglects the intimate relationship between many an individual's subscription to such ideals and his expression, if indirect, of a particular sexual desire.

Garrido's position may well be illustrative of an ongoing reluctance among some art historians to recognize the homosexual muse, inspiring the artistic representation of male or androgynous nudity. Such art, in their eyes, ought to embody higher ideals and, when this cannot be demonstrated, it is easily discarded as the vulgar subgenre of 'erotic art'. At times, the dimension of physical sensuality is merely denied and the critic's view projected subsequently upon the artist himself. Edgar Valenzuela, for example, relocates his own inappropriate doubt regarding the oeuvre's homoerotic content and speculates that the painter attributed feminine characteristics to his models in order to make them look androgynous and thus 'asexual'.[35] Surely, Herrán could not paint male nudity so consistently throughout his career without 'positioning' it within a wider, public narrative, here of national identity. But Valenzuela fails to see that the androgynous characters of Herrán's paintings and drawings remain icons, on a more implicit level of perception, of a peculiarly turn-of-the-century homosexual imaginary.

Fausto Ramírez, in various contexts, emphasizes the artist's adoption of androgyny as a particularly Symbolist narrative theme and even acknowledges how his languid, passive ephebes reflect 'sexual ambiguity'. But in the end, he too refrains from recognizing how such imagery may in fact originate from a personal impulse. 'Su originalidad', he rationalizes, 'fue convertir, traducir la temática y las preocupaciones simbolistas (mujer fatal, andrógino, relaciones desiguales y frustrantes entre los sexos . . .) a formas o expresiones de apariencia local.'‡[36] Ramírez, whose interpretation of Herrán's work is probably the most adequate,[37] ought to have noticed, however, that the localism of its imagery, of its indigenous cast, was a most efficient alibi for representing male nudity

*'implied by the descending figure of god, fashioned in a slab of stone, and the arrow placed on the bow, thus suggesting an upward movement. The Indian, while taking up the weapon, reminds us of the archetype of androgyny.'

†'An asexual Indian – which can be connected to that other modernist archetype, the androgyne, "with your neutered charm, your ephebe-like face, your flat breasts . . .", as the well-known sonnet of Amado Nervo goes – seems to come to the fore with closed eyes and his arms crossed above the head, focusing on the inner voice that leads him, and circled by a diadem of stars.'

‡'His originality was to convert and translate the symbolist themes and concerns (*femme fatale*, androgyny, unequal and frustrating relations between the sexes) into local shapes and expressions.'

outside the realm of the vulgar and the pornographic, of the suspicious or the pathological. Which, in its turn, reveals how, during the Porfiriato, the visual narration of sexual non-conformity was hooked up in a significant manner to tropes of cultural and ethnic exoticism.

The relationship between visual representations of nudity and their meaning is far more complex than is suggested by many historians or critics. It actually often combines different levels of signification, some of which are beyond the author's control, but some of which are unrightfully taken away from the artist by socially and culturally biased, omniscient art experts. Herrán's 'vitalism' expressed itself in images of sex and death simultaneously and reflected how both themes were intertwined in a Decadent aesthetic so prominent at the time. The immediacy of physical decay and death, the ambiguity of sexual roles, the relationship of both with religious concepts such as sin, culpability and redemption, are present in Herrán's work as well and contrast heavily with the optimism of his 'social' works. Homoeroticism is constantly present in all of his works, however, even when the artist addresses an abstract concept such as death. *Beso de la muerte* (1916) may reflect the work of his teacher, José Ruelas, or Munch, Böcklin or Rops. But it too cannot disguise the author's fascination for the male nude and perhaps guilt accompanying it. The work may in fact hold the key to an understanding of Herrán's life as a whole, where both guilt and social conformity impelled him to embrace public standards and to limit the expression of a less acceptable sexuality within the field of his artistic creativity.

A rewriting of Herrán's artistic biography obviously must be concluded with a close look at the studies, made by the artist, for the interior of the Teatro Nacional. An early version, titled *Friso de los Dioses Viejos* (1914), showed semi-nude Indians worshipping their gods. The lineature of their bodies is sharply drawn with a precise eye for the male anatomy. The representation of Aztecs is stereotypical at the same time, as idealized bodies reflect a peculiar exoticism. The almost identical faces, in profile, of all the men is both racist and, perhaps, inspired by a particular preference for men with exactly those facial features.

Most characteristics surface in other partial studies such as the drawing *Desnudo masculino* (n.d.), the *Panneau decorativo* (Plate 6) of 1916, or cover illustrations for *El Universal Illustrado* and *Revista de Revistas* (both in 1917). They reappear, finally, in the definitive studies of a triptych titled *Nuestros Dioses* (1918). Together, they show a symmetrical composition with, in the middle, an almost abstract figure, reflecting the sculpture of Aztec deities. To the right, the Spaniards are represented, worshipping Christ; to the left, the Aztecs venerating their own mother goddess Coatlicue, 'cuadrada, decapitada, sin ataduras antropomórficas'.*[38] Both religious symbols are integrated in one single image, both pre-Columbian and colonial, which reflects the artist's appreciation of *mestizaje* as Mexico's greatest cultural asset. It reminds us of the hidden message in *La raza dormida*. But the actual history of artistic production suggests that Herrán himself

*'made to look square, decapitated, without human-like characteristics'

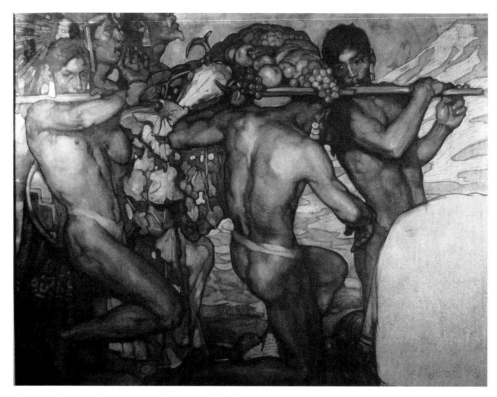

Figure 18 Saturnino Herrán, *Nuestros Dioses* (study) (1918), charcoal on paper, 110 × 145 cm, collection Alicia Udiña, courtesy of Centro Nacional de las Artes, Biblioteca de las Artes, Mexico City.

*'Like a painter, he drew each muscle and each centimetre of the bodily geography.'

†'the finery of its plumes and the even more appealing finery of their naked bodies'

was particularly driven by the panel on the left. Only a few small studies are kept of the right panel with Spaniards dressed to the nines, while he kept drawing and redrawing the left one: 'Dibujó como pintor, cada músculo y cada centímetro de la geografía de los cuerpos.'*[39] The charcoal sketches and watercolors, *Grupo de tres indígenas arrodillados*, *Grupo de cuatro indígenas arrodillados*, *Grupo de cinco indígenas* and *Nuestros Dioses* (Plate 5) collectively witness an almost obsessive drive to reach perfection – 'los atavíos de sus plumas y el atavío, más hermoso, de sus cuerpos desnudos'†[40] – and perhaps there is no more to it than that. But his choice to execute the Indigenous panel first may not have been purely coincidental in the light of other, minor facts. A drawing of 1910, for example, called *El beso* remained incomplete and again it is the male figure rather than the female one that is developed the furthest. A portrait of Alberto Garduño, holding a small sculpture of a male nude in his hand (1913), was preceded by careful studies of the sculpture only. *El hijo pródigo* (1913), too, was accompanied by various studies of the young man. Herrán copied work of Michelangelo (*The Dying Slave*) and Donatello (*David* in bronze), both works that suffuse a homoerotic atmosphere, but few sketches exist, on the other hand, that betray an equally vivid passion for the portrayal of women.

Herrán was represented at the art exhibition of 1910 that was organized by Gerardo Murillo, better known as Dr Atl. It embodied a reaction against the official exhibition of Spanish art at the 100th anniversary of Mexico's independence and against the cultural policy of the soon-to-fall regime of Porfirio Díaz. It ought to demonstrate how Mexico itself produced art that could stand comparison with Europe and at the same time was impregnated with a sense of national pride. *Indigenismo*, in this context, became politicized as the artistic expression of Mexican cultural identity. Alongside Herrán's images of pre-Columbian spirituality, there was Jorge Encisco's painting *Anahuac*, attributing both spiritual grandiosity and an aura of sensuality to the indigenous hero as well. Francisco de la Torre and Roberto Montenegro, in their turn, presented images of contemporary indigenous people as symbols of both national resurgence and artistic autonomy.[41] But soon artistic perceptions changed again and the very premises of romantic and sensualist Indigenism were challenged, partly by the Stridentismo movement of Maples Acre and Alva de la Canal, more so by the *machisto* ethic of a new generation of muralists.

Brazil's tropical Belle Époque

Economic modernization took place also in Brazil, where slavery was abolished as late as 1888 and a republican regime was installed the next year. The country witnessed a sequence of economic booms, even though they were regionally confined: sugar in the Northeastern states and mining in Minas Gerais, rubber in the North (Belém, Manaus), coffee in the state of São Paulo. Economic growth gave rise to urbanization. Old cities were sanitized (Rio de Janeiro,[42] Salvador and Recife), while new ones expanded rapidly (São Paulo, Belo Horizonte, Belém, Manaus).

The drive to modernization was marked considerably by a desire to replace the existing amalgamation of folk and imported cultures by a 'universal' European one, which explains the prominence of a neoclassical aesthetic, still current to some degree in the Old World. This is reflected not only in architecture and urban planning, but in the visual arts, which similarly subscribed to its themes and style.

Yet, neo-classicism was enriched by a new, turn-of-the-century aesthetic that drew its inspiration from contemporary art movements in Europe. On the one hand, there was clearly a move away from the predictable prescriptions of the Academy, while, on the other hand, mythology, religion and history remained favourite themes for the stylistically innovative artists as well. Examples of the latter are *Recompensa de São Sebastião* (1898) by Eliseu d'Angelo Visconti, *O despertar de Ícaro* (*c.* 1910) by Lucilio de Albuquerque, and *Caim e Abel* (1916) by José Ferreira Dias, Jr.

The dissemination in Brazil of a *fin de siècle* sensibility, however, gave rise to more daring expressions of bodily culture, sex and sensuality. The erotic became fashionable, partially due to the dissemination of European sexological theories. Relations between men and women were supported by new ideas on sexual attraction, even if they remained imbued with the imperatives of *machismo*. Fashion accentuated rather than disguised the feminine form, while male dress code remained rather austere: 'Mesmo a moda, com seus froufrous e joupons, corsets e pantalons, nada mais fazia de que realçar o conteúdo erótico do corpo feminino, aqui acentuado esbeltez de uma cintura, ali a opulência das ancas o do busto, e assim por diante.'*[43]

*'Even fashion, with its frou-frous and dresses, its corsets and slacks, reinforced the erotic appeal of the feminine body, now accentuating a slender waist, then the opulent thighs or breasts, and so on.'

There were 'dandies' in Brazil, among whom the writer João do Rio (1881–1921) undoubtedly was the most famous. He was known as the 'tropical Oscar Wilde'. But his presence was an exception to the rule that exuberance and refinement were now the monopoly of women. Men who adopted a frivolous and flamboyant pose were seen as sexual perverts in the new, modern Brazil.

What then, we must ask, was the place of an erotic male body in this new context? And, secondly, what does this reveal about the presence of a potentially hidden or codified trope of homotextuality? How, if at all, was a homosexual sensibility visualized?

Teixeira Leite claims that the male nude remained confined within the limits of the Academy. Outside, it would have been considered 'imoral o ao menos de mau gosto' ('immoral or at least in bad taste').[44] Yet alternative erotic work was increasingly produced, according to Mesquita, who points out that this included images of sexual diversity: 'Parallelmente a essas produções voltadas aos salões artísticos e meios literarios começam a aparecer outras formas de arte erótica, diversa daquelo erotismo institucionalizado de beleza idealizada e sublimada, que ganham o espaço de gabinete de colecionador. São imagens – pinturas, desenhos, pequenas esculturas, fotografías – referentes a sexo explicito, pedofilia, travestimento, homossexualismo, produzidas especialmente para amateurs.'†[45]

†'Parallel to these works, destined for the artistic salons and literary circles, new forms of erotic art showed up that were distinct from the institutionalized eroticism of idealized and sublimated beauty, and ended up in the collector's private cabinets. These were images – paintings, drawings, small sculptures, photographs – with explicit sexual content, pedophilia, transvestism, homosexuality, all produced for the amateurs.'

Explicit sexual imagery remained altogether rare in the fine arts, maintaining an academic rhetoric of idealized, de-sexualized beauty. The semi-pornographic, if exclusively heterosexual, works by the Brazilian Henrique Alvim Corrêa were anomalous, in fact, within the context of turn-of-the-century, 'decadent' art. The representation of nudity, male or female, still called for apologetic non-sexual narratives.

As elsewhere, history painting provided opportunities for depictions of male nudity, even when these were often bereft of sensuality in view of the grand historical narrative. They were discrete in comparison not only to the seventeenth-century ethnographic paintings of Albert Eckhout, but also to the early nineteenth-century drawings by Debret, Florence, Rugendas, von Martius or zu Wied. Brazilian artists, as opposed to their European teachers, were concerned less to exoticize their land than to visualize the course of history and progress, the advent of civilization and the mastering of the wilderness. Their works reflected the values largely of a Eurocentric Creole élite, either through composition or by means of hierarchic narrative. Nudity, in this context, became a signifier of inferiority, barbarity and heathenism.

Hierarchy is emphasized literally, at times, by the indigenous people's position in the picture's margins. Meirelles de Lima's *Primeira missa no Brasil* (1860) still shows the influential imagery of Eckhout, especially on the level of landscape painting, but the Indian is now witnessing the course of history, of which he is no longer in control. Likewise in the equally hierarchic depiction of the Indians in Pereira da Silva's *Fundação de São Paulo* and in Pedro Américo's *Batalha do Avaí*. Ettore Usai's monumental sculpture to the memory of father José Anchieta is a testimony also to Christianization and the cultural suppression of the indigenous population. The submissive positioning of the Indians turns their nudity into a carrier of social inferiority rather than exoticist, erotic appeal.

Yet as in Mexico, there was a countercurrent to nationalist and Eurocentric history painting. It focused on those populations on Brazilian territory who had become marginalized either in the wake of expansion, or as a result of economic exploitation. Most prominent among these were the indigenous populations or Indians, and the black slaves, imported massively from Africa and the Caribbean until the abolition of slavery in Brazil as late as 1888.

As elsewhere, *Indigenismo* was Eurocentric in itself and patronizing towards the Indian people and their cultural heritage. The depiction of the male – and female – body was immersed within the visual rhetoric of exoticism, reducing ethnographic variety to a single, static image of 'the Indian', *o indígena*. Nudity, in this context, was a signifier of Indian identity as well as a great excuse for creating erotic images that were socially acceptable because inscribed within the discursive trope of Indigenism.

It is virtually impossible for today's historian, moreover, to decide whether erotic impulse provoked an artist's imagery of indigenous people, rather than compliance with the expectations of a white, Creole élite. To an extent, the Indian's nudity was the outcome merely of an academic aesthetic, focusing on bodily structure. But a process of iconization pushed such exercises beyond ethnographic documentary and turned the Indian into a timeless and uprooted signifier of the exoticist gaze. 'The central themes of the élite have . . . made the Indian mysterious, turned him into folklore, focused on the grotesque and, finally, sublimated him, reproducing images that focus on the Indian's feathers, his muscularity, his bucolic environment, his historic immobility as idol', observes the Peruvian critic Mirko Lauer.[46]

Ethnographic precision accordingly was sacrificed to the idealizing image of autochthonous populations, drawn from international primitivist discourse rather than from local, anthropological observation. This can be noticed also in some Brazilian works. The *Índio simbolizando a nação brasileiro* (1872) is a sculpture by Francisco Manoel Chaves Pinheiro (1822–84) that neatly visualizes how indigenous heritage was mobilized as a

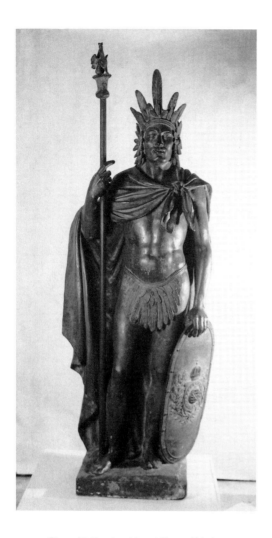

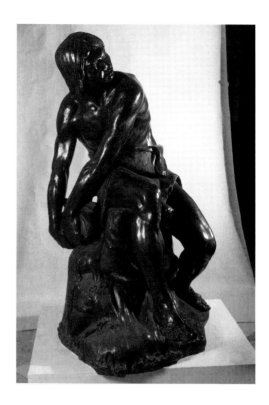

Figure 19 Francisco Manoel Chaves Pinheiro,
Índio simbolizando a nação brasileira (1872), terracotta,
192 × 75 × 31 cm, Museo Nacional de Belas Artes, Rio
de Janeiro, photo: Raúl Lima.

Figure 20 Candido Caetano Almeida Reis,
O rio Paraíba do Sul (1866), bronze, 146 × 120 × 97 cm,
Museo Nacional de Belas Artes, Rio de Janeiro,
photo: Raúl Lima.

vehicle for patriotic rhetoric, rather than as a legitimate object of representation within its own, autonomous context. The persistent influence of Brazilian Baroque remains visible in this work also, which only reluctantly subscribes to the aesthetic principles of academic sculpture.

A semi-nude seated Indian becomes an icon too in the eyes of Candido Caetano Almeida Reis (1838–89), who titled his sculpture *O rio Paraíba do Sul* (1866) and located the Indian figure in a remote, then still unspoilt area of Brazil. Yet another sculpture, by the Italo-Brazilian Luigi Brizzolara, is typical of a decontextualized iconic image of indigenous people. *O Guarany* is installed in front of the Teatro Municipal of São Paulo, along with a prototypical slave (*O escravo*), and even when an ethnographic reference is given, it is still an ideal type rather than an accurate representation of Brazil's southern indigenous population. A heroic role was ascribed to indigenous people in Rodolfo Amoêdo's (1857–1941) *O último Tamoio* (1883). Yet, it is telling that the painting simultaneously consolidates white supremacy over the indigenous tribes populating Brazil at an earlier time.

Occasionally, the male body is also embraced in images of Brazil's African population, yet here too the erotic is inscribed within a static, exoticist discourse of representation. Virtually all options are comprised within one single, homogeneous category, the slave. Whether he was presented as acquiescent in the face of his social inferiority, or as a member of the republics of runaway slaves in the so-called *quilombos*, he was depicted as a man without history, as a man on the margins of Brazilian society. See, in this respect, *Zumbi* by Antônio da Silva Parreiras (1869–1937), or the two iron statues flanking the main staircase of the Paraíso *fazenda* near Valença, Rio de Janeiro. They are fine examples of exoticist classicism.

Cecy e Pery by Horácio Hora (1853–90) is significant as well. It is an undated work painted by an artist who was black and who subscribed to the Primitivist trope of representation himself. It is undoubtedly a very sensual work, showing a black boatman manoeuvring his canoe across the water while, in the canoe, a white woman is lying asleep. One can hardly deny that the muscular, semi-naked body of the male character is on the same level with the white female one and, while an erotic complicity between both arises as one looks at the painting, one becomes aware of how this crossed socially acceptable boundaries even in a racially mixed country like Brazil. The transgressive power of sexual attraction, even if only suggested by the painting's subtle, controlled style, is emphasized not only by the female character's frailty, but also and equally by the sexual aura of the man. Yet here too, the painting's daring subtext is made harmless by situating the story in a remote, literary past.

Conclusion

Whereas the dissemination of 'gay' identity in Latin America has been relatively slow and remains predominantly limited to the major urban centres, it is nevertheless true also that European concepts of 'homosexual' identity became known at the beginning of the twentieth century onwards, giving rise to the cultivation by some of homosexual sensibility. This remained confined within the social boundaries of an educated élite, admittedly, yet was at times more clearly recognizable and tangible as its equivalent expression in, for example, nineteenth-century North American art. The various narrative contexts – the Academy, *Indigenismo*, Naturalism, Symbolism – reveal, in fact, how these provided opportunities for widely diverging visual expressions of what I have called 'homotextuality' in Latin American art.

Academic art, in this respect, was highly reminiscent of its European examples and harboured an equally ambiguous dialectic between the agenda of mimesis and portrayal within the confines of an exclusively male, homosocial art education programme. Homotextuality, as a result, was ubiquitous, yet hardly ever in a tangible, explicit way.

Symbolism, next, inscribed eroticism and physicality within the narratives of Decadence, imported directly also from the Old World and lending a somewhat prematurely *fin de siècle* feeling to the art production of newly modernizing cities in Latin America. At odds with the surrounding social realities, it was to please the local cultural élite, eager to lend itself respectable status by naïvely copying high art from Paris and Rome. Almost uncritically, so it seems, did the ruling classes welcome the Old World's visual iconography, even when, at times, this was clearly marked by homotextuality. To some degree, this may reflect the gradual dissemination of new insights, also imported from Europe, concerning sexual diversity. But homoerotic content, more importantly, could be pursued by artists precisely because it was carefully framed within wider narratives, and thus poorly perceived by most of its contemporary audience. To accurately see, one had to share the key to decoding and be a member of the man-loving tribe.

The relative openness of contemporary Latin American 'high culture' for images that, at close view, were inscribed within an explicitly homoerotic *imaginaire* proved to be short-lived, however. In Chapter 3, I will demonstrate that Modernism and, more particularly, the politicized aesthetic of Muralism and its offsprings were conducive to an eclipse, rather than further development, of images of a nascent *ambiente*. Heterosexism, in the name of formal innovation, pushed the visual expression of homotextuality into the margins of Latin American art production, only for it to resurface cautiously after the Second World War.

Notes

1 Quoted in Lucie-Smith and Boyd, *Life Class*, p. 10. Also, see N. Pevsner, *Academies of Art* (Cambridge, 1940), and the exhibition catalogue *Strictly Academic* (New York and Williamstown, 1974).

2 Solomon-Godeau, *Male Trouble*. Also, see Saunders, *The Nude*.

3 Solomon-Godeau, *Male Trouble*, pp. 26–30.

4 M. Praz, quoted in J. Sillevis, '"Le beau idéal"', *Maatstaf* (1984), p. 74.

5 On the growing stigmatization of homosocial arrangements, see M. Aerts *et al.*, introduction to conference papers 'Among Men, Among Women. Sociological and Historical Recognition of Homosocial Arrangements' (Amsterdam, 1983), pp. xi–xxii.

6 *Projeto Arte Brasileira: Academismo* (Rio de Janeiro, 1986), pp. 8, 24.

7 Independence was not achieved simultaneously everywhere. I merely mention the countries discussed in this book: Mexico 1821, Brazil 1822, Cuba 1898 (under US influence, however), Puerto Rico, under US control from 1898 onwards also.

8 See D. Ades, *Art in Latin America* (New Haven and London, 1989), pp. 27–30. On the exceptional situation of Puerto Rican art, see M. C. Ramírez, *Puerto Rican Painting between Past and Present* (Princeton, 1987), pp. 14–20.

9 As early as 1783, the Real Academia de las Tres Nobles Artes was founded by King Carlos III. In 1843, president Antonio López de Santa Anna promoted its re-opening after it had been closed during the War of Independence. See C. Bargellini and E. Fuentes, *Guia que permite capter lo bello: Yesos y dibujos de la Academia Real de San Carlos, 1778–1916* (Mexico, 1989), pp. 3–11.

10 J. Fernández, *Arte moderno y contemporáneo de México* (Mexico, 1993 (1952)), vol. 1, p. 61: 'Los desnudos masculinos eran frecuentes y alcanzan excelente construcción anatómica, pero los desnudos femininos no entraban en el programa de la moral y las buenas costumbres.'

11 See C. L. Taylor, 'Mexican gaylife in historical perspective', in W. Leyland (ed.), *Gay Roots: Twenty Years of Gay Sunshine: An Anthology of Gay History, Politics, and Culture* (San Francisco, 1991), pp. 190–202; J. Carrier, *De los otros: Intimacy and Homosexuality among Mexican Men* (New York, 1995); and I. Lumsden, *Homosexualidad: sociedad y estado en México* (Mexico and Toronto, 1991). In 1950, Octavio Paz acknowledged that homosexuality was treated with a certain indulgence in Mexico. See *El laberinto de la soledad* (Mexico, 1950), p. 43.

12 The original can be seen at the Museo Nacional de Arte in Mexico City. A bronze copy stands at the Avenida Alvaro Obregón, Mexico City.

13 'Anacreontism' refers to Anacreon, a Greek poet of the 6th century BC, and describes the revived passion for all things Greek since the mid-eighteenth century. 'The Anacreontic idiom', says A. Solomon-Godeau, 'in contrast to the asperities of Stoic manhood, celebrates a certain polymorphism (exemplified by the ephebe) as well as a demonstrable fascination with narratives of role reversal and gender ambiguity' (*Male Trouble*, p. 109).

14 See Vítor Meirelles de Lima's *A Bacante* (n.d.), Augusto Rodrigues Duarte's *Exequias de Atalá* (1878) or Eliseu Visconti's *Dança das Oréades* (1899).

15 See K. Dover, *Greek Homosexuality* (New York, 1980), pp. 157–8, on the relationship between Socrates and Alcibiades.

16 See A. Potts, *Flesh and the Ideal: Winckelmann and the Origins of Art History* (New Haven and London, 1994), p. 236.

17 See Solomon-Godeau, *Male Trouble*, pp. 127, 129–30.

18 See A. Mafra de Souza, in *Universo Acadêmico* (Rio de Janeiro, 1989), no page number.

19 See K. Hale, 'Thomas Eakins: artist of Philadelphia', *GCN*, 13 November 1982, pp. 8–9; T. Fairbrother, 'Sargent's genre paintings and the issues of suppression and privacy', in D. Bolger and N. Cikovsky, Jr. (eds), *American Art around 1900* (Washington, DC, 1990), pp. 29–49, and E. Lucie-Smith, 'The homosexual sensibility in Géricault's paintings and drawings', *European Gay Review*, 2 (1987), pp. 32–41.

20 Solomon-Godeau, *Male Trouble*, pp. 94–6.

21 F. Garrido (ed.), *Saturnino Herrán* (Mexico, 1988), p. 22.

22 J. A. Manrique, in *Tlacotalpan: De la pintura académica a la popular* (Mexico, 1995), p. 3.

23 See, on the European imagery of Atala, S.J. Delaney, '*Atala* in the arts', in J. Beauroy *et al.* (eds), *The Wolf and the Lamb: Popular Culture in France from the Old Régime to the Twentieth Century* (Palo Alto, 1977), pp. 209–31.

24 See C. Monsiváis, 'Ortodoxia y heterodoxia en las alcobas. Hacia una crónica de costumbres y creencias sexuales en México', *Debate Feminista*, 6, 2 (April 1995), pp. 183–210.

25 Details in *Exposición Homenaje a Ángel Zárraga, 1886–1946* (Mexico, 1969).

26 R. Meyer, 'Warhol's clones', *Yale Journal of Criticism*, 7, 1 (Spring 1994), p. 96.

27 C. Fuentes, in V. Muñoz, *Saturnino Herrán: La pasión y el principio* (Mexico, 1994), p. 10.

28 Garrido, *Saturnino Herrán*, p. 18.

29 *Ibid*., p. 27.

30 *Ibid*., p. 22.

31 F. Ramírez, 'La obra de Saturnino Herrán en el contexto del Modernismo', *México en el Arte*, 18 (Autumn 1987), p. 16.

32 In number 4 (29 March 1917).

33 Garrido, *Saturnino Herrán*, pp. 29–30.

34 See E. Showalter, *Sexual Anarchy: Gender and Culture at the Fin de Siècle* (Harmondsworth, 1990), *passim*, and B. Dijkstra, 'The androgyne in nineteenth century literature', *Comparative Literature*, 26 (1974), pp. 62–73.

35 E. Valenzuela, 'Saturnino Herrán (1887–1918)', *La Semana de Bellas Artes*, 70 (4 April 1979), pp. 12–14.

36 F. Ramírez, *Saturnino Herrán* (Mexico, 1976), pp. 28, 30, 35, 43–5.

37 See especially his text in *Saturnino Herrán: Pintor mexicano (1887–1987)* (Mexico, 1987), pp. 7–32, 74–7. Partially satisfying also is J. Valle-Castillo, 'El desnudo en Saturnino Herrán', *PLURAL: Revista Cultural del Excelsior,* 103 (April 1980), pp. 33–7. Fuentes also acknowledges the homoerotic dimension of the painter's numerous male Indian nudes. See in Muñoz, *Saturnino Herrán*, p. 10.

38 C. Fuentes, *El espejo enterrado* (Mexico, 1992), p. 109.

39 Muñoz, *Saturnino Herrán*, p. 52.

40 M. Toussaint, *Saturnino Herrán y su obra* (Mexico, 1920), p. 30.

41 See *1910: el arte en un año decisivo: La exposición de artistas mexicanos* (Mexico City, 1991).

42 See J. D. Needell, *A Tropical Belle Époque. Élite Culture and Society in Turn-of-the-century Rio de Janeiro* (Cambridge, 1987).

43 J. R. Teixeira Leite, *Dicionário crítico da pintura no Brasil* (Rio de Janeiro, 1988), p. 359.

44 *Ibid.*

45 I. Mesquita, in *O desejo na Academia, 1847–1916* (São Paulo, 1992), p. 18.

46 M. Lauer, 'Populist ideology and Indigenism: a critique', in Mosquera, *Beyond the Fantastic*, p. 82.

CHAPTER THREE

Modernism and the new politics of masculinity

(1910-70)

Introduction

The rejection of a *fin de siècle* aesthetic, if belated compared to Europe, opened perspectives for the dissemination of Modernism in Latin America and, along with it, of a sexual politics that was marked by paradoxical rigidity and, at times, even prudery. The logic of formal and aesthetic innovation often led to the dehumanization of visual imagery, to the eclipse of the human body. The abolition of a dimension of social documentary and local colour was reinforced by the consolidation of a predominantly heterosexist politics, if disguised by the presumably 'asexual' rhetoric of international abstractionism. 'Surely', says Lucie-Smith, 'the Modernists were . . . ferociously opposed to the Symbolists and to the Symbolists' allies, the Decadents. The drooping effeminates and androgynes . . . were just what they most disliked.'[1]

A similar outcome resulted from socially engaged modern art, itself deeply influenced by Mexican Muralism, not only in Latin America but elsewhere in the world as well. Socialist art's sexual politics often proved to uncritically reproduce standard norms of sexual and gender orthodoxy, lending it an, at times, explicit sexist and heterosexist outlook.

The visual expression of homosexual eros or identity was not altogether absent, however, as several artists adopted Modernism's language for coded imagery, made accessible to the understanding eye only by means of *Verdichtung* and ironic paraphrase. At times, as seen in the history of Cuban art, irony was seeping into the very visual rhetoric of a new masculinity proposed by the Revolutionary leadership. And, not surprisingly, it would soon give rise to controversy and repression. Homotextuality was soon denied legitimacy, whether simply by the overpainting of an originally too 'unmasculine' image of man as in a mural by the Mexican Roberto Montenegro, or by excommunication from the intellectual and artistic stage as with the Cubans Servando Cabrera Moreno and Raúl Martínez. Common to homosexual artists' attempts at including sexual variance in the arts, however destined to fail, was their subscription to the canons of artistic orthodoxy. Whether shaped after the agenda of formal innovation, or adhering to the revolutionary anthems of political art, the artists reviewed in this chapter all shared a wish for incorporation into the world of mainstream normality. Subcultural affirmation was a concept alien to them, as was any emphasis on local, cultural identity.

Machismo/Muralismo

Focusing on homotextuality, rather than on recognizably 'homosexual' iconography, allows the historian to record how even works that are formally inscribed within an asexual, political narration may be relevant. Not the author's intention, presumably dictated by sexual identity, but the question of pictorial poly-interpretability is crucial here in order to grasp how a dimension of homotextuality can, at times, lie predominantly within the realm of the viewer's perception. Whether the original intention was 'of a homosexual kind' or not becomes subject to what the artwork actually does. Put differently, homotextuality is not the gay artist's monopoly.

Such a deconstructionist approach, focusing on a text's – or painting's – relative autonomy, allows us to 'read' and understand it beyond a sexual taxonomy, which is essentially a socio-cultural construction limited both in time and space. This alternative approach allows for breaking down the apparently unsurpassable boundaries between 'straight' and 'gay' art or, for that matter, between 'straight' and 'gay' artists – a dynamic, moreover, that is actively simulated today by straight artists, for example, who deliberately produce imagery that they know will attract a gay audience or contain a commentary on gay desire.

In more remote times, when the debate on sexual identities was less prominent, less public and less polarized, that dynamic possibly played a role as well, if only implicitly, or by accident. The mechanism of reception operated then as well and we must recognize also that artists at the time may have been aware of the potentially homoerotic appeal of their works, even when they identified themselves as 'straight' artists, even when they were, in most cases, married, even when they would never have admitted verbally that a homoerotic dimension could actually be identified in their works. They were contributing to a strain of homotextual images as a result, and felt free to do so just because an artist's sexual identity was, at that time, considered less relevant than it is today. Especially in a Latin American context, this is not altogether hard to understand considering the near-ubiquity of a 'bisexual' sensibility despite strict moral codes that favoured heterosexuality and marriage and stigmatized 'homosexual' identity.

Attention must be paid, especially, to visualizations of (mostly male) labour in the arts because, in my opinion, they contain imagery relevant, if only indirectly most of the time, to the subject of this book. To be guided by the concept of homotextuality, rather than the limited and historical concept of 'homosexual identity', enables one to better grasp how images that are not recognizably inscribed within a homosexual *imaginaire* may nevertheless convey a potentially homoerotic message.

In a way, such may well have been a splendid alibi, illustrating how the communicative strain between 'gay intent' and 'gay understanding' can sometimes be very indirect. An artist's focus on themes that, at first sight, are hardly 'gay' may nevertheless allow him to invest a certain homoerotic gaze and present this to the outside world by means of seemingly innocuous narratives. That such an approach is nevertheless bound by the socio-political reality of creative process and limited by actual historical context is perhaps most clearly illustrated by a review of Mexican Muralism. This, in fact, shows how gay appropriation of visual language remained within the margins of an essentially heterosexist and homophobic trope of narration.

The Mexican example

Dr Atl, who became an intellectual mentor of Mexican *muralismo*, distanced himself in 1911 from much of the work that he had included in the art show of the previous year, and pleaded for a more *macho* praxis of the arts. If artists did not play a conscious, *virile* part in the social and political struggle of their time, then they were doomed to fail, argued Dr Atl,[2] who condemned not only academism, but also the turn-of-the-century cult of *décadence* and sensuality.

José Vasconcelos, Secretary of State for Public Education from 1921 until 1924 and first commissioner of murals by Rivera, Orozco, Siqueiros and others, pleaded in his turn for art 'saturated with primitive vigour', for new subject matter and for 'the sacrifice of the exquisite to the great, [of] perfection to invention'.[3] Vasconcelos's vocabulary – 'primitive', 'sacrifice of the exquisite to the great, perfection to invention' – reveals the masculinist premises underlying the politicized art of Mexican Muralism.

Herrán's work in particular seems to have become a target of criticism, according to Daniel Schávelzon, who stresses that the artist's representation of the Mexican people was seen as 'bourgeois' by the new generation of leftist Muralists. The foundation in

1924 of the Sindicato de Obreros Técnicos, Pintores y Escultores was symptomatic of the changing tide. Its manifesto, published in *El Machete*, echoed the Muralists' animosity towards previous bourgeois, intellectualist and sensualist art.[4] It targeted the expression, if implicitly, of any form of homoeroticism, commonly seen within a Socialist perspective as a 'bourgeois' deviation and symptomatic of the parasitic nature of that social class. The attack on refinement and perfection, likewise, was as much the expression of Muralism's 'vitalist', revolutionary aesthetic as of the implicitly homophobic call for rudimentary, 'masculine' art by its major advocates.

Abigail Solomon-Godeau recognizes a similar pattern in French Revolutionary culture, '[identifying] republicanism and civic virtue with masculinity, and the evils of the *ancien régime* with the "unnatural" power and influence of women'.[5] Homophobia indeed was inscribed, in Mexico as in France, within a more encompassing strain of sexism in general and, while French Revolutionaries fulminated against the frivolity of Rococo aristocratic taste, so did the Mexican soulmates take offence at the delicacies of decadent turn-of-the-century art. In both countries, the promotion of strict gender codes aligned with propaganda for social renewal and moral awakening, yet in both countries this entailed the sacrifice of advances made on the level of both feminist and gay emancipation.

The sexual and gender politics of Mexican Muralism can hardly be discussed in detail here, unfortunately, and I will merely point out how these were reflected in the absence, mostly, not only of any form of homoeroticism, but also of sensuality in general. When sex was represented, it was only as a metaphor of bourgeois decadence, conforming, in fact, with the animosity of the increasingly reactionary sexual politics of contemporary Socialism.

José Clemente Orozco, admittedly, painted scenes of prostitution during the beginning of his career. One painting actually shows a couple of lesbian prostitutes. But such images were part of male fantasy and objectification as much as of social documentary, and any speculation regarding Orozco's potentially positive portrayal of male or female homosexuality is swept aside by an engraving of his, called *Los anales,* that shows homosexual men as degenerate, pathetic and effeminate.[6] He subscribed to the implicit homophobia of Mexican Muralism also in a painting on canvas titled *Pomada y perfume* (1946). Homosexuality, again represented as effeminacy and vanity, is presented as a metaphor of corruption and inefficiency in a satirical portrayal of a general/president absorbed in the ritual of *maquillage*.

Orozco quickly dropped such themes altogether and exchanged them for political allegories of Mexico and America. His representations of both male and female nudes in the murals of the Escuela Preparatorio Nacional of Mexico City illustrate how these were symbols of national identity, rather than men of flesh and blood. They answered Dr Atl's call for masculine vigour and complied with the anti-decadent agenda of both Vasconcelos and the Syndicate: 'The influence of Dr. Atl's work . . . can be unmistakably seen . . . in . . . the superhumanly muscled nudes in "Youth". . . and in the colossal figures of "Tzontemec" and the human in the "Two Natures of Man".'[7] There is no life, but monumentality instead, no sensuality but symbolism only.

The simultaneous association of homosexuality with effeminacy and with political corruption can be seen also in Diego Rivera's mural at the Secretaria de Educación Pública. Especially homosexual intellectuals – Salvador Novo among them – became the target of Rivera's *macho* attitude as he perceived them as threats to the Great Revolution's goals. The mural *La historia de México* (1929–35) at the Palacio Nacional shows a corpulent, praying cleric, which, together with the figure's thick, luscious lips, suggest femininity – a charged and stereotypical representation of homosexuality, tied together with religious hypocrisy, political conspiracy and gender anomaly.

A stereotypical image of effeminate, bourgeois homosexuality can be seen also in Rivera's mural in the administrative building of the Universidad Autonoma de Chapingo, outside the Mexican capital. Here, a heavy-weight capitalist is represented with pale, powdered skin and bow-tied shoes. The figure emanates effeminacy just as the cleric in *La Historia de México*.

The remaining puppet-like figures in Rivera's murals are remarkably asexual, as in most Muralist works, and illustrative of the political rigidity of their messages. It was a rule from which Rivera hardly deviated in his mural paintings at the chapel of Chapingo (1924), which constitute a visual allegory of agriculture, commissioned by the Escuela Nacional de Agricultura, now Universidad Autonoma de Mexico, to which the chapel belongs.

Nudity, both male and female, is relatively ubiquitous here and not entirely free from an erotic undertone. On the chapel's west wall, half-naked miners are depicted and on one part of the east wall three naked women can be seen, whose poses remind the viewer of both swimming and gymnastics. Together, they represent *Fuerzas subterráneas*, however, which again sublimates their physicality and incorporates it into a more grand, cosmic scheme of earthly fertility. The same is true for the women portrayed in *Maduración* and *Floración*. They appear alongside symbols of ovulation, conception, and foetal development. The red, elliptic framing of a circular window suggests vaginal anatomy. Female nudity is a highly charged symbol of terrestrial fertility and is reinforced even by Rivera's depiction of the male *campesino* as the one who cultivates the (female) earth.

The mural's sexist code reproduces itself on the ceiling and on the north and south walls, respectively titled *Revelación de la camina, Tierra generosa, legítimamente poseída, Tierra fecunda, con las fuerzas naturales controladas por el hombre* and *Tierra virginal*. The possessor and cultivator is always male, while the possessed, cultivated earth is represented consistently as female. On the north wall, a naked man stands up with his legs spread.

His pose seems to anticipate active intervention, while, above him, a naked women lies down in a vault, suggesting passivity. The man is surrounded by the four elements: wind, represented by an angel's head, fire, shown as a naked man, earth and water, depicted each as *mestiza* women.

Rivera's gendered allegory of agriculture was conservative and reflected traditional Mexican conceptualizations of masculinity and femininity. The perception of anything homoerotic, especially in Rivera's paintings of naked, dark-skinned farmers on the ceiling, necessarily remains within the eye of the beholder only, but it certainly can be seen as the painter's most sexually explicit depiction of male nudity.

Exceptions to the rule of asexual, politicized *muralismo* were quite rare. Only a handful of murals present the human body in ways that are potentially erotic. Some of David Alfaro Siqueiros's later murals, for example, present male or female (semi-)nudity in more or less sensual ways. But here, as in most other Muralist works, the narrative context remained more or less political or religious and neutralized 'heretic' readings in advance.

Homoeroticism was thus erased from Mexican Muralist art. Only a handful of murals present male nudity as a potential carrier of sexual, or homosexual meaning. I have already commented upon the one executed by Zárraga at the Biblioteca de México, but this is far from explicit and the perception of a homosexual content remains largely within the eye of the beholder here as well. The allegorical narrative disguises any erotic connotation in general, and a homoerotic one in particular.

There is ambiguity also, due to the sublimation of an actual homoerotic gaze through asexual narrative context, in some murals by Roberto Montenegro (1880–1968). Male nudity, in fact, occupies only a limited space and the painter made sure each time that its erotic dimension was incorporated within the realm of either heterosexuality or spirituality.

Indeed, Montenegro's homosexual inclination is known and may well explain both his drawings after Aubrey Beardsley at the beginning of his career and the portraits made of fishermen while he lived in Mallorca from 1914 until 1919. One, *Pescador de Mallorca* (n.d.), can be seen at the Museo Nacional de Arte in Mexico City. Another one, currently part of a private collection in Palma de Mallorca, accentuates the man's long, muscular legs and torso. The figure reappears, finally, in the shape of a peasant on a mural panel for the Parlamento de las Islas Baleares.

The recurrent physical features of the men painted by Montenegro may indicate, as with Herrán, that there is more going on than mere stylistic convention. The returning image of long, athletic bodies in his other murals may indeed reveal the painter's personal weakness for men of such typology, be it sexual or aesthetic, but, in either case, having a homoerotic tenor. History, in fact, has shown not only that Montenegro did invest some personal emotion in his murals, but also that his audience actually perceived the

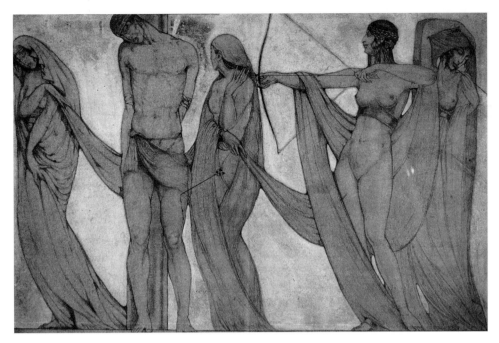

Figure 21 Roberto Montenegro, *El árbol de la vida* (study) (1921), pencil and gold-leaf on paper, 46 × 60 cm, courtesy of Instituto de Investigaciones Estéticas, Universidad Nacional Autonoma de México, Mexico City.

Figure 22 Roberto Montenegro, *El árbol de la vida* (detail) (original 1921 version), mural, *c.* 9.87 × 10 m, in former Iglesia de San Pedro y San Pablo, courtesy of Instituto de Investigaciones Estéticas, Universidad Nacional Autonoma de México, Mexico City.

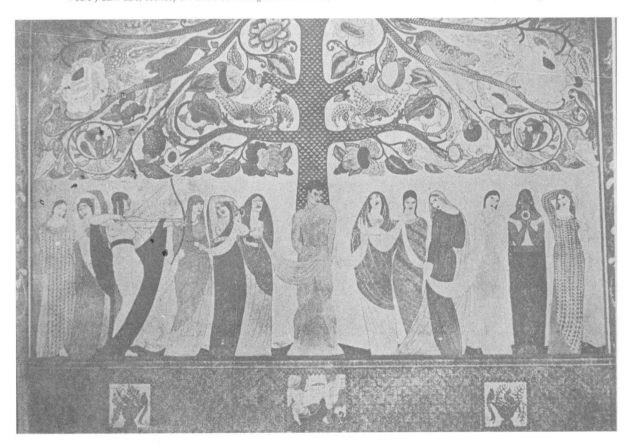

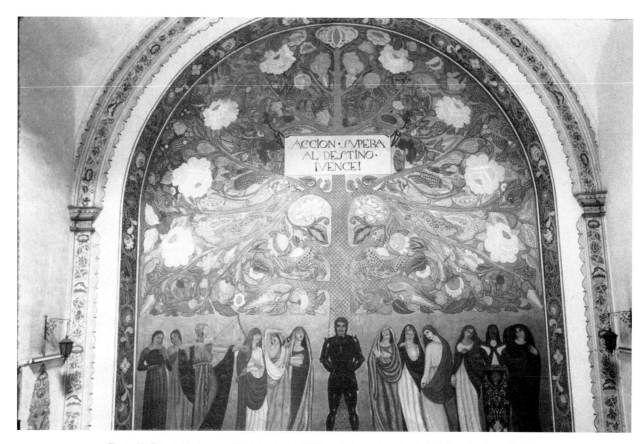

Figure 23 Roberto Montenegro, *El árbol de la vida* (1922 version), courtesy of Instituto de Investigaciones Estéticas, Universidad Nacional Autonoma de México, Mexico City.

male nude's erotic dimension and reacted accordingly. His mural painting *El arból de la vida* (1922), drastically changed during recent renovations (1944, 1984) and damaged by the earthquake of 1985, was already an adaptation of an original project that encountered opposition from José Vasconcelos. Drawings predating the actual work show a semi-nude man, slightly androgynous and reminiscent of Saint Sebastian, who is targeted by a woman with a bow and arrow. The original work was similar, if less refined, as can be seen only from a photograph today. Vasconcelos's Athenean philosophy of human mastery and civilization impelled him to pressure Montenegro and make sure that the original male figure at the centre of *El arból de la vida* was changed into a warrior, dressed in shining armour and looking not sideways but defiantly into the viewer's eye. It is clear that, implicitly, Vasconcelos's initiative was inspired also by considerations of *machismo* and homophobia.[8]

Male nudity appears in other paintings by Montenegro, including the frescos *La fiesta de Santa Cruz* (1923–4) and *Iberoamérica* (1924), both at the Convent of Saint Peter and Saint Paul in Mexico City. But here it is fully decentralized and pushed into the margins of the mural's iconographic narrative. The semi-nude men in *La fiesta de Santa Cruz* are

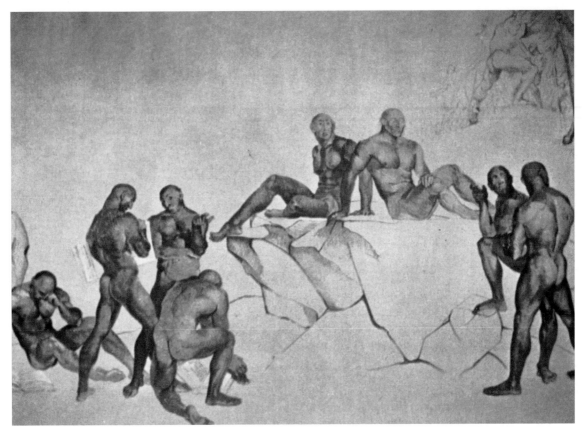

Figure 24 Pedro Medina Guzmán, *El pueblo de México y la Guadalupana* (detail) (1960), destroyed during the earthquake of 1985, photo: André Carens.

construction workers and artisans, no longer drawing the viewer's attention as was the case in *El arból de la vida*. Two other figures, said to be Xavier Guerrero and Montenegro himself, shake hands while the former glances at the latter, who seems to be aware of it. It would be unjustified to claim that this scene carried within itself a certain homoeroticism that trespassed social and ethnic boundaries – Guerrero was a *mestizo* – just as it carries a Socialist message about brotherhood and solidarity, but it cannot be excluded categorically either. Montenegro's work illustrates the at times highly coded character of homosexual expression. Biographical detail is disguised by the 'thickness' of narrative content, while nudity is de-eroticized through allegories of labour, cultural or ethnic difference, politics or religion.

A strategy of narrative de-eroticization of male nudity is applied also in two murals by Pedro Medina Guzmán (b. 1916). Their narrative context is very different – one is religious, the other a visual allegory of Mexico's social and economic policy – but there are some striking similarities between both that tend to corroborate a hypothesis regarding their underlying, if subtle, homoerotic content.[9]

The first mural, or series of panels rather, was never finished, nor does it still exist. It was attached to a wall of the old Secretaría de Industria y Comercio in the Mexican capital, but the building collapsed during the earthquake of 1985. The mural was destroyed.[10] It was titled *El pueblo de México y la Guadalupana* (1960) and one part, also uncompleted, was composed of men either working (the site seems to be an open-air mine) or resting. All of them are naked and have an identical anatomy: the same muscularity, the same facial features. One profile – round face, highly implanted Aztec nose, indented cheeks – is ubiquitous, as if it embodied not only a stereotypical image of 'the Mexican man', but also a projection of the painter's personal erotic preference.

The second mural, titled *Alegoria religiosa* (1958) can be seen at the church of La Piedad in the Colonia Narvarte, Mexico City. To the left, a group of good angels ascends towards God's outstretched hands, while to the right, one can see the story of the rebel angels who are fallen and whose image is copied after the Contrareformatory engraving *St Michael defeats the rebel angels* (1621) by Lucas Vorsterman.[11] Centrally, the Horsemen of the Apocalypse ride horses in the sky, while a victorious Christ sits on a beautiful white horse, surrounded by salvaged souls.

The bottom part is occupied, to the left, by stories of Genesis, Exodus and the New Testament, while to the right a scene depicts half-naked men fighting one another with various weapons and reminding the viewer of Antonio Pollaiuolo's Renaissance engraving of *Fighting men* (c. 1470–5). In the background, a visionary image arises of atomic catastrophe.

The allegory, remarkably enough, is represented as a mostly masculine affair, with only men being invited to the gates of Heaven or condemned to Purgatory and Hell. Again, these men are naked, which admittedly may be consistent with Christian iconography, but they show the same physical characteristics as those in *El pueblo de México*. The facial features, prominent in the latter, reappear in the scenes of this mural also, as in the naked man holding a text to the left, or the wrestling and fighting men to the right, or the falling and ascending angels on top. Male vigour seems ubiquitous in this mural and is reinforced by the painter's play with architectural elements. Concrete elements, sticking out of the wall on both the left and right sides, are used to stage half-naked men upholding or supporting these and exposing their virile muscularity while doing so. The high prominence of male nudity is at least remarkable and exposes the semantically homoerotic signature in the work of an artist who, at first glance, reproduces a Christian narrative tradition.

The erotics of labour in the tropics: Brazil

The impact of Mexican Muralism was felt in South America also, partly due to Siqueiros's visit to Brazil, Uruguay, Argentina and Chile in 1933. It coincided with an increasingly intense debate about the role of art in society, especially in Brazil where both the Sociedade

Pró-Arte Moderna (SPAM) and the Club dos Artistas Modernos (CAM) were founded the year before. They became major centres of debate about the social role of the visual arts, reflecting the growing politicization of daily life and, more particularly, the rise of syndicalist movements across Latin America.

It is interesting to see that in Brazil as well, this new tendency carried within itself a renewed emphasis on traditional gender roles, just as it had done in Mexico. Brazilian socially engaged art did not diverge from this pattern and adopted visual depiction of male strength and vigour as a metaphor equally of the working classes' combativity and Socialist utopia.[12] But here, too, room remains for alternative interpretation of an essentially ambiguous aesthetic, indulging in visual imagery of bulging muscles, sweat and energy. After the rather decadent representations of *fin de siècle* homoeroticism, this introduced a new, if implicit, aesthetic of a more butch and masculine tenor.

Labour had been a theme of Brazilian art for a long time and some early works, while focusing on working men, suggest a certain homoeroticism, even if probably purely accidentally. An example is the painting *Derrubador brasileiro* (1871) (Plate 7) by José Ferraz de Almeida, showing a young labourer who sits down to take a break and smoke a cigarette. He displays a 'musculatura meticulosamente delineada, que o suor faz rebrillar' ('meticulously drawn musculature, shining with sweat'), observes Júnior Motta Pessanha, who recognizes an atmosphere also of *lassidão* and tepid sensuality. De Almeida made the work while in Paris and the model was actually an Italian. The tropical heat is tangible, however, as is the resting worker's lassitude, his sweat, his tired eyes, his half-open mouth and the burning cigarette in his right hand.[13]

Other works also expressed the heroism of working-class men, implying, by the sheer emphasis on physical strength and moral courage, a certain homoerotic appeal. José Correia de Lima's grand portrait of the sailor Simon is one example (*Retrato do Intrépido Marinheiro Simão, Carvoeiro do Vapor pernambucano, c.* 1855); his *Eterna Luta* (1901), a bronze sculpture of a half-naked worker, is another.

Relevant also is the iconography of the so-called *bandeirantes*, colonists who penetrated the Brazilian interior during the seventeenth and eighteenth centuries in search of Indian slaves and minerals. They often clashed with Jesuit missions or with resisting indigenous tribes. Today, the *bandeirantes* have become a symbol for the self-made man, and artistic monuments and paintings representing them offer a possibility for depicting eroticized semi-nude male bodies. This is obvious, for example, in the *Monumento às bandeiras* (designed in 1920; executed between 1936 and 1953) by the Modernist sculptor Vítor Brecheret. Both *bandeirantes* or *mamelucos* and Indian slaves are sculpted on a huge, heroic bas-relief that is unmistakably homoerotic in its almost orgiastic assemblage of male nudity and physical strength. Brecheret's monument of the *Duque de Caxias* (1960) is an equestrian statue, also adorned by a bas-relief of *bandeirantes*, whose muscular torsos clad only in vests emphasize masculine, heroic strength.

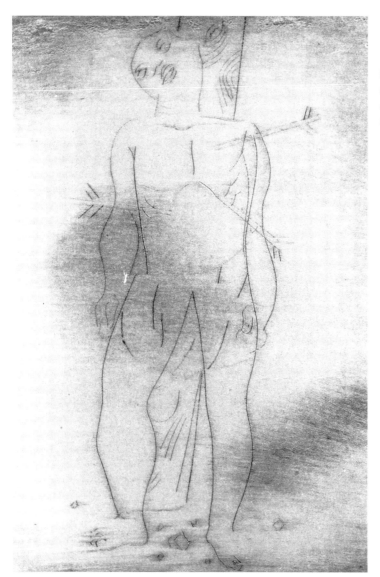

Figure 25 Cândido Portinari, *São Sebastião* (n.d.), engraving, 25.5 × 20 cm, col. Mario de Andrade, courtesy of the Instituto de Estudos Brasileiros, Universidade de São Paulo, São Paulo.

The heroics of labour is celebrated also in Amedeo Zani's monument of *Alfredo Maia* (1922), adopting male semi-nudity as a metaphor of labour and progress. The railroad developer Maia is visualized alongside a railroad worker, who is pushing a rock, symbolizing the construction of the new iron roads. Perhaps the Italian descent of the artist explains the sculpture's inspiration in a Fascist aesthetic. It surely is visible also in the *Monumento à Ramos de Azevedo* (1934) by Galileo Emedabili, an Italo-Brazilian like Zani, whose weaknesses for Roman facial features may well reveal a certain admiration for the new, Fascist aesthetic of 1930s Italy.[14]

Inspired by Socialist ideology, in contrast, was Cândido Portinari (1903–62), who is commonly presented as Muralism's greatest representative in Brazil. He also produced numerous, at times very famous, images of work and working people. He was married and there are no immediate indications that he was bisexual. Why, then, focus on his work here?

It is my contention that Portinari's oeuvre is a fine illustration of how a homotextual dimension can indeed exist against the odds of an artist's personal biography and profile as a heterosexual, married artist, whose interest in male homoerotic imagery usually remains nonexplicit. The artist is obviously interested in the male worker's body, which is more prominent than that of his female counterpart. The reason of course may have been purely aesthetic, just as academic art focused more on the male model for reasons of a technical kind. The male muscular structure is more articulated and thus offers more challenges to the artist, at least for many. 'Pictorial emphasis', says Jean Franco, 'is placed on bodies and limbs or on coarse, honest features, rather than on the features of soft, reclining nudes.'[15] Male bodies indeed dominate Portinari's most famous works: the series on Brazil's four national crops (sugar, cacao, coffee, rubber), and the murals at the one time Ministério da Educação in Rio de Janeiro *Ciclo Económico* (1937–47). Private, unpretentious drawings equally reveal the artist's fascination with the male body, among other themes, as can be seen in *Índio* (1938), a drawing kept at the Pinacoteca do Estado of São Paulo. *Torso de homem* (n.d.), *Índio em pé* (c. 1941), and *São Sebastião* (n.d.), three drawings originally part of the collection of Mário de Andrade, reveal a similar interest by the artist in the male body.[16] Men are the exclusive focus of interest also in small, independent works, such as *Pau Brasil* (1938), *O lavrador de café* (1939), and the well-known work, *O mestiço* (1934) (Plate 8). The latter's sensuality is undeniable. One can sense how the artist focused on his model's physical characteristics with great enthusiasm.

The empathic portrayal of masculinity is a constant theme throughout Portinari's oeuvre, and contrasts sharply with the relative absence of women. Is this not a significant fact? Does this not in itself lend a potentially homoerotic appeal to the artist's career? Again, the question is not: Was Portinari bisexual? Or even gay, if closeted? The point rather, especially in a Latin American context where homosexual libido did not necessarily imply adoption of an exclusive 'homosexual identity', is a historical understanding, allowing today's viewer to grasp how an artist's focus on masculinity was embraced by what one may call a 'bisexual *imaginaire*'. It did not call for definition as 'gay art', nor did an artistic focus on the male body compel the artist to question or redefine his sexual identity. The context of Naturalism, moreover, and of socially inspired portrayal of labour, facilitated the portrayal of semi-naked masculinity without addressing sexual identity.

The same applies to other Brazilian artists who adopted similar themes and focused on the male body more or less systematically: Hugo Bertazzon and Quirino Campofiorito. The sculptor Bertazzon (1897–1940) initially worked in a rather academic style that reflected influences of, among others, Rodin, Bourdelle and, eventually, Symbolism. Gradually, he started working according to the principles of Art Déco.[17] Thematically, he

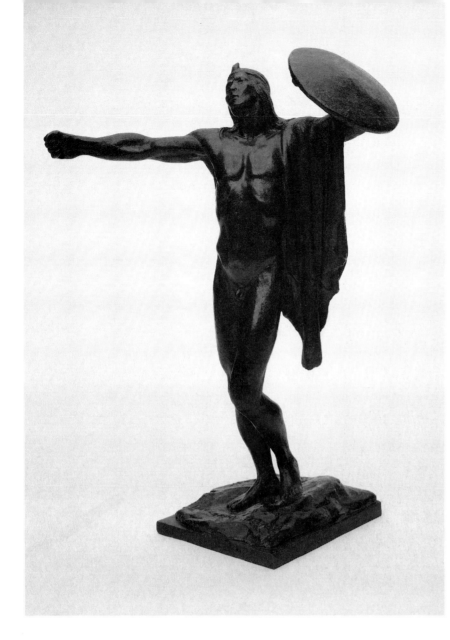

Figure 26 *(left)* Hugo Bertazzon, *Evocando Tupan* (1936), bronze, 37 × 27 × 20 cm, Museu Nacional de Belas Artes, Rio de Janeiro, photo: Raúl Lima.

Figure 27 *(right)* Hugo Bertazzon, *O arqueiro* (1930), bronze, 63 × 28 × 20 cm, Museu Nacional de Belas Artes, Rio de Janeiro, photo: Raúl Lima.

was inspired by classical mythology and Indian heritage, always focusing predominantly on masculine themes or narratives. *Prometêo* (1934) is a fine example of the first; the very sensual bronze statue *Evocando Tupán* (1936) is a belated, yet splendid and idealizing work in Indigenist tradition. *O vigia* and *O arqueiro* (1930) are equally inspired by *Indigenismo*. National folklore also provided imagery for rather heroic representations, three-dimensionally, of masculine power, reinforced, as in the series *Vida campestre* (1939), by the aristocratic appeal of horses.

Campofiorito (1902–93) is another artist whose numerous scenes of labour tend to focus on male workers especially. Nudity is faily scarce and the anatomy only schematically elaborated. Yet, an atmosphere of male bonding is tangible, interrupted only rarely by

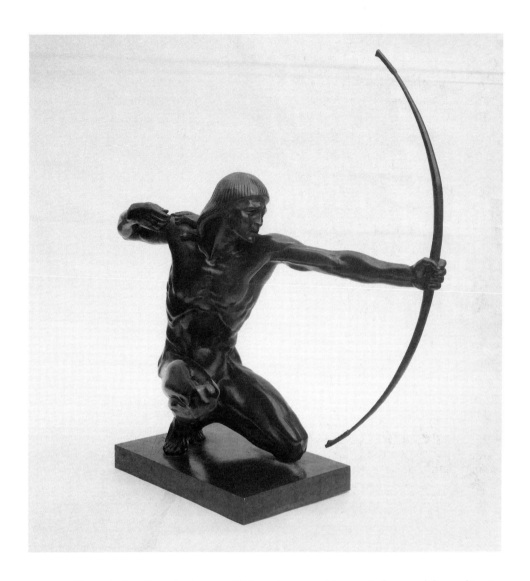

women. The painting *Hora de almoço*, which no longer exists, reminds one of the ambiguity of focus in *Labor* by the Mexican Saturnino Herrán. *Hora de almoço* shows two masons taking a break as a mother holds her child nearby. One of the men seems to be the child's father, yet his attention seems to be divided between his wife and child on the one hand, and his fellow worker on the other.

None of this is a clear and unmistakable indicator of homoerotic proclivity. One may actually point at the presence of women and children as a proof of the heterosexual, family-orientated values expressed by the artist, who was married to the artist Hilda Campofiorito. But a very large part of his paintings depict working men, more precisely drawn in general, and time and time again imbued with a subtle erotic undertone. As such, a semiosis takes place, comparable to the oeuvre of, for example, Constantin Meunier in Europe, or Rockwell Kent, Arthur Murphy and Hugo Gellert in the United States. While interpreting the latter two artists' work, Jonathan Weinberg has pointed out that the depiction of half-naked, muscular bodies in itself ought not to signify any homoerotic interest or message. In fact, they may be symbols merely of a proto-socialist rhetoric of labour heroism.[18] But Weinberg stresses that there may be another side to the truth as well. The social message, in fact, may be a strategy to make representations of male nudes less suspicious, less Decadent, less sexual – implying, however, that at first this may very well have been present in the artist's mind.

A certain homoerotic appeal surely may be located on the level of reception. The viewer, in fact, can hardly remain indifferent to the homosocial atmosphere of the then more rigidly divided worksite. The coffee plantation, the harbour or the construction site are *topoi* not only of production and work, but also of brooding, tropical eroticism. *Aquecendo a comida dos camaradas* (*c.* 1940), while apparently neutral, may perhaps illustrate best how Campofiorito was drawn by the camaraderie at the worksite and by its sexually charged atmosphere.

Cuba: revolutionary art and homotextuality

Despite an emphasis on the Cuban countryside, already present at the time of Cuba's so-called *Primera Vanguardia*, little art was produced on the island that combined depiction of labour scenes with an implicit homoeroticism. A heterosexist and *machisto* atmosphere is pervasive in the works of Carlos Enriquez, for example, whose portrayals of the *romancero guajiro* were always carefully presented in a heterosexual context. The power of *machismo* is striking also in the oeuvre of Víctor Manuel, Antonio Gattorno or Marcelo Pogolotti.

The more intimate, personal focus of painters belonging to the *Segundo Vanguardia* was even further removed from leftist-inspired art, then so prominent in neighbouring Mexico. The early, figurative work of Mario Carreño (b. 1913) contains images of cane cutters, whose raw physicality is striking, yet here too one notices a concern for formal innovation rather than a sensual, *a fortiori* homoerotic interest.

In the wake of the Cuban Revolution (1959), the arts were increasingly redefined, however, as instruments of education and propaganda. The foundation of the Escuela Nacional de Arte was to centralize artistic production and redefine the arts' agenda as geared at disseminating Revolutionary values and ideals.

It is not without irony, accordingly, that two of Cuba's most prominent artists of the Revolution – Raúl Martínez and Servando Cabrera Moreno – turned out to be irreconcilable with the increasingly rigid aesthetic of Revolutionary cultural politics. Their sexual identity was seen as incompatible with the *machista* code of the Castro regime, more particularly with the latter's increasing intolerance towards homosexual visibility and homoeroticism.

Both Martínez (1927–95) and Cabrera Moreno (1923–81) had initially set out as Modernist artists. Cabrera Moreno had experimented already with homoerotic work, yet most of his early work was semi-abstract with a more rigid, geometric version of the mythological universe characteristic especially of the work of his compatriot Wifredo Lam. Raúl Martínez too experimented with abstraction, then with Pop Art, but they both joined forces with the new Revolutionary regime in which they initially believed.

Pop Art actually became the vehicle for Raúl Martínez's Revolutionary art. '[El] transita así del "Yo" de sus derivas abstractas al "Nosotros"de la socialización *pop*.'*[19] His portraits of José Martí, of Che Guevara and of other Cuban heroes, often multiplied and always reduced to patchworks of vibrant colours, are widely known today. His active contribution to the genre of 'poster art' allowed for widespread dissemination across the island and abroad of Fidel Castro's revolutionary ideas. The anonymous peasant, factory worker, youngster and elderly, man and woman, all populated the paintings and posters of Martínez in an atmosphere of Revolutionary euphoria and Socialist optimism. Smiles abound, as can be seen in *Isla 70*, a painting that nowadays can be seen at the Museo Nacional de Bellas Artes in Havana, yet that was among the last ones made in the spirit of Revolution.[20]

Cabrera Moreno, for his part, dropped experiments with formal innovation and focused increasingly on heroic portrayals of Cuba's peasants and labourers, caught by Revolutionary enthusiasm while being the carriers themselves of that very Revolution. Work dating from that era is influenced, both in style and content, by the Muralism especially of José Clemente Orozco and David Alfaro Siqueiros. *Milicias campesinas* (1961), for example, reveals diagonal lines suggesting dynamic movement, as do the murals of Siqueiros in Mexico.

Cabrera Moreno was already an established artist and taught at the Academy of Cubanacán when the Revolution broke out, yet his position was threatened by the authorities' awareness about his active life as a homosexual man. In 1965, he was removed from his teaching position and put under surveillance for a period of five years.[21] Martínez, in turn, was declared an enemy of the Revolution, not because he was not known yet as a gay man – he openly shared his life with playwright, Abelardo Estorino – but because such information was considered irreconcilable with the public image of the Revolution.[22]

It is remarkable that, at least in the public work of both Martínez and Cabrera Moreno, the homotextual dimension becomes visible first in their Revolutionary works.

> Cabrera Moreno . . . documentó la gesta de campesinos, milicianos o macheteros y estetizó sus experiencias con su sensibilidad habitual, al punto de otorgarles el estatuto heroico que la cotidianidad les sustraía. Estos héroes del día a día eran generalmente bellos, suaves, ambiguos; y se balanceaban en una frontera, a menudo tensa, entre el erotismo permitido y la conocida homosexualidad de este pintor.†

*'[He] thus changes from the "Me" of his abstract works to the "Us" of pop socialization.'

†'Cabrera Moreno . . . documented the life of farmers, soldiers or cane cutters and aestheticized their experiences through his own habitual sensitivity, even to the degree of attributing to them a certain heroism that daily life deprived them of. These heroes of daily life were generally beautiful, handsome, ambiguous; and they were oscillating on the often sharp boundary between acceptable eroticism and the painter's known homosexuality.'

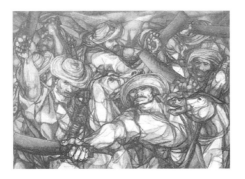

Figure 28 Servando Cabrera Moreno,
Milicias campesinas (1961),
oil on canvas, 140 × 201 cm,
Museo Nacional, Havana.

It may actually have been, continues Iván de la Nuez, that Cabrera Moreno became the official iconographer of the Revolution just because his eroticism went against the reticence of official discourse.[23] The Socialist-inspired images of Cabrera Moreno surely reveal a clear fascination, more or less tangible, for the male body, but this is always presented as a signifier of Revolutionary zeal, never as an object on its own. A rather implicit cult of virility is inscribed within the agenda of the Revolution and thus made acceptable to the ruling authorities.

A subtle homoeroticism can be noticed, next, in works by Martínez. *Ustedes, nosotros* (1969) does convey a message about homoeroticism, if only to a viewer informed about the artist's sexual identity. Some book illustrations also give implicit testimonies of their maker's homoerotic attraction, probably perceived as such only by *entendidos*, by 'those who understand' – which makes it harder to demonstrate. Never, of course, are such images isolated as homoerotic imagery on its own. In fact, the purpose of book illustration allowed for an expression of homoeroticism that remained unnoticed by those who were not capable of reading the signs.[24]

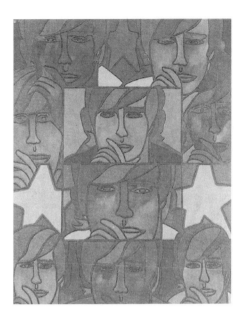

Figure 29 Raúl Martínez, *Ustedes, nosotros*
(1969), oil on canvas, 201 × 159.5 cm,
Museo Nacional, Havana.

At the same time, both artists produced a private oeuvre that was more explicitly homoerotic or at least made the sexual identity of the artists visible in less ambiguous terms. Political circumstances obviously are the main reason why such work has, as yet, gained little – if any – visibility or why, as in the case of Cabrera Moreno, it has been absorbed almost completely by private collectors.[25] I will briefly return to these works, however, in Chapter 4.

Puerto Rico

The slow development of a national Puerto Rican art explains in part why few if any images were produced that focus upon the island's lower classes. Most artistic production consisted of portrayals of the social and cultural élite. Yet, the work of the great local artist, Francisco Oller (1833–1917) contained the beginnings of what elsewhere became a tradition of social documentary. Oller embraced the debate on the abolition of slavery, focusing both on the cruelties inflicted on slaves ('El negro flagelado', destroyed) and on the slave's moral superiority. In paintings such as *La Ceiba de Ponce, Hacienda Aurora* and *Central Plazuela,* Oller documents the labour on the sugarcane fields and *engenios,* even when most attention goes into the depiction of the light and landscape rather than into social criticism. Following Oller were Manuel Jordan and Pio Bacener as well as Miguel Pou, Oscar Colón Delgado and Juan Rosado, who, while portraying the black population, remained patronizing and confirmed already existing racial stereotypes.[26]

Only in the 1930s were black people granted alternative images of themselves, partially inspired by the poems of Luis Palés Matos. A philosophy of *négritude* thus found visual expression in paintings by Luis Quero Chiesa and Rafael Palacios, yet, whereas their intention was to exalt black people, they simultaneously reinscribed their images within an at times even harsher stereotypical trope of visual representation than before.

The late, renewed take-off of art in the 1950s on the island of Puerto Rico stimulated renewed interest in the popular feasts and traditions, again diverting artistic language from Socialist-inspired criticism. The increasing degree of miscegenation and, as a result of it, the increasingly entwined social and economic interests turned blacks into a decorative rather than political topic of representation, as can be seen in work by, for example, Carlos Raquel Rivera and Rafael Tufiño. In a more general sense, the impact of Modernism postponed the development of a socially critical art and, along with it, of an art that focused predominantly on the working class. Images, as a result, of male labourers, imbued with eroticism either accidentally or purposively, remained hard to find until the advent in the 1960s of Puerto Rico's influential graphic school.

In Puerto Rico, too, progressive sexual politics were anathema to Socialist art. The Centro de Arte Puertorriqueño and, from 1957, the Taller de Artes Gráficas, led by Lorenzo Homar, were primarily inspired by the agenda of a political left. And, whereas the importance of Puerto Rican graphic art must not be underestimated, it is clear that its contribution to changing gender and sexual politics has remained limited. It would not be until the 1970s that visual imagery of body politics and sexual desire would become somewhat more acceptable, yet even then images with heterosexual content proved to be controversial. Considering the highly *machisto* orientation of the island, one would search in vain for more explicit homoerotic images.

The sexual politics of Modernism

The dissemination of Modernism in Latin America, if belated in some countries, was caught up within the wider debate of national or regional identity. Abstraction especially was proposed by some as a vehicle towards international recognition, a sign of economic and political 'modernity', whereas others felt that this implied denial of cultural autonomy, of locally rooted and socially relevant art.

The striving for a universally intelligible aesthetic did not 'regulate' art's sexual politics so much as give rise to a formal deconstruction of the human body, often simply eclipsing humanity as an object of artistic representation. Non-figurative art especially crystallized into a style that claimed to be detached from historical narrative and societal context alike. It pretended to be sexless also, even when close analysis at least of North American Abstract Expressionism has revealed an underlying, phallocratic rhetoric of artistic heroism, of sexism and even *machismo*.[27] Just as the 'International' style extolled itself above political debate, so too did it proclaim immunity from or indifference towards issues of gender and sexuality. And while the former proved illusive, if not downright misleading, so too did the image of a sex-neutral aesthetic disguise the actual (male heterosexist) gender of artistic praxis and production.

This justifies an enquiry into the hidden sexual politics of Latin American abstraction, even if only fragmentarily here, in the light of homotextuality in particular. Nelly Richard describes the issue from a feminist point of view, yet it can be extrapolated to the realm of queer criticism as well: 'To suppress or to neutralize considerations of gender (to make them insignificant) is tantamount to playing directly into the hands of the hegemonic male-dominated culture, one that skillfully hides the mechanisms of signification by which the absolute masculine is made equivalent to the universal-transcendent.'[28] An abstract painting isn't sexually neutral after all, and the deconstruction, moreover, of art practice's sexism needs to be accompanied by a parallel investigation of the heterosexism, if not homophobia, implied by the rhetoric of Modernism.

But the mechanism of disguise works both ways since some female, lesbian and gay artists also embraced the language of abstraction and subscribed deliberately to the myth of an ungendered aesthetic. Their motives were diverse and legitimate in view of the contemporary social context: the practice of hiding one's gender or sexual identity; the demand to be judged on professional merits primarily; the proof that, while on the margin of society, one can share equally in the praxis and debate of its centre. For today's critic, it is tempting to condemn this aesthetic of the closet pursued by gay and lesbian artists in the past. But one must be aware of the social reality of homophobia, in Latin America as elsewhere, and of genuine repression, for example during the Castro regime from the late 1960s until recently, or under the military regimes in Brazil, Argentina and elsewhere. In order to feel free to publicly acknowledge one's sexual identity, there must be a certain degree of social tolerance – a condition that has been fulfilled in most Latin American countries only recently, and the art historian must guard himself or herself against misplaced anachronism and unfair judgement.

The Modernist aesthetic was hardly conducive to the artistic expression of homoeroticism, largely because of the body's eclipse altogether from the range of representation. The elimination of eroticism is one of the major flaws, argues the critic Marta Traba, of Abstract Art, Op Art, Kinetic Art and even much Conceptual Art.[29] Yet, one must not discard Modernism prematurely since the language of non-figurative art did nevertheless provide tools for gay and lesbian self-expression. Just as (straight) women artists have frequently adopted abstraction to visualize women's culture,[30] so too can signs be detected in Latin American Modernism that reveal a 'gay sensibility', codified surely, yet containing unmistakable references to the social, cultural or emotional realities of homosexual experience. A process of 'meaningful mark-making' (Chadwick) may disclose a gay or lesbian *imaginaire* despite the artwork's abstract or semi-abstract character and notwithstanding the factually closeted lifestyle of the artist.

Weinberg, while commenting on some works by Jasper Johns, explains how a code of homotextuality may be geared to *hiding*, just as much as to *disclosing* the 'secret'. He sees Johns's strategy as one of 'concealment of that which signifies . . . [where] any biographically determined factors that might make up that content are not as important as Johns' insistence that there *is* a secret'.[31] A similar awareness must be applied to Latin American Modernism, especially when the political climate was repressive and social or sexual issues could not be addressed openly in the visual arts. The charged dimension of Modernism as a vehicle for national identity calls for hermeneutic deconstruction of 'signs' and 'marks' that carry a message about the place of sexual variance in such an ideological context.

Puerto Rico

The appeal of abstract art was perhaps most visible in Puerto Rico, trying to catch up with international art developments and to claim an image of cosmopolitan flair. On the island, chronically facing uncertainty about its cultural profile, a controversy developed, late in the 1960s, 'between those who defended a culture of national affirmation and those who advocated a "universalist" approach'.[32] Generally speaking, the battle seems to have been won by the Internationalists, who eagerly embraced abstraction as an aesthetic language transcending provinciality and folklore.

Some of the Puerto Rican abstract artists call for attention here in view of their homosexual identity, yet their very choice of abstraction may indicate that it could be adopted as a veil, behind which they could hide this biographical fact. Put less negatively, one may also claim that subscribing to the International style was an implicit, codified attempt to escape local social and cultural traditions, as these stood for sexism, heterosexism and homophobia. Abstraction being a peculiarly metropolitan product, reflecting values of individual emancipation, sexual liberation and public tolerance, evidently seemed more attractive in the eyes of local Puerto Rican artists wanting to escape and, often, migrating to Miami, New York or elsewhere in North America or Europe.

Among them figures Jaime Suarez (b. 1946), who bridged traditional artistic genres, combining painting, sculpture, architecture and especially ceramics. He adopted the latter technique in quite an innovative way, creating abstract shapes that lift ceramics above its often folkloric and anecdotal aesthetic. The *Totem telúrico* (1992), for example, is a column erected in Old San Juan to commemorate the Quincentenary of the 'discovery' of America , yet morphological transparency lends it a somewhat mysterious and timeless aura.

A similar, almost 'escapist' logic underlies the works of Jaime Romano (b. 1942), who, though born and living in the United States until the mid-1980s, returned to the island where he is now teaching at a university. Abstraction allowed him to communicate with the artistic centres of the world, whereas inscribing his art within a pictorial tradition of local, Puerto Rican imagery would have left him at the margins of artistic and critical debate. Only when established as an internationally renowned artist, did he return to his home island.

The pictorial universe of both Suarez and Romano leaves little room for speculation on how a covert homotextual dimension can be identified. In critical studies of their work, there surely is nothing to be found on this issue, as their authors consider sexual identity irrelevant to the creative process. But is it justified to simply discard the question as academic, as irrelevant? Perhaps Suarez's totem pole is a phallic signifier after all and a codified message to the gay audience of his own country? Perhaps not.

When we look at the work of Noemi Ruiz (b. 1931), the problem is, in the end, just as hard to resolve. Her abstract work is geometric, yet shows 'organic forms, concentric compositions',[33] all of which may be seen, according to Ann Gibson, as a way to express difference, namely feminine identity.[34] Yet, are there any conclusive indications that Ruiz in fact adopted a certain technique or style to express her identity as a female or lesbian artist? Ruiz, partner of Maria Emilia Somoza, herself an artist, has refrained from explaining whether or not she conceived her abstract work as part of a 'feminine' or 'lesbian aesthetic'. So, is not the issue of hidden, codified homotextuality a topic of speculation?

Cuba

In Cuba, abstract art was marginalized at the time when it became popular in Puerto Rico. It was replaced by the Revolutionary aesthetic of billboard, mural and poster art after the installation of the Castro regime in 1959. Until then, Modernism had developed slowly from the First Avant Garde (Víctor Manuel García, Carlos Enriquez, Fidelio Ponce) and Second Avant Garde (Amelia Peláez, Wifredo Lam, Mariano Rodriguez, Cundo Bermúdez, René Portocarrero). Yet only in the 1950s did abstraction take off decisively. The Grupo de los Once included Guido Llinas, Hugo Consuegra, Raúl Martínez, and especially Mario Carreño. A second group was heavily influenced by Argentinian geometric abstraction and other foreign artists such as Max Bill, while a third, semi-abstract group counted Antonio Eiriz, Humberto Peña, Manuel Mendive and the early Servando Cabrera Moreno among its members. Raúl Milián, Portocarrero's partner, also belonged to this group.[35]

Were gay and lesbian Cuban artists any more open about sexual identity when they subscribed to the international fashion of abstract art? Again, the identification of homotextuality is a hazardous task when faced with the dehumanizing aesthetic language of Modernist abstraction. It provided an excuse for most artists, in Cuba as elsewhere, not to disclose sexual identity directly and to keep art and biography separate.

Yet some artists adopted the agenda of formal innovation while simultaneously visualizing personal, social or cultural issues. (Homo)sexual identity is one of these, even when it can be retrieved only from underneath layers of codification. A pioneer role was played, in this respect, by Amelia Peláez del Casal (1896–1968). She studied for eight years at the Academia de San Fernando in Havana and spent another eight years in Paris, where she was exposed to work by Matisse, Braque, and Picasso. A major influence also was the Russian Constructivist work of Alexandra Exter, with whom she studied while living in the French capital.

Peláez returned to Cuba during the 1930s depression and combined a Modernist aesthetic with the colourful reality of the Cuban island. In her 'Cubist' still lifes, elements are recognizable, in fact, of colonial Havana architecture and of the country's flora and fauna, all caught within a thick black lineature and reduced to primary colours, typical at once of a Caribbean sensibility and Modernist purism.[36]

Peláez, who never got married, was what today we would call a lesbian. She lived with her lover, whom she presented to the outside world as a cousin.[37] She never presented herself as a lesbian in public, however, which is understandable in the context of Cuban sexism and heterosexism. But the adoption of a static label probably was alien to her, as was the sexualization implied by twentieth-century sexual labels.

A lesbian code pervades Peláez's Modernist aesthetic, however, as can be noticed, if only subtly, in her portrayals of women friends, resting in intimate spaces and interiors that radiate bourgeois *luxe, calme et volupté*. *Las hermanas lectoras* (1944), a portrayal apparently of two sisters, is the visualization at the same time of intimate female friendships, imbued, if covertly so, with a certain homoerotic tension. It is introverted, however, and the obvious narrative of family relationship anticipates criticism of homophobic tenor.

Perhaps the expression of homotextuality was more consciously pursued in her semi-abstract paintings of fruits and flowers. The flowers – for example, *Mar pacífico* (1943) or *Naturaleza muerta* (1955) – are symbolic carriers of femininity, while the fruits selected by Peláez – papayas and watermelons mostly – have feminine connotations, some quite visibly by virtue of their formal resemblance to female anatomy (breasts, vagina). *Frutería con sandías* (1964) (Plate 9) shows a bowl with large pieces of watermelon standing on a table in front of a window. The still life is innocent at first sight, yet contains a codified message that recurs throughout her artistic career and can be identified as 'of lesbian inspiration' in view of her biography. The selection of some fruits instead of others – why no bananas? – may well indicate that this was inspired by Peláez's desire to subtly express female homoeroticism within the frame of Modernist visual language.

A codified, if only implicitly 'lesbian', aesthetic seems to be present in the work of the Cuban artist Zilia Sánchez (b. 1934), who has long resided in Puerto Rico. Though influenced alike by Tápies, Dubuffet and Minimalism, she nevertheless reintroduced the human body into her art, by means of a far-reaching programme of abstraction and formal reduction. 'Se trata aquí', says Margareta Hernández Zavala, 'del erotismo más depurado por la severa preocupación formalista.'*[38]

This critic's ongoing analysis, however, is symptomatic of a more general reluctance, among audiences and critics alike, to see the lesbian connotations of Sánchez's sculptures, even when these are, at times, quite obvious. Zavala continues as follows: 'Se trata del delirio caribeño enmascarado, reprimido, escamoteado, presentado desde la esfera de lo permisible, de lo sugerido . . . el erotismo de la mujer, del cuerpo feminino, aquel tan parecido al propio.'†[39] Zavala, though aware of Sánchez's feminist affiliations, deliberately remains on the surface of things by merely emphasizing feminine eroticism. While suggesting the resemblance of the object's body with the one of the artist herself, she declines to call the lesbian dimension by its name. Marta Traba also heterosexualizes Sánchez's work, though an informed feminist critic herself, and reduces the formal language of the artist to a figuration of male-to-female penetration: '[Sánchez] crea una constante connotación rítmica al tema sexual, apoyada fundamentalmente sobre el contrapunto de erecciones y excavaciones.'‡[40]

A critic of the daily paper *El Nuevo Día* similarly reappropriated Sánchez's work for the realm of heteronormality and de-sexualized the work as a product of 'intellectualized Eros'. Though recognizing the presence of Uranian Aphrodite, he nevertheless claimed that this was sublimated by the formal perfection of divine contemplation – a common way, in short, to avoid the issue of female sexuality *outside* a male heterosexual perspective.[41]

Perhaps it comes as no surprise to find a more benevolent, if still covert, reading in a critical text by the Cuban gay writer Severo Sarduy. He first emphasized the sensuality of Sánchez's work, calling it 'un espacio de tactilidad' ('a realm of touching') in order to suggest that a 'lesbian' erotic may be implied. 'La voluptuosidad que inventa sus posibles' ('voluptuousness inventing its possibilities'), commented Sarduy, who declined to call that libidinous 'potential' by its proper name.[42]

It is remarkable indeed to see how the eroticism of Zilia Sánchez's works is widely recognized, yet deprived of an alternative contextualization within the realm of lesbian love. Yet another critic talks of 'nipples caressing nipples', while Enrique García Gutiérrez

*'Here, we are facing eroticism, purified maximally by severe formalist concern.'

†'It is about Caribbean delirium, masqueraded, repressed, presented from the sphere of what is permitted, suggested . . . the eroticism of the woman, the female body, in as far as it resembles one's own.'

‡'[Sánchez] creates a constant rhythmic connotation that is sexual and leans heavily upon the contrapunto of erections and excavations.'

praises the artist's elegant icons of feminine sensuality as the object of an exclusive, 'male gaze'.[43] Female *homosocialité,* however, is revealed in titles such as *Las Troyanas* and especially *Las Amazonas*, inscribing the semi-abstract, Modernist works within a homotextual discourse, at least recognizable for those on the inside. *Lunar III* (from the series *Las Amazonas*, 1970) is perhaps most telling as a suggestion of a female-to-female embrace. Each of the two women is represented as a semi-circle and the intimacy between them is made visual by the interplay of single nipple-shaped protuberances. Other works, like *Topología erótica* (from the series *Las Troyanas*, 1978) or *Topología erótica* (from *Las Amazonas*, 1980) are visual representations of emotional affinity between women, where spiritual character is emphasized through formal abstraction and purity according to the artist's Minimalist aesthetic principles.

Rene Portocarrero (1912–85), as is well known, was homosexual and shared his life with Raúl Milián (b. 1914), also a painter, whose work is predominantly abstract. The prominent couple was never hindered by Fidel Castro's regime, as opposed to Raúl Martínez, Servando Cabrera Moreno and Umberto Peña. Yet, public acknowledgement of an artist's homosexuality remains off limit. As recently as March 1995, Cuban television devoted an entire programme to Portocarrero but neglected to mention his lover even once.[44] What, then, allowed Portocarrero to get away with what became hazardous for Peña, Cabrera Moreno or Martínez?

A key to the answer, no doubt, is found in Portocarrero's oeuvre, which, like Milián's, was never explicitly homosexual. Girls and women actually populate many of Portocarrero's works, along with urban scenes of Havana, cathedrals, landscapes, flowers, butterflies, feasts and carnival scenes. His universe combines Spanish, African and Indian American heritage. It is composed of syncretic images of Afro-Cuban deities, combined with Christian mythology.[45]

There is a hidden homotextual dimension, however, in works that reveal a 'gay sensibility', comparable to the Mexican artist Chucho Reyes, who will be discussed later. Mythic figures, such as the *diablitos* and the angels, seem to embody a hidden reference to the world of fantasy and childish innocence, while his floral motifs are celebrations of colour, vibrancy and light. Though anything but explicit signifiers of homosexual eros or identity, it is possible that they were the product of what we awkwardly tend to call gay sensibility.

The very nondescriptness of Portocarrero's aesthetic as well as its apparent inscription within traditions of folkloric representation allowed him to escape the repression of homosexuals in Cuba in the 1960s. Even more, Portocarrero was embraced by the Castro regime as a painter of the people, while others, as we have seen, were ostracized on the basis of their sexual identity.

Portocarrero's lover, Raúl Milián, focused exclusively on works on paper. He started painting only in the 1950s, inspired by his friend's example, yet developed an entirely different style. Animals and gardens are themes that Milián shares with Portocarrero, yet his aesthetic is one of subtlety and discretion. The human figure seems to appear from thick mist, as if it is attempting to claim its own existence and transcend fear. 'Sus . . . hombres que luchan desde las sombras por afirmarse en el mundo, expresan el dilema interno de un hombre de extrema sensibilidad en un mundo de violencia desgarradora.' *[46] More precisely, the artist's sexual identity made him aware of society's challenge to an individual whose existential vulnerability is exacerbated by various forms of repression and intolerance.

*'His men, fighting from the shadows to affirm themselves in the world, express the inner dilemma of a man of extreme sensitivity amidst a world of destructive violence.'

Mexico

In Mexico, Muralism did not disappear from the art stage. The new campus of the Universidad Nacional Autonoma de México actually gave a new impulse to 'public art'. But the mid-twentieth century was characterized by an aesthetic *Ruptura*. Some artists leaned towards abstraction (Gerszo, Rojo, Carrillo, Felguérez, Ponce) while others developed a new language of small-scale, figurative art (Tamayo, Cuevas, Gironella, Toledo, Soriano, Guerrero). All returned to work on canvas, expressing a desire for artistic production on a more private, intimate scale.

'Modernist' expression of homotextuality, in Mexico as elsewhere, is rare and seems tangible only the work of Jesús Reyes Ferreira (1880–1977). 'Chucho' Reyes, as he is commonly known, was an avid collector of colonial Mexican art and craft, and he developed a great interest also in architecture. He was a friend of Luis Barragán and Mathias Goeritz. Deeply immersed in the universe of popular imagination, he nevertheless adopted themes from it merely to lend them 'modern' status. Thus, the frequently returning images of saints and Holy Christs, of popular feasts and *payasos*, of flowers and horses. His paintings and drawings of eroticized *gallos* and *gallinas* betray the artist's tribute to the vivid imagination of Mexican folk art,[47] yet their aesthetic rendering is clearly inspired by Modernism.

Recurrently, these images also expressed a homoerotic sensibility, if in a visual language that was so indirect that a non-suspecting audience failed to perceive it at all. He continued a tradition initiated in Mexican painting by the poet Xavier Villaurrutia, whose modest pictorial experiments expressed lightness and frivolity. Explicit eroticism soon evaporated from the artistic work of Reyes, but his semi-abstract emblemata expressed a 'gay' if not 'camp' sensibility that can be identified as such in the light of his personal biography. Figures such as *Payaso* are presented as a carnivalesque embodiment of homosexual *socialité*. Still, formal iconoclasm and flirtation with popular art are more important in Reyes's paintings than any kind of existential confession. In the end, straightforward gay images or explicit homoerotic ones were off limit for Chucho Reyes, who remained faithful to the agenda of Modernism and focused on formal innovation rather than subjective expression.

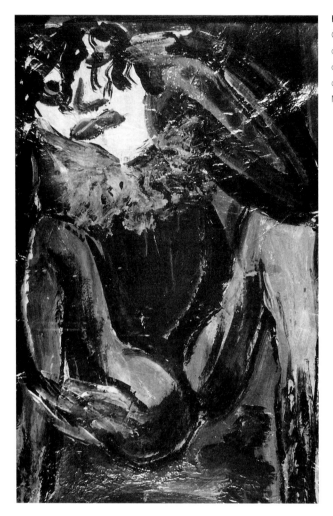

Figure 30 Jesus Reyes Ferreira, aka Chucho Reyes, *Payaso* (n.d.), tempera on china paper, 74 × 47 cm, private collection, courtesy of Centro Nacional de Arte, Biblioteca de las Artes, Mexico City.

Brazil

In Brazil, *Modernidade* is said to have taken off in the 1920s, more specifically during the Semana de Arte Moderna in 1922. European artists and writers visited Brazil (Cendrars, Marinetti), while Brazilian artists returned home after studies in Europe (Anita Malfatti, Tarsila do Amaral, Vicente do Rêgo Monteiro, Ismael Nery, Antônio Gomide). New, immigrating artists and architects like Lasar Segall and Gregori Warchavnik settled in Rio de Janeiro or São Paulo, then rapidly expanding and soon a centre of cultural renewal.[48] The year 1928 witnessed the publication of Mário de Andrade's landmark novel *Macunaíma*, while his brother, the poet Oswald de Andrade, published the *Manifesto Antropofágico*. Some artists in Rio founded the Núcleo Bernardelli in 1931. Artistic innovation in Brazil is put to the test at the Bienais de São Paulo held since 1951.[49]

Modernism – particularly abstraction and its spinoffs – turned the human body into a formal problem rather than an existential one. Eroticism and sexuality were pushed into the realm of provinciality. Still, major momentum must be attributed to Flávio de Carvalho (1899–1973), who adopted the language of Modernism while simultaneously elaborating on bodily sensation, sexual identity and gender roles. De Carvalho also paved the way for performance and body art in Brazil, more particularly for Lygia Clark and Hélio Oiticica, who will be discussed in Chapter 5.

De Carvalho adopted the erotic body as a prominent theme throughout his career, embracing both the male and female body in paintings, watercolours and drawings. But his life was one great performance also, giving rise to controversy on various occasions. As early as 1931, the artist attended a Corpus Christi pageant while wearing a beret. He was almost lynched by the crowd. He caused commotion also in 1956, when he walked the streets of São Paulo dressed as a woman. By wearing a blouse, a skirt and ballerina tights, he was commenting on the social construction of gender and adopting public performance as a means to do so.[50]

Conclusion

Naturalist imagery of male labour in Latin America as elsewhere was framed mostly by a mainstream, heterosexual gaze, and stressed the worker's masculinity and strength. The same is true for Naturalism's heir, Muralism, closely tied to leftist politics but still expressing male, heterosexist values most of the time. The Modernist canon, next, was marked by de-sexualization of both male and female bodies, as artists were interested primarily in formal deconstruction, and in the development of an increasingly abstract aesthetic.

And yet, even during these years of politicized art on the one hand and formal experiment on the other, artists who were homosexually or bisexually inclined adopted these visual languages in order to convey messages that were understandable to those 'who understood', that is men – and, to a lesser degree, women – who shared the codes of homotextuality and were able to uncover images of their own, largely underground gay and lesbian subcultures underneath the visual rhetoric of political art or, in the case of Modernism, of formal innovation. A certain body of work can be identified, allowing for the identification of a resilient, homosexual gaze, shared both by the maker and his audience. In Latin America also, artworks have been produced that, while formally celebrating labour or (socialist) revolution, also carry within themselves potentially 'gay' readings. Naturalist discourse itself framed such expression of homotextuality within the confines of an apparently asexual narrative and it was politically rather than sensually inspired. But there is evidence that, in some instances at least, the images of male nudity were perceived from within a homoerotic *imaginaire*.

Homotextuality surfaces sometimes in Abstract Modernism, also challenging a handful of artists to lend expression to their sexuality and desire according to its formalist prescriptions. That identifying such remains a hazardous task is evident, yet must not deter art historians from addressing the question and trying to retrieve the 'codified silences' implied.

Clearly, new figurative art, as developing alongside the overwhelming production of a so-called International style of abstraction, lent itself more easily to the production of recognizably homoerotic imagery. Still far removed from assertive, liberationist anthems, such images of *ambiente* were inscribed within the trope of empathic documentation and consisted largely, as will be made clear in Chapter 4, of intimate portrayals of homosocial friendship.

Notes

1 E. Lucie-Smith, *Adam: The Male Figure in Art* (London, 1998), p. 148.
2 Full quote in Desmond Rochfort, *Mexican Muralists: Orozco, Rivera, Siqueiros* (Singapore, 1993), p. 20.
3 *Ibid.*, p. 21.
4 See D. Schávelzon (ed.), *La polémica del arte nacional en México, 1850–1910* (Mexico, 1988), p. 312.
5 Solomon-Godeau, *Male Trouble*, p. 51.
6 See reproduction in Taylor, 'Mexican gaylife in historical perspective', p. 194.
7 L. Hurlbert, *The Mexican Muralists in the United States* (Albuquerque, 1989), p. 19.
8 This remains unacknowledged, however, by J. Ortiz Gaitán, *Entre dos mundos: los murales de Roberto Montenegro* (Mexico City, 1994), pp. 67, 90–7.
9 No monographic study of his work exists and very little biographical data can be found. See E. O'Gorman *et al.*, *Cuarenta siglos de plástica mexicana. arte moderno y contemporáneo* (Mexico, 1971), biographical index.
10 Personal communication by the CENIDIAP, Centro Nacional de Arte, Mexico City.
11 See a reproduction in P. Schatborn and V. van Rooijen (eds), *The Nude: Drawings, Prints and Photographs in the Collection of the Rijksmuseum Print Room* (Amsterdam, 1997), p. 25.
12 See A. Amaral, *Arte para quê? A preocupação social na arte brasileira, 1930–1970* (São Paulo, 1987), *passim*.
13 J. Motta Pessanha, in *O desejo na Academia, 1847–1916* (São Paulo, 1992), p. 47, also p. 65. Also, see M.C. França Lourenço, 'Revendo Ferraz Almeida', thesis, USP, 1981.
14 None of these connections are explained, however, in *Artistas Italianos nas praças de São Paulo* (São Paulo, 1992).
15 J. Franco, *The Modern Culture of Latin America: Society and the Artist* (London, 1967), pp. 146–7.
16 For details and illustrations, see M. Rossetti Batista and Y. Soares de Lima, *Coleção Mário de Andrade: Artes plásticas* (São Paulo, 1984), nrs. 392 and 401.

17 Very little has been published on Bertazzon. See a special issue, however, of the *Boletim de Belas Artes* (Rio da Janeiro, n.d.) devoted to his work (especially the article by H. Salvio).

18 J. Weinberg, *Male Desire: The Homoerotic Image in 20th Century American Art* (Mary Ryan Gallery, New York, 1995), p. 2.

19 I. de la Nuez, in *CubaSigloXX: Modernidad y sincretismo* (Las Palmas, Palmas and Barcelona, 1996), p. 72.

20 See *Cuban Poster Art: A Retrospective 1961–1982* (New York, 1983), *passim*. Also, see G.C. Echevarría, *Antología de un artista: Raúl Martínez* (Havana, 1995).

21 I. Lumsden, *Machos, Maricones and Gays: Cuba and Homosexuality* (Philadelphia, 1996), p. 234, note 28. This information was confirmed to me by the Cuban exile writer and playwright, Héctor Santiago, during an interview in New York City on 9 September 1996.

22 Martínez's memoirs are as yet inaccessible. Source: H. Santiago during the interview mentioned in note 21. Also, see R. González, 'Antonia Eiríz and Raúl Martínez: my painters say farewell', *Cuba Update*, October 1995, pp. 43–6.

23 De la Nuez in *CubaSigloXX*, p. 71.

24 See the illustrations on pages 20, 91, 220, 390, and colophon of a book by R. Martínez, *Un pueblo intero* (Havana, 1983).

25 H. Santiago claims that many works are still to be located in Spain, where the artist resided shortly before his death in 1981. Cabrera Moreno sold work to tourists also, who may not be aware of their significance both as part of Cuban artistic heritage and as material for this book.

26 I am greatly indebted to Marimar Benítez, whose study 'La representación del negro en la plástica de Puerto Rico' (1998) I downloaded from the cyber magazine *El Cuarto de Quenepón*.

27 On the sexual politics of abstraction, see A. Jones, 'Dis/playing the phallus: male artists perform their masculinity', *Art History*, 17, 4 (1994), pp. 25–38, and E. Crispolti, *Erotismo nell'arte astratta e altre schede per una iconologia dell'arte astratta* (Trapani, 1976).

28 N. Richard, 'Women's art practices and the critique of signs', in Mosquera, *Beyond the Fantastic*, pp. 145–6.

29 M. Traba, 'El erotismo y la comunicación', in *Zilia Sánchez. Tres decadas. Los sesenta. Los setenta. Los ochenta* (Humacao and San Juan, 1991), n.p. [7].

30 See W. Chadwick, *Women, Art and Society* (London and New York, 1996 (1990)), p. 366.

31 J. Weinberg, 'It's in the can: Jasper Johns and the anal society', *Genders*, 1 (Spring 1988), p. 170. Weinberg himself relies partially on C. Harrison and F. Orton, 'Meaning what you see', *Art History*, 7, 1 (March 1984), p. 81.

32 M. C. Ramírez, *Puerto Rican Painting* (Princeton, 1987), p. 31.

33 *Ibid.*, p. 32.

34 A. Gibson, 'Color and difference in abstract painting: the ultimate case of monochrome', *Genders*, 13 (Spring 1992), pp. 123–52.

35 For more information, see *CubaSigloXX. Modernidad y Sincretismo* (Las Palmas, Palma and Barcelona, 1996), and J. A. Martínez, *Cuban Art and National Identity: The Vanguardia Painters, 1927–1950* (Gainesville, 1994), *passim*.

36 On Peláez, see 'Amelia Peláez', in V. Baéz (ed.), *La enciclopedia de Cuba: Arquitectura. Artes plásticas. Música* (San Juan and Madrid, 1977), vol. 7, pp. 181–2. Recently, Peláez has been the subject of various retrospective shows. See *Amelia Peláez: Exposición retrospectiva, 1924–1967* (Caracas, 1991) and G.V. Blanc *et al.*, *Amelia Peláez: A Retrospective, 1896–1968* (Miami, 1988).

37 Interview with Héctor Santiago, New York City, 9 September 1996.

38 M. Hernández Zavala, in *Zilia Sánchez*, n.p. [4].

39 *Ibid.*

40 M. Traba, in *Zilia Sánchez*, n.p. [8].

41 S. Sacaluga, 'Las topologías eróticas de Zilia Sánchez', *El Nuevo Día*, 1981, quoted in *Zilia Sánchez*, n.p.

42 S. Sarduy, 'Las topologías eróticas de Zilia Sánchez', in *Estructuras en secuencia* (San Juan, 1970), n.p.

43 G. Brown, in *Estructuras en secuencia*, n.p.; E. García Gutiérrez, 'Eros y Zilia Sánchez', *El Nuevo Día*, 6 October 1991, p. 14.

44 Lumsden, *Machos, Maricones and Gays*, p. 232, note 34.

45 See *25 Años de color de Cuba: René Portocarrero* (Havana, 1988).

46 'Raúl Milián', in *Enciclopedia de Cuba*, vol. 7, p. 200.

47 No good study of Chucho Reyes's life and work exists as yet. See merely *El mundo de Jesús Reyes Ferreira* (Mexico, 1962) and *Homenaje a Chucho Reyes: Jesús Reyes Ferreira* (Mexico, 1984).

48 See N. Sevcenko, *Orfeu extático no metrópolis* (São Paulo, 1992), *passim*.

49 For more details, see the chronicle in *Modernidade: L'art brésilien du XXIème siècle* (Paris, 1988), pp. 373 ff. Also, see M. C. França Lourenço, *Operários da Modernidade* (São Paulo, 1995), and M. E. Boaventura, *O salão e a selva: Uma biografia ilustrada de Oswald de Andrade* (Campinas, 1995). On the development of art since the 1950s, see L. Amarante, *As bienais de São Paulo, 1951 a 1987* (São Paulo, 1989).

50 See L.C. Daher, *Flávio de Carvalho e a volúpia da forma* (São Paulo, 1984) and L. Amarante, *As bienais de São Paulo*, pp. 317–18.

CHAPTER FOUR

Postwar figurations of homosocial eros

(1 9 4 5 - 7 5)

Introduction

Non-figurative Modernism obviously did not monopolize the artistic scene, and alternative aesthetic languages developed alongside the ongoing experiment with formal investigation. New figurative art provided a channel for the expression of homoerotic desire, even when this remained discrete and highly codified. Although it allowed some artists to express their gay, lesbian or bisexual identity, this remained linked to an intricate code, developed to hide as much as to confess or reveal. Artists discreetly documented private friendships that were invested with male-to-male intimacy and portraiture especially offered itself as a privileged means of visualizing gay partnerships or love affairs. At times more daily life scenes were depicted that subtly documented homosocial eros, understandable primarily by an *entendido* or insider audience.

This mid-twentieth-century Latin American mode of expressing homotextuality was a 'minimalist' strategy compared, for instance, to contemporary developments of gay photography and art in the United States, France or Switzerland.[1] It was marked by discretion and uncertainty, intended more to give comfort to a small circle of initiates than to make oneself known as a gay man or woman to the outside world. José Quiroga has defined its code as a 'construction of privacy as spectacle', geared both at disclosure and disguise. How it operates was described poignantly by Sylvia Molloy, who pointed out 'the detours to which it resorts in order to name itself, the simulation it must engage in order to "pass", the codes it uses in order to be recognized even as it masks itself, and even the repression it exerts against itself as it internalized conventional prejudice'.[2] Such mechanisms at once reveal the limits of homotextual expression originating in some Latin American countries from the 1940s onwards and remaining in vogue until the rise of Gay Liberation movements in the late 1970s.

The 'spectacle of privacy' was not only closeted due to its ambiguous alteration between admittance and denial, but rooted in contemporary, medical and social discourses on sexual nonconformity. The adoption or 'quoting' by homosexual artists, male or female, of rather stereotypical representations of themselves was not different, in fact, from similar strategies in Europe or North America, where lesbian and gay artists subscribed to images that were common currency in society at large. Such apparently self-depreciative modes of expression did not necessarily confirm the existing socio-sexual state of affairs. In reality, they were subversive merely because they claimed the artist's right to visualize gay and lesbian subculture, even when such counter-representations remained inscribed within mainstream, stereotypical discourse. They were challenging also since they threatened to destabilize the organization of social life along the lines of gender. Gay men did so by presenting themselves as effeminate; lesbians by adopting the image of masculine-looking women.

Just as Romaine Brooks depicted herself as a 'butch' type, congruent with medical literature on cross-gender behaviour among lesbians and gays,[3] so too did a group of Latin American gay and lesbian artists present itself as the very embodiment of alternative gender ideals. The image of the limpwristed dandy, clearly visibly in Mexican art especially, thus undermined social and cultural convention, even though it is often considered 'politically incorrect' today. Frida Kahlo dressed like a man may well be seen at first sight as the deliberate adoption of a cliché, yet underneath the apparent conformism to wider discursive policy, there was a moment of reaction also and a claim to an independent, alternative representational politics. The often stereotypical outlook of 'homosexual art' from approximately 1945 until 1980 must not stand in the way of an understanding about its genuinely 'subcultural' and subversive intent.

Brazil: subtle affinities

In 1947, a book was published in Brazil that discussed homosexuality in the arts. It basically contained a single thesis on how the effeminate characteristics of some human figures by the Renaissance master Raphael were proof of the essentially 'mixed' (read: androgynous) nature of all people. Its author, Sílvio Marone, did not develop his point any further, nor did he investigate if any of the art of his own country would lead to similar conclusions. Yet, he relied on sexologists such as Marañon, Peixoto and Ribeiro to reiterate that the representation of homosexuality was tied up to a certain degree of cross-gender behaviour.[4]

The weight of sexological constructions of 'homosexual identity' is reflected in Brazil also in the work of some artists and cartoonists, portraying known homosexual personalities as visibly effeminate 'dandies'. Some representations of anonymous homosexuals also showed clear influence of medico-scientific discourse about gay men as members of a 'third sex'. Clearly, such new images of 'the homosexual' were distinct from before, when no such focus on a particular homosexual type existed. They announced a period of growing awareness among artists concerning the implications of sexual theory. Visual imagery of the male body, and of male nudity in particular, became increasingly 'suspect'. Social portrayal of new sexual identity can be perceived instead, playing down the erotic dimension and focusing on the clothes style and body language of homosexual men. Artists made sure, meanwhile, that the male body, when still considered valid as a topic of representation, was heterosexualized or, at least, bereft of erotic appeal.

Examples of both can be found in the work of Vicente do Rego Monteiro (1899–1970), though the artist's very long stay in Europe, rather than contemporary debate in Brazil, may have been more decisive for the genealogy of his early images of effeminate, possibly homosexual men.[5] *Explicações*, a watercolour of 1921 when the artist still lived in Paris, shows two men in discussion in a bourgeois salon. Their dress code is dandy-like, as is their body language: elegant positioning of hands and fingers, limp wrists even; luxurious bow ties and lacquered shoes. A similar, effeminate pose is taken by a man in *Figura ao vento* (1921). While facing a strong wind, he presses his knees together and carefully holds his colourful scarf. The delicate drawing of his eyes and eyebrows suggests mannerism and effeminacy. A portrait, finally, of Dr Alberto Cavalcanti (1922) shows a refined, elegant man with long – too long – fingernails and too refined facial features to be representing heterosexual masculinity.

The pattern is obvious still in *Arlequim e bandolim* of 1928, yet the artist, married since 1925 to the *parisienne* Marcelle Villard, exchanged it gradually for more virile representations of masculinity. Its tenor is undecided still in *Batismo do Cristo* (1928) – and even in *Casais* of 1946/7 – yet the move away from sexual ambiguity is blatant in some of his Modernist, Cubist-inspired images of male labourers (*Cabeça de operário*, 1923; *Os calçeteiros*, 1924), of hunters (*A caçada*, 1923; *O atirador de arco*, 1925), or of men involved in fights (*O duelo*, 1928; *O combate*, 1927).

The context becomes more heterosexual also, at least when the theme allows for it. A tennis game is played between a man and a woman. A soccer game obviously remains an exclusively male affair. Imagery that suggests sexual ambiguity disappears as the pictorial universe of do Rego Monteiro becomes exclusively heterosexual. This is

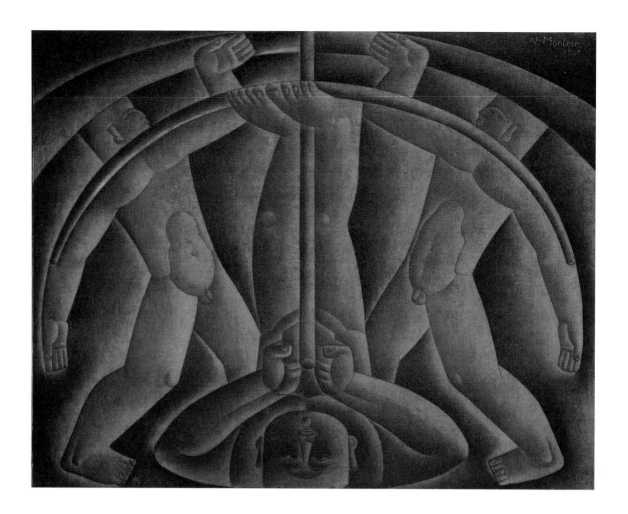

demonstrated also in his book of poetry, *Beau sexe*, published in Paris in 1950. Having become a protagonist of Brazilian Modernism, the artist stood at a distance from the sexual ambiguity characterizing some of his early work.

The call for Modernism allowed for physicality and subdued eroticism at an early stage. Anita Malfatti's male nudes, like *Nu masculino sentado* (1915/16) for example, are still imbued with a certain, if here female passion for male flesh. But gradually, both male and female nudes were pushed into the margins of artistic innovation or subjected to formal investigation instead. Only 'conservatives', such as Oswaldo Teixeira, Venere Bionda or members of the Grupo de Santa Helena kept choosing the human, especially female body as a self-supporting narrative theme. The body remains prominent also in the work of Emiliano di Cavalcanti, Vittorio Gobbis, Martinho de Haro and Ismael Nery, as of Flavio de Carvalho whom I briefly discussed in Chapter 3. Other artists created fewer or rather sterile images of the human body, however, and the male in particular was bereft of any erotic appeal. Clearly, formalist concerns were considered more important since classical narrative presentation of nudity had lost its intellectual attraction. Paintings of Alfredo

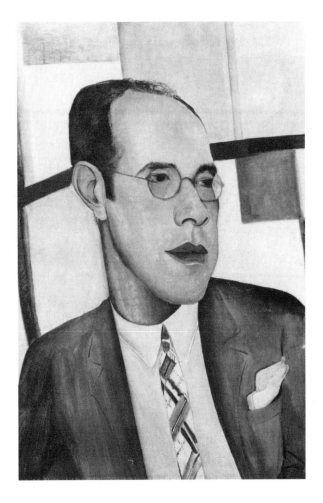

Figure 31 *(left)* Vicente do Rego Monteiro, *O atirador de arco* (1925), oil on canvas, 65 × 82 cm, Galería Metropolitana de Arte Aloísio Magalhães, Recife, photo: Romulo Fialdini.

Figure 32 *(right)* Lasar Segall, *Retrato de Mário de Andrade* (1927), oil on canvas, 73 × 60 cm, courtesy of the Instituto de Estudos Brasileiros, Universidade de São Paulo, São Paulo.

Geschiatti, Antônio Gomide, Fúlvio Penacchi and Enrico Bianco reflect this, as do the rather lifeless sculptures by Ernesto de Fiori of various, nondescript men.[6]

Was there no art, then, made during the first part of twentieth-century Brazil that revealed even an incipient code of 'homosexual art'? Certainly, no formal organization existed that gathered homosexually inclined artists around the theme of sexual identity. No group existed such as the literary circle Los Contemporáneos in Mexico, where homosexuality was among the common denominators bringing at least a few of its members together. In Brazil, the limited amount of 'gay art' *avant la lettre* is of a rather incidental kind, and even then its homotextual dimension is hard to demonstrate.

Perhaps Lasar Segall's portrait of Mário de Andrade (1927) reveals that in Brazil also a certain homosexual culture became visible underneath the layers of repression, self-censorship and, especially, adherence to an ambiguous, factually bisexual code of behaviour. The portrait exposes the writer's delicate features – codes that potentially revealed a certain upper-middle-class homosexual affinity at that time. It is known that Mário de Andrade was homosexual, even if a closeted one, which is understandable in

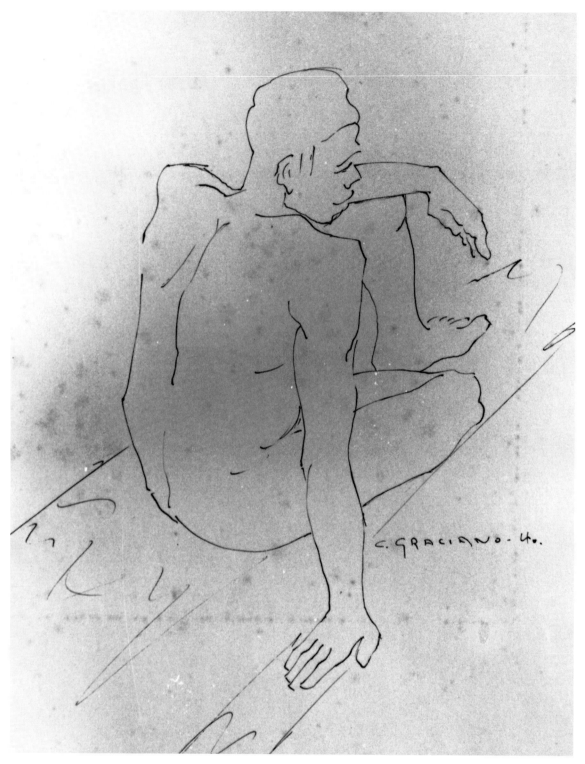

Figure 33 Clovis Graciano, *Nu masculino sentado (costas)* (1940), pencil on paper, 45.2 × 33.3 cm, courtesy of the Instituto de Estudos Brasileiros, Universidade de São Paulo, São Paulo.

view of his prominent role in introducing Modernism to Brazil. He was a protagonist, as said earlier, of the literary and artistic avant-garde and published his novel *Macunaíma* in 1928, while his brother Oswaldo wrote the *Manifesto Antropofágico*.

Visual expression of homosexual themes or sensibilities remained problematic indeed. They can be identified only underneath the aesthetic paradigm of Modernism or, at times, in some more private, often sketch-like works of artists who nevertheless prevented themselves from being explicitly profiled as 'homosexual'. This makes it hard to demonstrate if any particular image can be identified as 'homosexual' or not – unless, of course, such claims can be corroborated by additional archive research that would reveal a particular artist's actual homosexual proclivity.

No sound conclusion can be drawn, as a result, from isolated images that, when analysed thematically, may indicate a potential interest of the artist for either the homoerotic or a documentary of homosexuality. What indeed can be deduced from a picture such as Hugo Adami's *O fugitivo* (1934) (Plate 10)? Adami (b. 1900) focused on landscapes mostly, composed in vibrant colours illustrating the lush, tropical flora of Brazil. The picture of a semi-naked runaway slave asleep was inspired by an intention to portray his country's black and *mestiço* population along with Portinari and Teruz. Though blatantly erotic in itself, this painting does not allow for speculation on intended homoeroticism.

The sculptor João Batista Ferri (1896–1978) adopted sports as one topic among others for the arts. His *Atleta em descanso* (n.d.), now placed at the entrance of the Pinacoteca do Estado de São Paulo, clearly reflects the erotic appeal of sport activity and possibly allowed the artist to focus on the male body in a legitimate way. Yet, identifying this work as homosexually inspired is at this point closer to speculation than fact.

The same can be said for some of the works by Paulo Werneck, Joaquim Lopes Figueira Jr., or Clovis Graciano (1907–88), even when masculinity figures prominently in several drawings by the latter. Possibly, there was a more than purely aesthetic interest involved in drawings such as *Nu – dois rapazes* (1938), *Nu masculino sentado (costas)* (1940), or the empathic portrait of a dark-skinned young man (*Cabeza de jovem mulato*, 1941).

Subdued homoeroticism, whether conscious or unconscious, whether on the level of creation or of reception, may be discerned also in some isolated works by Helios Seelinger (1878–1965), though, again, this is hard to demonstrate unless documents support this as yet pure speculation. Clearly, his paintings of carnival scenes suggest that the artist was quite aware of the homosexual behavioural code. See the effeminate poses and limp wrists, considered characteristic of so-called *bichas* or *veados*. But this may be due to his familiarity with the bohemian neighbourhoods of Rio, where homosexual men used to socialize and had gained high visibility. Homosexuals traditionally become even more visible during carnival and society grants them a temporary right to 'camp it up'. Another work by Seelinger, *Luta pela vida* (1955), may indicate, however, that the artist was indeed keen to visually express homoerotic themes. While both a Futurist- and a Socialist-inspired image of hard life in the great industrial city, it prominently features semi-naked men whose sensuality is remarkable. Labour is given an almost orgiastic touch and attached to an awareness of the eroticism of male bonding.

Mexico: the heritage of Los Contemporáneos

In Mexico, a modern 'homosexual subculture' was clearly developing, even when it remained discreet and limited to the educated classes in the cities. In art circles, one witnessed the appearance of individuals whose lifestyles and identities approached that of self-identified homosexuals in metropolitan Europe and North America. They followed the example, perhaps, of critics such as Manuel Toussaint and Adolfo Best Maugard. Rivera's portrait of the latter is probably illustrative both of Rivera's homophobia as of Best Maugard's dandy-like pose. Work by Best Maugard himself undeniably reveals a sensibility that can be called 'gay' even in a Mexican context. His drawings of ballet scenes and of Mexican folk dances especially seem to verge towards campiness, while his self-portrait (*Autorretrato*, 1923) is a self-assured celebration of dandy life.

The writers' group Los Contemporáneos (1928–31) included Xavier Villaurrutia, Salvador Novo and Elías Nandino, all of whom were homosexual. Other authors, too, including the Columbian immigrant Porfírio Barba Jacob, identified themselves as such and expressed this, if subtly, in their literary works.[7] Of Mexican painters who maintained 'homosexual' lifestyles I have already mentioned Montenegro and Jesús Reyes Ferreira (the subject of Plate 11) in Chapter 3. Others were Agustín Lazo, Manuel Rodríguez Lozano, and Alfonso Michel.

André Breton, while setting up a show on Surrealism in Mexico, received help from the Peruvian poet and painter César Moro, who had arrived in 1938. The latter's openly homosexual lifestyle does not seem to have provoked any hostility from the guru of Surrealism, nor from any of his Mexican colleagues. 'For Moro', says Mac Adam, 'Surrealism (like writing in another language) offered a chance to express himself and his own kind of erotic vision openly. And while Breton and the Surrealists were not especially tolerant of homosexuality, they did not exclude or shun Moro for his sexual beliefs.'[8]

Public acceptance of homosexuality remained off limit, however, and the modern concept especially of 'masculine' homosexuals was more threatening than their effeminate counterparts. It uprooted the traditional pattern dividing the male population into active *hombres* and *machos* on the one hand, and *maricones* on the other. The taboo, as a result, was not lifted and perhaps became even stronger in a climate of social conformism, then

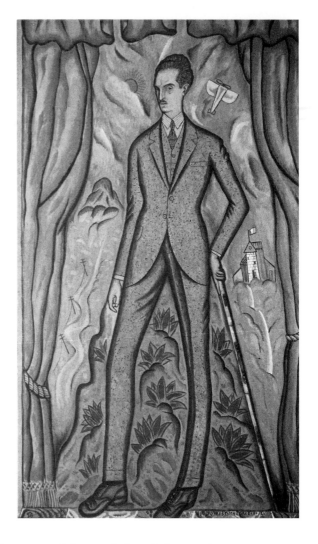

Figure 34 Adolfo Best Maugard, *Autorretrato* (1923), oil on canvas, 214 × 121 cm, courtesy of Instituto de Investigaciones Estéticas, Universidad Nacional Autonoma de México, Mexico City.

intense in Mexico. In 1934, a group of intellectuals pressured the newly founded Comité de Salud Pública to 'remove' homosexuals from the civil service. One ought to fire 'los individuos de moralidad dudosa que están detentando puestos oficiales y los que, con sus actos efeminados, además de constitutir un ejemplo punible, crean una atmósfera de corrupción que llega hasta el extremo de impedir el arraigo de las virtudes viriles en la juventud . . . [También] debe combatirse la presencia del hermafrodita, incapaz de identificarse con los trabajadores de la reforma social.'*[9] The new freedom remained limited as a result. Only relatively little explicit male nudity can be traced due to the increased awareness both among the artists and the public about its controversial potential. It appeared only incidentally and the tenor remained distant and objectifying.

Most artists, gay or straight, made sure that their incidental portrayals of nude masculinity could not be seen as expressions of a homoerotic gaze. Their style, expectedly, was cool and detached. The 'neutrality' of the painter's gaze is obvious, for example, in Juan Soriano's *San Jerónimo* (1942). It shows a naked man, possibly the painter himself,

*'individuals of questionable morality who are occupying official positions and who, while acting effeminately, not only are a criminal example, but create a corruptive atmosphere as well, that goes as far as to stand in the way of the development of virile virtue amongst the young . . . We must [also] fight the presence of the hermaphrodite, incapable of identifying himself with the workers for social reform.'

who sits on a chair. Behind him a small frame – a mirror? – showing a skeleton in an identical position. A stereotypical representation of homosexuality is obvious, next, in *La Playa* (1943), showing a beach scene with numerous people bathing, sunbathing and playing around. In the foreground, a tall, blond man is stretched out on the sand, eyes fixed on the viewer and his right hand leaning languorously on his hip. His pose is unmistakably feminine.

A speculative mind may recognize a homoerotic content in some of Guillermo Meza's work, even when both his male and female nudes are immersed in an undeniable sensuality and physicality. The contextualization is consistently heterosexual, however, as can be seen in *Pareja durmiendo* (1941) or *6 PM* (n.d.). The drawing *Orfeu* (1940) also reflects a 'pasión renascencista por el desnudo, . . . sensualidad formal del Barroco'*,[10] but the narrative's heterosexual content demands caution. The same goes for images of nudity in the work of Ricardo Martínez. *Los raízes del vallejo* (1946), though drawn in *Indigenisto* tradition, is actually focusing on the Indians' nude anatomy, but stylistic abstraction makes bodies into sculptures that are cold and distant and demonstrate the artist's apparent indifference.

Some physical sensuality is expressed in Julio Castellanos's painting *El baño de San Juan* (1937). The presence of naked boys (and girls) in and around a swimming pool may be compared to the pederastic tenor of Robert Riggs's *Pool* (c. 1933). At first sight, such an interpretation may indeed be just due to the frequent appearance of children in the painter's work in general. Yet, the artist's position seems rather detached and refutes speculation.

Several artists, known as bisexual or homosexual, were reluctant to express their sexual desire in a context of limited tolerance. Agustín Lazo, for example, abstained from painting male nudity, even though he was known to be homosexual. Others, however, produced work that allows today's art historian to identify a more or less explicit dimension of homotextuality.

Only three paintings by Alfonso Michel (1897–1957), *Torso masculino reclinado*, *La tempestad* and *El rio* (all dating from 1953), show male nudity in ways that are subtly erotic. Male nudity is only one among the themes of Michel's relatively small oeuvre, which includes female nudes and still lifes as well. The deliberate expressionism of its style almost neutralizes the effect and the bodies shown become like cold, lifeless lumps of human flesh.

The simultaneous play of involvement and detachment possibly can be explained by reference to the painter's biography. Michel was homosexual and his wealthy family supported his perpetual wanderings around the world in order to avoid a scandal in the conservative state of Colima, where he grew up. He spent time in California and especially Europe, sharing a studio briefly with Agustín Lazo while trying to give shape to his own artistic ambitions. Called a 'tropical *beatnik*' by Debroise, he both celebrated and loathed

*'Renaissance-like passion for the nude . . . formal sensuality of the Baroque'

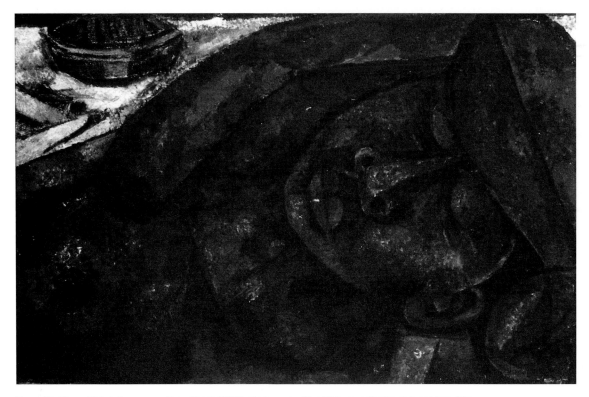

Figure 35 Alfonso Michel, *Torso masculino reclinado* (1953), oil on canvas, 36 × 55.5 cm, collection of Jorge López Páez, courtesy of Centro Nacional de las Artes, Biblioteca de las Artes.

his life of semi-opulence and aristocratic decadence. Behaving dandy-like, he cultivated a theatrical *mise-en-scène*, parody and bluff, yet he struggled with his sexuality for many years. He alternated longer-lasting relationships with freewheeling promiscuity. A photo exists of Michel posing near a Parisian *pissotière*, possibly documenting his life of cruising in the capital of France. While called 'the worst *guayaba* of the family' – his father made a fortune by trading tropical fruits – he once described himself with the neologism *agigolón*. He emphasized and embraced his gigolo-like existence of sexual exile and libertine eccentricity. 'La provocación agrega una nota de humor al oprobio: ésta es la única manera, quizás, de presentar su homosexualidad en aquella época. Ante una ignominia imposible de asumir socialmente, convierte su marginalidad en una razón de ser, no desprovista de cierta "poesía de lo patético".'[*11]

Though most of his private life has been kept secret by his family, one can nevertheless claim with certainty that both his life and work were marked by his sexual identity. Social

*'Provocation consists in humouring the disgrace: that is perhaps the only way to present his homosexuality in that era. Facing an ignominy, preventing social expression, he turns his marginality into a device for life, not bereft of a certain "poetry of the pathetic".'

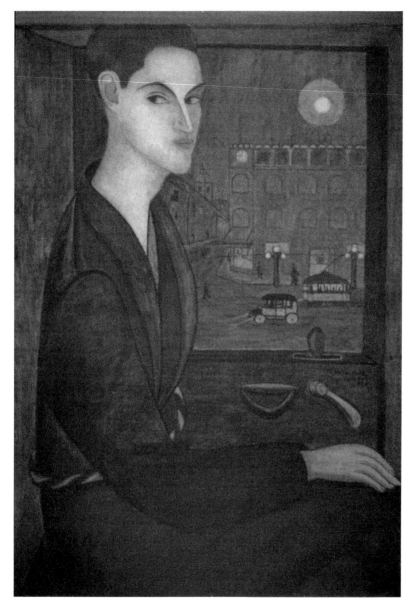

Figure 36 Manuel Rodríguez Lozano, *Retrato de Salvador Novo* (1924), oil on canvas, 200 × 130 cm, Museu Nacional de Belas Artes, Museo Nacional de Arte, Mexico City, courtesy of Instituto de Investigaciones Estéticas, Universidad Nacional Autonoma de México, Mexico City.

intolerance and self-criticism gave rise to his own personal ambiguity towards his painting career and to his somewhat mysterious 'posing' and frivolity. Perhaps his 'gay sensibility' is most tangible, suggests Debroise, in one worn photo of himself, lying half-naked on the beach at Tecomán. He seems to be hiding his face in the sand, while above, in French, is written 'l'inconnu' ('the unknown'). Feeling at odds with himself like a 'sailor on land', he thus seemed to want to express the lifelong uneasiness of a man whose sexual and social condition clashed with contemporary expectations.[12]

Manuel Rodríguez Lozano (1896–1971) never hid his homosexuality and expressed it with great candour in drawings and paintings, some of which are now kept in private collections.[13] A homoerotic undertone is clearly discernible in a series of nudes at the seaside and in a series of bullfighting nudes, where the *torrero*'s erotic appeal is reinforced by nudity. The model's look and bare nipple in *Retrato de un pintor* (n.d.) clearly reveals a homosexual gaze as well. Of a homoerotic tenor, also, are the illustrations by Lozano of a 1933 Mexican edition of Federico Garcia Lorca's *Oda a Walt Whitman*. *El pensador* (1936) (Plate 12) shows two strong, fully naked men walking on a rather ethereal-looking beach – there is a simplified image of an Aztec pyramid in the background – while a third, equally naked, man watches them. The viewer is invited to admire both men's beauty and to share a 'homosexual gaze'.

An altogether different expression of homotextuality in the arts is Lozano's portrait of Salvador Novo (*Retrato de Salvador Novo*, 1924), an empathic portrayal of the homosexual poet sitting elegantly in a car. In the night background is, probably, the Post Office building on the corner of the Calle de Tacuba and the Eje Central. The portrayal's underlying *gayacidad* documents the lifestyle of one of Mexico's known homosexual poets, yet also reveals something of the painter's own affinity and familiarity with Mexico's homosexual intelligentsia at the time.

Lozano's biography, though still too little researched,[14] reveals a homosexual lifestyle and one that wasn't hampered, for once, by scrupulous hiding or posing as 'straight' to the outside world. His studio attracted younger painters, including Abraham Ángel, Julio Castellanos and Tebo, with whom he maintained relationships that were more than just 'didactic'. Angel Torres Jaramillo, for example, better known as Tebo, was the son of a Nahuatl *peón* from Querétaro. Initially, he was Lozano's *mozo* or helper, but gradually he started to draw himself, encouraged by Lozano. A nude study of 1934 is an erotic portrayal of a naked man, whose legs are pulled up as he looks down distractedly.

Rodríguez Lozano's relationship with Ángel in particular drew wide attention: '[Era] una de las cosas bellas y reconfortantes que podían verse en México, donde los afectos altos y desinteresados, las efusiones espirituales, la fidelidad y la abnegación van siendo cosas del pasado,'* says José Juan Tablada in his book *Abraham Angel, el pintor niño* (1924).[15] Ángel died very young at age nineteen, so little can be deduced from either his biography or his limited, if suggestive, oeuvre. It is possible, however, that his portrait of the tennis player Hugo Tilghman (n.d.) contains a trace of vague erotic interest.

Rodríguez Lozano's amorous relationships were similar to the intimate friendships of French writer and artist Jean Cocteau. As Raymond Radiguet for Cocteau, so Abraham Ángel was the artistic genius-in-the-making for Rodríguez Lozano. The poet and *torero* Negro Muñoz was like Cocteau's Barbette. Rodríguez Lozano also adopted the role of a Maecenas, as did Cocteau, and did so while private support of the arts had been rejected by the Muralists.[16]

*'[It was] one of the most beautiful and comforting things one could see in Mexico, where high and disinterested feelings, spiritual effusions, faithfulness and self-renunciation had become things of the past.'

He was later sent to jail allegedly for the theft of engravings by Dürer, even though he had not been the thief. Homophobia, says Monsiváis, was the motive for his punishment.[17] Homoeroticism remained a controversial theme, expressed rarely in unequivocal images of male intimacy, more often as discreet, suggestive portrayals of intimate, if closeted friendships among men. Psychological portraits of 'friends' became coded documents of an incipient gay *ambiente* in the greater urban centres of Mexico.

Rodríguez Lozano's circle was one of these. Another one gained visibility in the work of Ben-Hur and his brother, Emilio Baz Viaud. Together, they visualized another, nascent network of 'male friendships' in the 1950s and 1960s Mexican artistic scene.

Ben-Hur (b. 1906) spent much of his adult life in New York City. Earlier, he grew up in the creative and eccentric milieu of his family. Not only he, but also his brother Emilio, as well as the children of his sister Maria, Marysole and Juan Wörner Baz, all pursued artistic careers.[18] Ben-Hur himself moved to the United States after having finished his studies at the Mexican art academy. In New York, he found work as an illustrator for various magazines, including *Time* and *Newsweek*, and considered himself primarily as a commercial artist with little real talent. He returned to Mexico later on.

One of his works is titled *Trompe-l'oeil with nudes* (1963). It is painted in almost Superrealist style, not very different, for example, from the Chilean artist Claudio Bravo. But a more significant resemblance, perhaps, can be recognized. The painting shows little reproductions of nudes, two male, one female, pinned against a wooden wall and looking very much like the work of one of America's best-known gay artists, Paul Cadmus. Emotional and stylistic affinities with Cadmus's work can also be detected in the painter's self-portrait of 1935. It is a subtle portrayal of vulnerability, not unlike those of the American artist and having the same moral exhibitionism. A drawing of a male nude, titled *Desnudo de hombre* (c. 1965), equally reflects Cadmus's numerous drawings of naked men in semi-languid poses.

Other, later work is distinct. Thus *Lámpara maravillosa de Aladino* (1926), which, while obviously inspired by Japanese prints, is a fine example of how the artist's gay sensibility was made legitimate by being placed in a less controversial, narrative context of Orientalism.

Ben-Hur's brother, Emilio Baz Viaud (1918–91), stayed in Mexico, studying architecture at the Academia de San Carlos. He was considered very attractive, wearing *huaraches* and jeans, very bohemian, and developed friendships with men employed in the arts. Among them figured Manuel Rodríguez Lozano, who played a major role in his life, and José Gómez Rosas, nicknamed 'el Hotentote', who was dark-skinned and made the decor panels for balls at the Academy. These included the so-called *perradas*, initiation rites for freshmen or *perros*, dogs, of whom Emilio was one. In the 1950s he set up a partnership with a certain Fischer and together they opened a gallery in San Miguel Allende, Guanajuato. The enterprise was short-lived and closed after four years.

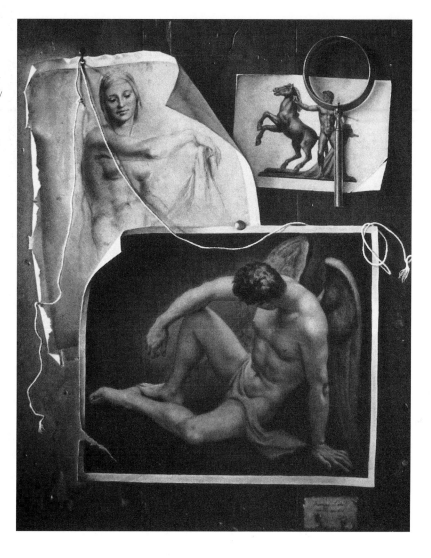

Figure 37 Ben-Hur Baz Viaud, *Trompe-
l'œil with nudes* (1963), tempera and dry
brush on cardboard, 63 × 50 cm,
collection of the artist, courtesy of
Centro Nacional de las Artes, Biblioteca
de las Artes, Mexico City.

In the 1960s, Emilio entered a monastery near Cuernavaca, where much attention was
paid to psychoanalysis. He took advantage, as he confessed himself, of the free sessions
offered there but was soon sent away.[19]

Much of Emilio's work consisted of portraits either of himself, like *Autorretrato del
artista adolescente* (1935) and *Autorretrato con camisa azul* (1941), or of his artist friends in
Mexico and the USA. Some of these portraits, like *José Gómez Rosas, el 'Hotentote'* (1941)
reveal no particularly 'gay sensibility'. But others undoubtedly do, even when such was
acknowledged only reluctantly by art critics at the time.[20] *Portrait of the painter George
Hutzler, aged [sic] 28, with his pet, Bimba* (1949) dates from his years at San Miguel de
Allende and acknowledges their friendship in a little note at the painting's upper left
corner. Emilio's portraits of Eduardo Parellón (1938) and of Vicente de la Barrera (1939)

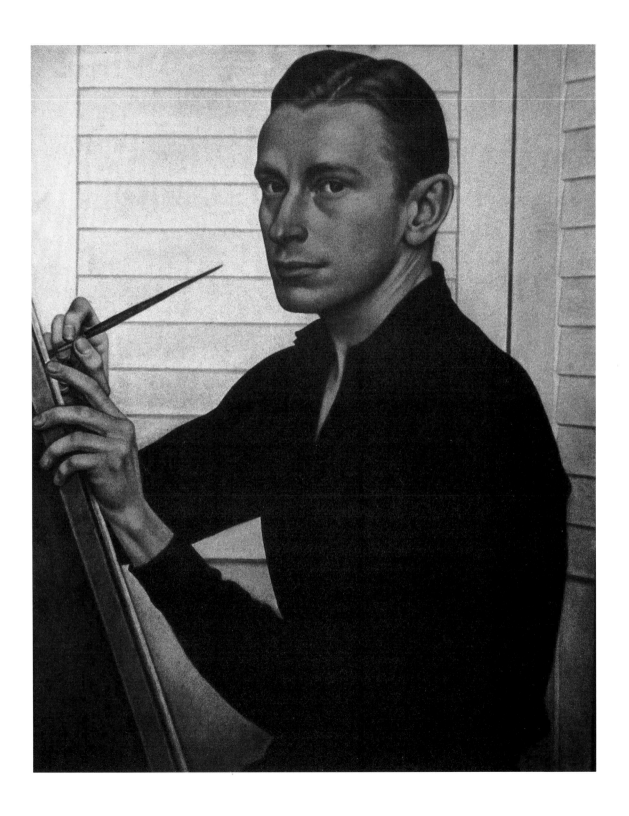

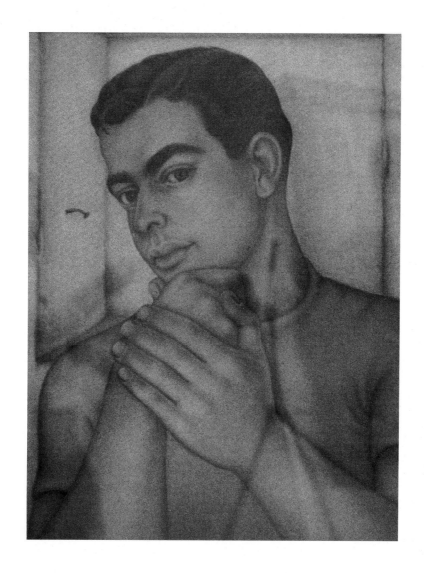

Figure 38 *(left)* Ben-Hur Baz Viaud, *Autorretrato* (1935),
watercolour and dry brush on cardboard, 60 × 48 cm,
collection of the artist, courtesy of Centro Nacional de las Artes,
Biblioteca de las Artes, Mexico City.

Figure 39 *(above)* Emilio Baz Viaud, *Retrato de Horácio* (1943),
watercolour and dry brush on cardboard, 80 × 56 cm,
collection of the artist, courtesy of Centro Nacional de las Artes,
Biblioteca de las Artes, Mexico City.

radiate an atmosphere of refinement in the former, of unmistakable sensuality in the latter. Complicity, finally, seems to have nourished the artist's inspiration in his *Retrato de Horácio* (1943), which remained, perhaps not without reason, in the artist's collection until his death.

Neither Ben-Hur's nor Emilio's artistic oeuvre is ever explicitly erotic, yet they document a pattern of male bonding that seems to have been coloured 'gay'. The portraits especially are valuable here as the covert visualization of friendship, possibly suggesting emotional and sexual intimacy among these men. Perhaps a last comment can be made about Emilio's *La calle de Cuahtemotzin* (1941), showing two men visiting a famous prostitution alley in the Mexican capital. One man holds his arm on his pal's shoulder, obviously as a sign of camaraderie and male bonding. This gesture, in fact, is still current in Mexico today and there is no connection to be read with homosexuality. But in the eyes of a homosexual viewer, this may nevertheless have had a secret meaning, as if a fascination for straight men is combined with the expression of male intimacy and this by means of the artwork itself. Such multiplicity of meanings constitutes one of art history's main challenges and is a recurrent theme when addressing the issue of an artist's sexual identity.[21]

It is impossible, of course, when surveying homotextuality in modern Mexican art, to omit the work of Frida Kahlo (1907–54). Her status as the wife of Diego Rivera hardly diminishes the significance of both her life and work within the context of a gay and lesbian *imaginaire*. Today – maybe especially today – Frida Kahlo's work is seen by artists and critics alike as a crucial contribution to the deconstruction of the art world's male prerogatives and to the recognition of gender and sexual diversity as legitimate objects of visual representation.

Though initially devoted to her husband, Diego, she gradually developed a more complex intimate life, especially after her husband started an affair with her sister Christina in 1934. Like Diego, she too had affairs – with men, such as the sculptor Isamu Noguchi and Leon Trotsky, but also with women, such as María Félix and Pita Amor. She assumed her bisexuality and expressed it, if covertly, in her art. 'Along with self-love and psychic duality, it is suggested in her double self-portraits, and it emerges in many of her paintings as a kind of atmosphere, a sensuality so deep that it was stripped of the conventional sexual polarities, a hunger for intimacy so urgent that it ignored gender', observes her biographer Hayden Herrera, whose description of homotextuality in Kahlo's work nevertheless remains rather vague.[22]

The most explicitly 'lesbian' work, undoubtedly, is *Duas desnudas en la selva* (1939) (Plate 13), showing two naked women – one dark-skinned, the other pale white – in a more or less intimate pose within the jungle. Yet, concrete social or geographic references are absent – which attenuates the painting's controversial content to some degree and codifies it within the realm of timeless mythology. The work thus can be read as an image of female bonding or of female solidarity across ethnic and social barriers.

Drawings and portraits of female friends can be seen as artistic recognitions of the model's sexual attractiveness, if only in view of the artist's biography. Mostly, the potential dimension of sexual attraction remains hidden behind rather traditional, if empathic portraiture as in *Retrato de Adriana* (1927). Only rarely does a portrait allow for speculation about sexual intimacy. The *Retrato de Eva Frederick* (1931), while labelled as 'semi-pornographic' by some,[23] is quite restrained in itself and calls for cautious interpretation.

The homotextuality of Kahlo's work is inscribed in a more complex gender code, making her paintings into works relevant not only for a study of 'lesbian' art, but also of 'women's art' in a wider sense. More significant, therefore, are changes of details especially from the 1940s onwards, when Frida emphasizes her growing independence by means of signifiers of masculinity. Her self-portraits thus show a gradual shift from refined, vulnerable femininity (*Autorretrato*, 1926) to almost masculine facial features, reinforced moreover by the artist's accentuation of facial hair (*Autorretrato*, 1945 and 1947) or, as in *Autorretrato con pelo cortado* (1940), by her adoption of a 'male' haircut.

Within a Latin American context, it is the absence rather than presence of unmistakably 'lesbian' images that makes Kahlo's work relevant also within the context of this book. For, as male artists frequently adopt a bisexual lifestyle without necessarily expressing this in their work, it would be unfair to expect a female artist to be visually explicit about claiming a similar right to sexual freedom. The integration of a handful of potentially 'lesbian'-identifiable works within her entire oeuvre perhaps demonstrates best how radical Kahlo's position was both as a woman and as a female artist. It may explain also why she is recognized by so many gay and lesbian artists today, not only in Mexico but worldwide, as a precursor who paved the way for more assertive artistic expressions of homotextuality and homoerotic desire.

Cuba: private revolutions

In Cuba, too, a covert homosexual subculture existed that was equally characterized by a textuality of the 'closet'. Literature predominantly provided a platform for gay expression, yet the vocabulary and syntax of homoeroticism remained highly coded. It was understandable only to a small élite of homosexual or bisexual intellectuals. The journal *Orígenes* (1944–56), founded by José Lezama Lima and edited jointly by Lezama Lima and José Rodriguez Feo, was a publication that allowed for sharing a homosexual sensibility, if always subtly so and in covert, often Platonic terms.

Lezama Lima stayed in Havana, working on the novel *Paradiso*. It remained unpublished until after his mother's death in 1966, and still is the most important 'gay' novel of Cuba.[24] Feo, on the other hand, travelled extensively in both the United States and Europe, contacting gay writers and boasting about his encounters with Stephen Spender, T.S. Eliot, Wallace Stevens, Luis Cernuda, André Gide and Jean Genet. Meanwhile, Feo seems to have had numerous amorous affairs with other men, yet for Feo culture – and, specifically, the journal *Orígenes* – became a sublimation of his homosexuality. 'Homosexuality', says Quiroga, 'is rendered productive by means of culture. It is as if . . . the spectacle of *Orígenes* . . . depends on the coded silence within this elliptical circuit of affections, as if *Orígenes* were not only a metaphor but rather a kind of pre-text.'[25]

Surely, homosexuality was a polemic issue, as is revealed in the preceding 'epistemology of the closet'. It not only gave rise to affiliations, such as between Feo and the novelist José Lezama Lima, but to rivalry and reproach as well. Feo criticized the Cuban art critic José Gómez Sicre, who was forced to leave Cuba earlier after a pederastic scandal. The widespread image, moreover, of pre-Castro Cuba as a 'gay paradise' calls for modification, since its parameters were limited in many ways. There was a discrepancy, first, between the city and the countryside; secondly between middle-class homosexuals, who had money as well as access to culture and information, and poor gay men and lesbians, who were not so fortunate.

But most importantly, the so-called homosexual haven of Havana was essentially a highly commercialized gay sex market, paralleling a straight one, and catering predominantly to an international tourist and expatriate community. It was tolerated only because of its pecuniary profits and limited, moreover, by the rigid gender system of *machismo*. Working-class men operated as 'trade' to foreigners while making sure to maintain the distinction between themselves as sexually 'active' and their clients as sexually 'passive'. Passive Cuban homosexuals in their turn adopted an effeminate code of behaviour and aligned themselves with feminine prostitutes.

The commodification of homosexual desire in the Havana underworld did not result in greater acceptance of a gay lifestyle elsewhere. Within the family and at work, the *locas* or queens were ridiculed or harassed. *Tortilleras* (or dykes), already less visible as such, were ignored or made objects of ridicule as well. 'If legal sanctions and official harassment were rare, this tolerance was due less to social acceptance than to overriding considerations of profit and the economic interests of the underworld that dominated the Cuban political apparatus.'[26]

After the Cuban Revolution of 1959 the commercialized sex circuits were wiped out, yet the *machista* system remained. Traditional gender expectations were gradually translated into an official policy of repression of homosexuality, seen as being of 'capitalist' inspiration and at odds with the requirements of the Revolutionary regime. The new policy resulted in the opening in 1965 of the so-called UMAP camps (Unidades Militares de Ayuda a la Producción), geared at re-educating 'asocial' individuals, including homosexuals.[27] It would lead to international protest and after three years the camps were dismantled, but homophobia remained inscribed within Cuban policy. The 1971 Congress on Education and Culture adopted a number of clearly homophobic resolutions and, though homosexuality was decriminalized in the Penal Code of 1979, it remained possible to arrest gay men and lesbians arbitrarily merely because they were said to violate 'public decency'. '*Antisocial* [became] a code word for allegedly ostentatious homosexuality.'[28]

Ian Lumsden claims that foreign critics have exaggerated Cuban oppression of homosexuals and the point must be made that propaganda is not Fidel Castro's monopoly.[29] Intolerance towards homosexuals and lesbians was part, moreover, of a climate of ever-increasing totalitarianism. Censorship of social, political and intellectual dissidence led to the Padilla affair of 1970 and to the disenchantment of most leftist intellectuals worldwide.

It is clear, nevertheless, that Castro's policy towards gays and lesbians was harsh and prevented a gay subculture from developing outside the confines of one's private room for many years. From the 1960s until the 1980s, it was impossible to claim greater freedom and visibility for gays and lesbians. This is reflected in the absence of clearly gay-inspired visual art. Many gay and lesbian artists actually got married to ward off suspicion and protect themselves.[30]

Only a handful of visual artists found the courage, in such a social and political context, to address matters of sexual identity or homosexuality in their work. I have mentioned the women's portraits by Amelia Peláez in Chapter 2, as I focused on Servando Cabrera Moreno and Raúl Martínez, if only with regard to their public work. Their remaining production, condemned to stay private due to political circumstance, bears testimony to how in Cuba discreet networks of same-sex friendships and relationships existed. Kept within the space of private houses, or – in the case of Cabrera Moreno – spread across the globe are unmistakably homoerotic images, discarded until now by Castro's cultural policy.[31] An attempt to set up a museum devoted to both by the head of the Cuban Film Institute (ICAIC), Alfredo Guevara, still has to materialize.[32]

The conscious marginalization of Cabrera Moreno and Martínez, along with the harassment by the Castro regime of Umberto Peña, Antonia Eiriz and others, remained sufficiently intimidating and cut off the way for more open visualizations of homo-eroticism, or of homosexual subcultural life. The oppressive political climate forced homosexual artists and intellectuals to leave the country, rather than pursue a career at home. They went into exile, along with numerous other dissidents, while parents, concerned about the Revolutionary educational regime, sent their children abroad. Then, in 1979, when the Mariel operation took place, a disproportionately high number of homosexual men and women left Cuba, never to return. From Europe, North America and other continents, they set about a campaign to make the dark sides of Castro Socialism known to the world.[33]

Puerto Rico: the visual politics of intimacy

Until fairly recently, there was limited tolerance only towards so-called 'erotic art' in Puerto Rico, an island whose population is exposed to the oppressive discourses of penal law, Roman Catholicism and the Evangelical churches of North American denominations. A *machismo encarcelador* (an imprisoning, oppressive *machismo*) equally precludes free expression of eroticism, especially by women artists. Female nudes by Luisa Geigel de Gandia were exhibited in the 1940s, causing a riot and provoking criticism. In 1947, an exhibition of erotic drawings by Julio Rosado del Valle was followed by a collective show on erotic art, yet both shows proved to be highly polemic and to make artistic expression of sexuality and eroticism into an ordeal. More controversy followed in 1961, when a show by Rafael Ferrer and José Villamil was considered too sexually explicit.

The ongoing climate of repression and censorship clearly nurtures the work of the painter Myrna Báez (b. 1931). Her visual language disguises as much as it reveals – a mixture, so it seems, of discretion on the one hand, and on the other, resistance against models of homosexual identity, disseminating itself on the island as communication with the USA has grown more intense.

Báez often 'quotes' great masters, copying or paraphrasing their female nudes mostly (among these, *La Gioconda*, 1973, after da Vinci; *La Venus roja*, 1979, after Velasquez; *Danae*, 1979, after Titian) and aiming at the renewal of images that have become common currency after multiple exposure in the media. *Susana despuès del baño* (1993), for example, reflects an old masterpiece, in this case Tintoretto's *Suzannah and the Elders* (1556), yet transcribes it within the context of life on the island of Puerto Rico.

Tintoretto, Giorgione and Titian, all masters of the Venetian school, have great sensual appeal for Báez, yet critics often overlook this in an attempt to de-eroticize the artist's quoting of them in her own work: 'Los desnudos de Myrna Báez repelen el erotismo y deben entenderse como elementos fundamentales de la composición. . . . Las poses de los desnudos de Báez no son seductoras.'*[34] Well, perhaps they are not seductive in any predictable, stereotypical way. The overweight, slightly older women in Báez's paintings are not objects of sexual attraction as defined commonly by a masculine gaze.

*'The nudes of Myrna Báez are un-erotic and must be understood as fundamental elements of composition. . . . The poses of Báez's nudes aren't seductive.'

Margarita Fernández Zavala, whom I just quoted, admits herself that voyeurism is included within the works of Báez. But she then moves on and 'explains' how Báez transmits the onlooker's gaze to the woman in the painting. The woman herself 'looks' at the landscape, from between the curtains, whereby the artist herself takes the place of the model in due course.[35] Fernández Zavala's analysis, while legitimate as an interpretation of Báez's feminist critique of the male gaze, is incomplete, however, since it throws away the baby with the bathwater. Not always are Báez's portraits of women in interiors purely autobiographical. Female nudity, at times, is presented as an object of contemplation by someone else, possibly – but not necessarily – another woman. Implicitly, Báez's universe reflects an 'alternative' gaze that may well be defined as inscribed within a *de facto* 'lesbian' *imaginaire*. It both defies and submits itself to the undecided character of Báez's representational vocabulary and her refusal to subscribe to an exclusive category of sexual identity. Final judgement is postponed deliberately, as Myrna Báez does not identify herself as lesbian.

Paintings like *Retrato de un sueño* (1989–90) and *Reposo* (1993) disclose itineraries, rather, into the model's psyche. Perhaps they are 'effective', as claims Maria Ramírez, 'in communicating the anxiety and alienation of the figures through the way in which the composition appears cut off and the figures compressed in its interior'.[36] But possibly the works are honest testimonies also of the artist's affection for the model – an affection that goes beyond mere physical desire and carries, within itself, the expression of a more spiritual bond between women. Báez, who is fascinated by the Puerto Rican landscape, is offering a codified image of woman-to-woman understanding that may be more redeeming, if less Platonic than suggested by Fernández Zavala. 'Báez's world', says Shifra Goldman, 'is one of women into which men occasionally wander'[37] – or, put differently, a world of women among women, self-reliant on the one hand, introspective on the other.

A more explicit homosexual 'graphesis', if turned upside down, can be found in the work of Susana Herrero Kunhardt (b. 1945). It is explicitly homoerotic, yet predominantly male – which calls for an attempt at understanding the underlying logic. Some recent works, like *Sin título* (1990), represent women, here one woman seen from above while she seems to be masturbating. But most other works show either single men (the series *Inudi*, after Michelangelo's *Ignudi* in the Sistine Chapel, Vatican), or male nude couples with their bodies intertwined in challenging positions and that, like Luis Caballero's, suggest a borderline activity between wrestling and sex (the series *Fuera de serie*).

Herrero Kunhardt's assertive vision, especially in *Fuera de serie*, has gained acceptance today, but critics have long questioned its validity. In 1976, a one-man show of her work was closed temporarily after voices arose about the works' presumably 'pornographic' content. It reopened after critics had defended it.[38] At times, the eroticism of her work is recognized without acknowledging its gay dimension.[39] Some focus on the artist's craftsmanship, while others feel a need to emphasize the spiritual and moral dimension of the work as a plea against intolerance and taboos.[40] Critic Enrique García Gutiérrez was the first and as yet only critic to explicitly address the homoerotic dimension of Herrero Kunhardt's oeuvre: 'Su primera consideración no es la de suscitar apreciaciones de un erotismo de provocación o sibarítico, aunque la sensualidad juegue un rol persuasivo en tan variados elementos como la ondulación suave de la línea, la

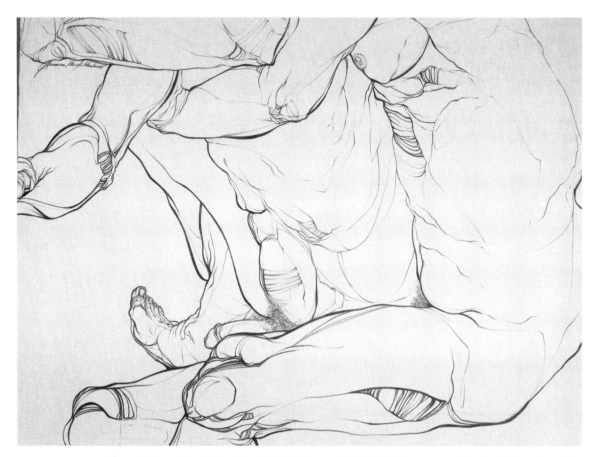

Figure 40 Susana Herrero Kunhardt, *Inudi* (1990), drawing, wax/oil, 76.2 × 111.7 cm, courtesy of the artist, San Juan, Puerto Rico.

*'It is not her first concern to evoke appreciations of provocative eroticism, even when sensuality plays a persuasive role on so many levels, be it the smooth undulating lines, the explicit depiction of genitalia, and in "Fuera de Serie", the intimate relations of the protagonists.'

†'Without moralizing, the art of Susana Herrero takes an outspoken position regarding the maker's responsibility not to remain silent on the most oppressing problems faced by contemporary society.'

explícita presentación de genitalia, y en "Fuera de Serie", la relación íntima de las dos figuras'.* At the same time, he expanded on the artist's sexual politics, hidden underneath an apparently timeless, academic signature: 'El arte de Susana Herrero, sin ser moralizante, conlleva una clara toma de conciencia ante la responsabilidad del creador de no estar al margen de los problemas más opremiantes que acostan la sociedad contemporánea.'[†41]

Herrero Kunhardt's drawings indeed recall the dramatic power of Michelangelo and Caravaggio, just as Myrna Báez had drawn from old masters for her imagery of the female nude. But underneath the timeless beauty of Herrero's nudes, there is a firm, if implicit, political message, first regarding the legitimacy of homosexual love, and second regarding gay people's vulnerability, both physically and socially, in the era of AIDS: 'My works of art', says Kunhardt, 'are related to the heroic homoerotic nudity that generates a dynamic and powerful icon. The drawings, lithographs and mixed media are a voyeuristic experience of interplayed convoluted poses which involves complex ethical, human and spiritual problems of contemporary life.'[42] The Renaissance, of course, has produced much imagery that has become quintessential in (male) gay iconography and its appropriation by Susana Herrero is inspired, partially, by her intention to extend it further into the present. But it is a postmodern appropriation since it is charged with an implicit message about the historicity of gay experience. The timeless Eros of her nudes gains a polemic aura as a signifier equally of Thanatos, leaving a bloody trace amidst the island's gay community.

Equally few in number are male Puerto Rican artists who produced imagery that can be defined as homotextual. Most traditional among them is Antonio Bou (b. 1944). His portrayals of young male friends are reminiscent of contemporary work elsewhere, likewise contextualizing homoeroticism within the decent and discreet atmosphere of male friendship. His portrayals of one such friend (*Estudios de Imanol*, n.d.) are given sexual aura by a slight accentuation of the boy's bulging crotch, whereas other works, such as a painting of Saint Sebastian are clearly inscribed within a homotextual *imaginaire*. Made for private circulation, probably among Puerto Rico's homosexual community primarily, they are becoming known to the wider world only today.

Conclusion

New after several decades of *machisto* rhetoric, also in the field of the visual arts, is a gradual, if careful presentation of the homosexual self from the late 1940s onwards. This is given a legitimacy of its own and diverges from previous iconographic narratives, such as academic, mythological, historical or *Indigenismo* art. The new figurations of homosocial eros do not require the narrative framing that characterized – and limited – its visual expression at the dawn of the twentieth century.

Still very much implicit are new portrayals of same-sex friendships, possibly suggesting intimate and sexual liaisons. Only reluctantly, artists allow the viewer to peek into their living room or bedroom, yet they do so by means of a visual narrative that suggests intimacy and complicity. Purely semantically, when dissecting these images on the surface, the art historian may not even find the key to such an understanding. Probably, the message was not even meant to be read by the outside world.

It seems that the portrayals of networks of friendships were meant to be noticed primarily – perhaps even exclusively – by those who themselves were 'in the game', those who 'understood', an understanding that is adequately stated in the Spanish and Portuguese word *entendidos*. These are images, therefore, of an incipient, self-assured *ambiente* that has not yet reached a high profile towards the outside world but reflects a growing consciousness both among the makers and the perceivers of such images. Resonating in the background are modern concepts of sexual identity that became more widely disseminated in countries until then marked by sharp divisions of sexual roles.

The example of European and North American Gay Liberation will soon make such images redundant or, put differently, too introverted. In the following chapter, I will describe how a new, more combative and activist visual language will be developed in the wake of nascent Gay Liberation movements in Mexico and Brazil at first, then in Puerto Rico and Cuba at a somewhat later stage. Yet, I will also demonstrate that, almost immediately afterwards or sometimes even coinciding with it, a postmodern critique will be attached to the newer outspokenly 'gay' and 'lesbian' art – a critique that merges with postcolonial criticism of cultural imperialism and of the patronage from a North American or European emancipatory model.

Notes

1 See A. Sternweiler, 'Von Quaintance bis Warhol – Schwule Kunst aus Amerika', in *Goodbye to Berlin? 100 Jahre Schwulenbewegung* (Berlin, 1997), pp. 245–6. Also, see R. Biederbeck and B. Kalusche, *Motivmann: Der männliche Körper in der Modernen Kunst* (Giessen, 1987), *passim*, and Cooper, *The Sexual Perspective, passim*.

2 J. Quiroga, 'Homosexual letters: the gender of correspondence', unpublished paper (1996), p. 2. Sylvia Molloy quoted by Quiroga.

3 See Chadwick, *Women, Art and Society*, pp. 299–300 on this theme.

4 S. Marone, *Missexualidade e arte* (São Paulo, 1947).

5 See, for more information, *Vicente do Rego Monteiro: Pintor e poeta* (Rio de Janeiro, 1994).

6 See *Expressões do corpo na escultura de Rodin, Leopoldo e Silva, de Fiori, Brecheret, Bruno Giorgi* (São Paulo, 1996).

7 For a general portrayal of Los Contemporáneos, see the introductory chapter of S. Novo, *The War of the Fatties and Other Stories from Aztec History* (Austin, 1994). For biographical profiles, see Foster, *Latin American Writers on Gay and Lesbian Themes* pp. 53–5, 281–6, 290–3, 450–2.

8 A. Mac Adam, 'Surrealism in Latin America. Editor's Note', *Review: Latin American Literature and Arts*, 51 (Fall 1995), p. 5. Further research may reveal more about Moro's homosexual life in Lima, Paris (friendship with the Vicomte de Noailles and the Chilean Armando Zegri) and Mexico City. See, for some details, M. Dreyfus, 'Interview with Emilio Adolfo Westphalen', *Review*, 51, pp. 50–6, and Foster *Latin American Writers*, pp. 263–6.

9 Quoted in C. Monsiváis, 'Ortodoxia y heterodoxia en las alcobas. Hacia una crónica de costumbres y creencias sexuales en México', *Debate Feminista*, 6, 2 (1995), p. 201.

10 R. Flores Guerrero, *5 pintores mexicanos. Frida Kahlo – Guillermo Meza – Juan O'Gorman – Juan Castellanos – Jesus Reyes Ferreira* (Mexico, 1957), p. 49.

11 See O. Debroise, *Alfonso Michel* (Mexico City, 1993), p. 17.

12 *Ibid.*, pp. 5–7.

13 Personal communication from D. Balderston, 25 February 1998.

14 See P. León, *Manuel Rodríguez Lozano (1895–1971)* (Mexico City, 1986); B. Taracena, *Manuel Rodríguez Lozano* (Mexico City, 1971), and J. Mesa, 'Los cien años de Manuel Rodríguez Lozano', *Boys & Toys*, 14 (November 1995), pp. 66–8, commenting upon the presumably 'homophobic' decision of the Instituto Nacional de Bellas Artes of Mexico not to organize a retrospective show for the centennial of Rodríguez Lozano's birth. Also, see M. Helm's *Modern Mexican Painters* (New York, 1968), pp. 130–5.

15 J. J. Tablada, *Abraham Angel, el pintor niño* (Mexico City, 1924), p. 37.

16 See O. Debroise, *Figuras en el trópico* (Barcelona, 1984).

17 Monsiváis, 'Ortodoxia y heterodoxia en las alcobas', p. 203.

18 See *Herencia y creación* (Mexico, 1991), pp. 1–19.

19 See A. Abelleyra, in *La Jornada*, 28 July 1987, p. 26.

20 See J. Crespo de la Serna, in *Excelsior*, 10 December 1944: 'impecable facture y gracia'; V. Groenberg, 'La expresión de Emilio Baz Viaud', *Nosotros. Magazine de Latinoamérica*, 10 March 1951: 'sensualismo'.

21 A single drawing of Ben-Hur and Emilio's nephew, Juan Wörner Baz, may justify similar speculations. It is titled *Amigos* (1967) and shows two boys sliding their leg into one and the same pair of trousers. This strangely recalls Paul Cadmus's play with lines in *The bicycle rider* and makes the position of both figures' bodies somewhat complicit.

22 H. Herrera, *Frida Kahlo: A Biography of Frida Kahlo* (New York, 1983), p. 198.

23 Thus, J. Keijzer, 'Broeken, laarzen en een Tehuana-kostuum', *Homologie*, 10, 4 (July–August 1988), p. 24. The author claims, however, that Kahlo's women portraits cannot be identified simply as works of 'lesbian art'.

24 See G. Pellón, *José Lezama Lima's Joyful Visions: A Study of* Paradiso *and Other Prose Works* (Austin, Texas, 1989). Also, see E. Lihn, '*Paradiso*, novela y homosexualidad', *Hispamérica*, 8 (1979), pp. 3–21, and D. Altamiranda, 'Lezama Lima, José (Cuba; 1912–1976)', in Foster, *Latin American Writers on Gay and Lesbian Themes*, pp. 202–11.

25 Quiroga, 'Homosexual letters: the gender of correspondence', p. 5.

26 L. Arguelles and B. Ruby Rich, 'Homosexuality, homophobia, and revolution: notes toward an understanding of the Cuban lesbian and gay male experience, part I', *Signs*, 9, 4 (1984), p. 687.

27 On Cuban homophobic policy in the 1960s and 1970s, see M. Leirner, *Sexual Politics in Cuba: Machismo, Homosexuality, and AIDS* (Boulder, 1994), pp. 25–43, as well as Lumsden, *Machos*, pp. 55–80. Very instructive also is B. Epps, 'Proper conduct: Reinaldo Arenas, Fidel Castro, and the politics of homosexuality', *JHSex*, 6, 2 (1995), pp. 231–82.

28 Lumsden, *Machos*, pp. 81–2.

29 *Ibid.*

30 See Arguelles and Rich, 'Homosexuality, homophobia, and revolution', p. 689. This information was confirmed by Héctor Santiago (9 September 1996, New York City) and Clara Morera (12 October 1996, New York).

31 See J. Bellechasse and I. Fuentes Pérez, 'Raúl Martínez: revolutionary or conformist?', *Unveiling Cuba*, 6 (January 1984), p. 11, and A. Pérez Vidal, 'Descubriendo Alfredo Guevara (entrevista)', *Contrapunto* (n.d.), p. 52.

32 Pérez Vidal, 'Descubriendo Alfredo Guevara', *Contrapunto* (n.d.), 52.

33 Regarding Castro policy against lesbians and gays, see the documentary film, *Conducta Impropia* (dir. Néstor Almendros and Orlando Jimenez-Leal, 1984), as well as the writings of novelist Reinaldo Arenas, Severo Sarduy, Héctor Santiago. Also, see Chapter 7.

34 M. Fernández Zavala, in *Entre cortinas: El gran desnudo caribeño. Pinturas y dibujos de Myrna Báez* (San Juan, 1994).

35 *Ibid.*

36 Ramírez, *Puerto Rican Painting*, p. 30.

37 S. Goldman, 'Modern art of the Spanish-speaking Caribbean', in *Caribbean Visions: Contemporary Painting and Sculpture* (Miami, 1997), p. 26.

38 See especially A.J. Molina, 'Obra de Susana Herrero', *El Mundo*, 25 January 1976, p. 6B.

39 For more welcoming views, see T. Tió, '¡Eso no se hace! ¿Por qué no?', *El Mundo*, 2 June 1983; M. Alegre Barrios, 'Susana Herrero Kunhardt expone en Holanda', *El Nuevo Dia*, 26 December 1990, p. 64; S. B. Cherson, 'El desnudo masculino clásico como arte actual',

El Nuevo Dia, 30 March 1990, p. 91. Denial of gay content is obvious in a review by M. Pérez Lozano, 'Cuerpos levitando embebidos', *Plástica*, 11 (November 1983), pp. 41–2.

40 J. A. Pérez Ruiz, 'Autonomía de lo profano', *Claridad*, August 1990, p. 14; R. A. Moreira, 'Sexualidad de lápiz y papel', *El Mundo/Puerto Rico Ilustrado*, 13 May 1990, pp. 4–5.

41 E. García Gutiérrez, in *Susana Herrero Kunhardt: Desnudos* (San Juan, n.d. (1990)). Also, see E. García Guttiérez in *Susana Herrero Kunhardt* (San Juan, n.d.).

42 Personal communication, 18 February 1997.

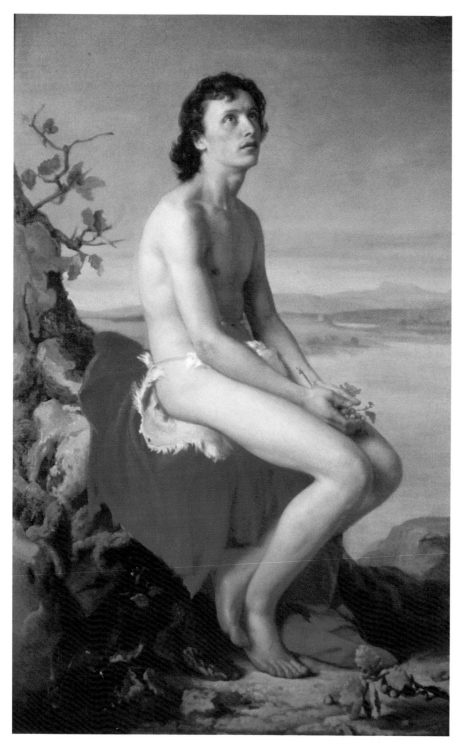

Plate 1 Luis Monroy, *El hijo pródigo* (n.d.), oil on canvas, 178.3 × 118 cm, Museo Nacional de Arte, Mexico City, courtesy of Instituto de Investigaciones Estéticas, Universidad Nacional Autonoma de México, Mexico City.

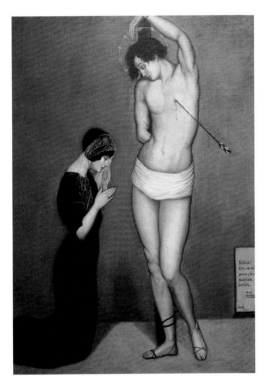

Plate 2 Ángel Zárraga, *Ex-voto* (1910–12), oil on canvas,
184 × 134 cm, Museo Nacional de Arte, Mexico City, courtesy
of Instituto de Investigaciones Estéticas, Universidad Nacional
Autonoma de México, Mexico City.

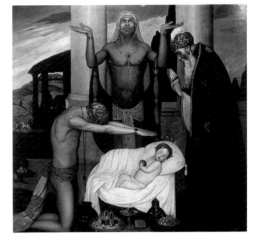

Plate 3 Ángel Zárraga, *La adoración de los Reyes Magos*
(1911), oil on canvas, 200 × 210 cm, collection Joaquín
Reda Vidal Soler, courtesy of Centro Nacional de las Artes,
Biblioteca de las Artes, Mexico City.

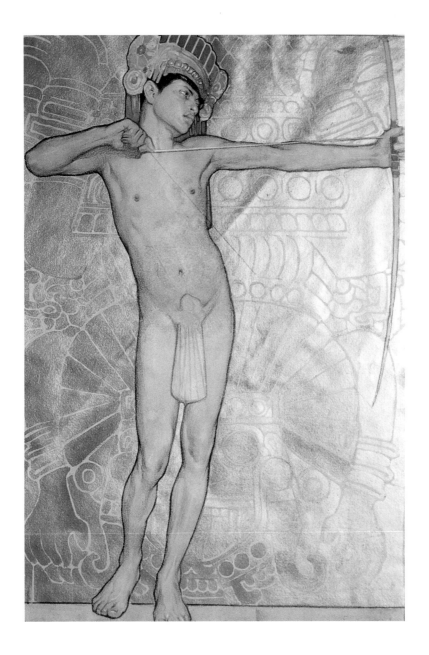

Plate 4 Saturnino Herrán, *El flechador* (1918), oil on canvas, 57.5 × 39.5 cm, Museo Nacional de Arte, Mexico City, courtesy of Instituto de Investigaciones Estéticas, Universidad Nacional Autonoma de México, Mexico City.

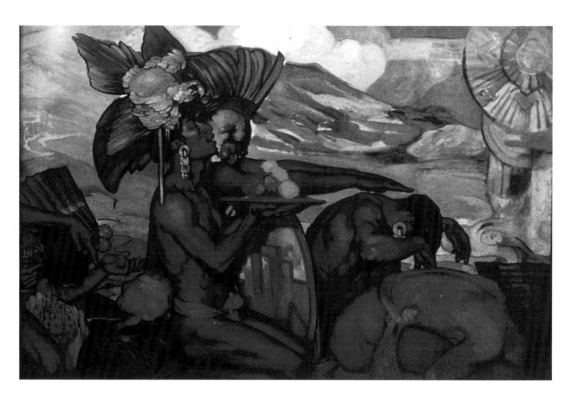

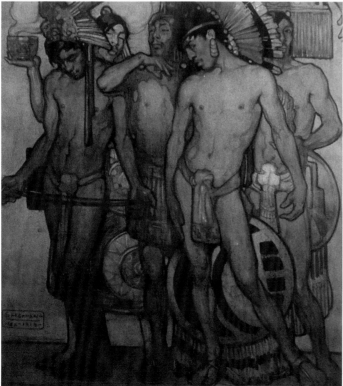

Plate 5 (*above*) Saturnino Herrán, *Nuestros Dioses* (detail) (1918), oil on canvas on wood, 532 × 116 cm, collection Alicia Udiña, courtesy of Centro Nacional de Arte, Biblioteca de las Artes, Mexico City.

Plate 6 (*left*) Saturnino Herrán, *Panneau decorativo* (1916), charcoal on paper, 42.5 × 39 cm, Museo de Aguascalientes, Mexico, courtesy of Centro Nacional de las Artes, Biblioteca de las Artes, Mexico City.

Plate 7 (*right*) José Ferraz de Almeida, *Derrubador brasileiro* (1871), oil on canvas, 227 × 182 cm, Museo Nacional de Belas Artes, Rio de Janeiro, photo: Raúl Lima.

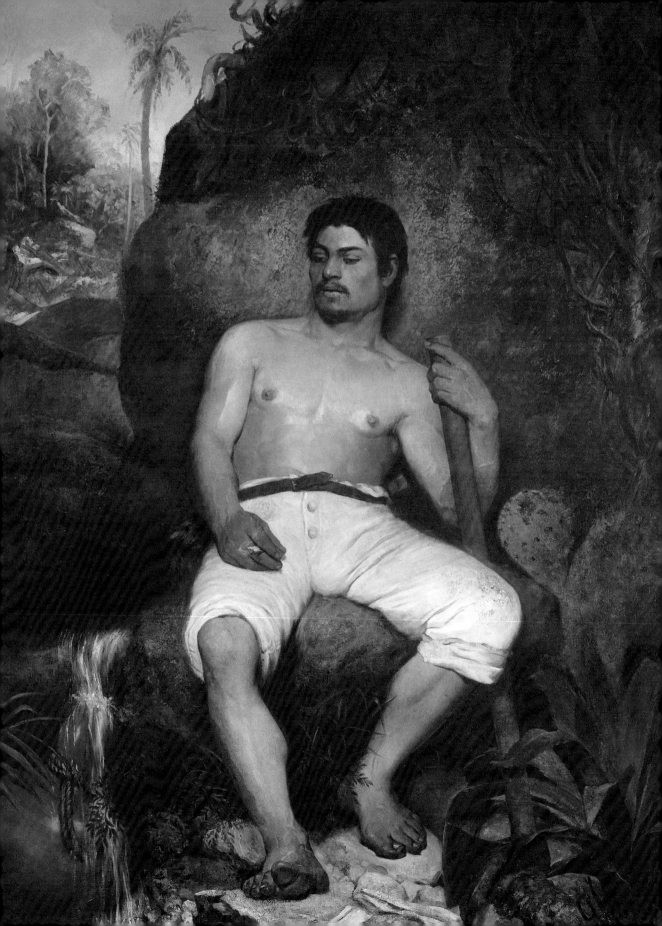

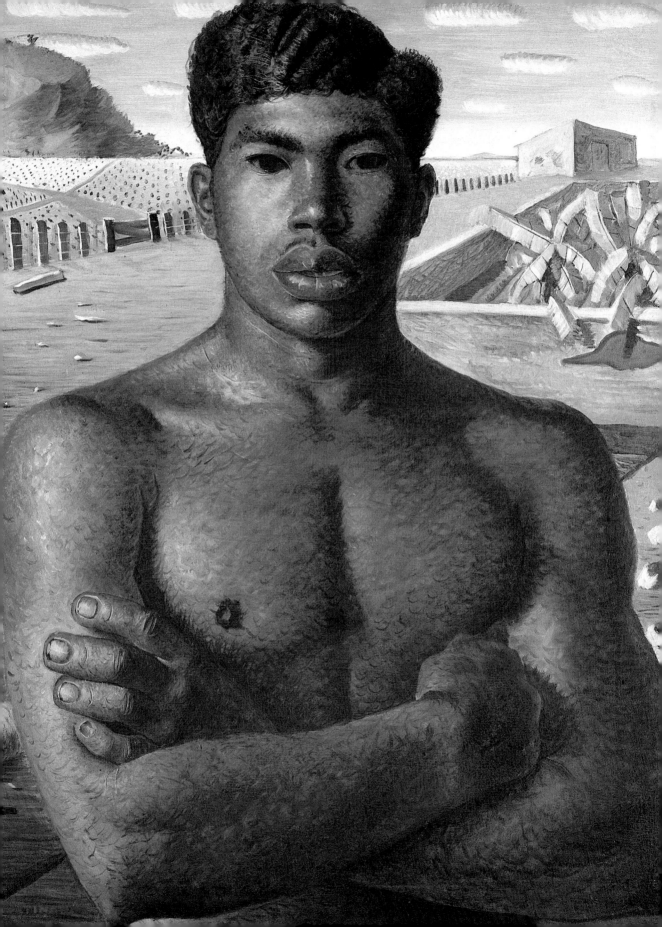

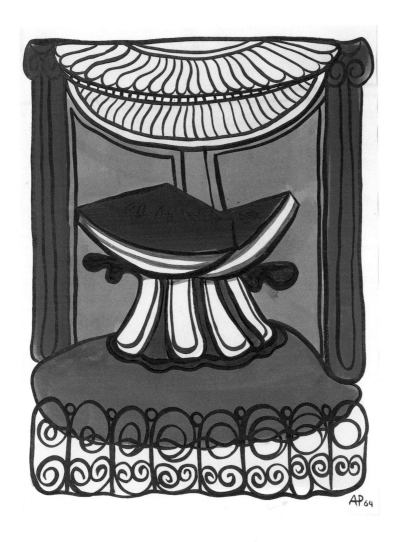

Plate 9 Amelia Peláez, *Fruteria con sandías* (1964), oil on canvas, 55 × 32 cm, private collection, courtesy of Christie's, London.

Plate 8 (*left*) Cândido Portinari, *O mestiço* (1934), oil on canvas, 81 × 65 cm, Pinacoteca do Estado, São Paulo, photo: Romulo Fialdini.

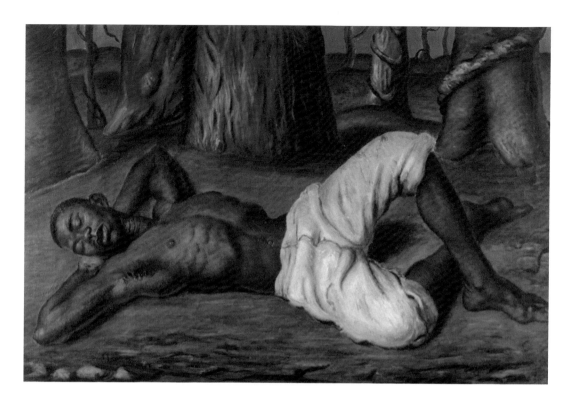

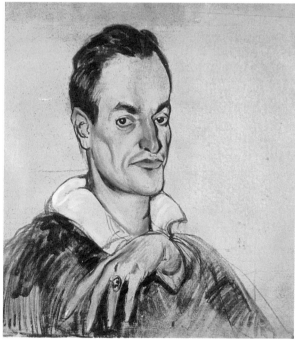

Plate 10 Hugo Adami, *O fugitivo* (1934), oil on canvas, 98 × 148 cm, Museo Nacional de Belas Artes, Rio de Janeiro, photo: Raúl Lima.

Plate 11 Roberto Montenegro, *Retrato de Jesús Reyes Ferreira* (1926), oil on canvas, 60 × 60 cm, Museo Regional de Guadalajara, courtesy of the Instituto Nacional de Antropología e Historia and the Instituto de Investigaciones Estéticas, Universidad Nacional Autonoma de México, Mexico City.

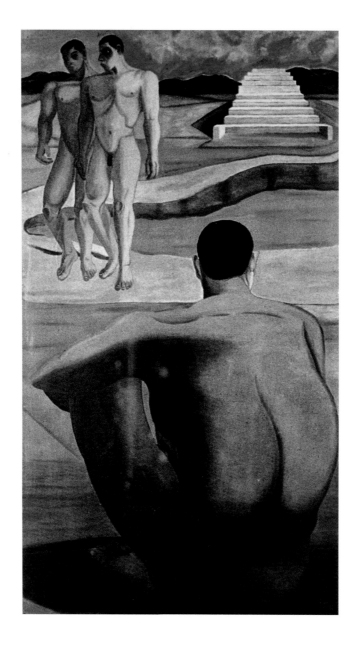

Plate 12 Manuel Rodríguez Lozano, *El pensador* (1936), oil on canvas,
200 × 130 cm, collection Nieves Bermúdez, courtesy of Centro
Nacional de las Artes, Biblioteca de las Artes.

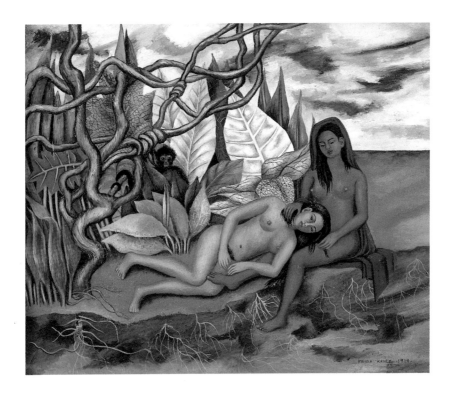

Plate 13 Frida Kahlo, *Duas desnudas en la selva* (1939), oil on sheet metal, 25.1 × 30.2 cm, courtesy of Mary Ann Martin Gallery, New York City.

Plate 14 Javier de la Garza, *Sálvese quien puede* (1986), acrylic and collage on wood, 198 × 150 cm, photo: Pablo Oseguera/José Ignacio González, courtesy of Galería OMR, Mexico City.

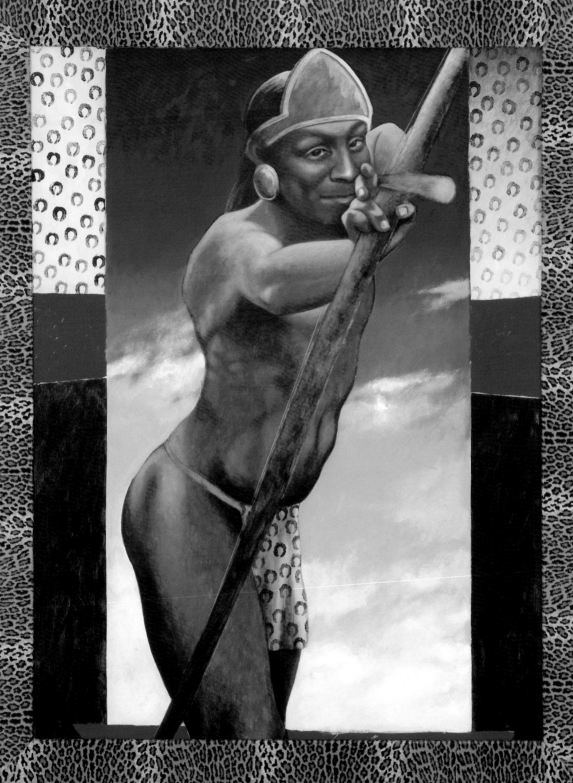

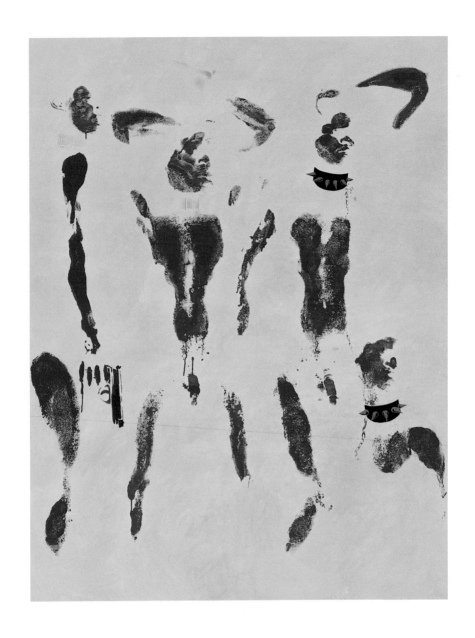

Plate 15 Ismael Costa Dias, *Os michês do Trianon* (1995), oil on canvas, 112 × 86 cm, courtesy of the artist.

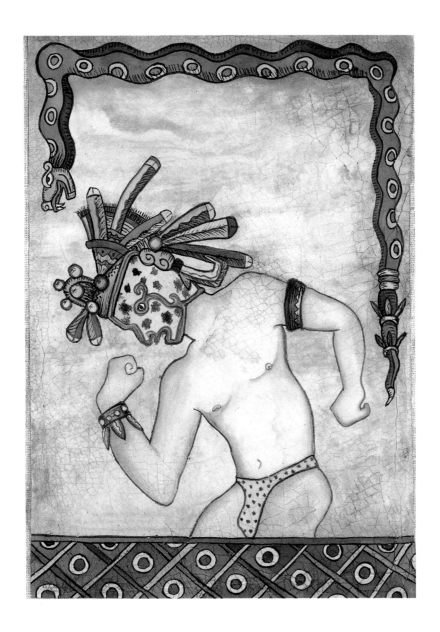

Plate 16 Teddy Sandoval, *Macho Mayan* (1993), watercolour on treated canvas, 17.8 × 25.4 cm, courtesy of Paul Polubinskas, Los Angeles.

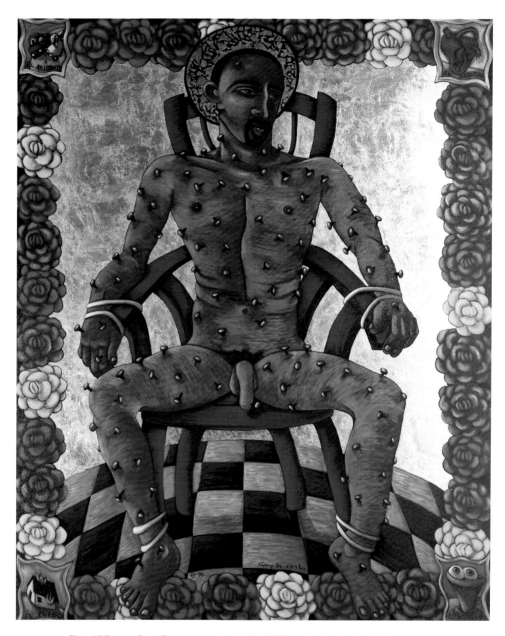

Plate 17 Tony de Carlo, *El santo protector del sida* (1996), acrylic, silver leaf, gold leaf on canvas,
122 × 152.5 cm, collection of the artist, Los Angeles,
photo: American Photo Repro Corp., courtesy of the artist.

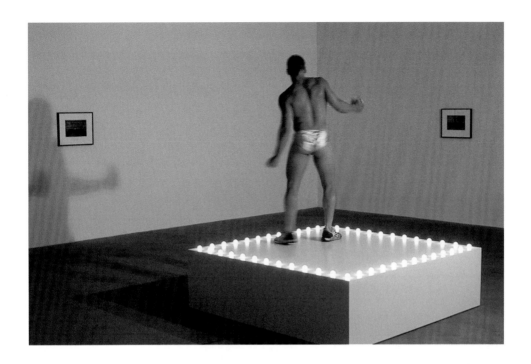

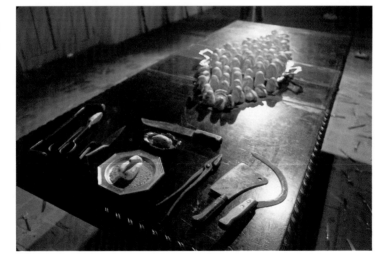

Plate 18 Felix González Torres, *Every week there is something different* (1991), installation (go-go dancing platform), photo: Peter Muscato, courtesy of Andrea Rosen Gallery, New York City / Galerie Xavier Hufkens, Brussels.

Plate 19 Ernesto Pujol, *Saturn's table* (1996), colonial table and chair, iron tools, 100 penises, size variable, courtesy of the artist, New York City.

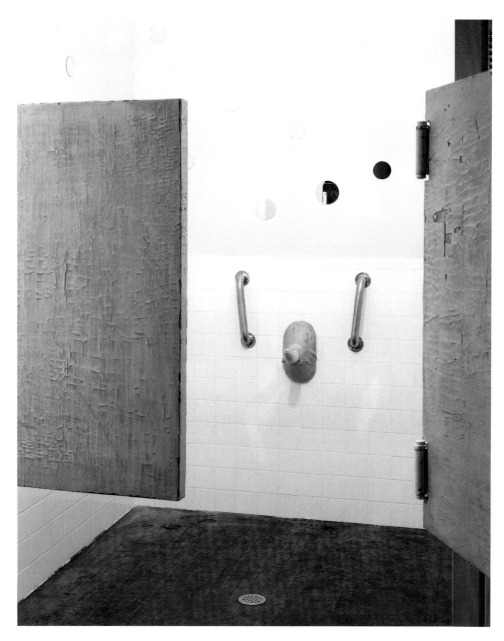

Plate 20 Maria Elena González, *Self-service* (1996), installation,
tiles, mirrors, chrome handles, rawhide,
photo: Robert Caldwell, courtesy of the artist, Brooklyn, New York.

Postmodern visions of *el ambiente*

(1975–today)

Introduction

Whereas in Europe or North America, quite a number of visual artists have presented themselves as 'gay' or 'lesbian', there are very few in Latin America who have turned the visualization of their sexual identity into a career, tied up more or less consistently with the more encompassing struggle for social and cultural emancipation of gay men and lesbians. Homotextuality surfaces recurrently in the work of numerous artists, though hardly ever contextualized as part of a struggle for Gay Liberation. Nor can their work be easily identified as 'gay' in the sense given to the word elsewhere in the 1970s and 1980s.

Homotextuality in the work of many a Latin American artist is of a 'queer' kind, as it surpasses the homogenizing and, to an extent, Eurocentric impact of Gay Lib. Even when subscribing to the political agenda of gay rights or, at least, of a fight against legal or social discrimination, artists often adopt a visual language that simultaneously comments upon the economic, social, and cultural conditions of the gay political movement in North America and Europe. Representations of homotextuality remain rooted in the specific social and cultural context of Latin American society and claim a right to diversity, primarily as a reflection of the diverse homosexual subcultures or practices existing there. Political organization of a gay and lesbian struggle took off relatively late and remains difficult and stochastic even today, which may explain the absence of a widely disseminated sense of 'gay community' and, in the arts, the presence or relatively higher visibility of 'alternative' homotextual imagery. Some images seem to buy into the repressive climate existing still, especially in more rural areas, and are characterized by a sense of pain, isolation and uncertainty. Other works present subgroups or practices within the 'gay' realm that had lost visibility in the Northern hemisphere because they were – at least for some time – considered 'politically incorrect'. Transgender people, for example, populate many a Latin American work by a gay (male) artist, as does effeminacy in a more general sense.

The intimate association of gay and transgender identity may seem to be conservative at first sight and to reproduce the oppressive gender politics underlying this representative pattern. But the cult of androgyny is one trope of representation only alongside others that aim at subverting an, in the eyes of their makers, all too familiar notion of 'gay sensibility'.[1] This rich iconography of *el ambiente*, when looked at more closely, is subversive by the mere nature of its eclecticism. It is avant-garde as it claims sexual and gender diversity, now esteemed highly within the context of today's gay, lesbian, bisexual and transgender orthodoxy in North America and Europe, yet omnipresent now as before in Latin American society.

While pushed into the margins of North American and European gay life and politics for many years, transgender people have only recently gained visibility once again and have been recuperated within the realm of the 'politically correct'. In work by Latin American visual artists, however, their uninterrupted and flamboyant presence alongside alternative, more 'masculine' representations of gay identity illustrates the distinct nature of social and sexual discursivity on this continent as well as the legitimacy of simultaneous, alternative politics of representation. As much of today's social life in Latin America is marked by hybridity, so too does the politics of visual representation of a gay and lesbian *ambiente* reflect the kaleidoscopic richness of real-life sex and gender practices.

A distinct 'gay' or 'lesbian art' seems to be delayed in Latin America, due in part to the fragility of Gay Liberation politics. Yet, this crystallizes into an avant-garde, postmodern and 'Post-Lib' politics of representation that claims the rights for expression of sexual diversity both towards the outside world and within the gay community itself. Latin American *ambiente* is a complex crucible of distinct sexual *imaginaires* and practices, which gains visibility by means of a visual language that transgresses the narrow confines of one-dimensional 'gay' politics. Modern visions of *el ambiente* thus turn easily into postmodern ones.

Mexico: *Liberación gay* versus deconstruction

The political organization of homosexual men and lesbians took off in Mexico only in the late 1970s. The Frente Homosexual de Acción Revolucionaria was founded alongside the Grupo Lambda de Liberación Homosexual and Oikabeth. The FHAR was inspired by socialist and anarchist ideology, but remained largely male and, at times, misogynist. Its policy was confrontational and short-lived. It ceased to exist in the mid-1980s, only to be succeeded later on by small initiatives (Guerilla Gay, Círculo Cultural Gay, Grupo Homosexual de Acción Revolucionaria, and the Colectivo Sol, founded by ex-members of FHAR and focusing on the organization of gay and lesbian archives and AIDS prevention).[2]

The impact of political activism on the visual arts was limited at first. Only incidentally, artists took on an outspoken activist position. The drawings by Enrique Guzmán (1952–86) published in the review *Tierra Adentro* in 1978 clearly expressed gay defiance against the outside world.[3] Guzmán was a troubled character, however, and the sudden surfacing of works with explicitly gay content was short-lived. They were made when the artist felt alienated from the official art world and faced a crisis, reflecting both existential anguish and creative uncertainty. Previous works by Guzmán disclosed messages about homosexuality as well, yet they were incidental, subtle and indirect.

His sudden focus on drawings with gay content was inspired by rebellion against Mexican sexual morality and a desire to make his sexual identity known to the malevolent outside world. They were distinct also in style. 'A pesar de su actitud rebelde y también pese a su rechazo frente a las imposiciones dogmáticas, Guzmán . . . se refirió a la homosexualidad de manera encubierta en muchas de sus obras anteriores a los dibujos del año de 1978 y no fue sino hasta aquella fecha que trabajó en la solución frontal de la homosexualidad como tema artístico sin emplear ya, para conseguirlo, recursos simbólicos ni tampoco sígnicos.'*[4] Guzmán committed suicide in 1986.

Gradually, the expression of homotextuality proliferated quantitatively, less so qualitatively. Many works of new 'gay art' are gathered in the yearly exhibitions during the Semana Cultural Gay (initiated in 1982) or in art shows focusing on AIDS (*De lo erótico, la tentación de existir*, 1987; *Por la vida, contre el SIDA*, 1988). Artists often remain faithful to a traditional 'gay' aesthetic, celebrating male nudity foremost. I merely refer to images by Fernando Andrade Cancino, Carlos Arias, Esteban Azamar, Gonzalo Ceja, Luis Fracchia, Antonio Helguera, Noé Hernández, Oliverio Hinojosa, Jorge Marín, Roberto Marquez, Jesús Meza, Alfonso Moraza, Agustín Portillo, Alfredo Torres Blanco, Gonzalo Utrillo and Reynaldo Velázquez.

Subscribing to a tradition of gay 'camp' are Paul Antragne, Arturo Ramírez Juarez, Froylán Ruiz and Salvador Salazar, whereas Luis Jaso's *Retrato de Farnesio* walks the thin

*'In spite of his rebellious attitude or of his rejection of dogmatic impositions, Guzmán . . . referred to homosexuality in a covert way in many of his works anterior to the drawings of 1978 and it wasn't until that date that he worked on homosexuality as an artistic topic, if without using symbolic means or signifiers while doing so.'

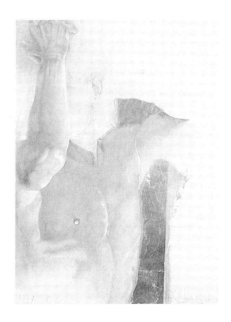

Figure 41 Roberto Cortázar,
Estudio para Judit y Holoferne (1994),
chalk and pencil on paper,
76 × 57 cm, Galería Praxis,
Mexico City.

line between friendly portrayal and frivolous parody.[5] Enrique Hernández creates three-dimensional works that document the social and architectural environment of gay cruising, while Ernesto Alvarez plays with gender transformation and hermaphroditism. The cartoons, finally, of Rafael Barajas are poignant commentaries on Mexican gender expectations. One of his drawings, *Pero eso si . . . soy mucho macho* (1989), is an ironic image of the stereotypical *macho*, sleeping in the shadow of his wide *sombrero* while carelessly flaunting a leg with stocking and woman's shoe.

Neoclassicism continues to allow for inscribing homoeroticism in an apparently legitimate canon even today, as can be seen in the works of José Nuño. His 'measuring' of male anatomy, more specifically of Greek and Roman sculptures, is reminiscent of nineteenth-century academic traditions and far removed from the representational politics of a more activist and gay-centred vision.

Timeless also in its return to the aesthetics of classicism is the work of Roberto Cortázar (b. 1962), which is simultaneously enriched by visual signifiers of homosexual bondage and sadomasochism. His large paintings and sculptures of mostly male nudes reflect Greek, Roman and Renaissance work, while documenting today's metropolitan gay subculture as well.

Art critics have often interpreted Cortázar's artistic message as a negative, melancholic one about the fragmentation of the human body, its annihilation in today's technological society, as a kind of romanticist reflex against a sobering rationality. Fernando Gamboa recognizes 'el artista crítico, cuestionador de las advertencias a una humanidad en grave crisis moral, a la que lanza una franca premonición'.*[6] Negativism is reflected also in the analysis of Gerardo Estrada, who interprets the representation by Cortázar of bodies as fragmented, dismembered, fetishistic as symbols of an incapacity for man to love or dream.[7] Few critics dare to acknowledge the creative and constructive dimension of the sensuality expressed in Cortázar's work. Héctor Perea, among them, describes Cortázar's anatomies as transcending 'el regodeo gustoso de los volúmenes para volverse verdaderos ensayos sobre el cuerpo y las pasiones del hombre'.†[8] Sylvia Navarrete emphasizes an 'erotismo doliente de efebos' ('a painful eroticism of ephebes') and situates Cortázar alongside the homoerotic works of Francis Bacon and Luis Caballero.[9]

Cortázar's own words capture best what his homoerotic paintings are really about: 'En mi obra no hay mensaje, no represento nada, sólo quiero que el espectador deje de sentirse siempre contestando cosas y pase al terreno de la sensualidad, quiero abrir los ojos a otros canales de sensualidad.'‡[10] Perhaps it is significant of a persistent form of Latin American *machismo* as well as prudery for critics not to want to see or explicate the work's gay dimension, even less the S/M and bondage scenes.

In the work of some artists, whether gay or not, homosexuality becomes a vehicle for addressing issues that trespass the province of sexual identity as such. Felipe Morales (b. 1959) adopts homosexual imagery in a rather carnivalesque blasphemous way. Francisco Toledo's (b. 1940) skeletons having anal sex – with bony dicks – evoke an aesthetic of homotextuality as a philosophical reflection simultaneously upon more 'universal' issues of life, disease and death (*Sin título*, 1989). Arturo Rivas (b. 1963) touches upon homosexual themes implicitly and from a mythopoeic perspective rather than from a narrowly defined 'gay' involvement. The homotextuality in Rivas's work is of an intellectual kind, and implies a commentary upon historical or literary themes. *Herodes y sus verdugos* (1995), for example, vizualizes the moral ambiguity of both Herod's infanticide and the life of Gilles de Rais. Other works by Rivas represent themes from classical mythology and the Bible equally imbued with an undercurrent of intellectually 'camouflaged' homoeroticism.

*'the critical artist, who questions the signs of a humanity in deep crisis, against which he warns [us] in an outspoken manner'

†'the tasteful shaping of volumes in order to become genuine essays about the body and passions of the male'

‡'In my work, there is no message. I represent nothing. I only want the viewer to stop feeling as if he should approve of things and to enter the realm of sensuality. I want to open eyes to other expressions of sensuality.'

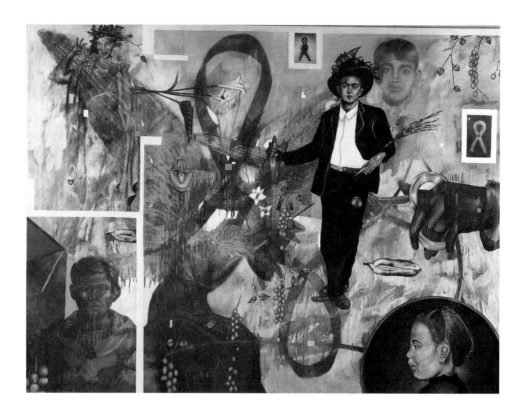

Figure 42 Arturo Elizondo, *Lejanía* (1995), oil on canvas, 198 × 262 cm, courtesy of Galería OMR, Mexico City.

Photographer Gerardo Suter (b. 1955) has produced work that is, to some extent, inscribed within the gay iconographic trope visible also in the oeuvre of Robert Mapplethorpe and, *a fortiori,* Rotimi Fani-Kayode. '[It] is centered', says Gerardo Mosquera, 'on a homosexual vision of the masculine body and simultaneously set within the ceremonialism and spirituality of the Yoruba tradition'.[11] Some of Suter's photoprints can be compared to photos by Mario Cravo Neto or Bauer Sá, both Brazilians, whom I briefly discuss later. Suter replaces Yoruba heritage with props and images from Pre-Columbian Mexico, impregnating his own gay *imaginaire* with reflections upon the distinct spiritual and sexual universe of his people's ancestry. Mosquera adequately described such an aesthetic as 'a kind of symbolic hierophany',[12] mediating between the body and its physical surroundings, the physical and the spiritual, the carnal and symbolic, culture and nature.

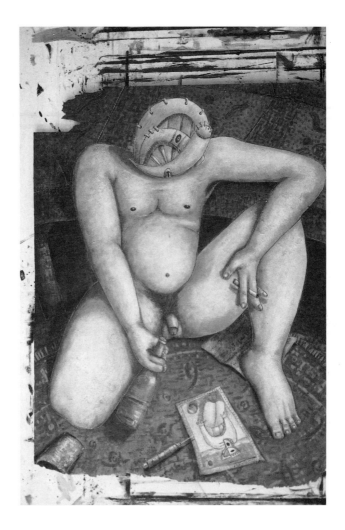

Figure 43 Mario Patiño, *Sin título*
(1998), acrylic on wood, 45 × 35 cm,
courtesy of the artist.

Arturo Elizondo (b. 1956) readily quotes from an international 'gay' collective *imaginaire*. *Lejanía* (1995), for example, includes a portrait of a man, most probably the French novelist Hervé Guibert, who died of AIDS. This fact is reinforced by the depiction of AIDS awareness ribbons, a symbol known in Mexico today as well. Nadar's photographic portrait of Arthur Rimbaud can be seen in *Espina enterada* (1994) alongside a self-portrait of the painter posing elegantly.

The work of Mario Patiño (b. 1962) is intellectually compelling as it often incorporates the visualization of gay identity within the much wider issue of gender hierarchy. He actually focuses on female nudity, leaving behind the province of his own sex, yet making clear, at the same time, that women and gay men share a common history of repression by Mexican *machista* society. Patiño portrays the woman's body not so much for its own sake – being gay, he would rather focus on his own sex—but as a metaphor of the victimization of inferior social groups by male dominance. Femininity, for Patiño, is a signifier of marginalization and oppression, directed not only at women, but at *maricones*, *tortilleras*, transvestites and transsexuals alike. Its visual representations are *fantasmas* that evoke a certain 'desdoblamiento del autor, una extraña identificación con un otro abstracto, con un opuesto que complementa la identidad autoral',* says the critic Juan Molina. The woman in Patiño's oeuvre is both *mujer-virgen* and *puta-santa*, a vengeful icon, a perverse and painful syncretism.[13]

*'[a] doubling of the author, a strange identification with an abstract other, with an opposite that completes the authorial identity'

Patiño, who lived in San Francisco for several years, but now resides in Pachuca, also addresses the male, homosexual body and often shows it as bereft of recognizable facial features. The head is mutated into robot-like machinery – a visualization of social alienation and marginalization that is reinforced by emblemata of substance abuse and violence. In an untitled work of 1998, a faceless man is holding a bottle of alcoholic beverage and seems to be lost in introverted contemplation.

Most interesting, no doubt, are the works of Javier de la Garza, Nahum B. Zenil and Julio Galán. They are immersed in so-called *gayacidad*, yet they are visualizations also of their maker's critical position towards a homogeneously applied category of 'gay art'. All three of them, moreover, are exponents of so-called New Mexicanism, which is replete, if only in an ironic and postmodern way, with symbols of cultural and national identity.

A universalist aesthetic of Modernism is replaced, in this context, by themes and styles traditionally seen as 'Latin American': the intertwining of dream and reality, a baroque sense of life's transience, vibrant colours and, at times, surrealist composition. It is not nostalgia, however, that prompts these artists to rely on signifiers of local colour. It is a critique or redefinition, instead, of cultural heritage, artistic tradition and market values. Their new aesthetic challenges the boundaries of traditional genres and embraces new sources of inspiration, some of which are old (popular art, *ex-votos*), while others reflect the integration of Mexico within the wider network of the global village and telecommunication (media, publicity).

While deconstructing ethnic, national and (Latin) American identity, as well as sex and gender roles, the new generation of Mexican artists defines new 'heroes', including 'proto-feminists' such as Frida Kahlo, Olga Costa, and even Miguel Covarrubias, whose depiction, while in the United States, of African Americans was very stereotyping but who did provide visual representations of cultural and ethnic diversity.[14] 'Mexican' and 'Chicano' realities invoke their commentaries on how cultural identity ought to be redefined in times of globalization, consumerism and migration. The sexual and gender politics of Mexico's postmodern artists reflects social innovation in the country's metropolitan centres especially, where feminism contributed to changing terms of communication between women and men.

Homotextuality, in this context, gained new significance in art, yet now reflected highly individual commentaries upon the growing visibility and homogenization of a Western-styled gay *ambiente* especially in Mexico City, Guadalajara and Monterrey. Critical distance is the common denominator of the transgressive allegories by Galán, of the introspective questioning by Zenil, and of the social parodies by de la Garza. They offer fascinating views of Mexico's changing libidinous economy, which derives from an obstinate past yet is eager to join Western permissiveness, one that is sceptical of a global commodification of sexual culture while increasingly aware of cultural authenticity and 'local knowledge'.

Best-known, worldwide, is Julio Galán (b. 1959). He was born in Muzquiz, Coahuila, and studied architecture, after which he moved to New York. There he stayed until 1990, when he returned to Mexico. Galán's oeuvre betrays influences of various kinds: Mexican folk art, *ex-votos*, calendars and commercial sign painting, lacquered gourds; comic strips, thrift-store paintings, children's books and cut-out dolls; Khnopff, Picabia, Kahlo, Magritte, Warhol, Bacon. Pellizzi pointed out how in the works of Julio Galán the familiar is exotic and 'the favored realm of an intense, pervasive eros, more repressed than sublimated, but also detached'.[15]

Explicit sexual scenes, in this context, are rare. A scene of homosexual 'bondage', a mirror image of one single man, can be recognized in *Anal e Isis* (1989), whereas *Niños con muchos huevos* (1988) shows in its centre a small *retablo*-like image of two young men kissing. *Las rosas envidiosas* (1987) shows a boy bending backwards and holding his head in desert sand. The boy thrusts his hips upward in a state of sexual arousal while, above him, drops of blood and semen and tears fall down from a rose in a vase with red liquid. A sculpture exhibited during the 1994 retrospective in Monterrey represented the same image though the erection was more pronounced.[16] *Cristóbal Cabrón* (1988), finally, and *Cavayo ballo* (1987) contain clearly homoerotic elements.

It is more interesting, however, to move beyond a simple identification of 'gay' content and to see how the representation of such matter is contextualized by Galán. Almost always, homosexuality is adorned with a sense of 'unattainableness', as the outcome not so much of incapacity, but rather of a kind of masochism. A constant awareness can be traced, says Jurie Poot, of *anamnesis*, of 'not being understood'.[17] Poot relates Galán's position to a Mexican custom, where a man suffering from unrequited love communicates this to his beloved and asks her/him to be seen with compassion. He then rightfully wonders 'whether that other person . . . really is someone else, for narcissism also seems to play an important part, in the sense that it seems as if he wants to unite with himself'.[18]

Recurrent is Galán's own portrait, mostly as a younger boy, asexual still and innocent. The painting *La lección del sí y el no* (1987) shows the artist as a boy masturbating at the view of himself dressed merely in briefs and socks. Another less

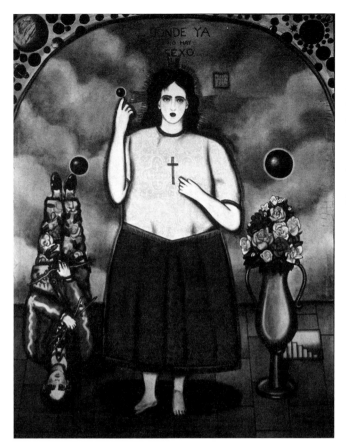

Figure 44 *(left)* Julio Galán, *Donde ya no hay sexo* (1985), oil and acrylic on canvas, 225 × 177 cm, collection M. Esthela E. de Santos, Monterrey, courtesy of Biblioteca de las Artes, Centro Nacional de las Artes, Mexico City.

Figure 45 *(right)* Julio Galán, *El hermano (niño berenjena y niña Santa Claus)* (1985), diptych, oil and acrylic on canvas, 147 × 244 cm, courtesy of Biblioteca de las Artes, Centro Nacional de las Artes, Mexico City.

sexually explicit work also reflects narcissism. *Siempre buscándote* (1988) shows the artist holding a small-scale model of himself in both hands. The image is covered with scraps of paper, symbols, so it seems, of lost harmony and ambisexual innocence. In *¿No te has dormido?* (1988) we see a young boy covering his eyes with both hands. His tears are transforming into roses, which in their turn transubstantiate into smudges of blood. 'One is reminded', says Elisabeth Heartley, 'of the kind of apocryphal miracles in which martyrs' blood turns to roses or causes blossom to appear in the winter snow'.[19] The roses here are emblemata of blood and passion. They attribute a sexual connotation to traditional religious imagery, according to Heartley, who rightfully emphasizes the presence of an outspoken religious sensibility.

Frequently, Galán's portrayals of the self are accompanied with a change or doubling of gender. *Donde ya no hay sexo* (1985) shows an emasculated or at least sexually ambiguous self, challenging traditional definitions of male and female genders as separate and incompatible. It is accompanied, to the left, with an upside-down image probably also of Galán himself, now as a young boy. The painting, when seen within the context of all his work, is at once feminist and 'gay' as it implies a critique of the social construction

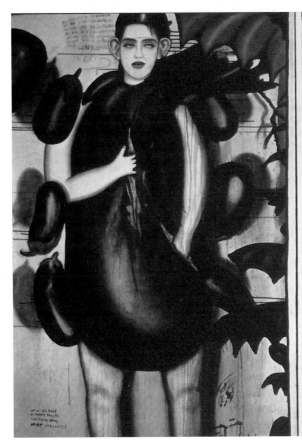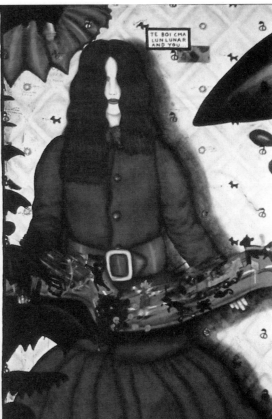

of gender. It projects a utopian return 'to an infant's state of pregenital sexuality in which everything is equally sexualized because sharp distinctions between categories like male and female, gay and straight, penis and vagina and even mother and child have yet to be formed'.[20]

A similar semantic process can be seen also in *El hermano (niño berenjena y niña Santa Claus)* (1985), showing the artist both as a boy in an eggplant costume and as his female *alter ego* in the shape of Santa Claus. It suggests a search, says Carol Damian, 'for a twin, a double, to satisfy his youthful curiosity and sexual confusions'.[21] In *Niños con muchos huevos* the desirable cross-gender projection is very clearly visible in the painting's centre, where Galán as a boy kisses Galán as a girl. *Los siete climas* (1991) shows the artist-dandy dressed in – the word is Dan Cameron's – a 'witch-doctor costume'. Black circular lines on his chest suggest female breasts, while past and present are merged by the simultaneous presence of an Aztec-like feathered hat and a contemporary clock.

Galán makes us believe that the association of homosexuality and femininity is not culture-bound, that is peculiar to a Latin American perception of sexual roles and identity, but desirable, instead, as a state of original, pure and innocent ambisexuality. All three paintings radiate an atmosphere of nostalgia, as if the artist wants to make clear how the homosexual's position is irreparably compromised by the loss of an original androgyny. The images of women in the oeuvre of Galán are disguised self-portraits – *efigies disfrazadas del propio artista*[22] – that embody the artist's aspiration for an original hermaphroditism now forever lost.

But Galán is also coming to grips with the complex reality of culturally different definitions of 'homosexual identity' and reluctantly acknowledges the extent to which a Latin American association of homosexuality with gender confusion reproduces itself on a more personal level. Traditionally, a label of homosexuality is applied to the passive, (read: feminine) partner in sexual relations among men only and Galán's imaginative world remains derivative of this to some degree. Carla Stellweg thus claims that:

> seen from the perspective of Mexico (the sexual constructs of an authoritarian male and macho society), (his) dreamlike journey through multiple metamorphoses could be viewed as a poignant example of the individual's rebellion against the collective and national role models. Of course there are many dense layers to Galán's psyche, persona, and imagery, but the most pervasive element comes from Mexico's complexity, confusions, and fusing of male/female roles.[23]

As provocative as Galán's images may be, they embrace simultaneously cultural convention and socially accepted codes. They are ridden with confusion, originating both from personal autobiography and from 'negotiation' with Mexican cultural heritage. They are 'Mexican' also in their rejection of North American and European deconstructive sexual politics, of a 'Western' pursuit of happiness. 'The atmosphere of penitence', says Max Kozloff, 'is but a screen for a lascivious guilt.'[24]

While Galán remains somewhat ambiguous about sexual identity,[25] this cannot be said of de la Garza and Zenil. The oeuvre of Nahum B. Zenil (b. 1947) undoubtedly seems the most explicitly 'gay' or certainly 'homosexual' of all. Yet, one must ask why his representation of gay identity is accompanied by a narcissistic visualization of personal suffering, by 'a ritual of sexual sado-masochism'.[26]

Sexual identity clearly is not the only theme in Zenil's oeuvre. It contains messages also about nationalism, family and religion. But it is virtually always self-referential and the artist himself is almost always represented as the artwork's main protagonist. He shares this narcissistic point of departure with Julio Galán, along with a deeply rooted sense of isolation and uncertainty. Luis Carlos Emerich emphasizes the artist's persistent awareness of guilt face to face with the undeniable truth concerning his homosexuality, yet indicates that Zenil's work is more militant than such an evaluation suggests. His recurrent presentation of psychic invalidity, of fear and frustration, is attached to a parody of Catholic and bourgeois morality each time the artist portrays himself embodying familiar images and icons of religion, faith, morality, marriage, procreation. Emerich calls this a personal kind of guerrilla war, based upon a rather radical libidinous ethic turning bourgeois conventions upside down.[27]

The homoeroticism in Zenil's work is often purely projective, therefore, and not visualized explicitly. *Retrato de boda* (n.d.), for example, merely contains a multiple self-portrait of the artist, figuring simultaneously as the bride and the groom, the father and the mother, the best man and the bridesmaid. It is a familiar pattern, central to his other works as well, where the homosexual bedevils conventional scripts of heterosexual happiness.

El corazón más sangriento (1990) draws from Catholic iconography and reproduces the familiar image as a self-portrait of the artist himself. At first sight, no gay dimension is perceivable, but underneath the careful quotation, there is parody in that the artist substitutes the original protagonist for himself and turns the painting's title into a superlative of personal suffering. Knowledge about his personal life allows for interpreting this as a critique of Catholic intolerance towards homosexual women and men. 'Zenil', says Debroise, 'doesn't claim to rework a symbology that has its own powerful connotations: medallions, icons, hagiographic paintings function in his work in the same way as in the original context. The intention, however, is deliberately, violently, profane. Closer to Buñuel than Sade, Nahum subverts sacred images to reveal, through slight modifications, their latent powers.'[28] The imposition of an explicitly 'gay' meaning upon existing discourses about nation, family and religion is a procedure of appropriation applied recurrently by the artist in order to contest the often homophobic and heterosexist nature of these moral narratives. By offering himself to the audience as a voyeuristic spectacle, he lures the viewer into taking a position towards his own personal dramas – and melodramas, as Edward Sullivan remarks[29] – and face their social origins.

Zenil's focus upon his identity as a gay man is at times poetic-oneiric, as in the seriograph *Otro sueño* (1983). Again doubling himself as two men riding a single horse, he depicts one as sporting a pair of angel wings. Below, a phallic protuberance, lifting up from underneath what looks like the sheets of a bed, contextualizes the scene as the visualization of an erotic dream. Both riders' joint direction, while chasing a herd of horses, now operates as the utopian dream of inner peace and acceptance. It is an image also of homosexual desire that trespasses the rules and regulations of Latin American society and thus achieves a moral status.

The homotextual perspective lends a very personal touch, moreover, to his postmodern quotations of religious imagery. Some icons of Catholic devotion, such as Saint Sebastian, obviously have been adopted by numerous other gay artists both from Latin America and elsewhere. Zenil reinforces the traditional iconography by both arrows and ropes and by showing himself as a Saint Sebastian tied to a traditional Mexican chair. The work's title, tellingly, is *Prisonero II* (1988) – which refers as much to the pain inflicted upon Saint Sebastian, as to the injustice done to gay men in Mexico today.

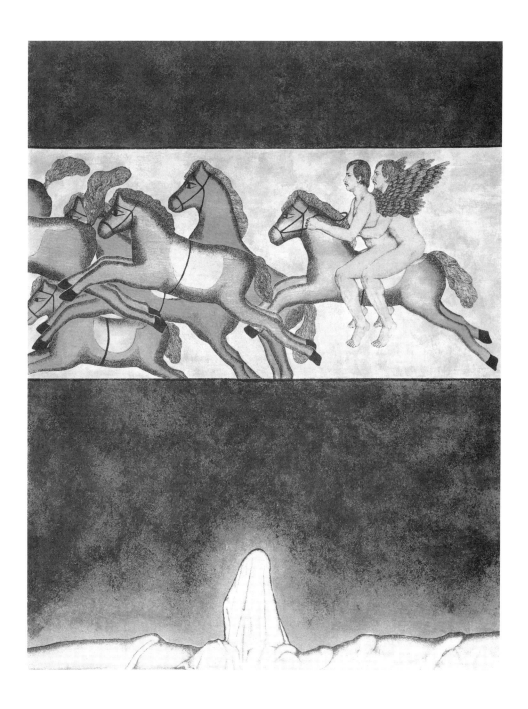

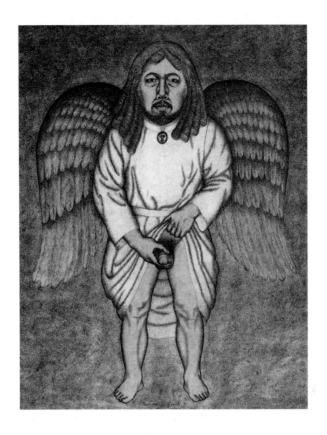

Figure 46 *(left)* Nahum B. Zenil, *Otro sueño* (1983),
seriograph, 72 × 52 cm, courtesy of Throckmorton Fine Art,
New York City.

Figure 47 *(above)* Nahum B. Zenil, *Autorretrato como ángel* (1991),
gouache and black ink on thick paper, 52 × 40 cm,
courtesy of Throckmorton Fine Art, New York City.

A greater challenge is implied in Zenil's narcissistic appropriations of less predictable religious figures, such as angels or Jesus Christ. *Autorretrato como ángel* (1991) presents the artist as an angel about to urinate which ironizes traditional devotionary imagery by virtue of scatological inference. In *San Miguel Arcángel* (1989), he portrays himself as Saint Michael having killed the 'dragon' of homosexual desire that lies underneath his feet in the shape of a naked man.

Yet, parody is not the only dynamic guiding Zenil's work. While portraying himself as one of Roman Catholicism's many heroes, he suggests 'both a close identity with these sacred subjects as well as a sense of auto-sacramentalization'.[30] Aside from a critique, accordingly, of the repressive power both of religious ideology and family values, he includes a visualization also of his intimate desire to be embraced and adopted by them. And, on a higher level, Zenil expresses his belief in a God who is good and forgiving: 'un Ser al que ahora concibo como muy amoroso y tan profundamente sabio que es capaz de perdonarlo todo'.*[31]

*'a Being whom I now estimate very loving and profoundly wise, so that it is capable of forgiving everything'

Socially, Zenil is the best-known 'out' gay artist of Mexico, if not of Latin America. Whereas his visual language is inscribed in Mexican culture and society, his political position regarding issues of sexual identity is clearly guided by an agenda of Gay Liberation, to which he actively contributed for many years. Along with José Maria Covarrubias, he organized the so-called Semanas Culturales Gays especially in the beginning years, and, as opposed to many others, Zenil is not reluctant to explicate his work's gay content when asked.

Some of the work of Javier de la Garza (b. 1954) is explicitly gay also, yet his expression of *ambiente* is often linked to the wider debate about the commodification of cultural difference both in trade and criticism. His work is generally considered as part of the New Mexicanism, which promptly made the artist develop an aesthetic vocabulary critical of such meta-discourse instead. But whereas de la Garza ironized the commercial exploitation of neo-Mexican identity, he equally played upon familiar visual representations of national ideology and subscribed to a somewhat postmodern ethic by attributing a carnivalesque code to his pictorial parodies. 'He was attempting', says Olivier Debroise, 'to underline the cheap gaudiness and incredible myth-making that was fundamental to the concept of a "national ethos".'[32] Merewether in his turn analyses de la Garza's baroque language as follows: 'For a while it undoes and de-mythologizes the iconography of *mexicanidad*, signs and symbols used in the past to signify a national identity, it also reveals a latent eroticism within the folds of this visual sensuality. Not only then is it a parody of representation, but reveals also within this a sentimental body.'[33]

De la Garza appropriated works by Saturnino Herrán and turned his romantic *indigenismo* into an object of ridicule. Such is obvious, for example, in *Sálvese quien puede* (1986) (Plate 14), which exchanges a turn-of-the-century fantasy about heroism for a portrayal at once cynical and humouristic of indigenous vulnerability in the face of genocide. An Indian warrior aims his bow and arrow at the viewers while embodying the artist's scepticism regarding any romantic construction of indigenous bravery that we may want to cherish. This lack of involvement, demonstrated by the painting's single protagonist, is reinforced, moreover, by the leopard-skin frame as a stereotypical accessory of exotic commodification. The model's 'bad acting' simply purveys a message against inappropriate appropriation.

De la Garza's critique of ethnic mystification is accompanied by a dismantling of Herrán's secretive homoerotic fascination and emphasizes rather than disguises the virtually naked Indian's sensuality. His muscular abdomen, hips and thighs, posed in a slightly provocative manner, are now presented openly as the legitimate focus of a homosexual gaze and as an indirect rebuttal of Herrán's hypocrisy in the eyes, that is, of today's audience.

The artist's 'cover version' of Herrán's *El guerrero* is imbued with criticism and parody. It is titled *Preparando el ataque* (1986) and represents an indigenous warrior taken directly from the popular calendar illustrations still sold on Mexico's streets today. His body build has more in common with Californian muscle studs than with the physical characteristics of Mexican indigenous people, which illustrates how 'sacred symbols [are embedded] in a context even more artificial than their own beginnings'.[34] But any idealizing perception is prevented by the warrior's appearance in front of a curtain and *passe partout* landscape, reminding us both of nineteenth-century photographic studios and of open-air photo sets, still common in many a Mexican market-place. Humour is implied also by the rubber ending of the warrior's arrow and by his narcissistic pose, which challenges both Mexican nationalist pathos and today's modern gay consciousness.

Critics rightfully stress the ironic dimension of such re-sexualizations of national themes, yet fail to recognize that de la Garza's imagery contains a subtle criticism also of the dissemination of 'Western' (read: North American) gay role models in the distinct cultural environment of Latin America. It thus includes a bitter commentary on Mexico's cultural and social scene, especially on its flirtation with the very signs and symbols that threaten the country's cultural autonomy and diversity.

The focus of diversity is perceptible as well in the works of 'queer' artists, who apparently subscribe to today's rewriting of the Gay Liberationist canon in both Europe and North America. They apply it to the rather uncritical copying of *gringo* gay identity by members of Mexico's middle class and combine criticism of mainstream 'gay' identity models with an attack on the still current representation of Mexico as being on the periphery of the art world. The annual art shows during the Semana Cultural Gay increasingly provide a platform for postmodern artists/critics of sex roles and gender identity, even when they are still attached to the politics of *Liberación Gay*.[35] A first show of 'queer art' (Rodrigo Saldana, Eduardo Abaroa) took place in Mexico City in 1995,[36] while a recent show in San Francisco gathered work by Rodrigo Aldana, Marco Arce, Aurora Boreal, Yishai Jusidman and Saúl Villa. Each in their own way offers images of homoeroticism and 'queer' sensibility that refute the altogether simplistic notions held by many still about Mexico's *ambiente*.[37]

But how is *el ambiente* reflected in art by lesbians or, for that matter, in 'lesbian' art? Surely, lesbian identity and eroticism remain less visible in Mexico, yet there are some female artists who focus on it in more or less explicit ways. Carla Rippey (b. 1950) is one of them, even though she was born in Kansas City and lived in the USA until she was about twenty. After a stay in Chile, she moved to Mexico.

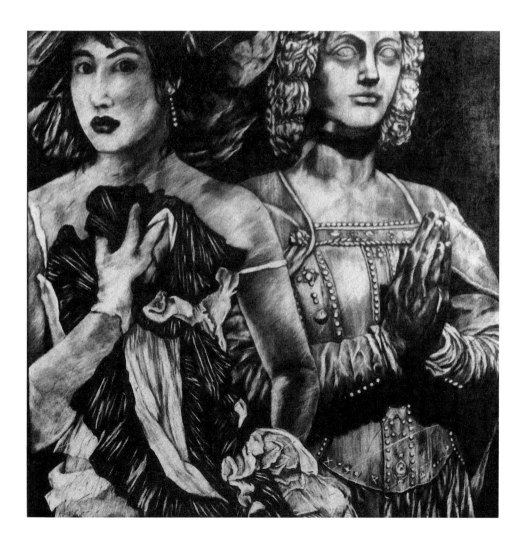

Lesbian content can be clearly identified in some of Rippey's works. *Quisiera ser como tú* (1989), though essentially an image of female narcissism, is to be understood indeed as inscribed within a lesbian *imaginaire*. Other paintings are blatantly lesbian, not only in sexual content and descriptiveness, but also in the out and courageous stand towards her audience.

Elena Villaseñor (b. 1974) presents herself as lesbian with greater clarity, as can be seen in works like *Saturnal* (1989) or *El beso*. The latter was used to illustrate the poster of the 1988 Semana Cultural Gay. Her images are transparent and straightforward representations of lesbian eroticism, if deliberately detached from explicitly sexual scenes. She opposes a secular tradition of presenting lesbian sex as an object of male voyeuristic desire.

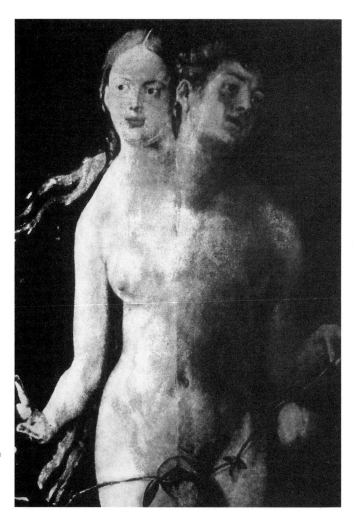

Figure 48 *(left)* Carla Rippey, *Como he de ser . . .* (1979), photo engraving on zinc, 55.5 × 38.5 cm, courtesy of Centro Nacional de las Artes, Biblioteca de las Artes, Mexico City.

Figure 49 *(right)* Carla Rippey, *Juego de damas* (1991), graphite and prismacolour on paper, 70 × 70 cm, collection S. Verduzco Rosán, courtesy of Centro Nacional de las Artes, Biblioteca de las Artes, Mexico City.

A similar aesthetic principle underlies the work of Consuelo González Salazar, whereas the photographs of Maritza López Castillo seem to claim voyeuristic pleasure for (lesbian) women. While focusing on the female nude, however, she deliberately abstains from predictably 'pornographic' poses and presents the naked female body as introvert yet vulnerable. The aggressive character of much male-produced and objectifying images of women is replaced by an aesthetic of isolation, self-centredness and reflection.

The cartoon-inspired images also of Patricia Torres (b. 1963) are subtle explorations of female sensuality. 'The mood . . . is almost filmic, nostalgic for the silent black and white era of the 1920s, manifested in the largely monochromatic surfaces, the use of flapper-style fashions and her unique non-perspective field.'[38] In *En el aire* (1989), two women are depicted, while another one lies on the couch. Only her legs are visible, as well as her left hand touching her genitalia (masturbating?). The two other women's pose reminds one of the famous *Gabrielle d'Estrées et la duchesse de Villars* (School of Fontainebleau, 1594), yet the original gesture of pinching a nipple has been changed. Instead, one woman holds a small, vulva-shaped heart in front of the other one's heart, thus evoking an intimacy that trespasses social friendship and suggests sexual complicity. Underneath Torres's claim to an unmistakably lesbian gaze lies a deconstructive message also about the relativity of gender roles. Her interiors are mostly domestic, but the objects implying certain feminine roles are deprived of meaning in the light of the women's fine erotic games.

Brazil: new understandings of *o entendido*

The heritage of years of military rule undoubtedly is responsible for the delayed appearance only from the late 1970s onwards of artists who were or are openly gay. Until approximately 1975 the country's dictatorial regime oppressed all leftist political movements and initiatives, feminism and gay activism included. Along with censorship against an incipient gay press, the police harassed or even arrested gay people. Homosexuality was bound to remain secretive, both in daily life and in the arts.[39]

Symptomatic of homosexuality's disguise was the original inclusion of the oeuvre of Hélio Oiticica (1937–80) within a Modernist aesthetic. An eclipse of the body, for example, was obvious in the artist's early work called *Metaesquemas*.[40] Gradually, however, Oiticica developed an aesthetic language that, when looked at closely, discloses an underlying 'gay' dynamic, even when this remains embedded within a vocabulary of Modernist, aesthetic innovation.

Oiticica was the son of an entomologist/painter/photographer and grandson of a philologist and anarchist, which exposed him from an early age to the intellectual debates of his time. His initial work, accordingly, was in tune with the Brazilian and international avant-garde of the 1950s. The *Metaesquemas* actually followed some geometric abstract works that he made as a member of the Grupo Frente, but which he abandoned soon afterwards for the more innovative, Neo-Concretist works of the early 1960s. These were his so-called *bólides*, *penetraveis* and *parangolés*.

The *parangolés* especially embody the artist's development away from art as an object on its own that can be looked at passively by an attentive audience. Along with Lygia Clark, Oiticica contested the autonomy of the art object (including, at times, performances as well) and proposed an aesthetic that was 'relational' instead. Anticipating Body Art, he made the human body part of the artwork/performance and made capes or *parangolés*,[41] which were carriers simultaneously of colours, materials and words. The first *parangolé*-performance took place at the Museu de Arte Moderna of Rio de Janeiro (1964), but its concept was closely tied to Oiticica's experience of life in the *favela* of Mangueira, more specifically to his participation in the culture of *samba* and carnival.

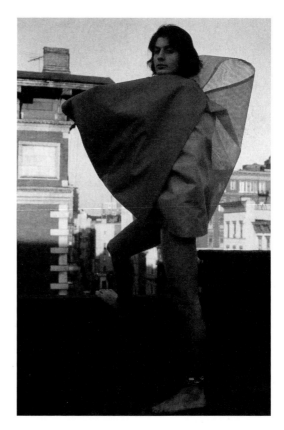

Figure 50 Hélio Oiticica, *Parangolé Cape 25* (1972), performance, courtesy of Art Space Witte de With, Rotterdam.

Mostly, the capes were worn by Nildo, Miro, Mosquito, Jerônimo, Rose and Maria Helena – friends of Oiticica and dwellers in Mangueira. Oiticica became a member of the *escola da samba* of Mangueira and a *passista,* one of the leading dancers during carnival. A work of 1966, *Bólide Caixa 18*, is a homage to 'Cara de Cavalo', nickname of a Mangueira outlaw, who was a friend of the artist until killed by the police.

There was a moment of transgression in all this, since the social boundaries between rich and poor are more real than is implied by the myth of miscegenation in Brazil. To an extent, sexual motives may have played a role as well, in view not only of the attraction of working-class men, but more radically also as a flirtation, both sexy and perverse, with alienation, physical danger and violence. Yet, though a middle-class intellectual, Oiticica conceived of his slumming as more than mere exoticism, more than a primitivist fascination for the spontaneity and improvisation of (black) working-class folk. Objecting to Brazil's ambition to adhere to the international avant-garde at the time, Oiticica preferred to emphasize how Rio was a habitat crucial to the creation of his work, and he developed a theory of performances that went against the grain of the commodification of art. But he adamantly resisted purist notions of national, Brazilian art and conceived of his work as 'the expression of non-transferable cultural possibilities through purely universal structures'.[42]

The *parangolé* is one of these, turning the idiosyncrasy of carnival into an artwork that is no longer tied to space or time. It is incorporated magically, says Oiticica, in a total life-experience (*vivência*) of both the spectator and the participant, while expanding the artwork's experience beyond the merely visual. 'The implication', says Guy Brett, 'is an overcoming of the dissociation of feeling and knowing, of mind and body, of self and other, of producer and consumer'.[43]

Oiticica obtained a Guggenheim grant to come and work in the United States of America. In 1970, he moved to New York where he lived at 81, Second Avenue until 1974. Until his return to Rio in 1978, he lived on Christopher Street, Greenwich Village. He called both addresses 'Babylonests' and 'Hendrixsts'. He led a gay lifestyle there and embraced the permissive mood of sex, drugs, and rock 'n' roll in an attempt, as phrased by the composer Pierre Boulez, to 'organize the delirium'. His life in New York City was not distinct, in this respect, from his amorous affair with the social ambiance of the Magueira *favela* in Rio itself. While he took notes, read and corresponded (the so-called *Hélio tapes*) in a sphere of intellectual curiosity and discipline, he embraced life to the fullest.

What in Oiticica's oeuvre discloses the author's homosexual identity? How does it reveal a body politic that can, all things considered, be called 'gay'? And what does this clarify about the liberation of homosexuality through art?

No single work of Oiticica contains an unequivocal reference to homosexuality, *a fortiori*, as the latter was never a focus of attention for the artist. His position was very much a Modernist one, as it addressed matters of form and aesthetics predominantly.

Yet, both the artist's creations and his ideas were inspired by an erotic impulse, even when this remained hidden underneath the jargon of formal innovation, coded within what Frederico Morais has called Oiticica's 'sensorial etymology'.[44] Along with the desire for social transgression, there is a clearly tangible impulse to cross the boundaries of gender and to loosen the fixity of sexual identity. 'Already Hélio's earliest *Parangolé* capes, as clothing, are by nature transsexual. They have no attachment to conventional signs of either masculinity or femininity', says Guy Brett, who further expands on the theme: 'Gay sexuality could be traced in his work, but all his proposals related to sexuality seem to be non-divisive, transsexual.'[45]

Transsexuality may not be the right term, as Oiticica's intention is to question fixed gender roles, rather than to claim a feminine realm for men (or vice versa). Metasexuality may be a better term to capture Oiticica's sexual utopia. It can be read also from the 'hermaphrodite' clothes-*bólides* of 1968, as well as from the artist's statements, in an unpublished manuscript, about the hermaphrodite identity of both *samba* and rock.[46] Texts originating from his stay in New York develop further how such new sexuality ought to be conceived. In notes in preparation for the book *Conglomerado*, one can distinguish a vocabulary that confirms the notion of utopian androgyny, of linguistic de-genderification: *multisexo, twowaynis, bilinguex*.[47]

Oiticica's position is postmodern *avant la lettre* as it entails a deconstruction of current sexual ideology. But his work remains simultaneously embedded in Modernism. It is a hybrid, in fact, combining the language of Constructivism (*Neo-Concretismo*) with a plea for 'participation', amalgamating Brazil's body culture, his own sexuality and *carioca* social reality at once. It is curious to see, in fact, how the eclipse of the body is revindicated in art that anticipated Body Art in both Europe and North America, and how art and desire became one another's reflection in a new praxis.[48]

Only since the late 1970s can one perceive some artists, both male and female, who consider homosexual identity a legitimate topic of artistic expression and act upon it in an assertive, exhibitionist way. The growing visibility of 'gay' art and artists is an effect, undoubtedly, of the so-called *Abertura*, leading to more political and cultural freedom, and eventually to the restoration of a more democratic regime.[49]

Greater gay visibility in the arts coincided with the rather brief development of a political gay movement, focused predominantly around the gay magazine *Lampião* in São Paulo and the Gay Liberation group Somos in Rio de Janeiro. But already in the early 1970s, its path was lightened by travesty shows and gala balls in gay clubs, as well as by the theatre performances of the Dzi Croquetes. These were influenced by the 'gender fucking' Cockettes of San Francisco and consciously turned masculine and feminine roles upside down. New developments in music, such as *Tropicalismo*, also supported the idea of homosexual liberation, even when Caetano Veloso, Gilberto Gil and Ney Matogrosso spoke discreetly still of ideal 'androgyny' and 'multiple' sexuality. The female singers Maria Bethânia and Gal Costa, who once let themselves be photographed while kissing each other tenderly, paved the way for a lesbian coming-out in music. Ângela Ro-Ro, Leci Brandão, Simone and Maria Lima let the world know that they preferred the company of women to that of men.[50]

The new, more positive climate inspired a handful of visual artists to produce images that were unmistakably 'gay'. Homosexuality did appear in the more private work of Arlindo Daibert (do Amaral) (1952–93), while Rodrigo de Haro (b. 1939) portrayed his *entendido* friends. One of his works, *Mimosas borboletas* (1971), shows a clearly camp collection of effeminate gay men in drag.[51] Some photographs by Alair Gomes (b. 1921) are implicit celebrations of masculine beauty. *Beach triptych* (1985), for example, is neatly inscribed within a visual trope of tropical sensuality and reflects Rio's sexual economy of desire.

In fact, only Darcy Penteado (1926–87) made gay sexuality into a central focus of his work. He was a book illustrator, fashion and stage designer, painter and society portraitist, but he also devoted his life to the cause of Gay Lib. Late in his life, he turned to literature, publishing *A meta* in 1976, and *Nivaldo e Jerônimo* in 1981. As a founding member of *Lampião*, Penteado focused increasingly on erotic images of the nude male. A show of his work in 1973 was devoted almost exclusively to this theme.

Penteado's approach was innovative due to his emphasis upon a masculine, even *macho* image of homosexual men. The tone is celebratory and in tune with the optimism of gay politics during the years of *Abertura*. In one drawing, a naked man is shown with his right arm uplifted into the air. In it, one can recognize the artist's strong aspiration to freedom not unlike that symbolized by the Statue of Liberty in New York. AIDS put a premature end to his career as both artist and gay activist.[52]

Some works of Glauco Rodrigues (b. 1929) are also interesting, if only indirectly so. They are 'tropical' visualizations, generally, of national historical narratives, as can already be deduced from titles such as *Retrato do Quati-Puru victorioso* or *Cartas de Pêro Vaz de Caminha*. Yet, a certain homotextual dimension surfaces regularly, if only as part of a more comprehensive semantic whole. One image of the large series *Cartas de Pêro Vaz de Caminha* (1971) contains a detail that unmistakably refers to homosexuality, more particularly to gay tourism and the codes of exoticism accompanying it. One can see a white man, probably a tourist, who embraces a black man in a rather amorous way and at odds with the factually segregated dating pattern of Brazilians themselves. Elsewhere, the artist 'quotes' the scene from Michelangelo's Sistine Chapel, showing God's hand touching Adam's, merely to position it amidst a beach scene, where bathers of Ipanema mingle with the indigenous inhabitants of Brazil. Yet another scene contains a visual

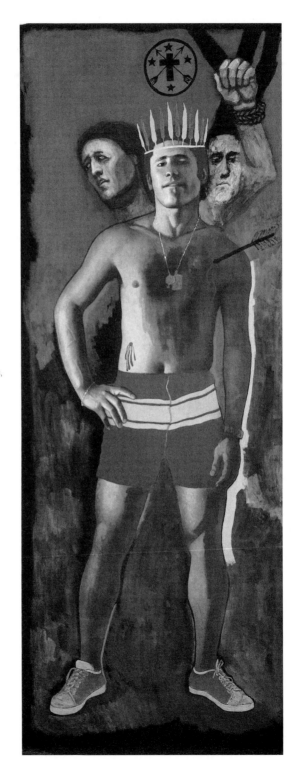

Figure 51 Glauco Rodrigues, *Meu Brasil brasileiro (São Sebastião)* (1986), acrylic on canvas, 220 × 100 cm, private collection, photo: Romulo Fialdini.

quotation of Saint Sebastian, now situated amidst an exclusively male group of beach tourists. Could it be the so-called Bolsa, that is the short stretch of Copacabana beach where gay men tend to converge and socialize? Saint Sebastian is the topic of another painting, titled *Meu Brasil brasileiro* (1986). It is a syncretic image, really, of a modern-day *malandro*, adorned with Roman Catholic status.

A subtle play of desire can be noticed, finally, in *Paz na tarde* (1989), showing four figures in a coloured vacuum. One woman looks away while a man and woman play badminton on the beach. To the right, Glauco Rodrigues included a faithful copy of *O derrubador brasileiro* by Ferraz de Almeida, whose gaze is now focusing on the white male player's behind.

The Gay Liberation movement was aborted prematurely in Brazil, yet gay visibility spread across the country. In cities other than Rio or São Paulo, gay groups were founded and one among them, the Grupo Gay da Bahia in Salvador, is currently one of the most active ones. It focuses on ongoing problems of homophobia, gaybashing and even assassination, while simultaneously promoting HIV-prevention and addressing the needs of people with AIDS. To the outside world, it presents an image that questions the picture of Brazil as a gay paradise.

Politicized 'gay art' remains virtually nonexistent, however, as most artists who do adopt homosexuality as a theme tend to focus on the erotic aspects instead. Thus the *carioca* painter Luiz Pizarro (b. 1958), who was part of the so-called Geração 80 and whose ardent images of the masculine body are reminiscent at once of José Clemente Orozco and William Blake. Their vibrant colours correspond to the light of Rio de Janeiro, attributing an air of *Tropicalismo* to the artist's representation of nude virility.

The canvases by Paulo Sayeg (b. 1960) show men riding horses and reveal an umistakable fascination for the masculine body. His Chinese ink drawings, while stylistically very distinct from his other work, show sexual scenes with an often clearly homosexual twist.

Clearly inscribed within a trope of homosexual *imaginaire* are the works of Geraldo Porto (b. 1950), residing in Campinas. They are reminiscent of the photographers von Gloeden and von Plüschow, while their style is deliberately academic also, paying tribute to the Academy's implicitly homosocial aura. Other work by Porto combines a formal language, adopted from both Klee and Torres-García, with a quest for spirituality and gay sensibility.[53]

A different style characterizes the work of *paulista* Florian Raiss (b. 1955). His sculptures and paintings of crawling men (*Sem título*, 1994) seem to oscillate literally between the beauty and the beast, between animal-like alienation and recognition of human purity. His terracotta masks of movie stars such as Mae West, Gloria Swanson,

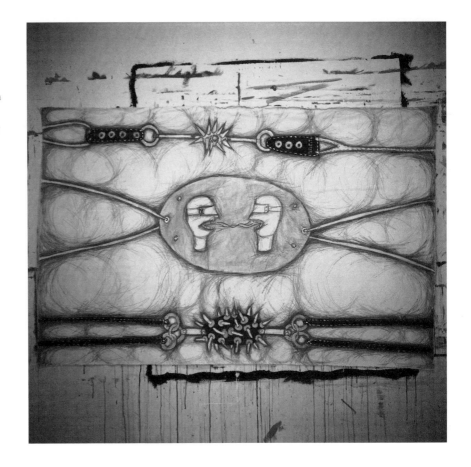

Figure 52 Edilson Viriato, *Sem título* (1996), mixed media on canvas, 65 × 83 cm, photo: Odilon Ratzke, courtesy of the artist, São Paulo, Brazil.

Joan Crawford and Marlene Dietrich are inscribed, on the other hand, in what is widely recognized as the realm of 'camp'.[54]

The work of Curitiba-based artist Edilson Viriato (b. 1966) consists of paintings, graphic work, collages, installations and performances, all together offering a compelling image of gay desire and sexuality tainted by the tragedy of AIDS.[55] He also curated a show in Curitiba, focusing entirely on AIDS and the arts. Some of Viriato's own works are playful, such as the fur bunnies with protruding erections, while others are contestatory and critical. His collages in particular seem to yearn for discursive continuity with gay politics in the Northern hemisphere.

Most intriguing, however, are his graphic work and paintings. They radiate an aesthetic that is complex and eclectic, expressing both sexual desire and the finality of life. Death and, on a less dramatic scale, religious disapproval are the inevitable watchdogs of Viriato's vitalism, searching at once for sexual gratification and spiritual peace and plenitude. *Sem título* (1996) is one among the works exhibited during his show 'Vida – morte – dor – prazer' in a defunct gas station that had not been renovated yet. The dirty environment intensified the artist's imagery of gay sadomasochistic eroticism, expressed by either black lilies – a symbol of 'forbidden love' – or latex hoods and masks. The heads of two individuals seem to communicate or perhaps even make love, yet their exchange threatens to be separated by the pulling force of strings. Connecting devices are made ambiguous by thorny objects that may signify separation by death as well as suggest an atmosphere of bondage and restraint. The canvases themselves are given the appearance of human skin, upon which his graphic figures appear as roughly edged tattoos. Viriato, like most of his contemporaries, adopts the subject of AIDS not so much as a tragic endnote to sexual liberation, but as a powerful symbolic signifier within the context of his S/M-inspired eroticism.[56]

In the work of some other artists, too, homotextuality surfaces in a somewhat more complex way as part of larger deconstructive discourses on culture and society. Not homoeroticism, but the social and cultural construction of homosexual identity is the focus of interest for some artists also in Brazil. At times, this verges towards social documentary. At other times, it focuses on secondary aspects of metropolitan gay life, or on the commodified, urban aspects of a gay *imaginaire*.

Disguised homosexual sensibility may be detected, for example, in the solitary nightly cityscapes by Luis Gregório Novaes Correa (b. 1951). They visualize the desolate late-night city centre of São Paulo, populated by a few people, possibly cruising gay men. *Luzes amanhecendo* (1975) is a watercolour that shows three of them, walking through the city at dawn. One has his arm around the second one. At first sight, the image illustrates the alienation experienced by people living in the large metropolis of São Paulo, and reminds one of Edward Hopper's desolate urban scenes. But this may be a portrayal also of that city's nightly gay subculture, more precisely of its architectural components and the liberating feeling of urban anonymity.

An example of the latter is *Os michês do Trianon* (1995) (Plate 15) by Ismael Costa Días (1968). It shows the blue imprints of three naked male bodies on a yellow canvas – a technique not unlike the 1960s 'boy art' of Yves Klein. They represent male hustlers, operating in the small park across the street from the Museu de Arte de São Paulo. Two of them are wearing leather-studded wristbands, as if to emphasize the ritual of potentially sadomasochistic exchanges with their clients. The image, while semi-abstract when looked at from too close, gradually reveals a poetic documentary instead of the homosexual and bisexual economy in metropolitan Brazil.

The work of Adir Sodré (b. 1962) is relevant also in this context, as some of his portraits seem to contain an ironic comment upon a metropolitan gay *imaginaire*. He portrayed the transsexual and national cultural hero(ine) Roberta Close, whose rosy hermaphrodite body dominates a painting as colourful as those of Henri Matisse. He calls him/her a 'neo-modern nymph', thus emphasizing the celebrity's urban artificiality along with her/his mythological appeal to a gay audience especially. Sodré's portrait, next, of American cult figure Divine visualizes the latter's fame even in Brazil, yet the work's exaggerated, Pop-like aesthetic reveals the artist's scepticism towards North American cultural imperialism and an uncritical adoption of a commodified 'gay culture' by Brazil's metropolitan gay community. Sodré, who resides in the rural state of Mato Grosso, deliberately distances himself from a commercialized *ambiente* and deploys an ironic stance in both his life and work.

Implicitly rejecting a highly profiled 'gay' identity is the work of some Brazilian artists who inscribe their work in an Afro-Brazilian tradition, for example, the white artist Mario Cravo Neto (b. 1947) and the black one, Bauer Sá (b. 1950), both black-and-white photographers whose visual universe shows great affinity with black culture and embraces the distinct sexual order that goes along with it. For neither is homosexuality a theme or motive – in fact, neither of them is gay – yet their images of black men are deliberately imbued with sensuality and eroticism. The distinction homo/heterosexuality is theoretical rather in the symbolism of Afro-Brazilian syncretism. It makes its artistic expression into one of potentially polymorphous sexuality and embraces homosexual eros without naming it. Thus, photographs like *Lelicana* (1994) by Sá or *José da Paixão* (1982) by Cravo Neto may be read equally as recognitions of masculine sex appeal, even when both images of male nudity are contextualized otherwise.[57]

While 'gay' art had surfaced and spread since the late 1970s, there were increasingly signs that this very concept would soon become obsolete, or at least questionable. Perhaps this is not surprising, since sexual boundaries have always been rather flexible and fluid in Brazil. Local gay artists surely had followed international trends, exposed as they were to these by, for example, the São Paulo Biennials. In 1967, work by Andy Warhol and David Hockney was exhibited. In 1981 followed Gilbert and George; in 1983 Keith Haring. Later, Salomé followed along with the Argentinian gay artist, Guillermo Kuitca.[58] The example also of North American and European gay subcultural politics had strengthened their artistic vision.

Yet, as 'gay' art became more visible worldwide and became common currency also in Brazil, it soon lost much of its revolutionary appeal. Criticism arose against the 'provincial' character of self-centred 'homosexual art'. As gay people grew sceptical themselves about the narrow political agenda of Gay Lib, they adopted a less activist stance, which was reflected also in the visual arts. A younger generation attempted to deconstruct 'modern' sexual discourse and aimed at surpassing the pigeonholing of sexual taxonomy by adopting a more detached and critical approach. The critic Adriano Pedrosa acknowledges, accordingly, that some artists are actually lesbian or gay, but nevertheless dismiss the fact as merely biographical: 'Unlike European and particularly North American art circles, in Brazil these concerns rarely come about.'[59]

Most prominent among the young, 'queer deconstructionists', though dead at the early age of thirty-six, is José Leonilson Bezerra Dias (1957–93), better known as Leonilson.[60] Leonilson abstained from turning his sexual identity into a cause for militancy – 'Não que eu seja um defensor que sai com uma bandeira'* – nor did he present his art as 'gay art'. Ambiguity is a keyword in his work, not from a closeted position –

*'Not that I was a militant who would sport a banner.'

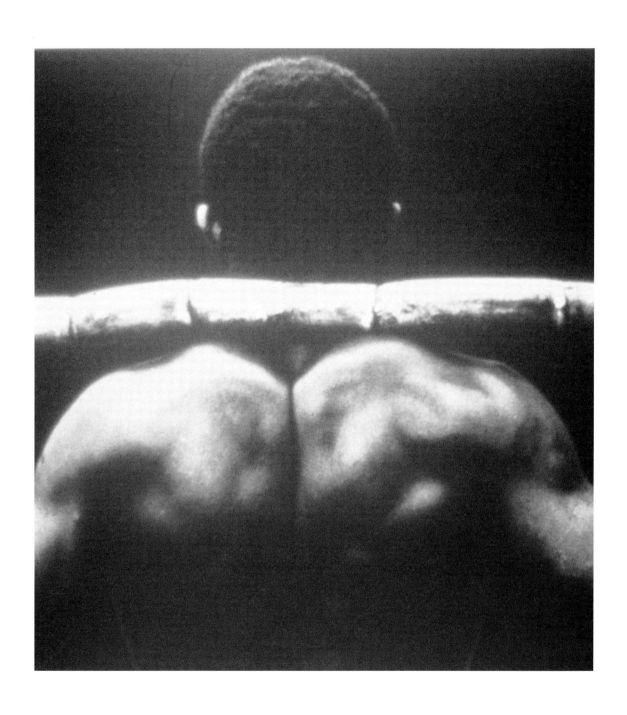

Figure 53 Bauer Sá, *Lelicana* (1994), black-and-white photo, 56 × 49 cm, courtesy of Throckmorton Fine Art, New York City.

he never denied being homosexual – but as part of a postmodern claim about the fluidity of desire and the historicity of both 'gay' and 'heterosexual' identity. There is an undeniable 'desire to mark the expression of subjectivity', says Pedrosa, who described the artist's confessional mood as essentially a 'quiet and intimate one'.[61] Yet, another critic, Lisette Lagnado, claims that Leonilson's work did entail a cultural activism that was related to the political dimension of a late twentieth-century *usage des plaisirs*.[62]

Leonilson's career took off against the background of Brazil's so-called Geração 80, a group of artists including, among others, Alex Vallauri, Beatriz Milhares, Daniel Senise, Jorge Guinle, Luis Zerbini, Leda Catunda and Leonilson himself. Each of the artists' works was distinct, yet collectively they were influenced by the Italian Transavanguardia and called for a new experience of the pleasure of painting. Most went their own way afterwards, including Leonilson, who adopted embroidery as his trademark technique. After conceptual experiments concerning the 'metalanguage' of art, he focused increasingly on subjective destiny, especially after his positive HIV-diagnosis in 1991.

Already at an early stage, between 1983 and 1988, Leonilson disclosed his sexual identity, even if in a semi-abstract manner. Influenced by both Paul Klee and the Brazilian Pop artist Antonio Dias, he included imagery of spurting fountains, repeatedly used the word 'boys' and fetishized homoerotically charged elements of Ancient Greek culture. Towards the end of the 1980s, however, Leonilson adopted new techniques, influenced eclectically by Oiticica's *parangolés*, by Eva Hesse's weavings and by Shaker design. His decision was inspired not so much by the example of Italian *arte povera*, since necessity, rather than luxury compelled him – and other Latin American artists – to use poor materials of all kinds.[63]

His artistic language increasingly reflected a deeply rooted unease, springing as much from his position as a gay man as from a 'romantic' awareness of marginality. A 'solitary nonconformist' or *inconformado*, he acknowledged the contradictory feelings given with existence and artistic creation, and represented life as hiding within itself not one but many truths. Certainly, a search was involved also as to how to express gay desire. How, without falling into the traps of 'gay sensibility' and 'camp', can one visualize the homoerotic? How to name it without adopting a vocabulary, imposed from above, by a culture (the politicized USA) that is not his own?

Two strategies of representation are indicative of the artist's awareness of outsidership. First, there is the use of words and phrases in different languages, at times deliberately misspelled, to emphasize not only a sense of exile, made tangible, moreover, by his numerous trips to Europe and the USA, but also that the adoption of any vocabulary of life is necessarily inadequate and limiting. Implicitly, this may entail a critique of sexual vocabulary, pinning people down on the confining triad of heterosexuality, bisexuality and homosexuality, where nomadic desire is called upon to take one position.

Secondly, Leonilson also violated grammatical rules – Lagnado calls this 'gender syllepsis' – by attributing an erratic gender to certain substantives (*O ilha*, 1990). In its wake, the boundary between male and female sex is uprooted, as can be seen in *O Penelope* (1992) and part of the installation at the Morumbí Chapel, called *Los delicias* (1993). The association of delight with plural masculinity may be a coded signifier of the pleasures of promiscuity, just as other works, titled through gender syllepsis as well as through a fusion of plural and singular, may refer to the disastrous effect resulting from it in the shape of physical deterioration and disease: *Os solidão* and *Os ruinas* (both part of *Rapaz dividido*, 1991). That message can be retrieved also from *Grandes homens, mesmo veneno* (1991), expressing a gay man's frustration in view of physical attraction on the one hand, and the risk of contamination by HIV on the other.

The emblematic imagery of Leonilson is perceptible also apart from the coded messages about AIDS. These, in fact, were the logical continuation of works documenting the artist's subjective desire as well as the social reality of homosexual life in contemporary Brazil. Leonilson participated in the society life of both Rio and São Paulo while sharing in the permissiveness of European and North American metropolises: 'A gente ia para Europa, e a situação . . . era de abertura total.[64] Nos anos 80, houve isso. Houve uma quasi permissividade. . . . Onde você pisava, a loucura estava estabelecida. As pessoas se drogavam, tinha aquelas festas, tudo. Quando se aproximou o espectro do Mal, você ja não tinha controle da loucura das coisas.'*[65] The visualization of life in the fast lane, if there at all, is toned down into almost cryptic, hieroglyphic signs. A small drawing of 1991, titled *O cometa*, shows nothing but a tiny urinal and the text '*Olhos verdes/O cometa*'. The work is part of a series called *Os dedicados* and was made for friends. When asked by Lagnado if a reference to Marcel Duchamp was involved,[66] Leonilson replied: 'Nem um pouco. É mais uma sacanagem relacionado com o banheiro público. É um símbolo de perversão, como os caras que guardam o cabelo da mulher. Fetiche. Esta imagem aparece três vezes: usei na mesa do Centro Cultural, no bordado em seda bege, *Mr. One Night Stand*, e neste desenho.'†[67] The furtive character of a sexual rendezvous is emphasized by the fetishized representation of the site of action, while the mentioning of one physical detail ('green eyes') reveals a level of romantic intimacy despite the sexual encounter's anonymous context. A similarly cryptic work, yet unmistakably homotextual, is *O vapor* (1991), of the same series, and documenting an equally nameless sexual adventure in one of the gay bathhouses of Brazil. It merely shows a playing card with three red crosses in one diagonal and two red hearts in the remaining corners: 'Esse trabalho é muito próximo do trabalho do mictório. Ambos são meio pervertidos e fetichistas. O vapor remete a sexo.'‡[68]

The romanticism of nomadic desire was challenged after the artist's positive diagnosis in 1991 and new works followed that carry a message of warning, frustration, pain or regret. An engraving, titled *Mesma saliva, mesma veneno* (1991) is somewhat hysteric in

*'People went to Europe, and the situation . . . was one of total openness. In the 1980s, that's how it was like. There was an almost absolute permissiveness. . . . Everywhere you went, there was madness deeply rooted. People took drugs, there were these parties, anything. When Evil showed its face, you no longer had control over the madness of things.'

†'Not a bit. It is more like something dirty, related to the public bathroom. It's a symbol of perversion, like those guys who keep the hair of a woman. A fetish. The image appears three times: I used it once on the table in the Centro Cultural, once on an embroidery in beige silk, *Mr. One Night Stand*, and in this drawing.'

‡'This work is very close to the public bathroom one. Both are pervert and fetishist environments. The steam leads to sex.'

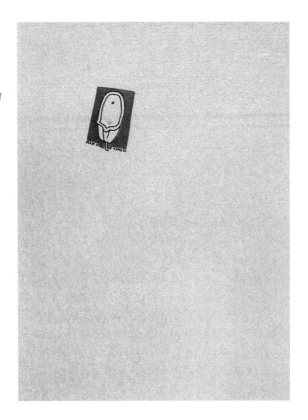

suggesting transmission of HIV through saliva, but other works assess more realistically what he is really facing. *Moeda de artista, dias contados* (1985) seemed premonitory, says Lagnado, possibly referring also to the transience of artistic success. But other works of the same years clearly reveal Leonilson's awareness about AIDS. During the last three years of his life, he made several embroideries and drawings that tell how he has dealt with the disease.

O perigoso (1992) is an emblematic sequence of images witnessing the artist's coming to grips with new reality:

> The first drawing of the series has the identity of a *corpus delicti*: a single drop of his own contaminated blood. What could have become a trap of literalness (from the use of dangerous blood to the simple representation of a rosary) is in fact a tale of the painfulness of lines and strokes that are weakening but refuse to surrender or succumb to self-pity. Illness, supported here by a range of flowers (daisies, primulas, Easter lilies), is elevated to an allegorical dimension alongside the lily wreath, a Christian symbol of innocence and death.[69]

Leonilson's work on AIDS is different, here, from much other more politicized 'AIDS art'. It is a reflection primarily upon the moral consequences of the illness from within the consciousness of the artist himself.

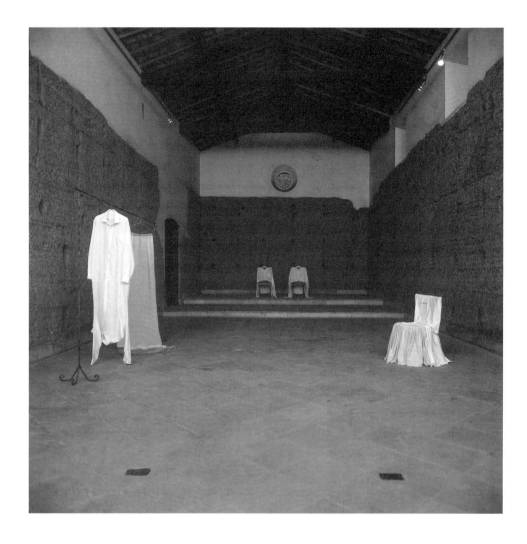

Figure 55 Leonilson, Installation at Morumbí Chapel, São Paulo (1993), courtesy of Projeto Leonilson, São Paulo, photo: Eduardo Brandão.

Eventually, moreover, his works become testimonies of martyrdom, embroideries like *ex-votos*, traces of funeral remains. *J. L. 35* (1993) is one of them; *Se você sonhe com nuvens* (1991) another. Perhaps the installation at the Morumbí Chapel, briefly mentioned above, is the most serene expression of loss, not only of the artist's own individual life, but of the gay community collectively. The work 'transmits a disturbing silence' (Lagnado) as personal suffering is reinforced by the virtual emptiness of the religious architectural environment. Yet, while the work is inscribed in a Catholic context merely by virtue of the site, it is simultaneously a critique thereof that entails a rather iconoclastic attitude towards misplaced stoicism. The installation is a testimony, not of the acceptance of suffering, but of the artist's and gay community's desire for adequate protection against the 'plague'. Thus the chairs, covered with shirts that read 'do falso moral' and 'do bom coração'.

At the same time, it remains imbued with a (Catholic?) desire for purification and redemption, stressed by the use of light fabric (voile) and the absence almost entirely of colour. Two shirts, sewn together at the bottom and hung up, so that one is upside down, represent Lazarus resurrected after four days in the grave. It is a subtle expression of hope, along with an aspiration to immortality. Lagnado, from whom this analysis derives, thus catches the installation's soul: 'Sensuality comes to the surface like a catharsis, an epiphany of a possible aesthetic model, in which the body's *via crucis* translates the need to express faith. Leonilson redefines the divine through a critique of authority and the hypocrisy of the Church.'[70]

Leonilson's oeuvre illustrates how the personal is political, even when no purposive intention directed the creative process. AIDS forced him to evaluate praxis and discourse alike and to question the premisses of Gay Liberation also in Brazil. The autobiographical is a screening at once of the content of identity, and of the teleology of sexual, specifically homosexual desire. In due course, his work became a strategy of resistance against the deterioration of his body, while the body inspired artistic production as the carrier of death and desire, *eros* and *thanatos*. 'Work = body = work', says Lagnado, who recognizes a source of redemption in what she calls the 'poetry of ellipsis' of Leonilson's post-1991 work.[71]

'Mapping sentimental memory' (Ivo Mesquita) is central to the oeuvre of Leonilson. It is postmodern largely as an attempt to untackle obstinate associations between sexual nonconformity, immorality and disease, and as a strategy of resistance also, deconstructing the fixed parameters of personal identity: 'Imagens, palavras, gestos são metáforas aptas ao conceito pós-moderno de *self* – deslocado, fragmentário, carregado de informação que parece ser importante e imediata, mas que é freqüentamente elusiva e ilusiva. . . . (Ele) quer evitar narrativas fixas e certezas fáceis.'*[72]

Contemporary lesbian artists too stay far away, in Brazil as elsewhere, from rather predictable celebrations of homosexual eros. Their work, like Leonilson's, sheds critical light on traditional tropes of homotextual representation and embraces a more complex aesthetic of female-to-female desire. Both Valeska Soares (b. 1957) and Rosana Monerrat (b. 1967) create end-of-the-century social commentaries upon 'modern' subjectivity, while suggesting that their sexless creations can be interpreted in various ways. By doing so, they both deconstruct common categories of sexual and gender identity, whether gay, bisexual or straight, and offer an essentially 'postmodern' critique of the limiting effect of such categories upon human desire.

*'Images, words, gestures are adequate metaphors of the postmodern concept of the self – dislocated, fragmented, loaded with information that seems to be important and relevant, but that often is elusive and illusory. . . . [He] wants to avoid fixed narratives and easy certainties.'

Puerto Rico: *machismo* notwithstanding

Massive migration to the United States has made the situation of gay men and women in Puerto Rico somewhat distinct from other countries in Latin America and the Caribbean. Rather than developing a Gay Liberation movement on an island where homosexuality is still a felony, most middle-class homosexuals find it easier to move to cities abroad, especially New York. There, many end up participating in the metropolis' bustling gay life. Other, mostly working-class homosexual or bisexual immigrants do not so easily adopt today's notion of 'gay identity' and find themselves oscillating between an alternately exoticist or racist gay community on the one hand, and a persistently homophobic Puerto Rican community on the other hand.

Those who stay behind or, after several years of life in North America, return home, face an almost endemic homophobia there – a fact exacerbated by the advent of AIDS. An island widely popular for its sexual opportunities and a cheap destination for charter tourists as a result is easily lured into scapegoating homosexuals as the primary risk group. Many homosexual tourists frequenting the island have only intensified this process of marginalization, leaving gay men with HIV in particular in a state of great social uncertainty. Migration to New York, once a way out, is not really attractive anymore, considering the city's high seroprevalence. In fact, many who emigrated while still healthy have seroconverted since.

It comes as no surprise, accordingly, that artists, to the degree that they actually deal with issues of homoeroticism or homosexual identity, often adopt a rather complex way to lay it bare. Arnaldo Roche Rabell (b. 1955) has become one of the island's most prominent artists.[73] The homotextual dimension of some of his work is hidden in both the image and the creative process. Jointly, they produce 'gay' images that are hardly recognizable at first, yet come to the surface after close inspection. Roche's work is closely related to his personal emotions, rather than to any political or sociological observation of Puerto Rican sexual politics. Yet, it is remarkable how the artist's idiosyncratic visions are revealing of the hardship faced by homosexual artists on the island or, for that matter, within the community of Puerto Rican exiles.

Dreams and visions are the artist's raw material, intense and often violent, provoked by his recurrent headaches, so he claims.[74] But his paintings are not simple, mimetic visualizations of what he himself can see. Already at the stage of artistic creativity, he intervenes and regulates those dreams by the use of vital technique. Painting, for Roche, is like a ritual, a ceremony, and a medium for self-communication. 'His paintings', says Garcia Gutiérrez, 'are like exorcisms in which his own image is seen as protagonist, either a victim of himself or of his models or victimizing them.'[75]

To obtain the goal of exorcism, Roche adopts the so-called *frottage* technique, which consists of laying a blackened canvas across a body or an object, then scratching across the surface in order to lay bare the underlying layers of usually red or yellow paint. Thus, an imprint is made on the canvas of the figure or object lying underneath. It is an intense creative act, involving 'physical intimacy and spiritual communication, immediate touch and conceptual knowledge'.[76] The relationship between himself, his subject and the medium of painting itself is personal, psychological and tangible.

Homotextuality, in this context, is contained within the creative process. The making of a painting actually requires communication, both verbal and tactile, with his model. In theory, this goes for work with male or female models, and Roche indeed makes works representing both women and men. Yet, the women mostly represent mother images, as can be seen, for example, in *El origen* or *Maria del Mar*, both works of 1986. Men, on the contrary, appear in quite different ways, collectively revealing the artist's special relationship to them already on the level of the physical creation of an artwork.

Roche's work becomes fascinating since the painting becomes an expression simultaneously of sexual desire and of the ghosts that haunt his mind and make him aware, at times, of the nature of his sexuality. Visualization of homoeroticism is anything but predictable in Roche's work and impregnated instead with a far more comprehensive agenda. 'The presence of homoerotic feelings . . . can only be interpreted as symptomatic of what Arnaldo Roche – man and artist – considers a main theme of his art: the existential and social alienation that he experiences – trapped in his own image and imagery and provoking a violent confrontation between the model and the artist,' says Garcia Gutiérrez again.

The idiosyncratic homosexual *imaginaire* of Roche can be seen, for example, in *El matador de dragones* (1985), a work that already shows stylistic maturity and is much harder to understand than some of his early work. *Alsino*, for example, is an early work of 1973, showing the protagonist of a novel by the Chilean Pedro Prado. The man is represented naked in front of the featherwings that allowed him to escape, then, like Icarus, fall. The figure's nudity clearly shows the young artist's fascination for the male body, yet such straightforward images would soon be exchanged for far more complex renderings of homotextuality.

El matador de dragones is one of those cryptic, hard to 'decode' images, showing a strong yet unappealing man who flaunts an erection. Simple depiction of physical beauty has now made way for an image of apparent ugliness. The aesthetic or sensual quality of the male nude is no longer the focus of this more recent work. Allegory rather seems to direct this work, showing how the man holds the cut-off head of the artist himself. In his other hand, he holds a knife, yet he is facing resistance by a man outside the picture who reaches for the head. Could it be the artist, who is facing the dragon slayer? And if so, who or what, then, does the latter represent?

Despite the artist's use of homoeroticism as a metaphor for social marginality, one may indeed wonder if a more direct social commentary is involved. Perhaps the dragon slayer stands for the object of Roche's own desire, while the cut-off head represents his alienation as a gay man? If so, then the character outside the picture's frame may well be homophobia personified: homophobia, present not only in the artist's own environment, *a fortiori* in his homeland itself, but possibly also in his own mind.

A similar play with meanings may rule *Me llevan*, a painting of the same year. Here, one can see the silhouette of a (black?) man, literally running off with Roche's large head in both hands. This man exhibits an erection also, symbolizing both erotic tension and fertilization by nightmarish creatures, again possibly related to ambiguous feelings about his own sexual desire.

Whereas these works suggest a rather problematic, self-repressive attitude towards his own sexuality, there are other paintings that reveal Roche's critical stance towards the homophobia and heterosexism persistent in society. Puerto Rican *machismo* is the target, for example, in *Miedo de Esteban* (1988). It is yet another complex work, showing a large male figure trying to escape an even larger rooster-like creature, symbol, as is known, of masculinity. Masculinity or, perhaps, the dominant ideology of male-centred homophobia – which may explain the artist's choice of the name Esteban as a reference to the gay icon Saint Sebastian.

Homoerotic sensuality surfaces also, either as semi-abstract charcoal drawings of male nudity, doubled like Rorschach stains (*Vulnerable*, 1985), or in works on canvas. *Casi despierto* (1989) shows a faun-like figure waking up in a private room. The scene's voluptuousness is emphasized by the figure's apparent morning erection. Through the windows one can perceive high-rises, referring undoubtedly to Chicago, which the artist has made into his second, adopted hometown. Inside, there are imprints from leaves, imported by the artist from Puerto Rico and symbolizing the power of memory, inner geography.

Homoeroticism can be identified, next, in the oeuvre of Carlos Collazo, Enrique Renta, and Néstor Millán. Collazo (1956–90) painted in a variety of styles, including abstraction and figuration. Only towards the end of his life, when dying of AIDS, did he paint self-portraits that lend a particular homotextual dimension to his work. They all deal with the more intimate aspects of his disease, deliberately presenting the artist as a bald, older man. This way, Collazo wanted to reduce the self-portrait to its essential, while presenting a metaphor for the ordeal of a dying artist. The visual documentary of physical decay, brought on by terminal illness, is at once sober and assertive, personal and universal: 'Su faz es un modelo accesible', says his friend and colleague Maria de Mater O'Neill, 'para documentar los síntomas del envejecimiento, el progresivo desgaste de la vida. En ellos no se lee la particular historia del pintor sino el destino común del hombre, que desemboca en la muerte.'*[77] Yet, the self-portraits also carry the imprint of the devastating effect of AIDS upon the island's gay community and lend a purely historical and documentary dimension to them.

*'His work is an accessible model to document the symptoms of becoming old, of the gradual waste of life. In them, one doesn't read the painter's particular history, but the common destiny, rather, of mankind facing death.'

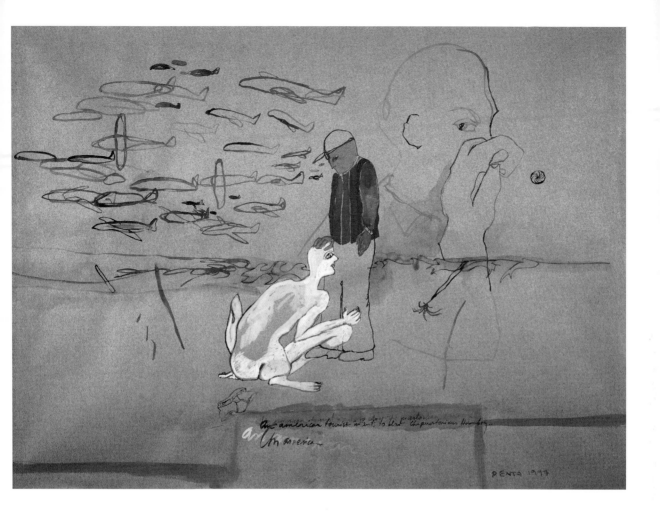

Figure 56 Enrique Renta, *Incidente (The American tourist wants to blow the Puerto Rican homeboy)* (1997), watercolour on paper, 45 × 55 cm, courtesy of the artist, San Juan, Puerto Rico.

Enrique Renta (b. 1959), while initially adopting abstract expressionism, has gradually adopted a new figurative aesthetic that is undeniably inspired by gay sensibility. Recognizable through images of bodily atrophy are scenes of homosexual desire. 'Las composiciones . . . [de] Renta pueden leerse como audaces poemas existenciales donde el artista revela que entiende la importancia de la comunicación y el amor entre los hombres.'*[78] While incidentally documenting patterns of postcolonial sexual exploitation – as can be seen in *Incidente* (1997) – Renta adopts painting as a medium primarily of self-discovery that is fundamentally autobiographical and introspective. His art, says Renta, is commenting upon the fate of a marginalized minority, facing death, violence and uncertainty. Yet, while visualizing gay social and intimate experience in a Puerto Rican context, Renta at once inscribes 'provincial' commentary within a universalist narrative about the human condition. 'The common thread is existence, survival, art as an exercise

*'The compositions of Renta can be read as audacious existentialist poems, in which the artist reveals that he understands the importance of communication and love among men.'

against the existentialist illusion of impotence, singing the importance of pain, freedom, self and memory as catalysts of change.'[79]

The most explicit and 'out' homosexual among contemporary Puerto Rican artists is painter and photographer Néstor Millán (b. 1960). Perhaps his openness about sexual identity was facilitated by his familiarity with gay life in a city such as New York. There, he was confronted not only with the city's racial, ethnic and sexual complexity, but with many stories also of disease and personal loss, provoked by AIDS.[80] Still, the biographies of Roche and Collazo demonstrate that exile as such is not enough. What moves Millán is his political awareness as well as a certain combativity as a gay man, even when his visual language is anything but predictably activist.

His oeuvre is a contemplation about masculine identity, more precisely about 'its power, its intimacy and its encompassing vulnerability'.[81] At first sight, his models seem to be unaware of the painter's or photographer's eye and their spontaneity blends nicely with the surrounding architectural environment of rooms and gardens. The domestic atmosphere lends warmth and intimacy to Millán's visualization of a homoerotic gaze. *Butterfly chair II* (1995) almost makes you feel the late afternoon's sun as one follows the model's dreamy gaze outside.

But, on closer inspection, the image is not idyllic, but a still frame of tragedy unwrapping itself as the painting's narrative is inscribed in history. Millán's small-scale paintings of resting men gradually reveal themselves as testimonies of reinvention, reinvention by gay men of themselves in the wake of both the AIDS crisis and increasing homophobia. 'The physical barriers . . . between the viewer and the nude, between myself and the models, symbolize . . . the sexual frustration and repression of the past decade', says the artist in a recent interview.

> Being gay during the crisis of the AIDS epidemic has scarred my artwork – literally. In a sense like the Puerto Ricans, the gay population has been forced to redefine itself and its conduct in a new era. An era where the spontaneity of body contact, emotion and expression was replaced with obstacles: fear, sickness and death. In my artworks, the male is an alienated protagonist either because of his nakedness which might be forbidden or because of his sexuality.[82]

Melancholic testimony of vulnerability in the face of AIDS is the theme also of recent photos, taken in derelict buildings alongside the island's western coast. While apparently personal and subjective, they contain subtle criticism of society's indifference and ongoing heterosexism, as well as of the 'bureaucratic excess and frivolous medical protocol' that stands in the way of an efficient treatment or cure.[83]

Some work by Millán can be seen as positive 'gay' art. Yet, it must be said that occasionally a certain ambiguity arises, resulting, it seems, from the artist's outsider position as a homosexual. The photoseries *Against straight lines* and *With other men* (both

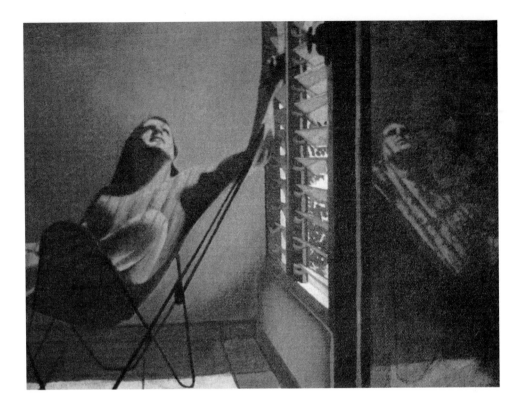

Figure 57 Néstor Millán, *Butterfly chair II* (1995), acrylic on canvas, 23 × 30.5 cm, courtesy of the artist, San Juan, Puerto Rico.

dating from 1987) are outspoken in their gay content and offer compelling images of homoeroticism. But images are included also that seem to question gay assertiveness. In *Against straight lines* one man is seen while veiled – a 'sign of penance', says one critic,[84] and one wonders why such sceptical footnotes to gay self-realization reoccur throughout the work of Néstor Millán.

Millán, who resides alternatively in Puerto Rico and the USA, seems critical of the limited freedom granted to gay men not only on the island but among the Puerto Rican community in New York as well. Repression is a recurrent theme that transcends homophobia and extends itself to the notion of displacement in a geographical sense. The bicultural focus of his own life remains marked by 'vulnerability, insecurity, and rejection'.[85]

AIDS, in this context, is only one focus besides others, allowing the artist to address the more universal and inevitable conditions of life. Sensuality, in all his works, is compromised by ephemerality, eventually also by age and death. He uses average-looking bodies, even with pot bellies at times, rather than idealized images of masculine eros. 'El erotismo', says a critic, 'de sus desnudos masculinos no es una delectación en el cuerpo del varón.'*[86] These psychological apsects are visualized by a rather introspective mood.

*'The eroticism of his masculine nudes is not like he's taking pleasure in the man's body.'

It is not surprising, in the light of persistent *machismo* on the island of Puerto Rico, that critical reviews are somewhat apologetic about Millán's paintings and photographs of the male nude. Excursions on male nudity in Ancient Greek and Renaissance art are to claim legitimacy for the controversial topic in Puerto Rico today.[87] But Millán's courageous position clearly paves the way to more acceptance both of artistic imagery of homoeroticism, and of a gay *ambiente* in real life.

While not gay himself, Víctor Vázquez (b. 1950) also addresses the impact of AIDS on Puerto Rico. Explicit references to the gay community are absent, as an implicit message is sent out about how HIV and AIDS affect not only homosexuals but anyone. A photo installation, *El reino de la espera* (1991) comments on the epidemic's devastating effect on a friend, whereas other works are a mythopoeic documentary that reconciles historical reportage with cultural processing, social criticism activism with religious interpretation, sorrow with consolation.

This diachronic temporality is crucial to Vázquez's aesthetic, says José Fernández, allowing for mediation between past and present, between the cosmopolitan and the local. Thus, the importance of ritual, sacrifice and redemption, briefly, of the 'mythological capacity to justify social reality'.[88]

For this reason, too, Vázquez's imagery is inscribed within the visual universe of syncretic Afro-American religion. His adoption of *Santería* imagery and symbolism is anything but nostalgic, but marked by a contemporary awareness of crisis, transience and death. Along with Caribbean artists such as María Magdalena Campos-Pons, Marta Maria Pérez and José Bedia, he adopts hybrid Afro-American religious imagery as a language of metaphors for commenting upon contemporary history and society instead of as a means of visualizing static religious ideas. The universal, rather than local aspects of *Santería* are emphasized against the postmodern background of social and cultural *bricolage*. The recurrent use of birds, mostly chickens, points at transcendence and liberty, yet their appearance with broken wings or, worse even, while entirely plucked refers to the fragility of such aspirations in real life. Vázquez attaches an ironic use of such familiar iconography to the manipulation of gender and suggests that a balance can be found, says one critic,[89] in a fusion of *yin* and *yang*, of life and death, of the masculine and the feminine. It is a coded comment, in fact, upon the insanity of rigid gender roles.

Out lesbian artists are as yet rare in Puerto Rico, despite, or maybe because of the presence on the island of a feminine yet ambivalent pictorial universe like Myrna Báez's. In fact, only María de Mater O'Neill (b. 1960), who herself worked as a printmaking assistant to Báez, seems to embrace the topic of lesbian identity voluntarily and openly. Yet, such remains enclosed within a 'less provincial' investigation of feminine, more particularly Latin American feminine identity. She frequently confronts the island's sexual puritanism with ambiguous erotic enigmas, says art critic Teresa Lopez, and combines

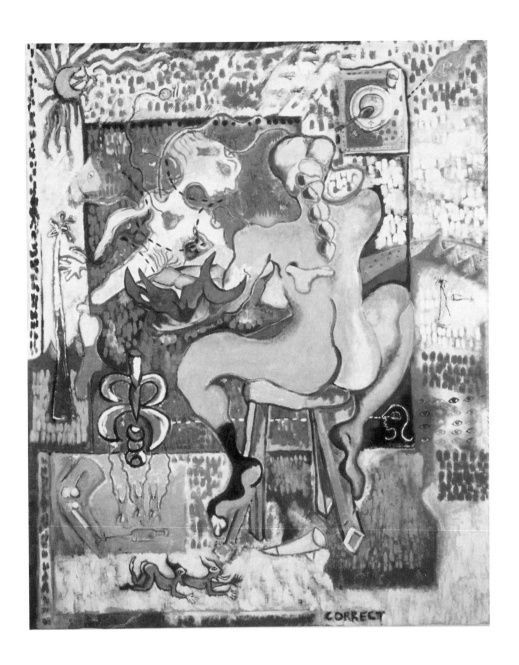

Figure 58 Maria de Mater O'Neill, *Autorretrato no. 8 (desnudo frente al espejo)* (1988),
oil on canvas, 183 × 157.7 cm, courtesy of the artist,
San Juan, Puerto Rico.

the exploration of sexual identity with an obstinate and ongoing investigation of Puerto Rican national identity.[90]

O'Neill explores sexuality through autobiographic portraiture mainly, as did her mentor Myrna Báez, yet she diverges drastically from the aesthetic of intimacy characterizing Báez's interiors. *Autorretrato no. 8* (1988) visualizes introspection quite differently and positions the central, female figure amidst a plethora of crudely drawn paraphernalia.[91] Referring alternatively to Willem de Kooning's *Terrible women* and a Transvanguardia aesthetic of the personal and the concrete,[92] de Mater O'Neill identifies the search for cultural and sexual identity as the development of a visual language that at once confirms and criticizes Puerto Rico's ambivalent sexual morality.

In more recent work, O'Neill adopts the visual language of comic strips to attach a critical questioning of local mores to postcolonial criticism. A lesbian superhero is a crossing between Superman and a politically correct, feminized Tarzan, whose main target is the island's contemporary art critic and who contests the latter's continuing and deliberate neglect of issues such as gender, sexual identity and AIDS.[93]

AIDS confronted O'Neill when friend and painter Carlos Collazo turned HIV-positive, then died. She made a video documentary about him, as a tribute but also as a means of informing her surroundings of the destruction and loss for the Puerto Rican artistic community, struck violently by the disease.[94]

Other works focus on the island's physical geography as a metaphor for the island mentality of *Puertorriqueños*, upon the sea as conveyor of Caribbean cultural identity. O'Neill frequently publishes on Puerto Rican and Latin American women's art and combines an artistic career with numerous initiatives to promote the study of Caribbean artists. The cyber art journal *El Cuarto del Quenepón*, co-edited by herself, offers information on Puerto Rico's contemporary art scene and stands at the vanguard of artistic exchange through the Internet.

Cuba: the limits of visibility

After the stigmatization of Martínez and Cabrera Moreno, homoeroticism vanished from Cuban art for many years. The unchanged policy of repression towards sexual diversity as well as persistent homophobia and *machismo* intimidated artists from exploring such a theme in their work.

Only since the late 1980s can one observe small signs of change. There are indications that the Cuban policy towards homosexuality has indeed lost something of its vigorously oppressive strength and that gays and lesbians are actually gaining greater freedom, greater visibility. Proof of such are a first show of Cuban homoerotic art, set up by Fidel Pérez at the Centro Cultural Yara in the early 1990s, as well as the government-subsidized film *Fresa y chocolate* (1993), based on a short story by Senel Paz. *Gay Cuba* (1995), a documentary film by Sonja de Vries, also portrays a rather optimistic image of gay and lesbian life today, while on stage homosexuality is dealt with in a rather assertive manner by stage director Carlos Díaz. At the more marginal Teatro Sótano, plays are presented that show gay cruising scenes as well as frontal male nudity. Musicians address homosexuality with greater audacity and explicitness while *Ocánia: pasión infinita* was staged 'replete with transvestites and effigies of erotic angels'.[95]

But too far-reaching visibility and political association remain unacceptable to the Castro regime and police oppression especially threatens gay and lesbian freedom even today. Raids take place more or less regularly.[96] Minimal claims to gay and lesbian rights are still bound to be smothered by the authorities. The advent of AIDS in Cuba also has given rise to so-called *sidatorios*, where HIV-positive people are quarantined in exchange for free medical care – a drastic measure that severely offends the civil rights of people with HIV and AIDS.[97]

The regime's ambiguity towards homosexuality may explain why the so-called Renaissance of Cuban art embraces homosexuality only reluctantly.[98] Certainly, the inclusion of racial or ethnic alterity seems to be less subversive, as is the eclectic use of artistic styles celebrating cultural *mestizaje* and syncretism. 'Se [proclaman] transvanguardistas y posmodernos por cuanto la posmodernidad implicaba lo mestizo, lo exótico y la alteridad. . . . Se [pronuncian] en favor de . . . su derecho de liberarse de prejuicios para potenciar toda suerte de mestizajes, sincretismos y eclecticismos (entre concepciones estéticas distintas, entre el mito y la magia, entre lo culto cristiano y el yoruba).'*[99]

Until now, critics have abstained from addressing this and deliberately or not contribute to the persistence of a conspiracy of silence against the expression of homosexual identity and eroticism in Cuban art. Yet, the postmodern aesthetic of recent Cuban art allows for homotextuality to surface again. This occurs in ways that are distinct from the Gay Liberation-inspired art of contemporary Mexico or Brazil. An implicit homotextual dimension is present, as such, in the performances of Manuel Mendive Hoyo (b. 1944). However, one searches in vain for recognizable gay imagery, symbolism or personalities, as Mendive draws heavily upon Cuba's African-American heritage. Sexual identity, in this context, is not divided into homosexuality versus heterosexuality, nor does he imply the adoption of a certain, recognizable body language or vestimentary code for homosexual women or men. Mendive's 'inclusion' of sexual variety is more fluid and reflects an Afro-American construction of sexual identity, perceptible in other parts of the Caribbean and Brazil as well.

Participating in the world of *Santería*, Mendive adopted its visual and symbolic language in his art, cognizant of its relative tolerance for gender deviation, while critical towards a 'Western'-style construction of 'gay identity'. *Santero* festivals indeed draw

*'They [declare themselves] as transavantgardist and postmodern in so far as postmodernity implies the *mestizo*, the exotic, alterity. . . . They [present themselves] in favour of . . . their right to liberate themselves from prejudices in order to pave the road to all kinds of *mestizaje*, syncretism and eclecticism (between distinct aesthetic concepts, between myth and magic, between Christian cult and Yoruba).'

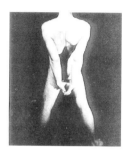

large groups of homosexuals, which is explained by the plasticity of Yoruba ritual itself. The *orixá*'s or spirit's gender is not fixed and *santero* initiates, commonly known as *iyabós* or 'brides', can be either women or men. Not all African religious organizations embrace sexual diversity, however. The cult of *Abakuá*, for one, is not only homophobic but sexist as well.[100]

The inarticulate yet embracing nature of *Santería* sexual politics is transposed to Mendive's work, both in his graphic work and paintings, and in his adoption, in a more recent period, of Performance and Body Art. Quotation is not literal, however, as Mendive creates a more vivid mythology, a *mitogénesis viva*, and trespasses cultural localism. Implicitly, such includes a sexual message also, carried out most prominently in the joint enactment of music, dance, body painting, pantomime, ritual and spectacle. The performances, while bringing to life the artist's self-styled Utopia, are *topoi* of alternative sexualities as much as of cultural, ethnic and religious diversity. Homosexual eros, while remaining implicit and unspoken of, is pervasive nevertheless in Mendive's comprehensive human cosmology.[101]

There are signs in Cuba also of artists adopting a more straightforward, assertively 'gay' aesthetic. Among them are Reynold Campbell, Eduardo Hernández, Adrián Morales and Abigail González – young artists who, for the first time since Cabrera Moreno and Martínez, are producing images that are clearly inscribed within a gay *imaginaire*. Homotextuality is either homoerotic, as in the works of the painter Reynold Campbell (b. 1971) and the photographer Eduardo Hernández (b. 1966), or it is subjected to a process of 'camp', as in paintings by Adrián Morales (b. 1965). Different strategies are used, partially reflecting the artists' divergent subjectivities, of course, but there is quite a striking difference between the almost carnivalesque codification in Morales's work (see, for example, *La revoleón*, 1988) and the easy-to-grasp homoerotic dimension of photographs of male nudity by Hernández (*Homo ludens*, 1994).

Legitimacy is attributed to the lesbian imagery of 'neo-erotic' studio photographs by Abigail González (b. 1964). In *Untitled* (1994), the artist actually quotes from pornographic canons, yet claims a lesbian gaze to what was staged initially as arousing imagery for men. A naked woman, lying on a bed, admires herself in a mirror held up by another naked woman. There is a reference to Edouard Manet's *Olympia*, yet the black maid is now replaced by a white woman, the flowers by a mirror and the look towards the (male?) viewer by one into a reflecting mirror. The mirror's image is a subversive quotation of *L'origine du monde* by Gustave Courbet.

Other works, such as an untitled one from the series *Ojos desnudos* (1998), show women in the intimacy of their bedroom or bathroom. These images are equally defined by an outspoken lesbian gaze, rather than a traditional, male one. They reappropriate the subject of the lesbian body, which for too long has remained a masculine prerogative.

Perhaps most significant is the work by René Peña (b. 1957), who, while not gay himself, produces images that address the social and cultural construction of sexual identity and gender. These surface indirectly only in his series *Ritos I* (1992) and *Ritos II* (1994–5), explorations of Yoruba religion, really, that are nurtured by a psychoanalytic understanding of phallic eroticism. But a work like *Don algodón* (1993) is unmistakably inscribed within a visual trope of sexual diversity. It shows a man with a muscular torso and feminine make-up, enacting imagery of 'gender-fucking' as part of an anti-*machismo* critique. A series of prints titled *El cocinero, el ladrón, su mujer y su amante* (after Peter Greenaway's film) also discloses the gap between what Cubans pretend to be to the outside world and what they do or are within the intimacy of their homes. An untitled work (1998), finally, is inscribed within the same, ironic narrative and shows the artist with heavily painted lips and a spoon in front of his right eye. The partial vision, caused by the spoon, is a metaphor almost of the double standard, allowing for sexual encounters among men as long as they do not violate the rules of gender bipolarity.[102]

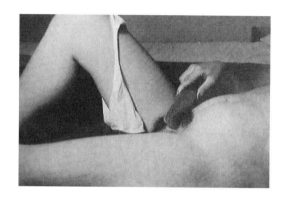

Figure 60 Abigail González, *Sin título*
(from series *Ojos desnudos*) (1998),
black-and-white print, 10 × 15 cm,
courtesy of Fundación
Ludwig, Havana.

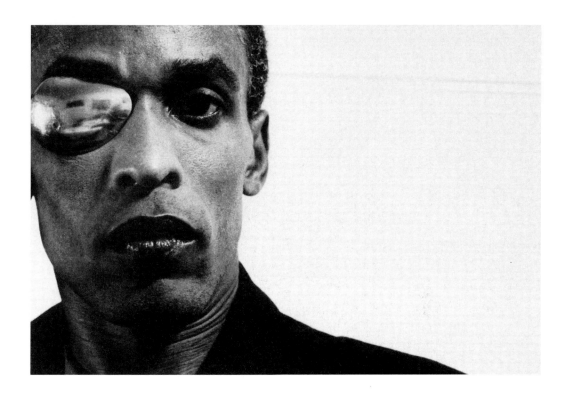

Figure 61 René Peña, *Untitled* (1998), black-and-white print, 30 × 40 cm, courtesy of Galerie Geukens and De Vil, Knokke, Belgium.

Conclusion

The outlook for homotextuality in contemporary Cuban art is typical of developments in Puerto Rico and, *a fortiori*, in Mexico and Brazil. The chronological overlapping of 'gay' art, reflecting the social construction of modern homosexual identity, and its 'queer' deconstructions within the perspective of postmodern and postcolonial criticism can be perceived in the four countries discussed in this book.

Such is due, as we saw, to the relatively late start of the Gay Liberation movement, styled after North America and Europe – approximately ten years later. By the time that gay identity was embraced by homosexual men and women in Latin America both as a model of personal identity and as a weapon for political emancipation, voices arose that questioned the epistemological and discursive premisses on which gay identity was rooted.

The time had come for eclecticism and 'deconstruction', itself nourished in part by postcolonial criticism. The dissemination of Gay Lib was not unequivocally welcomed, partly because it was culturally imperialist, not always intentionally, but in fact. It proved inadequate in its reflection of white, middle-class, male values. It provided no real answers to people of different skin colour or ethnicity, to the poor, or to the transgender people, who were facing a rising popularity of the *macho* clone.

Rooted in the distinct, local realities of subcultural bisexual and homosexual life, the 'gay' art of Mexico, Brazil, Puerto Rico and even Cuba soon evolved to become its very own deconstruction or, better, ironization and readaptation. Artists developed an alternative homotextuality.

This new trope of homosexual self-expression is both advanced and conservative, carrying within itself many of the ambiguities characterizing today's societies in Latin America. It is accommodating to the reality of fluid sexual boundaries, of diverse homosexual subcultures, simultaneously existing and in permanent interaction with one another.

At the same time, the new 'queer aesthetic' remains a mirror image of persistently hierarchical sexual role models, most clearly visible in the omnipresent effeminate *loca*, *bicha* or *mariposa*. Coexisting and interacting with the more egalitarian 'gay' model, the traditional bipolarity of 'active' versus 'passive' sex partners, each superficially demarcated by 'male' versus 'female' gender, whether homosexual or heterosexual, testifies to the persistent reality of widespread homophobia.

Representational tropes of homotextuality, at once repressive and enlightened, visualize an inherently fragmented Latin American *ambiente*. A factually 'postmodern' dynamic directs visual expression towards a paradigm of *bricolage* while negotiating between internationalism and 'local speech' (Geertz), between multiculturalism and an agenda of social and political emancipation. Rooted, in this context also, in the postcolonial deconstruction of cultural identity, it remains influenced at the same time by local patterns of inequity, specifically between men and women, between 'heterosexuals' and 'homosexuals'.

This evidently explains why, despite an apparently detached and ironic positioning, disclosure of one's sexual identity remains a hard issue for visual artists in Latin America today. It actually contributes to some of the flaws of this very book, since not every artist discussed in this book will feel comfortable about being included here, even when I do not explain the production of homotextual imagery as inherently reflecting sexual, i.e. homosexual or lesbian identity. The very fear of association has actually withheld some artists from cooperating with me.

Similar judgements, justified by circumstance or not, have moved many to leave their home country and seek sexual freedom abroad. Exile, deliberate or, in some cases, forced upon them by homophobic policies or regimes, has been embarked upon disproportionately frequently, compared to heterosexuals. It has contributed also to the multicultural outlook of gay and lesbian communities in Europe and especially North America today. These patterns of migration have provoked new cultural debates that, as I will describe in the next chapter, are carried also in the widely varied artistic output of gay and lesbian artists of Latin American descent.

Notes

1 See C. Blas Galindo, 'Cultura artística y homosexualidad', in *Ex profeso* (Mexico, 1992), pp. 18–19.
2 See I. Lumsden, *Homosexuality, Society and the State in Mexico* (Toronto and Mexico City, 1991), and C. L. Taylor, '*El ambiente*: male homosexual social life in Mexico City', Ph.D. thesis, University of California, Berkeley, 1978 (esp. ch. 6).
3 *Tierra Adentro*, 16 (December 1978), p. 13.
4 C. Blas Galindo, *Enrique Guzmán: transformador y víctima de su tiempo* (Mexico, 1992), p. 25. Also, see *Enrique Guzmán (1952–1986): precursor de su tiempo* (Mexico, 1995).
5 On Jaso, see H. Covantes, *La pintura mexicana de la ingenuidad* (Mexico, 1984), pp. 91–5.
6 See F. Gamboa, quoted in the catalogue *Cortázar: postmodernidad y Romanticismo* (Mexico, 1995), p. 12.
7 G. Estrada, in *Cortázar*, p. 9.
8 H. Perea, in *Cortázar*, p. 15.
9 S. Navarrete, 'Roberto Cortázar', *CURARE*, 6 (April–June 1995), p. 7.
10 R. Cortázar, in an interview by Marcela Garcia, *El Norte*, 1986, quoted in *Cortázar*, p. 14.
11 G. Mosquera, 'Two Mexican photographers', *Atlántica*, 15 (Winter 1996), p. 182.
12 *Ibid.*, p. 183.
13 Thanks to Juan Molina for letting me quote from his as yet unpublished paper 'Como un otro sin nombre. Mujer y violencia en la obra de Mario Patiño', n.p.
14 Rare characters in Covarrubias's oeuvre may be seen as homosexual, yet seem to be attached to the world of dance, revue theatre and show business exclusively. Their representation is stereotypical also: effeminacy, frivolity, flamboyance.
15 F. Pellizzi, 'On the border', in *Julio Galán* (New York, 1989), n.p.

16 See, on this sculpture, E. J. Sulllivan, 'Sacred and profane. The art of Julio Galán', *Arts Magazine*, (Summer 1990), p. 55.

17 J. Poot, in M. Cervantes and B. MacKenzie (eds), *Julio Galán: exposición retrospectiva* (Monterrey and Mexico, 1993), p. 55.

18 *Ibid.*, p. 57.

19 E. Heartley, in Cervantes and MacKenzie, *Julio Galán: exposición retrospectiva*, p. 44.

20 *Ibid.*, p. 43.

21 C. E. Damian, 'Julio Galán', *Latin American Art*, 6, 1 (1994), p. 58.

22 J. M. Springer, 'Julio Galán. Nostalgia de lo inalcanzable', *Art Nexus*, 59 (July–September 1994), p. 51.

23 C. Stellweg, in *Uncommon Ground: 23 Latin American Artists* (New York, 1992), p. 17.

24 M. Kozloff, 'Memories of the future', *Artforum* (October 1991), p. 108. Also, see L.S. Sims, 'Julio Galán', in *Nuevos momentos en el arte mexicano [New Moments in Mexican Art]*, p. 50.

25 Also, see the text by the artist in *Arturo Elizondo. Obra reciente* (Mexico, 1995).

26 C. Merewether, 'Forces of history/symbols of desire', in *Nuevos momentos*, p. 29.

27 L.C. Emerich, 'Nahum B. Zenil – An den Grenzen der Vernunft', in *Bilder und Visionen*, p. 154 (pp. 154–69).

28 O. Debroise, 'Nahum B. Zenil', in *Nuevos momentos*, p. 83.

29 E. J. Sullivan, in *Nahum B. Zenil: Witness to the Self/Testigo del ser* (San Francisco, 1996), p. 9.

30 *Ibid.*, p. 15.

31 Nahum B. Zenil in an interview of 1995, reprinted in *Nahum B. Zenil: Witness to the Self*, pp. 25–31.

32 O. Debroise, in *Javier de la Garza* (New York and Mexico City, 1992/3), (n.p.)(p. 8).

33 C. Merewether, 'Popular culture and the imaginary', in *Nuevos momentos*, pp. 95–6.

34 F. del Paso, 'Javier de la Garza', in *Nuevos momentos*, p. 107.

35 Before that date, more modest cultural initiatives were taken from 1982 onwards that gradually developed towards the yearly Semana Cultural Gay.

36 See a review by O. Debroise, 'No soy crítico (NSC)', *CURARE*, 6 (April–June 1995), pp. 14–15.

37 See R. Gallo's introductory text in *Tendencies: New Art from Mexico City* (San Francisco, 1995).

38 C. Smyth, *Damn Fine Art by Lesbian Artists* (New York and London, 1996), p. 122.

39 J. N. Green, 'Beyond carnival: homosexuality in twentieth-century Brazil', Ph.D. diss., UCLA, Los Angeles, pp. 315–19.

40 See *Hélio Oiticica: Grupo Frente 1955–1956/Metaesquemas 1957–1958* (Rio de Janeiro, 1996).

41 Originally, 'parangolé' is Brazilian slang, meaning an animated situation, sudden confusion or agitation between people. Oiticica transmitted the original meaning to the capes, used during the turbulent performances enacted by people wearing these capes.

42 Oiticica paraphrased from quotation in G. Brett, 'Hélio Oiticica: rêverie and revolt', *Art in America* (January 1989), p. 119.

43 Brett, 'Héilo Oiticia', p. 114. Paraphrase from H. Oiticica, 'Anotações sobre o parangolé', in L. Figueiredo *et al.* (eds), *Aspiro ao grande labirinto* (Rio de Janeiro, 1986), p. 71.

44 F. Morais, quoted in Brett, 'Hélio Oiticica', p. 115.

45 G. Brett, 'The experimental exercise of liberty', in *Hélio Oiticica* (Rotterdam, 1992), p. 233. Also, see 'Fait sur le corps: le *parangolé* de Hélio Oiticica', *Les Cahiers du Musée National d'Art Moderne*, 51 (Spring 1995), p. 43. João Trevisan is more decisive about Oiticica's 'desire for the bandits of the slums', yet his research is predominantly guided by a rather militant Gay Liberationist rhetoric. See *Perverts in Paradise* (London, 1986), p. 118.

46 'Discovery of hermaphrodipotesis', 1969. See Brett, 'The experimental exercise', pp. 234, 238.

47 Oiticica also addressed issues of gender transgression in a film, titled *Agripina e Roma Manhattan* (1972), as well as in a slide series, titled *Neyrótika, Não Narração* (1973). He played a role also in a documentary, *One Night on Gay Street*, directed by Andreas Valentin, New York, 1975.

48 Without elaborating on this, I gladly refer to C. Basualdo, 'Quelques annotations supplémentaires sur le Parangolé', in *L'art au corps* (Marseille, 1996), pp. 257–73.

49 E. MacRae, *A construição da igualdade. Identidade sexual e política no Brasil da 'Abertura'* (Campinas, 1990), *passim*.

50 Trevisan, *Perverts in Paradise*, pp. 119ff., and Green, 'Beyond carnival', pp. 320ff.

51 *Borboleta* is the Portuguese equivalent of the Spanish derogative term *mariposa*, and is used by some gay men in Brazil also. By doing so, they make the word into one of their own and turn its pejorative connotation around. See W. R. Dynes, 'Portugayese', in S.O. Murray (ed.), *Male Homosexuality in Central and South America* (New York, 1987), p. 185.

52 See reproduction in W. Leyland (ed.), *Now the Volcano* (San Francisco, 1979). I have not been able to locate or fully identify this work.

53 Personal communication by the artist, 17 November 1997.

54 Personal communication, 10 November 1997. Also, see M. Pacheco Fiorillo, 'Subversão, mas sorrateira', *Istoé*, 279 (28 April 1982), p. 4.

55 The show took place at the city's Museu de Arte Contemporâneo in 1993.

56 See A. Araújo, 'Obra recente de Edilson Viriato. O teorema do final de milênio', in *Edilson Viriato: VI Bienal de Havana, Cuba. Brasil* (n.l., n.d.), n.p., and *Edilson Viriato* (Curitiba, n.d.).

57 No monography on Sá is available. On Mario Cravo Neto, see P. Weiermair, *Mario Cravo Neto*, (Zürich, n.d.).

58 See Amarante, *As bienais de São Paulo, passim*.

59 M. Pedrosa, 'El arte de la vida: una nueva generación/The art of life: a new generation', *Poliester*, 2, 8 (Spring 1994), p. 17.

60 The use of first names is very current in Brazil. Even presidents are often referred to by their first name: Getulio, Jucelino, Fernando, Itamar, Fernando Enrique . . .

61 A. Pedrosa, in *Leonilson: São tantas as verdades/So many are the truths* (sic) (São Paulo, 1996), p. 22. Also, see A. Tager, 'AIDS abstracted', *Poliester*, 3, 9 (Summer 1994), p. 15: '[The] paintings are more poetic than narrative. He created networks of hieroglyphics and symbols, which he wove into elusive and allusive allegories.'

62 L. Lagnado, in *Leonilson*, p. 29.

63 Pedrosa, in *Leonilson*, p. 22.

64 The use of the word 'abertura' is not coincidental. In Brazil, a political *Abertura* took place from the late 1970s onwards, after a military regime had been installed in 1964. A political gay movement also grew as a result of the more relaxing political climate, yet it was modest in comparison to the high visibility and freedom in cities such as Los Angeles, New York, London, Paris, Munich or Amsterdam, all places visited by Leonilson between 1981 and 1991. See MacRae, *A construição da igualdade*.

65 Leonilson, interview by L. Lagnado, 30 October 1992, published in *Leonilson*, pp. 95–6.

66 More precisely, to Duchamp's infamous *Fontaine*, 1917, first exhibited at a show of the Society for Independent Artists in New York. His then used pseudonym was R. Mutt (read: Aar-moot, like the German word *Armut*, poverty).

67 Interview by L. Lagnado, 27 November 1992, published in *Leonilson*, pp. 117–18.

68 *Ibid.*

69 Lagnado, in *Leonilson*, p. 54.

70 *Ibid.*, p. 64.

71 *Ibid.*, p. 71.

72 I. Mesquita, in *Leonilson*, p. 195.

73 On Roche, see E. Garcia Gutiérrez and M. Bonesteel, *Arnaldo Roche Rabell: eventos, milagros y visiones* (San Juan, 1986), and E. Garcia Gutiérrez, 'Arnaldo Roche. Agonista: la lucha por la identidad', *Revista Plástica* (September 1987), pp. 19–28.

74 See M. Bonesteel, in *Arnaldo Roche Rabell: eventos, milagros y visiones*, p. 13.

75 E. Garcia Gutiérrez, in Sullivan, *Latin American Art*, p. 133.

76 H. Sturges, *New Art from Puerto Rico* (Springfield, MA, 1990), p. 70. Also, see R. Pau-Llosa, 'The imagination as dialogue in the painting of Arnaldo Roche', in *Arnaldo Roche Rabell* (St Louis, MO, 1988), p. 2.

77 M. de Mater O'Neill, in *Carlos Collazo, 1956–1990: exposición homenaje* (San Juan, 1994), pp. 23–6.

78 M. Alvarez Lezama, 'Una mescla de poesia, pasión y realidad virtual', *El San Juan Star*, 28 September 1997, p. 16.

79 Artist's statement, 15 July 1998.

80 See the text on Millán in *The Decade Show* (New York, 1990), pp. 42–3.

81 See quote in *Néstor Millán: en otros cuerpos* (San Juan, 1996), n.p. Also, see the works exhibited at the Museo de Arte e Historia de San Juan in 1993 (*Néstor Millán: tempus fugit*, text by E. Garcia Gutiérrez).

82 N. Millán, in L. Dodson, 'New generation photography', *Photographos Magazine*, 48 (April 1996), n.p.

83 Thus Millán in 'Universos personales', *Extra Cámara Magazine* (Summer 1996), n.p.

84 C. Biasiny-Rivera, 'American voices: Puerto Rican photography in the U.S.', *Fototest* (1994), p. 42.

85 Millán, quoted in R. Weiss, 'Néstor Millán', in *Cambio de foco* (Bogotá, 1992/3), p. 58.

86 J. L. Navarrete, *Breaking the Margins* (Caracas, 1993/4), p. 136.

87 M. Alvarez Lezama, 'Millán's art conveys beauty, tragedy', *San Juan Star*, 18 March 1993, n.p; E. Garcia Gutiérrez, 'Néstor Millán: el espectador como intérprete', *El Nuevo Día*, 19 May 1996, pp. 10–13; and M. Alvarez Lezama, 'Nude male expressiveness', *San Juan Star*, 19 May 1996, p. 16.

88 J. Fernández, in *Víctor Vázquez: la casa de las almas (instalación media mixta)* (Hato Rey, 1998), n.p. Also, see E. García Gutiérrez, 'Víctor Vázquez, testigo de la muerte', *El Nuevo Día*, 21 July 1991.

89 F. Castro, in *Víctor Vázquez: el cuerpo y el ave* (San Juan, 1996), p. 11.

90 T. Lopez, *Paisajes en tiempos de ansiedad. La obra de Maria de Mater O'Neill* (San Juan, 1991), p. 3. Personal communication by de Mater O'Neill, 3 June 1998.

91 See I. Romero-Cesareo, 'Art, selfportrait and the body', *Callaloo*, 17, 3 (1994).

92 Lopez, *Paisajes en tiempos*, p. 3. Also, see *Autorretrato* (joint exhibition by Collazo and de Mater O'Neill) (San Juan, n.d.).

93 Personal communication by de Mater O'Neill, 3 June 1998.

94 *Un retrato de Carlos Collazo*, dir. by Sonia Fritz, colour, 15 min., video, San Juan, 1994.

95 See Lumsden, *Machos, Maricones and Gays*, pp. 126–7.

96 Thus in October 1997, when a gay club, El Perriquitón, was raided shortly after international patrons Jean-Paul Gaultier and Pedro Almodovar had left the site. Recently, new initiatives to 'clean' the streets of prostitution and homosexuality seem to push gay men and women further underground again.

97 See Leirner, *Sexual Politics in Cuba*, pp. 43–52, 117–49, and Lumsden, *Machos, passim*. Today, the *sidatoria* have become more open again.

98 The term was coined by Luis Camnitzer (*New Art from Cuba*, Austin, TX, 1996) as a means of describing the innovative trends of Cuban art in the 1980s and 1990s. He too notices the paucity of so-called 'gay art'.

99 M.L. Borràs, in *CubaSigloXX*, p. 37. Also, see *The Nearest Edge of the World: Art and Cuba Now* (Brookline, MA, 1990), as well as various critical texts by G. Mosquera.

100 See Lumsden, *Machos*, pp. 47–8.

101 See E. Hernández, 'Cuadros móviles, filosofía 'mala rabia', *Cartelera*, 252 (25 to 31 December 1986), p. 3. Also, see *Manuel Mendive* (Kyoto, n.d.).

102 See E. Hernández, 'De donde se habla de René Peña, el cocinero, el ladrón, su mujer, su amante y el Quijote', *Atlántica*, 15 (Winter 1996), pp. 58–62.

CHAPTER SIX

Queer visions of Latino/a exile

Introduction

A joke circulates that numerous young artists of Latin American descent came to the USA 'in order to graduate'. While referring literally to getting their degrees at colleges or universities, the phrase is understood by many also as code for 'coming-out' as lesbian or gay. Compared to the oppressive sexual climate of their home countries, North America or Europe are seen as places of both sexual experimentation and psychological growth.[1]

The liberating effect of exile is easily overshadowed, however, by an awareness concerning the segregated structure of gay and lesbian life in North America and by solidarity with gays and lesbians of other ethnic minorities, equally kept adrift from a white-centred middle-class gay and lesbian community. A cross-fertilization thus took place between cultural expression of ethnic identity on the one hand, and of sexual and gender identity on the other, often prompting negotiation between both.

Many socially and economically disadvantaged, others socio-economically privileged and well-off, Latino/a gay and lesbian artists were and are facing the challenge of survival in communities that carry within them numerous threats. The relatively high prevalence of HIV and AIDS is among its most dramatic ones, alongside homophobia (from within, but not exclusively) and racism (from outside, but not exclusively). The survey in this chapter reflects this and addresses how disease and death, loss and uncertainty, heterosexism, gay-bashing, Eurocentrism and racist attitudes cloud the pink horizons of Latino/a gay and lesbian people and communities.

Yet, it is not all misery and pain that nurtures their artistic creativity and many works are celebrations, exuberant or intimate, quiet or loud, of beauty, sensuality, self-realization and sex. Some artists claim the beauty of Latino people, while others consciously deconstruct recurrent narratives of its presumably 'exotic appeal', yet they share a visual language that is positive and redeeming beyond the confines of socio-anthropological documentary.

Several artists trespass – or even abstain from – the province of gay or lesbian expression, partly in order to avoid the trap of pigeonholing and of media and commercial marginality. Their refusal to be labelled as a 'gay' or 'lesbian' artists often collides with scepticism towards any qualification of their work as 'Latino' or 'Latina'. Instead, they experiment with visual media and language, materials and techniques, or focus on themes of general politics, ecology, postmodern consciousness.

In this chapter, I will focus on art by gay and lesbian artists of Mexican, Cuban, Puerto Rican and Brazilian descent, whether born in or having emigrated to Europe or North America, who consider the visual expression of homotextuality as part of their artistic message. Obviously, the picture remains selective and I do not claim to have covered all artists fitting the category. Nor is it the story of all Latino/a gay and lesbian artists in exile, of course, but it may well set the frame for additional study.

New frontiers of queer Aztlán

If profound and well-documented studies exist about 'Chicano' art, then it must be said at once that few have paid attention to the issue of bisexual and homosexual identity in art production by men and women of Mexican descent. Women's art has received much attention, as can be concluded from Shifra Goldman and Tomás Ybarra-Frausto's *Arte Chicano* bibliography (Berkeley, 1985) as from various studies on Chicano women artists, published in recent years.[2] Lesbian, gay and transgender identity or imagination remains buried, however, apart from a handful of curatorial and documentary initiatives.[3]

The omission may be explained, partly, by the male-centred and, at times, sexist character of the Chicano movement, already oblivious often to the contribution of women artists. Neither sexism nor heterosexism are male prerogatives, however, and animosity towards alternative sexualities is present also amidst the Chicano community's female population. *Machismo* and *Marianismo*[4] being the binary code that regulates traditional Mexican and Chicano society, this clearly does not embrace potentially subversive gender variety, especially not, as is the case for Chicano culture, when cultural identity is at stake.

Among the first in Los Angeles to react against the overwhelming heterosexism and even downright homophobia of parts of Chicano society was the group ASCO. Their critique remained implicit, however. Never did any of the group's statements contain an explicit reproach of homophobia, nor did any of its members ever proclaim themselves to be gay. It was indirectly and in a 'carnivalesque' way only that Harry Gamboa, Jr., Gronk, Willie Herrón, or Patssi Valdez included coded messages about sexual identity in their improvisational performance style.

The word ASCO was adopted in 1973, two years after the group first gathered in 1971. It means 'nausea' and reflected the group members' disgust at Chicano marginality, as much as the criticism of 'politically correct' Chicano intellectuals, who took offence at the group's aesthetic language, their use of graffiti, their guerrilla theatre.[5] More artists joined the group later on, including, among others, Teddy Sandoval, Mundo Meza and Cyclona, a drag queen whose real name is Robert Lagorretta.

ASCO calls for attention in this book, largely as an exponent of Performance Art, whereby the latter is described as 'a type of "theatre" that depends for communication on the use of visual objects (including the body of the performer) used in certain configurations rather than being based on a written text with a plot which is orally performed'.[6] Performance was the group's privileged medium of expression from its early beginnings, when East Los Angeles witnessed great social upheaval. There were the 'walk out' and 'blow out' actions of high school students, who challenged the inferiority of segregated Chicano schools. The journalist Rubén Salazar was killed on 29 August 1970 when violence broke out during a demonstration against the war in Vietnam.

Most of the members of ASCO attended high school during these turbulent times, yet the first public art actions of Gronk, Valdez, Meza and Cyclona were about gender diffusion more than about the problems faced by the Chicano community of East LA. The men among them would dress in drag, long, velvet robes layered with satin, silk and lace, then walk arm in arm across the busy sidewalks of Whittier Boulevard. In *Cockroaches Have No Friends*, a one-act play produced by Gronk, Cyclona grabbed another actor's imaginary genitalia, made of a water-filled balloon and two eggs. He smacked the eggs to the floor, shocking an audience of non-suspecting families with children. The show thereupon was cut short by the police.

A first major performance took place in 1971, again right in the public eye, on the corner of Eastern Avenue and Whittier. Herrón's face was grimed as a *calavera*-like Christ, while he was wearing a white robe with a brightly coloured *sagrada corazón*. Gronk personified Pontius Pilate (also known as Popcorn). 'He wore a green bowler hat, flaunted an excessively large beige fur purse, and carried a bag of unbuttered popcorn.'[7] Gamboa was a zombie-like altar boy, wearing an animal skull headpiece 'to ward off unsolicited communion'.[8] Herrón carried a huge cross, covered with gold spray-painted squiggles, and performed the Catholic ritual of the Stations of the Cross.

Eventually, the cross was erected in front of the US Marine Recruiting Station as a sign of protest against the war.

The 'camp' stylistics of ASCO gave rise to controversy, along with the group's publication *Regeneración*. Rumours about unorthodox religious sects surfaced in East LA, triggering speculation about the involvement of Gronk *cum suis*. Politically correct Chicanos took offence at the latter's visual imagery, saying that it left them with a feeling of *asco*, of nausea. The blasphemous effect of the grotesque was continued, moreover, when the group turned Muralism into a life show. Muralism, by then, had gained respectability as a serious means of cultural expression, yet it was challenged by the new performance of the group. Valdez was dressed as a Virgin of Guadelupe in a black *crêpe* gown, while wearing an aluminium *calavera* on the back of her head. Gronk figured as a Christmas tree, 'embellished with three inverted lime-green chiffon dresses, red glass bulbs and a five-point acrylic star painted on his face'. The happening was completed by Herrón, who figured as a 'Walking Mural', tired of its environment and walking away.

Provocative clothing remained a trademark of ASCO. Virtually all members subscribed to the fashion of platform shoes, sometimes one foot high. Herrón was arrested 'for skipping in his hand-painted monster platform shoes', and Gronk, in fact, was attacked by an irate *cholo* who did not appreciate his turquoise and black footwear – read: who could not handle the gender-defying message of contemporary fashion. To an extent, ASCO's costume politics reflected the unisex fashion of its time. It was also significant as part of a Chicano politics of appearance, if an admittedly controversial one that went against the grain of the community's strict gender roles. Its transgressive character also conflicted with religious sensibilities, turning the proto-'queer' performances of ASCO into a critique of hypocritical Catholic sexual politics.

Homosexuality briefly moved to the forefront even as some ASCO artists united into the so-called Butch Gardens School of Art. In 1979, for example, the group presented *La historia de Frida Kahlo*, in which Gronk performed a musical number and danced with Teddy Sandoval, dressed in high heels and a strapless gown. An accompanying flyer read: 'Art only exists beyond the confines of accepted behavior'. It was a call, if subtle and indirect, for coming out as gay men and contributing to Gay Liberation this way.[9]

Explicit recognition of homotextuality was warded off soon, however, by Gronk (b. 1954). He dropped the topic almost completely as he moved into the mainstream of the Los Angeles art scene. 'I am what I do', he says, 'I am my art' – which is a legitimate reaction against misguided and sensationalizing speculation on his sexual identity.[10] Gronk now likes to profile himself as an 'archaeologist', tracing the despair, anxiety and creativity of the Angelino experience, painting the city's danger, its mystery, decadence and pain. His works have moved away from the Performance Art of ASCO and are portrayals of the both glamorous and sordid milieu of LA nightlife, no longer defined predominantly by social life in the Chicano community.

He remains critical, however, towards an art community that now welcomes the 'token' Latino artist, as much as he strives to pass beyond an all too predictable 'Chicano' aesthetic.[11] Meanwhile, speculation abounds as to the real identity of La Tormenta, a recurrent character in Gronk's work. Is she the artist's *alter ego*? A reminiscence of the ASCO-era play with drag? And may one not recognize a particularly gay or, at least, 'camp' creativity in *Josephine Boneapart protecting the rear guard* (1987)? The name 'Boneapart', while clearly referring to the historic Josephine Bonaparte, surely suggests a game with words – 'leg bones apart' – and emphasizes availability. The 'rear guard' is a phallic structure, covered with a condom, reminding the viewer of a reading lamp with a semi-transparent shade.

The world of transient sex in cheap hotels is captured in works that simultaneously seem to refer covertly to anonymous sexual encounters, whether gay or straight. The names of women, as in *Bonita in pink* (1987), may be those of drag queens and transvestites, not unlikely in and around the real-life hotels in rundown areas of Los Angeles. Hotel Senator, for example, is a real downtown hotel, and a *spiritus locus*, says Max Benavidez, of sordid romance, of sleaze. Yet, whereas these sites are locations on the edge of LA's Barrio, they are simultaneously turned into philosophical commentaries upon the destitution and solitude of the postmodern urban dweller: 'Gronk has melted media, form and content into a searing statement on the moral perversity of both inflicted and self-imposed estrangement', observes Benavidez, who captures well how the local colour of Chicano urban geography is turned into metaphor by the artist himself.[12]

The eclipse of 'gay visibility' in Gronk's work parallels an eclipse of ethnic identity, at least on the level of predictable stereotypes. This is revealing of the artist's strategy of resistance, of his claim to authenticity and personal integrity amidst ongoing, simplifying discourses that would present him not only as a token Chicano artist, but also as a prototypical 'militant gay' artist. It is his ASCO heritage, perhaps, that explains best why Gronk took so clear a stance against biographical readings of his work.

Some Chicano artists apparently share Gronk's ambiguous policy, while others see no harm in publicly acknowledging their sexual identity. At least not in the end. The LA-born artist Teddy Sandoval (1949–95) originally did so rather covertly only by participating in the Mail Art movement. To him and many others, it was a safe outlet for the expression of gay concern or sensibility. Biron, a photographer and one-time contributor to Mail Art, also owns a coloured xerox Valentine message sent by Sandoval and showing the artist in full drag.[13]

He temporarily joined the ASCO group and gradually developed an aesthetic that covered matters of 'life, death, sex, chance, pride, and decadence all woven together with the forces of Nature as the thread that ties these juxtaposed symbols together'.[14]

His visual language increasingly reflected Los Angeles's multicultural society and incorporated numerous references to a Chicano gay subculture along the way. Such is reflected, for example, in the painting *Macho Mayan* (1993) (Plate 16). Mexican heritage is visualized by the figure's mask, loosely referring to the Pre-Columbian Mexican pantheon. In fact, the dark spots on his face as well as his flattened nose refer loosely to the Mayan deity Xaman Ek, God of the North Star and an *ad hoc* symbol, perhaps, for the northern territory of Aztlán. The serpent above, however, may well signify Kukuklan or his later Aztec counterpart, Quetzalcoatl.[15] A 'carnivalization' of semantic content takes place, however, as the presumed deity is depicted, rather campily, as a *macho* body builder exposing his biceps on Venice Beach.

Miguel Angel Reyes (b. 1964), was born in Colima, Mexico, and arrived in the United States at age eleven. He is active today as a commercial illustrator and an artist, focusing on the male model with great insistence. He illustrated a book of poetry, *Moribundo* by Michael Gregg Michaud, and painted a handful of murals at different sites in Los Angeles. One, called *Amistades* (1995), portrays the artist's personal friends mostly, interspersed with roses, tulips, lilies, bamboo and reeds. An earlier mural, titled *Mar eterno* (1992), depicted gay and non-gay communities in their joint battle against AIDS. It shows five figures in a pool. The central figure, a person with AIDS, is held by his partner, while a heterosexual couple shows concern.[16]

Both dance and 1970s and 1980s fashion photography are major sources of inspiration for Reyes, who aims at capturing the soul, rather than the physical resemblance only of the people portrayed. His models are often clubgoers, dancers and models, and one can clearly grasp the sensuality of Los Angeles's Chicano *ambiente*. Some men look masculine, while others represent the transgender spectrum of Latino gay life. All are given equal documentary value, yet psychological portrayal is tangible only in some. Others look like depersonalized representations of clublife typology.

Gradually, Reyes focused more on men whose appearance is less refined, less delicate. The tough, streetwise *cholo*, while often reiterating Chicano intolerance towards out and visible homosexuals, obviously has become an icon of gay imagination also for the artist himself. *69* (1995) is one such portrayal that captures the sexiness and gay appeal of the non-gay-identified, yet potentially bisexual *cholo*. It ironically comments upon the ongoing problem of homophobia within the Chicano community, and this despite educational efforts and growing Latino gay assertiveness. The objectification, through painting, of a sex object, now close and intimate, then again out of reach, is a possible strategy of contestation, adopted by Reyes to emphasize both solidarity and schism within the Latino community. It is significant, then, that Reyes's portrayals of real-life friends veer somewhere between the butch masculinity of his *cholo* dreams, and the overly mannered, glamourized and often transgender-identified patrons of clubs like Circus or Arena.

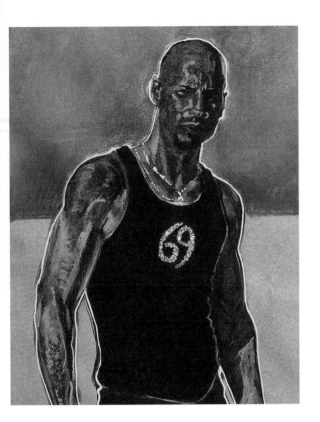

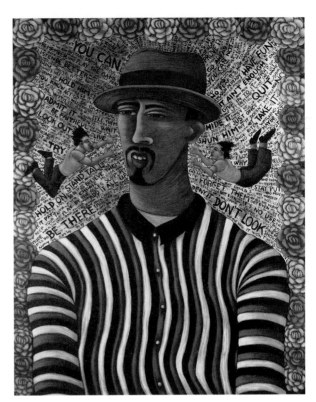

Figure 62 *(left)* Miguel Angel Reyes, *69* (1995), pastel on paper, 30.5 × 50.5 cm, courtesy of the artist.

Figure 63 *(right)* Tony de Carlo, *Don't listen to them* (1997), acrylic, silver-leaf on canvas, 122 × 61 cm, collection of the artist, Los Angeles, photo: American Photo Repro Corp., courtesy of the artist.

The erotics of transgression or, more precisely, the attraction of 'trade' pervades the work also of Tony de Carlo (b. 1956). In many of his paintings, a tangible fascination can be perceived for the heterosexual ambiance of the *cholo*, yet de Carlo challenges the latter's *macho* image by attributing elements that are commonly perceived as 'effeminate'.

De Carlo's cultural background is complex. He was born in Inglewood, California; his mother is an American of German-French descent, and his father a Mexican of Italian descent. Tony de Carlo lived alternately in California and Kaneohe, Oahu (Hawaii). While in between a Chicano community and a fictitious, 'white' Los Angeles, he felt drawn, nevertheless, to the Latino universe of imagination, as to the social realities of the LA Barrio.

In many ways, de Carlo's aesthetic derives from Latin American heritage, or, better put, the rather stereotypical discourses about what art of this continent represents: Baroque, religious imagery almost at a level of kitsch, sensuality, surrealism, magic realism, colourful palette, 'naïve' style. The festive palette is intensified even in works like *Jesus and the Anthuriums* (1996) where the pain and vulnerability of a crucified Christ is smoothed by the surrounding red anthuriums. But de Carlo's choice is eclectic and far from inspired solely by the pictorial universe of his Mexican roots. 'My art', says de Carlo, 'is Hawaiian, it is Latino, it is neither. It is a page of my American life.'[17] The anthuriums are a recurrent theme, a bit like the calla lilies in Diego Rivera's work, yet they are taken from the flora of Hawaii. The work *El santo protector del sida* (1996) (Plate 17) depicts a naked man, sitting down while his entire body is pierced with nails instead of arrows, as in the exemplary image of Saint Sebastian. The picture is framed with painted red gardenias, similar to Hispano-American baroque painting, yet the saint's gold-leaf aureole is taken from Russian icons.

De Carlo recurrently appropriates token imagery from Colonial Latin America, yet now within a gay context. Elements of popular, Catholic devotion are incorporated within empathic representations of the *cholo* universe in particular that exerts a powerful influence upon the artist's erotic imagination. In *Don't listen to them* (1997), a *pachuco* is depicted with a goatee, red lips and dressed in a striped shirt. The semi-religious atmosphere is re-appropriated here by the image of flying men reminiscent of the angels in Colonial American art, by means of text captions that reflect Hispano-American banners quoting from the Bible and painted in between the visual scenes. Catholic moralism, however, has been replaced by fragments of contemporary discourse surrounding the AIDS epidemic and containing at times contradictory calls for safer sex and lively expressions of sexual desire alike.

The politics of gay desire surface in other works also, showing a Chicano boxer, for example, whose appearance is impregnated both with masculinity and femininity. The gracefulness of the boxer's Madonna-like face is reinforced by a crown as well as by the burgundy robe, still exposing the boxer's virile chest. It represents 'a cholo *boxer* elevated to sainthood status', says the artist, who doesn't deny that, underneath the dimension of erotic appeal, there is a subtle criticism also of the rigid gender roles characterizing the Chicano community at large.[18]

In another painting, de Carlo portrays a *pachuco*, dressed in a zoot suit, pierced by arrows like Saint Sebastian. The underlying gay iconography here too is obvious. Seen through the looking-glass of a gay male gaze, the arrows become symbols at once of the artist's sadomasochistic sensibility and of his awareness of vulnerability in the light of AIDS.

The epidemic is the underlying theme also of *Urban survivors* (1995), representing two men who embrace each other rather ambiguously. One holds an arrow in his right hand, making him into the other's executioner, into the man with HIV about to infect his partner. Alternatively, one may read an image into it of solidarity between seropositive and seronegative gay men, as the encounter is charged with deeply felt tenderness and empathy. The cityscape of towering high-rises accentuates the epidemiological reality of seroprevalence in the urban surroundings of Los Angeles, even when, stylistically, they remind the viewer of Honolulu rather than LA.

Sandoval, Reyes, de Carlo, as well as Fernando Torres and Mike Moreno, are members also of ¡VIVA!, a group of gay Latino writers, actors, performers and artists founded in 1988. The initiative sprang from attempts within the Chicano community of Los Angeles to address the problem of HIV and AIDS. Its spokesman, Luis Alfaro, conceived of the project as a support network for local Latino/a artists and a coalition advocating for Latino/a gay, lesbian and AIDS visibility in other venues. I will not discuss ¡VIVA! or Luis Alfaro's work here, as they consist of theatre predominantly.[19] One notable visual art initiative, though, was the so-called *joteria* project, playing with the words *loteria*, which is a popular card game in Mexico, and *joto*, a derogative term yet here an alternatively appropriated word for 'homosexual'. It consists of a series of small canvases, each measuring about sixteen by twenty inches, showing homoerotic imagery, instead of the common images of the traditional *loteria* game.

The identification with the Chicano community is less intense in the work of Roberto Gil de Montes, a bicultural artist who targets American society as a whole, as opposed to Reyes, de Carlo, Torres or Moreno. Gil de Montes (b. 1966) lived in Mexico during the first sixteen years of his life, then moved to Los Angeles only to return to Mexico after fourteen years. But the Mexico of his memories had disappeared and he returned to Los Angeles. Visual elements of the Mayan Bonampak murals, of Mexican popular art, *retablos* and *ex-votos* can be identified, yet they seem to be suspended in a spaceless and timeless universe, marked by dislocation and nostalgia.

Gil de Montes addresses issues of sexuality and gender, focusing at times on the duality between male and female. His images of Latino nightlife in Los Angeles embrace the role-playing that occurs both in a heterosexual and a homosexual context. Inevitably almost, AIDS is an important theme in his work. Carla Stellweg describes one painting, *Yo no soy monkey* (1991) as an image of time ticking away: 'The male figure, wearing a pair of white jockey shorts, has his eyes closed, and seems entranced, while a monkey, donning the cone-shaped hat, is staring point blank into our eyes. On the left, an hourglass filled with red powder is beginning the countdown – the virus has begun?'[20]

Aside from Los Angeles, San Francisco also is a magnet for gay and lesbian artists of Chicano descent, primarily because of the city's worldwide appeal as a 'gay capital'. Gay and lesbian art often remains within the boundaries of the Chicano community there and artists gather themselves into a kind of spiritual community between the gay enclaves of Castro Street, Polk Street and South of Market on the one hand and the Mexican and Central American neighbourhood of the Mission on the other. They exhibit in the Galeria de la Raza/Studio 24 rather than in a more mainstream gay art gallery elsewhere in town.

Since the early 1990s, collective shows have been organized by the Alliance of Lesbian, Gay and Bisexual Latino/a Artists (ALGaBiLA). They are a major platform for exposure for Chicano/a gay artists, whose work does not gain easy access to mainstream galleries. Chico Xavier Garza, who took the initiative, followed the example of the Mexican show 'Ex Profeso' (1990)[21] and included work of his bisexual father Xavier Garza Galindo, who had died of AIDS earlier. He conceived of the show as a collective act of coming out towards the Latino community itself. Such was felt to be inevitable as many of the participating artists were already partaking of the city's gay scene elsewhere. The shows included drawings by Tom Hernández, paintings by Jorge de Baca, Mario Patiño,[22] Rodrigo Reyes, Eugene Rodriguez and José Mario Alvarado, sculptures by Javier Perez, and photographs by Philip Ávila-Ruíz Garcia. Mixed-media artists Domingo Nuno and Ralfka Gonzalez also exhibited there.

The 25th anniversary, next, of the San Francisco-based Galería de la Raza gave rise to an exhibition titled 'Queer Raza. El corazón me dio un salto' ('The queer race. My heart skipped a beat'). The curators Nao Bustamante and Eugene Rodriguez conceived of the show as at once historical and educational, aiming both at the visualization of growing Latino/a gay activism and the fight against racism, homophobia, and AIDS.[23] Daniel Contreras and Dolissa Medina, next, made clear which issues were involved and how gay Latinos/as were facing the problem of fragmented identities:

> As we have learned, past generations of Queer Chicanos/Latinos had to negotiate these identities within a framework of fragmentation. Subsequently, we lacked any substantial body of Queer Raza history as a model for self-definition. Still, we had the lessons of the Chicano and the gay rights movements. We knew that somewhere, others like us yearned for a union of these experiences with those of the self. And so the interior migrated outward. For some the journey did not necessarily involve physical relocation; for others leaving home was part of that initial quest for sexual freedom. But no matter how varied our individual experiences, we all arrived in the San Francisco Bay Area as Queer Raza. We are all sexual immigrants who never really left home.[24]

Prominent also, if less closely linked with the Latino ethnic community, is Jerome Caja (1958–95). Caja was a regular patron of the gay bar scene south of Market Street. When he died, a memorial service was held in the South of Market gay bar, Hole in the Wall.

Caja played an important role in San Francisco's late 1980s radical queer scene, where he performed as the most unlikely go-go boy in clubs like Chaos, Uranus and Screw. His 'post-apocalyptic', deconstructive drag was in tune with the visual language of his miniature paintings in nail polish, with the obscenity of his subject matter and with the polymorphous perversity of his sexual *imaginaire*. He explored the pagan roots of eroticism, twisted by his Latino Catholic awareness. Perhaps his Latino heritage prevented him from talking about his HIV-positive status and, later, AIDS.

For Caja, the AIDS epidemic was not a subject of social talk, nor could it be controlled or prevented from spreading 'as long as the generative, or passionate act is tied to self-annihilation'.[25] Fatalism and irony reign in a work like *Bozo fucks death* – Bozo being a nickname for Jesus – or *Death gives kitty a happy treat* (1994). A series of paintings made from the ashes of Charles Sexton, an artist friend, are striking in a smilar manner. In one of them, one can see Sexton devour himself – an image provoked, says Caja, by the debilitating force of self-pity.[26]

Gay and lesbian artists of Mexican descent evidently live in New York also. Yet, despite this city's reputation as the capital of proximity, they find it hard to fully partake in the largely white-defined commercial art scene there. Gay art being confined within the circuit of alternative art spaces and galleries only partly allows for inclusion of the art made by ethnic minorities within the metropolis' gay and lesbian community.

Max Carlos Martínez (b. 1961) is New York based and produces a pictorial universe that is at once frivolous and tormented. Some works are collages, setting homoerotic attraction against the background of appropriated Modernist paintings by Braque, Léger or Delaunay. The collage's protagonists are also taken from art history, be it Gainsborough or El Greco. 'My collage work', says Martínez, 'involves the deconstruction and reapplication of master works incorporating pop iconography and cartoon sentiment.'[27]

His paintings suggest the diaphanous medium of stained-glass windows and lend ephemeral status to male nudity (*None*, 1996). A series titled *Housewife battles self* (1994) shows the mundanity of Chicano domestic life, yet radiates a campy sensibility at the same time. It is 'a vividly coloured domestic Apocalypse, couched in a language of archangels and demons lifted straight from popular religious pictures'.[28] One angel 'in a pink Chanel dress' is actually an image of the artist, who retrogressively witnesses the process of acculturation to which his family was subjected after having emigrated to the United States. Martínez's self-portraits are testimonies of the homophobia faced during those years and attempts at exorcizing 'the demons of self-oppression' that went along with it.

Federico Correa (b. 1946), finally, while born and raised in Salinas, California, now lives in Norfolk, Virginia, and produces paintings that are inscribed within the great Spanish traditions of Goya and Roman Catholic sensibility. The emotional flamboyance and intensity of his work are a reflection, so he admits, of his own guilt-ridden attitude regarding his sexual identity. His vivid, yet ambivalent images of either the carnivalesque or morbid, good or evil, strike a universal chord while at the same time testifying to the artist's Latino cultural heritage. Homosexuality recurrently comes to the surface, if only as a narrative enclosed within a more philosophical investigation of human existence. The male body, flaunting a huge erection, while lying on top of a birthday cake (*Birthday*

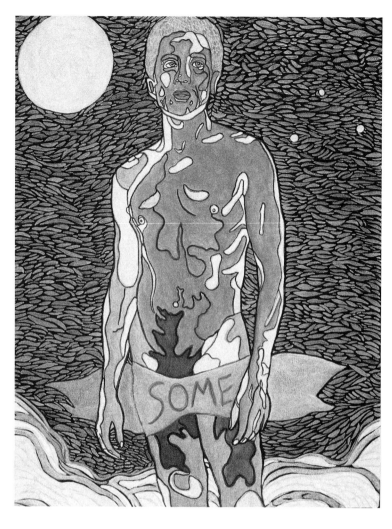

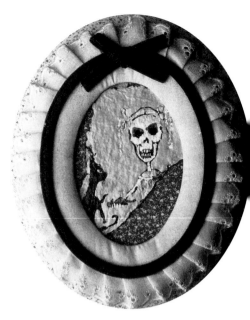

Figure 64 *(above)* Jerome Caja, *Death gives kitty a happy treat* (1994), mixed media, 21.5 × 18 cm, courtesy of Paule Anglim Gallery, San Francisco.

Figure 65 *(top left)* Max Carlos Martínez, *None* (1996), acrylic on canvas, 46 × 30.5 cm, collection of Mauricio Lafitte-Soler, courtesy of the artist, New York City.

Figure 66 *(bottom left)* Federico Correa, *Birthday cake* (1988), oil on canvas, 20.5 × 18 cm, courtesy of the artist.

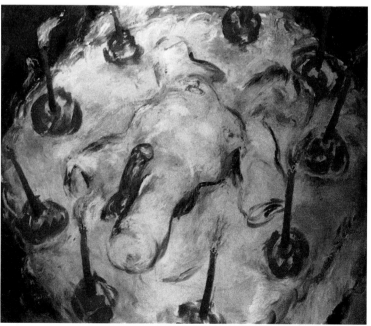

cake, 1988), is a signifier of both the family dogma's grip, and the gay man's desire to escape from it. The body's severed limbs and the penis' reddened appearance are visual icons of homosexuality's stigma. The image, says Correa, 'is soaked in [the] hypocrisy [of] Catholicism and family tradition. It is thickly coated with subdued violence, destruction and cruelty . . . all in the name of love!'[29]

Lesbian Chicana artists call for attention here, particularly in view of their relatively low degree of exposure in both a mainstream context and the male gay art world. Mostly, their work remains within the confines of shows and galleries curated or run by women. Female participants at the ALGaBiLA shows in San Francisco were the painters Norma Austin and Ester Hernández, the photographers Virginia Benavídez, Celina Cárdenas, Desi del Valle, Nereyda Garcia-Ferraz, Catalina Govea, Lea Morales-Shadburn and Patsy Rico (of Honduran descent), and multimedia artists Juana Maria de la Caridad, Celia Cárdenas, Xochipala Maes Valdéz and Rebecca L. Tarin.

The Esperanza Peace and Justice Center in San Antonio, Texas, operates as 'a Latina/o, mujeres, queer, cultural, gente based community center rolled up into one',[30] and organizes speaker forums, art shows, film festivals and so on, all as part of a more general art policy that wants to 'bring together [women] politics and culture into the arts'.[31] Recently, it initiated Visions de Esperanza, a youth media project, and Mujerarte, a women of colour arts cooperative, while it was the first organization also to set up an AIDS art show and a gay and lesbian art show in San Antonio.

The centre almost closed down due to pressure by conservatives, including within the male gay community, who considered its policy as biased towards people of colour, racist and sexist. Work by the lesbian artist Laura Aguilar especially was one of their targets, thus lending particular poignancy to her own claim that, whereas each has an unalienable right to self-expression, not every one has equal opportunities to do so. Some of her photographs, often self-portraits or images of heavy-weight women, impelled conservatives to object against what they perceived as 'pornographic and obscene'.

The works of Los Angeles-based and self-taught photographer Laura Aguilar (b. 1959) are compelling social commentaries that lay bare the mechanisms of stereotyping and marginalization in mainstream society. Going against the grain of a predictable aesthetic, Aguilar portrays either herself or close friends and relatives, collectively presenting proud affirmation of cultural and sexual diversity. Such is the case in *Sandy's room* (1990, mural-size remake 1993), a tribute to Myrna Báez, and in two series, *Latina lesbians* (1986–90) and *Clothed/unclothed* (1991–2). In the former, objectification is cut off by including captions handwritten by the models themselves. The latter is a series of diptychs and triptychs, showing individuals or couples dressed at first, naked next. The models, while real-life people, show pride and confidence, whether belonging to an ethnic, cultural or sexual minority.

Aguilar produces a poignant image of sexual and cultural self-affirmation also in *Three eagles flying* (1990). It is a photographic triptych, showing an American flag on the left-hand side, a Mexican one on the right, while in the middle the artist portrays herself bare-breasted, wrapped in both flags and tied with ropes. The work comments on its maker's bicultural status, connecting the meaning of her own name – *aguilar* (Spanish) = eagle – to the eagles symbolizing both the United States and Mexico. Not being accepted as fully American because she is a Chicana, nor as genuinely Mexican because, being dyslexic, she is hardly fluent in Spanish, she nevertheless presents herself boldly as a woman who has turned dystopia into a source of pride. '[While] acutely aware of her separateness, [she is] comfortable enough with herself to present us with a personal vision that is both intimate and authoritative', says Diana Hulick.[32] It is remarkable, in this respect, that her breasts are bare, as if suggesting, says Yvonne Yarbro-Bejarano, 'the impossibility of completely imprisoning or constructing her body through monolithic definitions of race or nation'.[33]

Aguilar, being a large woman also, further develops her aesthetic of self-affirmation in a series of fifteen black-and-white self-portraits (*Nature self-portraits*, 1996) that defy common conceptions of physical beauty. '[She] creates a visonary dialectic', says Berta Sichel, 'bent on transforming conventional concepts of attractiveness.'[34] Posing fully nude while sitting or lying in a harsh, desert-like environment, Aguilar lends an almost sculptural presence to her own body while simultaneously avoiding the camera's lens and presenting herself in a self-contained, introspective manner. While playing with the contrast between the arid, rocky surface of her surroundings and the vulnerability of the flesh, she at the same time suggests some sort of mimetic continuity, reminiscent of a primitive earth goddess.[35]

Aguilar being light-skinned, as her mother is half-Mexican, half-Irish, adds yet another dimension to the complex composition of her personal identity – which brings us to the core of Aguilar's work as multilayered and hard to pin down within a single category. Her lesbian sexuality also adds to the opacity of Aguilar's individual identity, comparable to, for example, Tony de Carlo, and gives rise to ironic upheaval and deconstruction not only of 'mainstream' values, but also of the standards and norms of their respective ethnic communities. 'Aguilar's deployment', says Yarbro-Bejarano, '[of a queer sensibility] in the context of racial difference and sexual sameness demonstrates its remarkable flexibility to describe an "insider/outsider" position determined by multiple factors and shifting according to context.'[36]

Chicana lesbian sexuality is in your face also in the work of Marcia Ochoa and Ester Hernández. At play in both artists is 'a lesbianization of the heterosexual icons of popular culture'[37] related to the postmodern tropes of appropriation and irony. Ochoa (b. 1970),

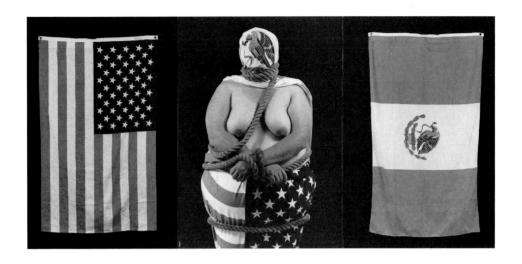

Figure 67 Laura Aguilar, *Three eagles flying* (1990), black-and-white photograph triptych, 60.96 × 152.4 cm, courtesy of the artist.

Figure 68 Laura Aguilar, *Nature self-portrait, no. 7* (1996), black-and-white photograph, 40.64 × 50.8 cm, courtesy of the artist.

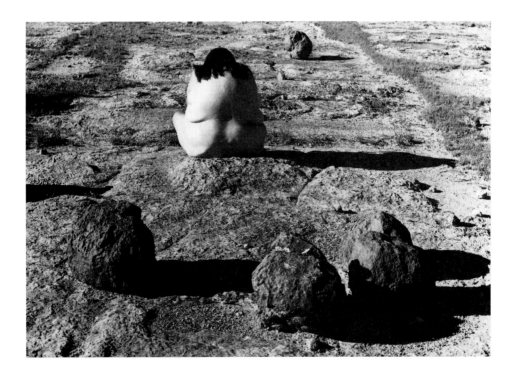

both a poet and a photographer, self-published *La ofrenda* in 1991. This so-called 'chapbook' shows images of herself naked while holding a heart in both hands. These images contrast with the artist's self-presentation elsewhere in the book as 'butch' and imply a kind of shuffling of butch–femme codes. 'The butch image on the back cover, completely clothed, legs slightly spread and arms crossed in a stance of non-availability, bespeaks the agency of touching and desiring, and completes the image of the same body as object of desire', suggests Yvonne Yarbro-Bejarano.[38] At stake here also is a lesbianization of Aztec blood sacrifice as well as the Catholic ritual of transubstantiation.

La ofrenda, a serigraph this time by Hernández (b. 1944), is a bold display of lesbian identity, 'quoting' the aesthetic of home altars so common in Chicano culture and appropriating them in an alternative context. Such a strategy 'provides the frisson of "exotic", "primitive", "savage" or even "criminal" alterity. Within the context of working-class Chicano culture, the female body merely replaces the male's as the normative site of the venerating tattoo', comments Yarbro-Bejarano, who describes the work as a 'lesbian body-as-altar, [where] the lesbian context presses the religious icon transgressively into [a] representation of lesbian desire.'[39]

Other works of Hernández also play with the familiar image of the Virgin of Guadelupe, who is both virgin and mother and opposed to the *puta*, to Malinche, that ambiguous cultural icon of Mexican identity and the loss of it. The *puta/virgen* dichotomy penetrates Mexican and Mexican-American society in fundamental ways and appropriation of the virgin image for lesbian purposes evidently challenges the deeply rooted notions of sex and gender among Mexican-Americans. Hernández's strategy here converges with Gloria Anzaldúa's project of 'unlearning the *puta/virgen* dichotomy, of reading the pre-Columbian mother back into Guadelupe'.[40]

A double strategy to challenge Mexican-American notions of both ethnic identity and femininity can be perceived also in the work of Monica Palacios, which equally provoked criticism even by gay white men. Palacios (b. 1969) calls her performances 'part stand-up comedy, part performance art, part chihuahua'[41] and, while performing, she tackles the notoriously heterosexist, racist and male-dominated world of stand-up comedy. *Latin lezbo comic* (n.d.) contains an autobiographical narrative rather than the one-liners that almost completely define the outlook of traditional stand-up comedy. In it, Palacios positions herself not only within Mexican-American society but deliberately outside the mainstream gay community ('I really wanted to live in West Hollywood so I could be a hip-happenin'-homo, but I didn't want to devote my life to – pastels'). *La llorona loca: the other side* is another performance act by Palacios also covering the interrelating dimensions of sexual identity, culture and ethnicity.

If homophobia is a reality amidst Chicano society, then it may not be all that distinct from the homophobia present amidst American or European society at large. The fact is that numerous artists have found or defined opportunities to visualize and comment on issues such as sexual identity, gender and, inevitably, AIDS. Such is due partly to the artists' courage and perseverance despite the threat of homophobic backlash. But the rich production of Chicano gay and lesbian art is a sign also of a more embracing attitude towards sexual and gender variance that may stem from the hybrid heritage of Mexican and Mexican-American society itself. This being a *mestizaje*, really, of diverse Pre-Columbian cultural systems and a relatively 'accommodating' Hispano-American Catholicism, may well explain, along with the assertive stand of the artists themselves, why homoeroticism and homosexuality are an unmistakable part of Chicano art today.

Artistic challenge for a *Nuyoriqueño ambiente*

New York City's large Puerto Rican community – larger than the island's entire population – harbours a substantial gay and lesbian community and some of its artists address both ethnic and sexual identity at the very crucible of metropolitan life. To a degree, homotextuality in *Nuyorican* visual arts reflects concerns that are similar to the images of a gay and lesbian *ambiente* produced on the island itself. But the very process of migration and incorporation within the North American gay and lesbian subculture, though inadequate, has prompted artists to address these issues in an innovative and, often, deliberating way. Even AIDS, while devastating in its effect and tied up with an often troublesome dynamic of social stigmatization, is addressed by some among them as a point of departure for more ambitious and comprehensive reflections on both fate and faith of *Nuyorican* lesbian and gay artists.

A distinguished role, in this context, was played by René Santos (1954–86), at least until his premature death due to AIDS. His work displays a peculiar 'gay sensibility' retrievable despite a highly codified aesthetic. Critic Davis Deitcher claimed in this context that one must pay attention to what the silences say about the gay character of Santos's work: 'I think that once again it's work that has as much to do with concealment as it does with revelation, and this makes his work for me gay.'[42]

Santos indeed hardly produced images that were in any way recognizable as 'gay'. But the expression of gay focus is evident, if hidden inside the artist's visual vocabulary and mode of painting, marginalized in the wake of Modernism and condemned to the realm of sentimental kitsch. His fragmentary reproduction of family portraiture, at times substituting a two-dimensional image of the bourgeois frame for the actual picture itself, signifies the artist's awareness of himself as an outsider both as a gay man and as a person with AIDS. Critical distance directs the pictorial freezing of super-8 movieshots also, as well as paintings that seem to reproduce stills from Hollywood films. Ironic play can be perceived in his portraits of dogs, symbols of the suburban happiness of nuclear families in one instance, companions of the lonely in another.

Most revelatory of the artist's homosexual inspiration and 'camp' sensibility are his photomontages of the late 1970s. They consist of stills from B-movies and text excerpts from pulp novels of all kinds. At times, the artist shows up within the confines of the text, sometimes even in drag, as Renée – an ambition that René Santos cherished in real life too, yet without going so far as turning into a drag queen as such. 'The result', says Deitcher, 'was transcendent camp, which repositioned the popular form of the illustrated Spanish "novella" from buses and subways to the galleries of New York.'[43]

The artistic career of Santos coincided largely with the heydays of Gay Liberation in New York, yet its aesthetic language was at odds with the rhetoric particularly of masculinity regained. It was more attuned to the discursive universe of the drag queens who had triggered the Stonewall riot in the first place yet were marginalized once white, middle-class gay militants took over. This would lead to a rather limited visibility of minorities within the American gay scene until its manifest contestation in the wake of early 1990s 'queer' politics. The call for recognition of cultural, sexual and gender diversity within the gay community itself gave rise to a growing prominence of minority artists too, who now saw a chance to co-define the parameters of representational politics.

It comes as no surprise, however, that such is not an easy task considering the power politics of New York City's art scene and the ongoing 'ghettoization' of art by ethnic minorities. Many a gay or lesbian artist, accordingly, finds access to their audience only through initiatives taken within these communities themselves. Though an opportunity on the one hand for expression on the crossroads of ethnic, cultural and sexual identities, it is often also a handicap and an impediment to disclosure of any artist's universal appeal.

Illustrative of this dilemma is the presence of (mostly male) gay artists in the *Nuyorican* initiative, called O.P. art. It is a loose configuration, really, of Puerto Rican artists, yet today the group's cohesion seems to be somewhat lost. The group showed collectively in both New York and San Juan.[44]

Sex and gender identity are prominent issues for most members of O.P. art, especially for José Luis Cortés, Axel Reyes, Abnel Rodríguez and Alberto Valderrama. But their careers demonstrate that coming out as a gay artist is easier through the channels of their own ethnic community than within the larger gay community itself, even within the cosmopolitan context of New York. What unites them is their self-identification as 'Puerto Rican gay' artists, rather than as 'gay' artists, because their affiliation with the white, largely middle-class and upper-middle-class gay community elsewhere in the city is rather problematic and weak.

The artistic career of José Luis Cortés (b. 1962) was triggered by his finding out of his HIV-positive status in 1981, and, along with it, by a positive acknowledgement of his own identity as a gay man. He soon embarked upon a series of works that are at once vitalistic and critical of the forces that stand in the way not only of a cure for and tolerance towards people with AIDS, but also of acceptance of homosexuality. Cortés's fate indeed is not only closely related to the AIDS crisis amidst the Puerto Rican community both on the island, where he lived until 1990, and in New York City where he has lived since. It is intimately linked also with the particular outlook of a gay and bisexual subculture within that same community and with the ambiguous, at once embracing and repressing, attitudes of Puerto Ricans towards sexual nonconformity. Determined to take control over his life and to comment upon these mixed realities, Cortés focused on self-portraits especially (*El calvo*, 1996) as these allowed the artist to find himself and position himself assertively within the world. They also functioned as a source of courage in the light of public indifference towards HIV and AIDS, and of stigmatization, within the Puerto Rican community, of homosexual women and men.[45]

The radical stance in the face of AIDS is obvious also in his portrayals of local churches, which come across both as bastions of religious bigotry and homophobia, as well as potential sites of reflection, compassion and reconciliation. '[They] avoid mere topicality', says one critic, 'for a clear-eyed view of Decade Two of the AIDS era.'[46]

Cortés altogether trespasses the ghetto of AIDS art and produces poignant imagery of vital lust, phallic power and sadomasochism. Here, references to ethnic identity are obliterated in exchange for a more universal visual language commenting upon issues of role-playing, sex, desire. During so-called Pork nights at the gay club The Lure, he painted a huge mural (1996), where erect penises are interwoven with a semi-abstract pattern of lines and surfaces, mostly in black, grey and white. The patchwork surfaces accidentally remind one of work by Joaquín Torres-García, yet function here as reinforcement of the priapic atmosphere that characterizes gay *socialité* at The Lure. A similar mood radiates also from elegant, wooden totempoles that have been decorated in Cortés's trademark patchwork aesthetic of white, grey and black. Bondage is a theme in yet other self-portraits showing the artist wearing a leather hood.

The current work of Cortés includes a painted inventory of pornography shops, peep-show parlours, and xxx-rated 'art palaces', most defunct now in the wake of sanitation and gentrification processes around Times Square, 42nd Street and 8th Avenue. One such recent work, *Eros* (1997), shows the façade of a porno movie theatre, now closed, yet once an important landmark of gay *socialité*. *Eros/virus* (1997), showing the entrance of that very same cinema, not only documents the architectural dimension of gay and bisexual cruising, but witnesses the ambiguous interaction between sexual freedom on the one hand, and health threats on the other: hardly visible, yet unmistakably there, one can perceive how the word 'virus', printed on newspaper, surfaces from underneath a still slightly transparent coat of acrylic paint.

Abnel Rodríguez (b. 1964), born in Santurce, Puerto Rico, resided in New York from 1985 until 1987, then studied at the Universidad de Puerto Rico and returned to New

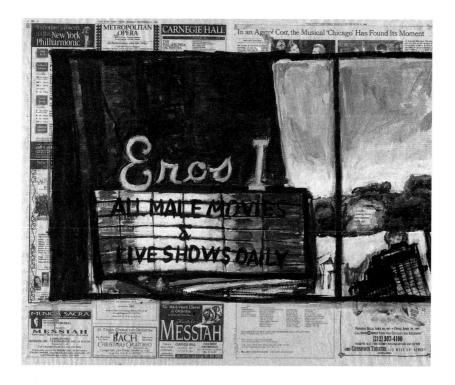

Figure 69 José Luis Cortés, *Eros* (1997), acrylic on print, 56 × 66 cm, courtesy of the artist, New York City.

Figure 70 Abnel Rodríguez, *En la mente de Dios* (1995), mixed media on canvas, 76 × 76 cm and 76 × 76 cm, courtesy of the artist, New York City.

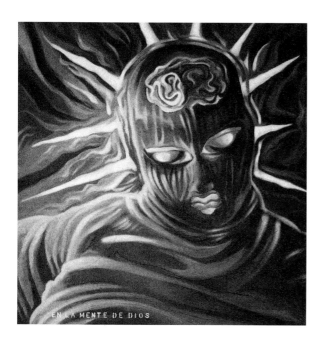

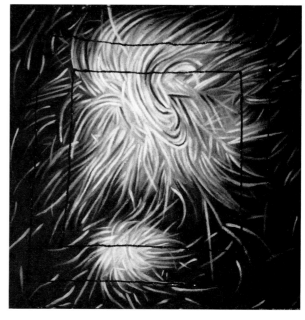

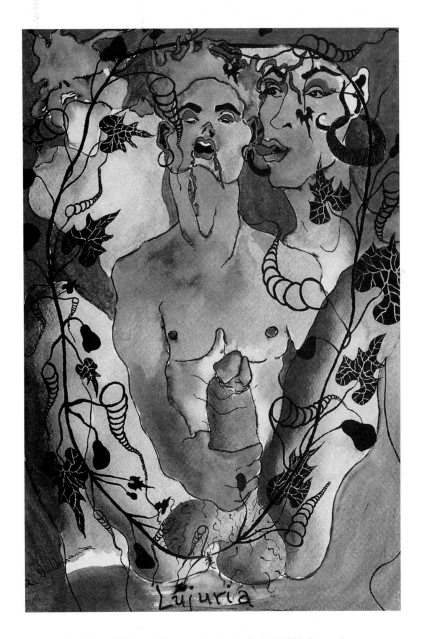

Figure 71 Alberto Valderrama, *The seven deadly sins: 'Lujuria'* (1993–5), gouache on paper, 30.5 × 43 cm, courtesy of Andy Glasgow, Washington, DC.

York in 1990. His choice for life 'in exile' was inspired partly by a wish to graduate, in his case, at Pratt Institute. But for Rodríguez too, 'graduating' was an excuse to go and live a gay life in the big city, far away from the constraints of family, religion and social oppression. It was an escape, also, from his mother's devotion to the Pentecostalist Church. He had experienced a 'horrible childhood' as a result[47] and after having spent time amidst the drag queen scene 'Para las 15' of San Juan, he decided to exchange Puerto Rico for the bright lights of the big city.

Many of the artist's works reflect the weight of his religious upbringing and show images of an ambiguous God, a source at once of strength and pain. The diptych *En la mente de Díos* (1995) is an emblematic work that visualizes God as a masked man. Flames around his head take the shape of an aureole, while, inside his skull, one can see a brain. It stands for the artist's uncertainty about what goes on in God's very own brain and reflects his scepticism towards religious doctrine about (homo)sexuality.

Rodríguez, knowingly HIV-positive since 1985, expresses criticism towards institutionalized religion also in *Santo Cristo del Retrovir* (1992), a large oil on canvas, unmounted, and a tribute especially to his deceased lover, Juan. The painting's title can be read from a text banner on top, mentioning, along with it, 'Wellcome 100 mg'. The undisguised reference to AZT clearly positions the work within the realm of 'Art against AIDS', yet its political dimension is attenuated by the artist's attribution of this work to his deceased lover. The painting accordingly reads as an *ex-voto*, entirely within the tradition of Catholic devotion, and based upon a belief in faith's efficacy. The ambiguity of religious doctrine is accentuated, however, by the welter of roses at the painting's bottom, and by the sharp-edged triangles around the central image of God. They indicate, says Rodríguez, that 'being attracted to God is, like S/M, being attracted to pain'.[48]

The duality between positive and negative, warmth and pain is obvious also in other partly religious, partly blasphemous imagery: the image of God's eye that looks like the inside of a rectal tube (*Ojo de Díos*); the sacred blood that makes dirty (*Sacra sangre*); or, most clearly, in the recurrent images of fire. Fire, that 'can cleanse and purify, but . . . also represents the punishment of hell'.[49] Small, circular paintings simultaneously show the fire both as *chispa vital*, sparkle of life, and *fuego consumidor*, a symbol in Pentecostalist religion especially of what awaits the unrepenting.

The balance is more towards the positive and constructive in a series of small pastels (1995), which show flames alongside male hands, feet, genitals, buttocks. In other work, too, Rodríguez shows the less grim and more playful sides of life: documentary photography of the gay scene both in Puerto Rico and New York, small-scale drawings and pastels of drag and leather queens, intimate portrayals of friends and lovers.

Alberto Valderrama (1957–95), while born and raised in Puerto Rico, lived in West Hollywood from 1978 until the next year. After a stay on the island, Valderrama returned to the USA, this time to New York City, in 1982. After initial work on paper, Valderrama started a series of drawings on treated fringed canvas and moved on to oil paintings next. In San Juan, he painted a mural depicting the breasts of a woman, served on a dinner plate. While confronting reactions from feminists, he objected that the scene was inspired by Federico Garcia Lorca's poem 'Romance de la Guardia Civil Española' about Rosa de los Camborois. This woman had cut off her breasts to offer them to God and purify herself in the act.[50] Valderrama withdrew to the Blue Ridge Mountains of Virginia in 1990, yet remained present in New York until his death of AIDS. He originally signed his work with 'Alberto', later with 'Valderrama', 'Incognito' or 'Nina Ciclonefence'.

His series of comic strips, *The adventures of Señorita Cosa*, allude to the camp expression 'Miss Thing' and contain sexually charged fantasies depicting sexual encounters between men. In one of them, the setting is the forest of Puerto Rico; in another one may recognize personalities from the New York City gay scene. Many contain lessons for everyone to practise safer sex. More compelling, however, is the unfinished series titled *The seven deadly sins* (1993–5, only six were completed). They show plenty of sexual imagery also, including enormous penises and androgynous people who combine both male and female traits in one person. Transgender people fascinated Valderrama, who himself was proud of his own 'in-between' status, both man and woman. In one painting, he presented a portrait of himself as an androgynous man-woman centaur, with both sets of organs, a pair of wings and the lower body of a horse. There was a philosophy attached to it that was highly derived from pre-modern speculation on the virtue of androgyny. He also admired lower vertebrates, as they are equipped with both male and female sexual organs, yet he was aware also that his own fascination was rooted in Puerto Rican attitudes towards sexual nonconformity. Young Puerto Rican gay men feel 'constrained by the sexual roles placed on them by society and the Church, and therefore entered that netherworld of men who dress as women'.[51] Valderrama's message, accordingly, is critical of traditional Puerto Rican norms and values regarding sexual morality, yet reiterates them partly by subscribing to the equation of gay and transgender identity.

The photographer Axel Damian Reyes (b. 1967) inclines towards explicitly homoerotic imagery that is somewhat influenced by, among others, George Platt Lynes. It is distinct, however, as an expression of gay assertiveness so lacking in the work of his tormented predecessor. The tone of Reyes's work is refined and erotic, capturing the male body's attractiveness through studied *clair obscurs*. The body often seems to hover above ground and becomes immaterialized by juxtaposition with images of floating flowers and leaves. The narcissistic presence of his models is accentuated by elements such as mirrors, or the shining light of a single lamp – all of which reinforces the gay sensibility underlying Reyes's visual language.

Other artists, not belonging to O.P. art, combine visual commentary on sexual and ethnic identity alike. Among them Reyes Meléndez (b. 1962), who documents Puerto Rican – and in a wider sense, Latino – gay experience in a subjective and poetic way. He

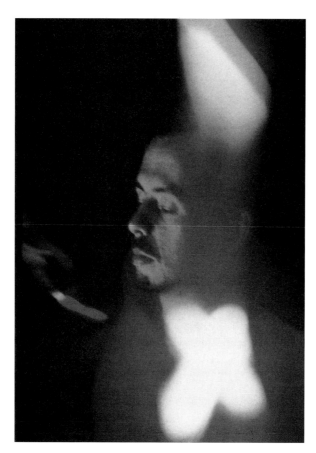

Figure 72 Reyes Meléndez, *Perfect strangers (Wolf)* (1997), colour photo print, 54 × 40 cm, courtesy of the artist, New York City.

downplays the sharp edges of HIV prevalence amidst his own community and focuses on the human and emotional aspects of homoerotic alliances instead. *Perfect strangers (Wolf)*, a very recent photographic work, reveals the artist's desire to see beauty underneath the clouds of sombre premonitions and to document the individual lives of people: 'hybrid, mutant, lonely, perverted, distorted, always in transition, perhaps like myself'.[52] Working with special light effects that make his models look blurred and unfocused, he seems to emphasize how many encounters in the fast city of New York remain fluid, transient and ephemeral.

The conceptual and installation artist Miguel Ventura (b. 1954) was born in San Antonio, Texas, then lived in Mexico for fifteen years. After his studies in Princeton and Boston, he studied printmaking with Saúl Villa in Mexico City, yet now has settled down in New York. His work is conceptual and includes drawings, paintings and book illustrations as well as multimedia works, installations or self-published books. The so-called *Notebooks of Mademoiselle Heidi Schreber* (1995)[53] depart from Daniel Paul Schreber's *Memoirs of My Nervous Disorder*, commented on earlier by both Freud and Lacan, yet now presented by the New Interterritorial Language Committee. This is a mock organization that publishes various other texts, along with fragments from Schreber's memoirs, in German, Spanish, English, Swahili, Arabic and Cantonese. 'The accompanying polyglot text', says Roberto Tejada, '[is] a ceaseless assault on fixity and its self-contradictory phobia of all things hybrid – namely sex, species and language.'[54]

At first sight, there is very little connection with any explicitly gay content, nor is there, for that matter, in his installation *NILC baby T-shirts* (1995), yet Ventura's conceptual approach fundamentally criticizes essentialist discourse, endemic in much gay political rhetoric. It also questions the latter's tendency to frequently wipe out ethnic and cultural variety within the gay community.[55] The T-shirts are signifiers, therefore, of an alternative discourse and one that, as yet, remains unanswered: no real bodies are wearing the T-shirts, which are doomed to remain like empty containers of utopian displacement. 'The T-shirts . . . are empty coverings for non-existent youths, hanging uninhabited on the walls, their use value extinguished – never fulfilled.'[56]

While an organization like O.P. art attracted many a male gay artist of Puerto Rican descent, there are far fewer 'out' lesbian artists whose work is relevant within the context of this book. One among the few is Frances Negrón-Muntaner (b. 1966), a video artist, poet, publicist/reporter and critic, who is strongly influenced by Black Audio/Film Collective and Sankofa. She addresses issues both of cultural and sexual identity, more precisely of Puerto Rican identity both on the island and in the United States. For her, 'the cinematic space has become a proposal for the re-signification of "home"'.[57]

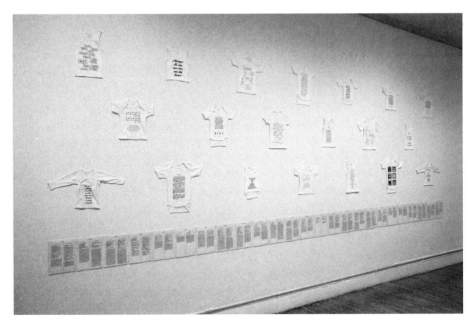

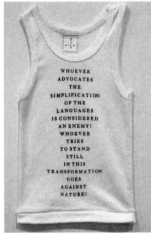

Figure 73 Miguel Ventura, *NILC baby T-shirts* (1995), installation, mixed media, variable dimensions, courtesy of Art in General, New York City.

Negrón-Muntaner, who resides in Philadelphia, claims, in this context, that Puerto Rico's affiliation with the United States, while potentially neocolonialist, enhances opportunities also, all the more since the United States are becoming increasingly 'Latinized' themselves. By saying so, she goes against the grain of Puerto Rican nationalism.[58]

The incorporation of Puerto Rico within the realm of USA influence indeed offers chances for sexual liberation while nothing stands in the way of affirming one's own cultural variety even on the level of sexual politics. The fictitious video-documentary *Brincando el charco: Portrait of a Puerto Rican* (1994)[59] illustrates the artist's vision of displacement and, more particularly, of the cultural dysphoria faced by Puerto Rican gay women in exile. It is a story of a young, light-skinned lesbian who had left the island when her lesbianism had been revealed to her father. When he dies, she faces the dilemma of returning to the island or staying in the United States.

The director herself plays the main role of Claudia Marín, who is presented as a lesbian. The representation of lesbian identity is deliberately non-sexual, which is inspired by the artist's refusal to pin down her identity upon sexuality as such and to counter representational traditions, presenting lesbians as titillating material for straight men. It is a choice made in order to avoid simplistic messages about the presumed liberating effect of 'marginal' sex. When trying to capture the complexity of sexual identity, one must be prepared to look beyond the merely physical.

Negrón-Muntaner addresses the issue of appropriation with regard to Gay Liberation, and states that as a homosexual man or woman from Puerto Rico, one has a choice between being 'gay' in the American sense, or nothing at all. 'Primero se habla en Inglés y después se traduce' ('First one talks English. Then, one translates'), says Negrón-Muntaner, who claims that the adoption of an American model of sexual liberation does not necessarily go against the grain of Puerto Rican culture but can be incorporated (translated) into it. The issue, rather, is patriarchy, forcing lesbians and gay men to seek voluntary exile abroad as long as its structural violence is not contested on a wider scale.[60]

Cuban-Americans: the sexual politics of gay exodus

For Cubans, motives for exile were mostly political and economic, yet their migration abroad was inspired at times also by sexual motives, particularly after the initiation by the Castro regime of a quite repressive policy towards homosexual men. The institutionalized homophobia, embodied in the UMAP camps, was to boost the masculinist outlook of the Revolution and triggered the exodus, to a degree made possible by the regime, of gay men.[61]

Before the Revolution, Havana had been a playground for adventurous Americans and one of the largest brothels of the Western hemisphere. Middle-class Cuban gay men, however, took advantage of journeys abroad to flee the *machismo* inherent to Cuban society and pursue alternative sexual pleasure elsewhere.[62] After 1959 and, with greater urgency, after 1965, this became a necessary way out of the grip of repression and enforced 'rehabilitation'.

Among those who went to Europe and who simultaneously addressed sexual identity in their work figured Angel Acosta León, Roberto García-York and Ramón Alejandro. Acosta León (1930–64) was a homosexual artist who emigrated to Paris in 1964, but his story soon took a tragic turn, potentially revealing the difficult situation faced by homosexual artists in Cuba. On the way back to Cuba, he committed suicide by throwing himself off the ship. His work, while limited in quantity, was the object of a retrospective exhibition in Havana some years ago,[63] but no questions were raised on that occasion regarding the artist's motives for ending his life. Homosexuality undoubtedly played a role,[64] suggestive of the Cuban authorities' position in this respect.

Roberto García-York (b. 1929) moved to Paris in 1964. While starting as a fashion designer in Cuba, he soon developed a style that was labelled by critics as 'surrealist'. Yet, it is a gay sensibility that underlies García-York's aesthetic and that was captured well by a critic as *les folies York*.[65] The nude male figures prominently in mysterious landscapes that are only vaguely reminiscent of planet earth. They are utopian images of homosexual self-realization, influenced, if subconsciously, by the nascent Gay Liberation movement in France, yet expressions also of the artist's visionary spirit and imagination.

Ramón Alejandro (b. 1943) travelled to Buenos Aires and Montevideo, then Brazil and Spain, and subsequently settled in Paris in 1963. While in France, he produced a graphic body of work impregnated with eroticism. Some of his drawings were exhibited during the First International Exhibition of Erotic Art in Lund, Sweden, and Aarhus, Denmark (1968). In 1974, he participated in a group show titled 'Images érotiques et obscènes' (Galerie Images, Paris). Alejandro got married, raised a family and nowadays resides in Miami. He grew increasingly fascinated also by both Eastern and Western philosophy, which is reflected in the nostalgic landscapes of his later pictorial universe.

The early drawings exhibited in Lund, Aarhus and Paris are of an explicitly erotic kind. They seem to carry within them a clearly visible cult of phallicism, mixed with either humour or anxiety. The drawings suggest pansexuality, yet at times they are clearly homoerotic. In one drawing, a rather effeminate man observes an old lady, sitting next to him at a table and whose face is shaped like a male gland. The man's facial expression betrays fascination and withdrawal at the same time. Another drawing shows a naked man, falling down while being besieged with flying male genitalia, which may again reveal the artist's ambiguity towards sexual nonconformity, or, rather, his cautious criticism of the ubiquitous regulation of sexuality by society.

A more relaxed celebration of anal sex, whether heterosexual or homosexual, is blatant, on the other hand, in *Cosmogonie* (n.d.). This drawing shows a crystal-like rock in the ocean, with palm trees on the narrow beach. On top of the rocky surface are erect penises, penetrating the protruding anuses of small, frivolous clouds. The image's scope is universal at one level, yet the flora invokes the tropical island of Cuba. The winged genitalia inscribe the drawing within the pictorial ambience of a Hispano-(American) Baroque aesthetic.

Alejandro maintained friendships with other, openly gay artists and writers. He illustrated Severo Sarduy's book *Epitafios* (Miami: Universal, 1994) for example. Yet, calling Alejandro's work 'gay' would not only violate the diversity of his oeuvre but would be at odds also with the artist's essentially bisexual visual language. Bisexuality, if not in praxis, then to a greater or lesser extent in artistic production, was a pattern, moreover, that can be noticed frequently, possibly more frequently even among Latin American artists, whose sexual politics are less rigid or reifying than among those working in an Anglo-Saxon context. Not that the playing of both heterosexual and homosexual registers could be pursued with spontaneity and ease, nor that the expression of the homoerotic side occurred in an atmosphere of openness and acceptance. It surely remained controversial and all too often led to the marginalization of artists, even during the years of sexual liberation when Alejandro lived in Paris. Exile to more sexually liberal cities across the globe did offer opportunities, however, to explore one's own sexual libido more independently. And the distance from home may have facilitated the discovery by some of their sexual identity, whether bisexual or homosexual.

Interesting also as a story of coming out in exile is the career of Juan González (1942–93), a Cuban who chose the United States rather than Europe as his newly defined, adoptive motherland. Gonzaléz was born to a wealthy family of Camagüey and as a child already raised his mother's suspicion of non-conventionality when he kept drawing numerous portraits of feminine Hollywood stars. Such, obviously, was not a boy's pastime and this initiated a persistent feeling of 'not fitting in' in the mind of the artist. He turned shoeboxes into shadow theatres and fabricated mahogany shrines with opening doors and devotive figurines. Later, when an adult, and after the Castro regime had expropriated the family possessions, he got married, probably due to social or family pressures. He left for Knoxville, Tennessee, where he stayed with relatives of his mother-in-law. His wife joined him, but he moved to Miami later on, again alone. He left his family in 1969 and spent time alternatively in Miami and New York.

González engaged in what may be called a second exile, when he fled the Cuban community of Miami and decided to spend time in New York City instead. The Cuban community there seemed less close and inwardly orientated – which allowed him to fully come out as a gay man. He did not join the more militant sides of Gay Liberation, however, and never turned homosexuality into an object of political art, 'except in the broad sense that for the gay man or woman, the personal is always political'. Even AIDS was addressed by him in a 'subjective, spiritual, elegiac, and intimate way'.[66]

The emergence of homoeroticism becomes visible soon, yet remains carefully staged all through the artist's career. It is a constant game of revelation and concealment, inspired in part by the ongoing awareness of marginality, eventually vulnerability in the face of homophobia and AIDS. Social conditions are not the only defining force, however, as González is aware, on a more philosophical and introspective level, of the inner contradictions brought on by sexual desire. From the beginning, the French novelist Jean Genet had a profound influence on him: 'Genet's lyrical and baroque dreams', writes Irene McManus, 'of sin, sacrifice, redemption, and ascension, his unconventional but authentic preoccupation with God, his homoerotic fantasies and rituals, all had a profoundly awakening effect on González.'[67] Other influences both from the field of literature and the visual arts were Federico García Lorca, Truman Capote and Tennessee Williams, then classical art, Michelangelo, Khnopff, Seurat, Hockney, Cornell.

The homotextuality of González's visual language is subtle and allegoric. The male body is present as a symbol, rather than simply as the embodiment of gay desire. In an *Untitled* collage (1974) two decapitated, nude male bodies can be seen as they fight each other. The missing heads symbolize conflict between spirituality and sensuality, or, perhaps, a yearning for Platonic love despite strong physical desire. A peacock in the middle, symbol of male vanity, inscribes the work within the realm of narcissistic homosexuality.

Something of Julio Galán's quest for asexual androgyny, for spiritual hermaphroditism can be perceived in *La cuña* (1976), even when this work is deserted by humanity. It is an image of a *cuña*, or cradle, white, but no baby is lying in it. The image sprang from the artist's friendship with one of his cousins, a girl who found it hard to live up to her family's expectations. González, who experienced a great affinity with her, speculated on how an ideal, androgynous being could be born from a spiritual union between them, from a *coniunctio* of opposites (he male, she female). The mental exercise was triggered by the uneasiness, experienced by both his cousin and himself, towards the social and sexual roles traditionally imposed upon them.

Some works by González – *Irish red (portrait of Patrick)*, *A la cabeza del Bautista en Sevilla*, *El soñador*, *Double portrait of Jimmy, N.Y.C.*, *Still life in red for Manuel* – are portrayals of some of his (possibly gay) friends, just as he painted allegorical images also of his female friends or of some of his relatives. His portraits are fairly detached, yet not uninvolved either. They are discrete visualizations of individual people who played a role in his life.

Or, at times, of unknown strangers, who caught his eye. In *Whistler* (1981), for example, to the left of a self-portrait, one can perceive a housepainter on a ladder. The scene is set in Morocco, visited by González in 1980. One can see the painter observe the artist. This brings about complicity of a physical kind: González, who, while there,

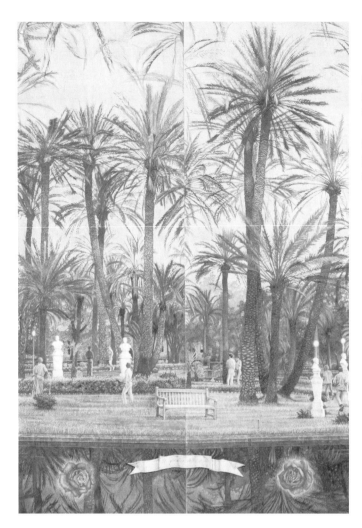

had visited not only Paul Bowles but the Chilean painter Claudio Bravo, also 'tried to make him very sensual. Morocco has so many sensual-looking people. I have him there as a companion in this space that is a cage.'[68]

The anonymity of gay cruising is made tangible also in *Bathers of Blenheim* (1982), which suggests an atmosphere of male bonding, not unlike the works of Walt Whitman or Thomas Eakins. Or also in *Il giardino delle sorelle* (1987), which depicts the Piazza Reale in Palermo, Italy. It is an archetypal image almost of any city's public park, commonly a site for gay men to make contact in the afternoon or at night. Significantly, all of the figures in this painting are men. One is even naked, and all seem to be keeping an eye on everyone else – which is typical of the visual promiscuity implied by cruising.

AIDS changed all this. While spending some time in Philadelphia, the artist saw a newspaper photo of a flooded city and considered the image a brilliant metaphor for the disaster, hitting the gay community especially. He used it as inspiration for *After*

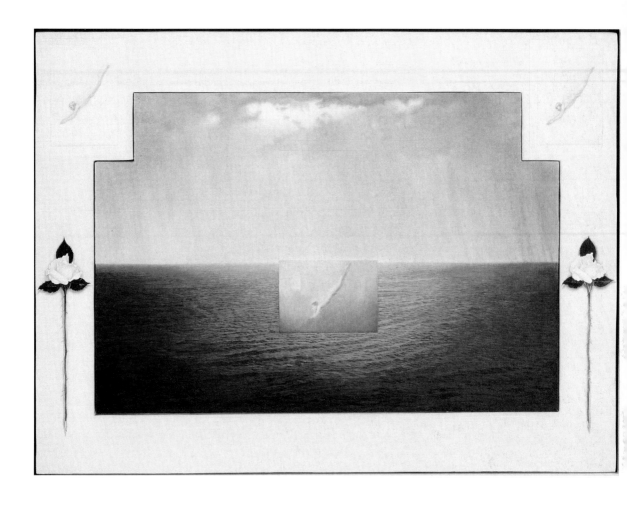

Philadelphia (1982–4), an allegoric panorama including an image of himself while riding a horse. The latter symbolizes masculine sexuality, threatened by the surrounding floods of water.

González tested HIV-positive in 1984. Two years later, his partner Patrick died and González himself died on Christmas Eve 1993. Several of his later works are discreet comments on the AIDS crisis, far removed from the loud, contestational art of Gran Fury or similar. *New York, Year 1986* is devoted to his lover and shows the cityscape of New York. Pigeons fly off the roofs as a man stares into the horizon, his back turned to the viewer, his hands resting in his trouser pockets. Two semi-nude men in jeans sit on identical rooftops, mirror images of one another, yet one is looking away, the other is looking at the first one. Above them, where ominous clouds transform into a white sheet, one can see a wreath of white roses, symbolizing love and martyrdom, innocence and transcendence. 'González reinvents the rose crown of the Spanish painters and the red thorns of Redon to create a visual miracle – a royal crown of grace – for a city suffering from AIDS.'[69]

AIDS is the *Leitmotiv* also in *Mar de lágrimas* (1987–8) and in *In his silence* (1988). The latter departs from Alexandre Falguière's 1867 sculpture of the boy martyr Tarcisius, whose image is connected to Saint Sebastian and adopted as a tribute to a deceased friend, Angél. The self-portrait *Blue* (1993) is perhaps the most clinical vizualization of AIDS ever made by González, and a visible portrayal of physical decay. The artist, now facing death, is suffering from cytomegalovirus and presents his life as in decay. The cracks in the image reinforce the message, as does the use of black, funeral wax, laid on with a spatula. The blue symbolizes loss of memory while the goldleaf underneath reminds one of *estofado*, a technique adapted for polychrome Baroque altars where 'veins' of gold are made visible underneath the painted colours.[70]

The diver's journey (1989), finally, is one of a series of three paintings inspired by the Diver's Tomb at Paestum, Italy. Paestum was described by Pliny, Horace and Ovid as a place where roses bloomed most easily, yet González attributes a more than documentary place to roses in each of the three paintings. Together, they symbolize mystical Trinity and inscribe the classical theme of the diver into a Catholic tradition. In *The diver's journey*, a diver appears threefold, twice in black and white, to the left and right top, and once, in colour, in the middle, caught in a small rectangular frame. Together, they form a triangle turned upside down, yet another symbol of Trinity. The sea is black and its surface morbidly tranquil. Rain pours from a heavy, grey sky – taken, supposedly, from Martin Johnson Heade's *Newburyport Marshes* (1865–75, Museum of Fine Arts, Boston). The image's suggestion of death is reinforced by the thin, black frames, yet the diver seems to be cut loose from destiny's heavy weight. It looks as if his dive into the deep water is spiritual rather than physical, a transcendence of death.

Deliberate exile by some was followed by more or less compulsory expatriation of others, most acutely in 1979. The so-called Mariel operation was targeted at the 'unwanted' individuals, many of whom belonged to the lower social class of Cuba, many of whom were homosexuals, intellectuals and other so-called undesirables.[71] Some of the artists were young and at the beginning of their career. Others, like Carlos Alfonzo and Juan Boza, already had their merits recognized, yet were expelled nevertheless.

Juan Boza (1941–91) was also born in Camagüey, but, when facing repression, emigrated to the USA in 1980 after having received artistic training at the San Alejandro Academy and the Taller Gráfica Experimental in Havana. Though surrounded by *Santería* and carnival in Cuba, he did not think much of these cultural phenomena until he took up residence in New York City.[72] From then on, they became a major topic of interest for the artist. He started creating Afro-Cuban altars, devoted to the *orixás*.

Boza's inscription of his work within the Afro-Cuban tradition of *Santería* does not unveil to what extent a homosexual vision was implied or not. Yet, traditionally, *Santería* is more tolerant towards gender variation and actually attracts a considerable number of homosexual men. Boza did not explicate this dimension, yet one may ask if its very implicit incorporation by the artist is a sign of recognition precisely of the social and cultural tolerance towards homosexuals at least among some segments of traditional Cuban society. Boza had become a *santero* himself.

The recognition of homosexuality, admittedly, was limited and closely tied to ritual contextualization. It wasn't necessarily extended into the practice of daily life. For Boza, however, the search for cultural and sexual identity was merged within one, single Afro-American aesthetic. 'Gay recuperation' remained within the boundaries of the artist's Cuban heritage. It was given a new discursive rhetoric, in fact, that was at odds with current visual idioms of Gay Liberation and underlined the outsider position of Cuban and Cuban-American homosexuals in the face of both their ethnic and sexual community. Conservative at first, when looking only at the formal elements borrowed directly from Cuban *Santería* itself, Boza's visual language is also radical within the context of today's Western society. '[A] background of the "old" together with the new universal influences are the fundamentals of my aesthetics and visual creation', says the artist,[73] who, as a dispossessed person both socially and sexually, aimed at involving himself with both secular and spiritual ancestry through his art.

Carlos Alfonzo (1950–91) initially took part in group exhibitions sponsored by the Cuban government, yet in 1980 he was sent away along with the other exiles of Mariel. He took up residence in Miami until his death of AIDS at forty. He had gained access to galleries and collectors, building a steady reputation and sharing happiness with his lover Carlos Artiga. Artiga also died of AIDS in 1992.

While in Cuba still, the artist's life was marked by hardship and uneasiness, caused in part by traumatizing military service and a brief, unhappy marriage. In his early work, the sea often appeared as a metaphor for potentiality, as a 'vast, unexplored frontier . . ., a place of passion tied to the Afro-Cuban rituals. Its flowering waters also embodied passage, and ultimately, freedom.'[74] Such imagery, while typical perhaps of any islander's artistic sensibility, reflected the threat of censorship and oppression that was pending above him like a sword of Damocles as the Castro regime grew more homophobic.

Still, Alfonzo discreetly assumed his homosexuality, inspired in part by the examples of José Lezama Lima and the Spanish poet Federico García Lorca, in part also by the sensual Afro-Cuban poetry of Nicolás Guillén. Anticipating the coded homotextuality of his later work, Alfonzo even exposed his sexual identity in works such as *Estrellitas volando* (1979). This contains decorative creatures, engaging in forbidden sexual encounters, says Olga Viso,[75] yet was sufficiently covert in order not to alarm the Cuban authorities.

Eventually, Alfonzo was ostracized and fled the island during the epoch of Mariel. His works, until then exhibited in the University of Havana, were removed and his name obliterated from the Cuban art scene. In Miami, Alfonzo's style became mature, remaining

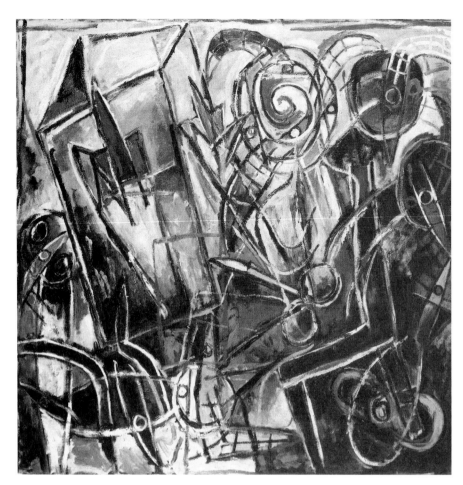

Figure 76 Carlos Alfonzo, *Sin título* (*c.* 1990), oil on canvas, 244 × 183 cm, private collection, courtesy of Sotheby's, New York City.

largely semi-abstract and containing pictographs alongside recognizable elements taken from Afro-Cuban culture, flora and fauna. There are hands, lips, phalluses, and so on, all submerging into some kind of expressionist, vividly coloured chaotic whole. The traumatic experience of exile was one returning aspect of his work; sexual experiment another.

Alfonzo's oeuvre never discloses anything explicitly 'homosexual', as his semi-abstract aesthetic didn't lend itself to anecdotal disclosure. Yet, underneath the violence of shape and colours, the artist's gay sensibility or experience do surface repetitively. In an untitled and unsigned work, *Sin título* (*c.* 1990), one can recognize a person seated on a chair and holding up his knife-like fingers. His penis is visible also, yet it doubles as a paintbrush while his testicles look like the symbol for infinity. Other paintings tell about a memorable sexual encounter or, increasingly, about the death from AIDS of yet another friend. Never, though, is the visual expression of gay experience the leading principle of his work. It is subjected, rather, to the artist's idiosyncratic stylistic concerns, making the homotextual dimension of his oeuvre into one that is both revealed and disguised by polysemic juxtaposition.

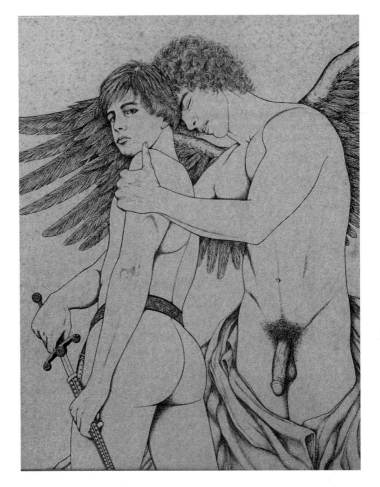

Figure 77 Jaime Bellechasse, *Guardian angel* (*c*.1985), pencil and ink on cardboard, 60 × 45 cm, photo: Miriam Armenguer, courtesy of Daniel Fernández, Miami.

Towards the end of his life, when turning ill, Alfonzo created a series of dark canvases (*Grief*, 1988, and *Blood*, 1991) as well as drawings focusing on human blood. As with Felix González-Torres, whose work will be discussed below, these blood drawings and canvases were premonitions of imminent death, metaphors of contagion and disease. 'I want to explore blood', said the artist, 'not in realist rendering, but as a metaphor.'[76] Ink drawings of that year also, the *South Miami Hospital series* (1990), betray the artist's growing sense of grief and solitude, exhaustion and despair.

Among the younger Mariel *émigrés*, there was Jaime Bellechasse (1956–93), who left the homophobic climate of his home country behind and developed a 'gay' lifestyle while residing in New York. He later moved to Miami, where he subsequently died of AIDS. His work is clearly recognizable as impregnated with homosexual themes. It focuses on male homoerotic sensuality in the first place and aims at attributing positive, redeeming value to love between men. The American gay lifestyle, as an alternative to Cuba's rigid sexual and gender codes, is embraced rather than criticized. For Bellechasse, the positive sides of the North American gay community outweighed the inner divisions and persistent racism within that community, as it also provided practical solutions for someone who was facing harsh repression while still in Cuba.

Felix González-Torres (1957–95) obviously calls for attention here also, especially since his work does not subscribe to the self-complacency of the modern-day gay community, but is critical of the social and cultural construction of sexual identity. González-Torres also raised awareness regarding the futility and impertinence of pigeonholing his work as 'Latin American', a crime of which this very book is guilty, if only factually and by virtue of my focus on homotextuality in Latin American art.

While a Cuban by birth and an 'out' gay man, González-Torres developed an aesthetic language that questioned the ideological presumptions upon which labels such as 'gay art' or 'Latino art' are built. The at once intellectual and emotional characteristics of his oeuvre hardly leave anyone indifferent, though it is not always equally well understood.

Born in Guáimaro, Cuba, Felix González-Torres moved to Puerto Rico at first, then, in 1979, to New York City, where he studied at the Pratt Institute as well as at the International Center of Photography. In 1987, he joined Group Material, a collective of conceptual artists that had already existed since the year he arrived in New York and profiled itself against the highly marketed and commercialized art scene of the 1980s. Inspiration for Group Material as well as Gonzaléz-Torres was found in the writings of Benjamin, Althusser, Barthes and Foucault, along with the feminist art of Cindy Sherman, Jenny Holzer, Barbara Kruger, Sherrie Levine and others. Male artists, too, subscribing to the postmodern canon of 'deconstruction' (Baldessari, Majore, Prince, Welling) or redefining the tenets of Modernism (Bleckner, Halley, Koons, Wool and others) created a background against which González-Torres was to define his own idiosyncratic oeuvre.[77]

The artist's belonging to New York City's gay community obviously compelled him to join those artists who had made sexual identity and desire into an object of artistic investigation. Among them were Robert Gober, Nan Goldin, Keith Haring, Michael Jenkins, Zoe Leonard, Donald Moffet, Jack Pierson and David Wojnarowicz. They were 'intrepidly and quite candidly exploring the social construction of homosexual identity. Their goal, however, was not to establish a new counterimagery that would somehow be more "truthful" about the social, psychic and sexual realities of gay life, but, rather, to repudiate any unitary notion of (representational) truth.'[78] By appropriating existing tropes of representation that reflected straight, hegemonic discourse, these artists, including González-Torres, aimed at infiltrating an already existing art system and questioning its complacent and tendentious orientation. Thus González-Torres explained and justified the guerrilla tactics of this new kind of 'gay art': 'We should not be afraid of using such formal references, since they represent authority and history. Why not take them? When we insert our own discourse into these forms, we soil them. We make them dark. We make them our own and that is our final revenge.'[79]

Such a strategy, while leading to frustration for some extreme rightist enemies of 'immoral art', managed to convey an interesting series of messages to a more enlightened, understanding audience. The homotextual dimension remains subtle and never exclusive, nor explicit. A billboard *Untitled* (1989), which is entirely black and mentions major monuments of gay and lesbian history, is perhaps the most explicit of all. Other works, however, incorporate the audience's potentially divergent attributions of meaning, congruent, in fact, with the postmodern declaration of the author's death.

The billboards, shown across Manhattan, of an empty bed (*Untitled*, 1991) do not reveal if two men slept in it or otherwise. In fact, the artist did not provide any clue as to whether the bed witnessed sleep, sexual intimacy or death. For the artist, the presentation of an image of privacy on the city's walls contained a comment on the Bower vs. Hardwick case and demonstrated that, at least in the USA, 'privacy' is no longer an unalienable right. Yet, it was up to the viewer to suggest his own interpretation, according to his or her judgement and independently from the artist's own, in the end personal and private intention. The effect was aimed at purposively by the artist, who anticipated reductive definitions of his work as 'political commentary'. It was not so much about politics, as an act of politics, that is a way to trigger action and 'make this a better place for all'.[80] The image of a private site – the bedroom, wrinkled sheets, and dented pillows – on the city's public walls and streets aimed at reinforcing the collective endeavour of reading, critique and interpretation. The artists did not even add a second, more revealing title between parentheses this time, leaving an open end to interpretation.

The latter is a common strategy, however, applied by the artist many times. While often using the neutral *Untitled* as the main title, he commonly enriched this by adding one or two words between brackets – words that often disclosed the work's gay content, yet never explicitly. A fine example is *Untitled (perfect lovers)* (1991), showing two battery-operated clocks that indicate the exact same time. The work was included in González-Torres's one-man show at the Hirschhorn Museum in Washington, DC and actually provoked a visit by a congressman favourable to censorship and family values. The man left frustrated, as the homosexual content of which he had heard did not correspond to his own rather narrow ideas of 'pornographic' art. Such play is revealing, in fact, of the unexpected, codified and yet open-ended homotextual dimension in González-Torres's oeuvre, making it into a very compelling form of both (post-)feminist and conceptual art. 'Two clocks', said the artist himself, 'side by side are much more threatening to the powers that be than an image of two guys sucking each other's dicks, because they cannot use me as a rallying point in their battle to erase meaning. It is going to be very difficult for members of Congress to tell their constituents that money is being expended for the promotion of homosexual art when all they have to show are two plugs side by side, or two mirrors side by side, or two light bulbs side by side.'[81]

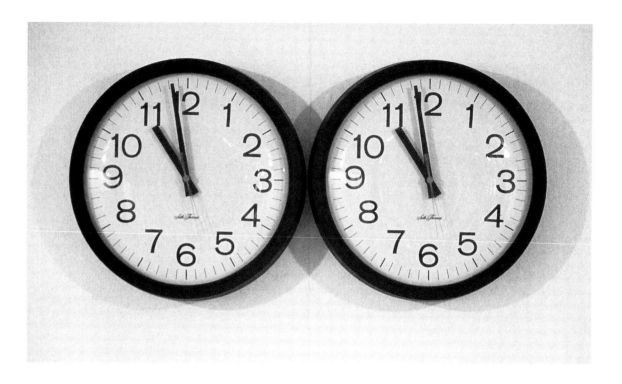

Figure 78 Felix González-Torres, *Untitled (perfect lovers)* (1991), two white-faced clocks, photo: Peter Muscato, courtesy of Andrea Rosen Gallery, New York City/Galerie Xavier Hufkens, Brussels.

Untitled (perfect lovers) was part of a larger installation, including *Untitled (Alice B. Toklas' and Gertrude Stein's grave, Paris)* (1992), as well as *Untitled (lover – Paris)* (1993). The whole 'alluded to libidinal desire', says Nancy Spector, 'while remaining intentionally elusive. Its leitmotif of paired objects suggested erotic coupling; the fact that the objects were identical intimated that the desire was to be construed as homoerotic.'[82]

Similarly, the homotextual dimension is revealed at second glance only in the captions between parentheses: *Untitled (loverboy)* (1989), showing curtains veiling a window, or *Untitled (North)* (1993), with strings of lightbulbs hanging down vertically and cluttering on the floor. This work allows for several interpretations, yet the word 'North' is a cryptic reference to the artist's lover Ross, who lived north in Toronto for several years. The procedure can be found also in *Untitled (loverboys)* (1991), an installation/assemblage of blue-and-white candies, collectively forming the total weight – 350 pounds – of both the artist and his lover. 'The central problem with all of his work', said a newspaper critic, 'is whether we'd "get" any of it without the one-trick labels, which claim . . . that the work is "Untitled" before stating the point in the parentheses.'[83] Put otherwise, rather than reducing an artwork's content to the province of 'gay art', it is crucial for today's artists to 'deconstruct' the very logic of such labelling activity and to turn common divisions upside down. 'Labels are very useful', said González-Torres, 'when you want to be in control. Actually, more than anything I think the work is about form. I'm a sucker for formalism and yes, it does include certain interpretations because everything we see in culture we ascribe to the language. We ascribe to it a narrative.' But for him, the balance between form and content is volatile: never is one of the two poles privileged over the other. This very strategy distinguishes González-Torres's oeuvre from any other 'gay' artist, in fact, as it refuses to participate in a discourse of reification and marginalization and calls for its critical dismantling instead.

The work of art itself gains historical momentum not merely from its formal qualities or fixed social or cultural contents. In fact, the audience's perception itself is crucial to the artistic process and is consciously played upon by the maker himself. *Every week there is something different* (1991) (Plate 18) nicely illustrates this. At first, the viewer – and critic – is offered a rather conventional exhibition of black-and-white photographs, showing the one-word inscriptions on the Roosevelt monument near the Museum of Natural History of New York. The words say: 'Statesman', 'Scholar', 'Explorer', 'Humanitarian', 'Patriot'. . . . But then, one week later, only three of the photographs – 'Soldier', 'Humanitarian', 'Explorer' – are withheld and go-go dancers come in at various times to dance on a platform, lined with small white lightbulbs. 'In such a contrived and kinky context', says Spector, 'the photos quickly acquired different shades of meaning; their bold inscriptions slyly reminded one of the Village People . . . whose members flaunted and parodied stereotypical macho roles with camp bravura. Posturing as "real" men, these male musicians lampooned gender role-playing while revealing the erotic underpinnings of homosocial behaviour.'[84] Simon Watney also recognized a pattern of appropriation, presenting the semi-naked go-go dancer at once as a soldier facing the war zone of homophobia, anxiety and censorship; a humanitarian in his relation to the everyday reality of AIDS in New York City's gay community; finally, as an explorer 'who has dared to set out against all the dreadful pressures of homophobic education and popular culture. He has come out as a gay man . . . and has now stepped courageously into the spotlight of exhibitionism.'[85]

The next week, the artist removed the dance platform as well as the photographs and put down a carpet of silver-wrapped candies, titled *Untitled (placebo)*. Now, the political dimension is becoming clear as the candies stand for placebos given to AIDS patients in the drug-testing programmes by the federal government. At the same time, they are to 'humour' the viewers, who, by taking off one candy, are lured into the subtext of homoerotic desire and homophobia. Formal elements, borrowed from both conceptual and minimal art, thus reinforce an essentially social message about the current problem of AIDS and homophobia.

AIDS evidently is a major theme also in the work of González-Torres, whose lover not only died from it, but who knew about his own seropositive status as well. A series of smaller, graphic works as well as small-scale installations bear witness to the artist's dealing with loss and disease. *Untitled (bloodwork – steady decline)* (1993) contains thirteen drawings of grids, each with a diagonal straight line plotted from the upper left to the lower right. The graphs, while visualizing the declining T-cells in the body, are simultaneously metaphors of imminent death. Once again, Nancy Spector: 'The extraordinary scale of loss created by the AIDS crisis has induced a new cultural understanding of time, a "heterochrony" in which the future aspirations of modern-day youth coexist with a projected life span that contradicts their hopes and dreams.'[86]

Untitled (chemo) (1991) and *Untitled (blood)* (1992) are simple bead curtains, separating two spaces in an apparently innocent way. Yet, when contextualized against the background of AIDS, they too become signifiers of clinical realities. The red beads refer to bloodcells, in which the HIV virus is located predominantly. Chemotherapy is a treatment for AIDS-related (and other) cancers; having to pass through the curtain reinforces the viewer's sense of having to undergo such treatment.

Some of the candy piles, finally, such as *Untitled (portrait of Marcel Brient)* (1992) and *Untitled (a corner of Baci)* (1990), carry within them minimalist messages of microscopic disintegration and cellular decay while equally representing the artist's –and any individual's – courage also 'to be able to let go'. Premature loss due to AIDS is an underlying dimension also in the more intimate works made for his lover Ross, as well as in the public billboard *Untitled* (1990), depicting a verbal message on the right to health care for all.

The body, though central to all these works, remains invisible as the artist chose to de-emphasize the figurative. His work, while immersed in the very concrete situation of the artist both as a gay man, as a person with AIDS and, more marginally, as a Cuban-American, adopts the aesthetic languages of minimalism and conceptual art so that its meanings remain open-ended rather than confined to a single, specific gender, sexual or ethnic configuration.

González-Torres eschewed easily defined roles as a 'gay', 'queer' or 'Latino' artist, just as he also avoided sentimental imagery of AIDS. His work is deeply impregnated with his everyday experience as an American of Cuban descent, whose sexual identity made him grow aware of politics. Yet, rather than playing the chord of simple oppositions – 'us' versus 'them' – he preferred to tackle aesthetic language in itself. He created a Brecht-like alienation, forcing members of all parties and constituencies to open their eyes to the power of discourse itself. He thus pointed out how discourse frames both policy and daily life, not only in relation to AIDS but also with respect to wider issues of sex, gender, race and ethnicity. His concern was to 'draw attention to the workings of the various social and psychic mechanisms of displacement, disavowal, and projection which are actively at work in homophobic discourses, and thus also in the larger cultural process which constitutes and maintains individual and collective subjectivities. Such work is thus intended to intervene at a level prior to the self-consciously political.'[87]

Compared to González-Torres, few artists gained the same intellectual depth, nor did they produce an equally compelling aesthetic language that was both poetic and political, private and public. Nor did most other gay male Cuban-American artists aim at deconstructing surrounding reality in such a systematic and coherent way. The Cuban or, in a wider sense, Latino aspect of one's identity becomes somewhat redundant in the work especially of younger artists, who, while born to Cuban parents, identify primarily as Americans. Or, when facing ongoing processes of marginalization within the USA, as Cuban-Americans. Their growing awareness, in fact, of their minority status despite being born 'American' is an impulse at times for them to go and search for their social and cultural roots.

Ernesto Pujol (b. 1957) surely goes furthest in tracing the genealogy of his own identity and produces work that comments clearly on Latino sexual politics. 'My art work', says Pujol, 'has to do with memory and the deconstruction of the male gender in traditional Latin American society. I am particularly interested in how the white upper classes of Latin America construct oppressive heterosexual masculinity.'[88]

Illustrating the above was the artist's recent one-man show in Cuba itself – the second one only, after Ana Mendieta's, of a Cuban-American artist. *The children of Peter Pan* (1996) consisted of a series of installations, five in total, that clearly shows a thematic closeness to recent developments in Cuba, more precisely, of the ambiguous policy of the late Castro regime towards homosexuality. More historically, the show included a commentary also on the uprooting experiences of so-called *bitonguitos* or 'little princes', bourgeois children – like Pujol – who were sent abroad by their parents as the Revolution spread across the island.

Peter Pan, in this context, is a signifier of childhood memory, coinciding, says Gerardo Mosquera, with the loss of Cuba as the artist's 'foundational myth'.[89] But it is a gay metaphor also, claims Pujol, reinforcing the experience of uprootedness and isolation.[90] The show included *Rocking chairs*, which consisted of nine rocking chairs placed on a carpet of split peas (*chícharos*) and sugarcane waste (*bagazo*). The latter signifies the produce that once enriched the Cuban upper class; the former symbolize inferior food products, now essential to the ordinary Cuban's diet. On the mahogany chairs, small white ceramic genitals were placed, 'connoting the innocence of those not able to decide their future'.[91] The chairs, positioned three times three, acknowledge the input of black culture also, as it accompanied and enriched the artist's white, Creole descent. Three, in Afro-Cuban religion, stands for Elegguá, the *orixá* protecting children as well as the spirit of the road. Pujol thus adopts a local, indigenous character as if to bless *ex post facto* the child's journey into exile.

Saturn's table (1996) (Plate 19) was another of the five installations, set up specifically for the site in Havana. It is a compelling work that directly addresses the metaphor of castration. 'I think', explains Pujol, 'that, just like feminist women artists have worked

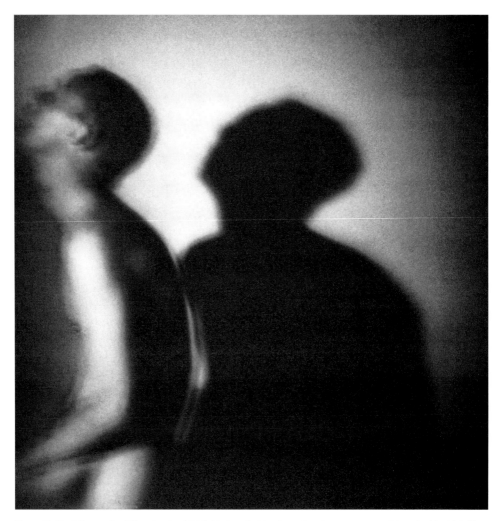

Figure 79 Frank Franca, *David from London* (1996), black-and-white photo, 51 × 51 cm, courtesy of the artist, New York City.

with the metaphor of rape for the past thirty years, homosexual artists must be courageous and use the metaphor of castration . . . to deconstruct and undo traditional heterosexual patriarchy.'[92]

Such a position, while immediately relevant to a discussion of sexual politics, here within a Cuban context reminds one also of how castration is often applied as a tool of representation in a more strictly political sense. In her study of French Revolutionary art, Abigail Solomon-Godeau emphasizes 'how fantasy, sexuality, and sexual politics [were] actively at work within the terrain of the political'. Images of castration became signifiers, in this context, of regicide; images of family romance reinforced the new post-Revolutionary reconstruction of civil and family law.[93] *Saturn's table* carries within itself an ironic reversal of French post-Revolutionary art, castration thus becoming a vehicle for criticizing the Castro regime (regicide) and its reactionary policy towards sexual diversity.

Performance artist Ricardo Zulueta (b. 1960) was born in Cuba, grew up in Miami and now resides in New York. He only reluctantly admits to covering issues of (homo)sexual identity, arguing that such explicitness would unnecessarily pigeonhole and marginalize his work. Instead, he develops his very own aesthetic, as exemplified, for instance, in *Therapy IV* (1988). The act of performance actually looks like a tableau, says Lucy Lippard, '[that is conceived] as vignettes of specific (but unidentified) historical situations'.[94] Like Felix González-Torres's work, Zulueta's critical distance is telling of his critique of sexual taxonomy – a taxonomy that has been imposed upon most of Latin America by virtue of a dominant Eurocentric discourse, including sexological theory and the social regulation of sex.

Frank Franca's photographic work, on the other hand, shows affinity with a more traditional brand of 'out gay art' and openly acknowledges the sexual dimension of gay identity. Franca (b. 1961) was born in Havana and grew up in Mexico, Spain and Florida, yet now situates his work within the gay (male) community of New York, to which he belongs. Nothing in his work indicates scepticism or plain refusal of the label 'gay'. In fact, his work for the gay community itself, especially within the context of AIDS prevention and education, demonstrates the artist's commitment to the gay cause. He produced the photowork of the Day without Art poster of 1995 as well as an entire series of rather explicit photos used by the Gay Men's Health Crisis as illustration material for mini-posters about the risks of unprotective sex. He contributed as a project artist and designer also to Electric Blanket, an early initiative to raise people's consciousness about HIV and AIDS through art.

His other photos are poetic celebrations of gay male sexuality, often verging towards the harder edges of S/M. This occurs in a rather playful way, however, as opposed to the coldness of much work focusing on similar themes. In a recent series, the pictures remain deliberately blurred in order to reinforce the sensual and at times orgasmic experience (*David from London*, 1996; *José in chains*, n.d.) of single, masturbating men.

Fascinating, next, is the work of Maria Elena González (b. 1957), one of only a few 'out' Cuban-American lesbian artists, and one who, like González-Torres and Zulueta, refrains from presenting her works within the confines of 'gay' or 'Latino' art. Maria Elena González produces an oeuvre that is undoubtedly most intellectually compelling. It is feelings, however, and sensations, that trigger the process and allow for the spectator to penetrate into the complex layers of meaning that constitute the body and consistency of her work.

González left Cuba with her family in 1968. She arrived in Miami, where she became part of the large Cuban community. She settled down in New York after studies in Miami and San Francisco, where she 'came out'. Exile, however, was not inspired by a desire to come out or to make that process easier by moving to another country. Already at the early age of seven, her mother had become aware of Maria Elena's development towards a lesbian identity and had supported this by calling her *invertida*, sympathetically and at odds with the homophobia so thriving in other parts of Cuban society.

Recurrent concerns in González's works are ecology, cultural identity – more specifically, the position of Latin American and Latin(o/a) artists on the art market – and sexual politics. At times these are reflected in the artist's use of materials (wood, rawhide, wax, latex, tiles, metal, pubic hair, or feathers), yet the message is often encoded within subtle plays of signification. Cuban identity is hardly expressed through visual language or objects taken from her native country, except, perhaps, the rawhide that is used for *congas* too. In *Telling tales*, mahogany tongues are hooked up to a wooden beam – a subtle reference to *Santería*.

The feminist dimension, most relevant here, is not made visible simply by addressing women's issues, but rather by informed, visual commentary upon, among other things, the context of artistic production. New -isms, including feminism, contain a potential threat of new manipulations, says González, who prefers to remain alert in view of commodified ideas.[95] Perhaps this explains why the 'lesbian' content of some works by González extends to a commentary upon the ongoing invisibility of lesbian art while she trespasses the province of 'gay' art by deconstructing the artificiality of sexual labelling, even of gay and lesbian politics. A fine installation, titled *Self-service* (1996) (Plate 20), consists of a small bathroom-like space, tiled and equipped with tiny, circular mirrors as well as two handles. The room is accessible to the audience, which is drawn infallibly by the phallic device against one wall. The device is named Gloria, like the clichéd image of a glory hole. It is made of polished wood and rawhide, and attached so as to suggest auto-erotic pleasure. It not only invites the viewer to consider use of Gloria, no matter what one's gender or sexual identity may be, but also to embrace the originally lesbian-inspired environment as an opportunity for introspective criticism and a more outward questioning of any label's artificiality. In a way, *Self-service* can be seen also as a post-feminist transcription of Judy Chicago's *Menstruation bathroom* as well as of Faith Wilding's *Womb room*, first by deliberately widening the range of femininity beyond the reproductive cycle, and secondly by drawing attention to sexual pleasure, whether heterosexual or homosexual, female or male. The installation thus lends itself to multiple pleasures while simultaneously challenging current taxonomies of gender identity and sexual desire.[96]

House of games (1996) was installed at Rotunda Gallery (Brooklyn) and consisted of children's games (basketball, merry-go-round, pin-the-tail-on-the-donkey, Chinese checkers). The installation, while accessible for children, provided intellectual commentary at the same time and contained a powerful political message about the contemporary attacks on artistic expression. In subtle ways, the games had been given sexual

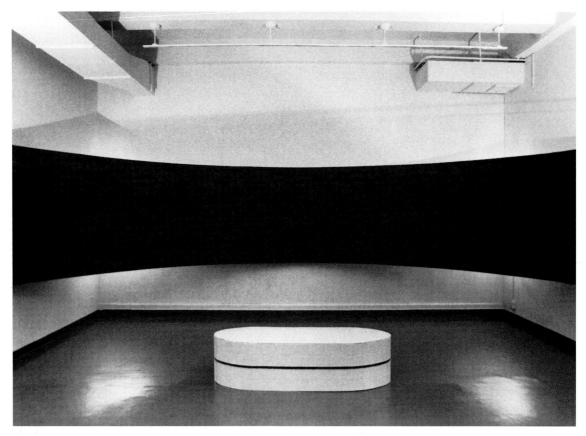

Figure 80 Maria Elena González, *Persistence of sorrow* (1996), installation, rubber, wood and vaseline, photo: Bruce Schwartz, courtesy of the artist, Brooklyn, New York.

connotations also, yet these were to be discovered only through the visitor's participation and play.

The active, tactile dimension is an omnipresent dimension of González's art and can be noticed in smaller works also. *Audrey* (1994) looks like a *boudoir* table at first, yet hidden within is a stylized representation of a *vagina dentata*, symbol of the pressures that stem from rigid gender roles. A tube, whose interior is covered with nasty nails, or, in another work, plastic fish-shaped soy sauce containers that smell fishy, are in-your-face reminders of sexist politics as well as of voyeurism thrown back at you. In *See saw* (1995), two World War Two hospital splints are installed upon a curving metal base. The splints are covered partially with female pubic hair and defiant celebrations of lesbian sexuality.[97]

Death – 'the enormous presence of absence'[98] – is the central theme of *Persistence of sorrow* (1996), an installation that harbours the names of numerous lost family members and friends. The concept reminds one of the well-known AIDS Quilt, yet it trespasses the province of AIDS and its elaboration is marked by a quite different approach. The visitor enters inside an oval, sepulchral space that has been dimly lit and is covered with

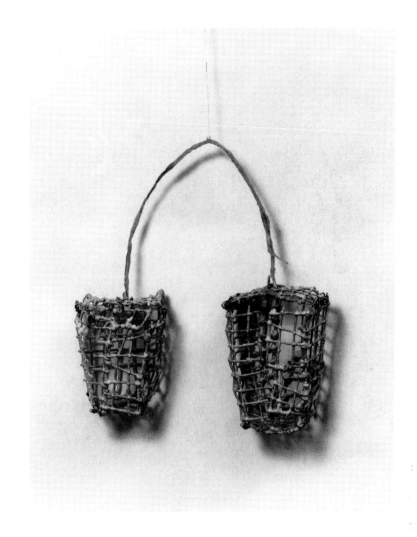

Figure 81 Linda Matalón, *Yoke* (1996), wire, wax and cloth,
89 x 40.5 x 18 cm, collection of Marc and Livia Strauss,
photo: D. James Dee, courtesy of Jack Shainman Gallery, New York City.

neoprene all around. On the surface, braille names can be felt that have been gathered from the artist's own relatives and friends. They are part of a network that has been decimated by death and disease. The names stick to the viewer, subsequently, since they are covered with a shiny smudge of Vaseline. The tactile moment, important in *Shelter* (1994) also, has now become the crux of an artistic experience and calls the viewer to share the sorrow brought on by disease and death.

The Brooklyn-born Cuban-American artist Linda Matalón (b. 1958) works with wax, wire, cloth and, sometimes, tar to suggest the shape of infirm, disabled bodies – an aesthetic language triggered by the AIDS epidemic, to which she felt closely related as an 'out' lesbian Latina artist. But there is a more upbeat dimension to her work also and a subtle reference to the vaguely erotic attractions experienced by the artist as a child. Her father owned a shop in the garment district of New York, where she spent hours as a child sitting on the big cutting tables where women were at work with big scissors. This atmosphere resonates in the works of 'embodied abstraction', made with techniques like sewing, weaving and wrapping.[99]

Matalón's work is influenced by Brancusi and Eva Hesse especially, whose minimalist sculptures imply deconstructive commentaries upon the social construction of gender and sexual identity. This is aimed at equally by Matalón, whose biomorphic sculptures (*Yoke*, 1996) seem to 'embody' fluid sexual desire. Vaguely reminiscent of body parts, both female and male, the often hanging sculptures become signifiers of vulnerability. Shifting morphologically from sexually undefined legs to phallic shapes to female breasts, they are marked by visual indeterminacy, says Liz Kotz, beautiful and yet unsettling.[100] 'They seem to be imbued', says another critic, 'with a protective desire, not to contain objects, but to protect desires, wishes, and intentions.'[101] Categories of masculinity and femininity seem to become obsolete in the work of Matalón, who thus continues the sexual politics of Hesse and lends a new, more radical dimension to her 'lesbian'-inspired work.

New *cidades maravilhosas*: Brazilian gay artists in exile

The political climate of Brazil between 1964 and the renewed democratization towards the late 1980s evidently triggered the exile of numerous homosexual men and women, some of whom pursued an artistic career when abroad. They often partook in the emancipatory process of homosexuals in Europe or North America, while subscribing to the middle-class model of 'gay identity'. But underneath the apparent adoption of a reified model of sexual identity, traces remain of Brazil's most complex and often sophisticated sexual culture – a culture marked by fluid boundaries, by pragmatic discrepancies between discourse and behaviour, by role reversal and by an almost constant ironization of sexual orthodoxy. Caught by the metaphor of 'carnivalization', this complex play of sexual desire remains visible in the art production of gay Brazilian artists in exile until today. It can be perceived, for example, in the art work of Claudio Mesquita, the one-time lover of the deceased political agitator and gay activist Herbert Daniel, with whom he lived abroad for several years. Both of their exiles were politically inspired predominantly, as they were critical opponents of the military regime in 1970s Brazil. But their prolonged stay in Paris was an opportunity for sexual liberation also.

The years of political *Abertura* made politics into a less urgent motive for migration or exile, but Brazil still harbours problems when it comes to sexual politics. Especially middle-class gay men and women, who have the economic means to emigrate, now tend to choose residency in Miami, New York, Paris, Amsterdam, London or Sydney in order to feel free in their pursuit of happiness. This very economic aspect explains why, as a group, these Brazilian *émigrés* are less visible and blend in with middle-class communities rather inconspicuously.

Some of the artists among them welcome life abroad as a ticket to gay self-realization, whereas others maintain a somewhat more covert position. Often, the latter reflects the relatively common pattern in Brazil of men who are factually bisexual yet define themselves as 'straight' and eventually get married and raise children.

Or they are straight, but find the social and artistic climate abroad to be more welcoming of imagery that, at home, may be considered controversial. One such story is laid bare in the artistic production of Sérgio Ferro (b. 1938), who resided in Paris for many years and who, while trained as an architect, is a prolific visual artist as well. As a neoclassicist, he draws heavily upon Ancient Greek, Roman and Christian iconography, and does so in a style that is influenced by great masters such as Titian, Veronese, Giorgione and Michelangelo.

Ferro, who is married and a father, cannot be called a 'gay artist', even when his oeuvre demonstrates an outspoken focus upon the male body as a topic of visual expression. Male (semi-)nudity abounds, even when at times heterosexualized by the painting's thematic narrative. Ferro's commercial success may well explain why he is reluctant to publicly acknowledge the potentially homoerotic content of many of his works, but he factually produces images that appeal to a homosexual *imaginaire*.

Numerous are his works representing the male nude. They show Adam, Saint John the Baptist, and Saint Sebastian among others – all figures allowing the artist to focus on the male nude as did the academic artists of the nineteenth century. More contemporary themes, including a series on Vincent van Gogh, also focus on the masculine body while the narrative context may have allowed otherwise. His *Projeto painel Bandeirantes* (1995) is perhaps the most explicitly eroticized visualization of the male bonding that characterized the pioneers of the Brazilian Far West. A huge panorama of masculine strength and muscularity extends itself from left to right and reiterates the epic monumentality, already striking in the *Monumento ás bandeiras* of Vítor Brecheret.[102]

In his own way, Ferro insists on transcending common, limiting categories of sexual identity that supposedly define artistic output in a linear, almost mechanical way. Leaving aside the artist's sexual identity, as I have done at various instances elsewhere, I do recognize a certain 'postmodern' refusal to subscribe to the altogether static taxonomy of modern sexual science. Perhaps, progress can be discerned in homoerotic work made by straight artists, if only in the sense that a male artist's focus upon the male body and, for that matter, of a female artist upon the female body can actually be appreciated apart from speculation on the maker's sexual identity.

Entirely different is the artistic career of the photographer Samuel Costa, who envisioned Paris as one of Europe's capitals where artistic growth and sexual liberation went hand in hand. Working for gay magazines such as *Gai Pied Hebdo*, he actively contributed to the gay movement by taking both documentary and erotic photographs. He laid much focus on the actual diversity of gay subcultures worldwide and documented such by photographs, including ones taken in his own country, Brazil. But for him, partaking in the bustling gay life of pre-AIDS Paris was a natural way out of the complexities of his own country's sexual labyrinth and he actively pursued the visualization of gay freedom by means of images that, like Franca's in New York, celebrated his newly found community's positive values and integrity.

Europe's 'Gay capital' Amsterdam naturally harbours foreign gay artists, especially since the Dutch authorities are relatively welcoming of gay partnerships, internationally composed or not. The city on the canals has become the home of mixed-media artist Claudio Goulart (b. 1954). *A man can hide another* (1994) and *Interior portrait* (1995) are installations commenting upon the HIV-positive body and lay bare the awkward interaction between attractiveness and disease. The artist's presentation of himself, either dressed or naked but always blindfolded, awakens an uneasy feeling for the viewer. Are we entitled to admire his physical beauty – and, conversely, is the artist entitled to pose seductively while his inner body is threatened by decay? How honest must one be? Is disclosure of one's serostatus inevitable, or is one entitled to keep it secret?

In Geneva, Zaqueu Guimarães (b. 1963) is studying at the École des Beaux Arts, while already active as a video artist. *Untitled* (1998) is a video documentary about his boyfriend's life as an HIV-positive person. While documenting the challenge of combination therapy and compliance faced by his partner, Guimarães reflects on the ambiguity of increased life expectancy in a still very gloomy, medical perspective.

The USA attracted Brazilian artists also, who settled down in San Francisco, Los Angeles, New York or increasingly also Miami, where a large thriving Brazilian expatriate community exists. The drawings by New York-based artist Luiz Fonseca are clear, straightforward images of gay male eroticism verging towards a degree of explicitness that is political rather than pornographic (*Masturbation*, 1976). They celebrate Gay Liberation and still exhale some of the 1970s euphoria, soon to be ended by the tragedy of AIDS.

As such, they are different indeed from the more recent photographic work by Ferenc Suto (b. 1960), also currently residing in New York. These contain subtle homoerotic imagery, yet they are printed on a very small scale. The prints are hidden behind paper 'veils' also, as if to emphasize that the gay male gaze has become somewhat clandestine once again, notwithstanding Gay Lib.

Marcelo Maia is a New York City-based photographer, who focuses on the beauty especially of Brazilian and North American black men. His work, while stylistically different and often imbued with effects of *clair obscur*, exhales a fetishistic dimension not unlike Robert Mapplethorpe's and equally inscribes the black man's physical difference within an eroticizing homosexual gaze. While commenting upon racist representations of the 'ugly' black race, it merely subverts such a code by attributing positive connotations to it. Yet, whereas Mapplethorpe at times went too far in objectifying the black male as a sexual 'stud', Maia himself makes an effort to let his models speak and to let his audience discover their soul. His work remains largely aestheticizing, however.[103]

Other gay exiles from Brazil are Luis Montoya, Carlos Pisco, Geo, and Hely Lima, all of whom produce more or less recognizable 'gay' art that is, admittedly, uneven in quality. Documenting Gay Liberation in North American cities, these artists seem to embrace exile as a way out of Brazilian homophobia. At the same time, their work is often romantic and derivative of a kind of *bossa nova* naïvety. Reluctant, all of them, to leave behind the carnivalesque, they collectively create a visual documentary of high expectations in metropolitan America.

The growing number of artists who no longer feel reluctant to disclose their sexual identity must not mislead us into believing that sexual diversity has become less problematic within some of the USA's Latin American communities, the Brazilian one included. Problems of homophobia, heterosexism and sexism remain strong forces, even when the 'accommodating' and pragmatic nature of Latino Roman Catholic heritage provides islands of tolerance and acceptance. It is clear, however, that the rigid gender system, implied by *machismo*, requires gay men and lesbians to conform to a higher degree than in other communities of the USA and to live up to current expectations of *tortilleras* and butch dykes, of sissies and *maricones*. The struggle for cultural autonomy and resistance against such limiting choices is still ongoing.

Meanwhile, there are signs that homotextuality is no longer adopted as a source of iconographic representation only by gay or lesbian artists. Straight artists, too, increasingly aware of the impact of AIDS on the artistic community, include images of *ambiente* in their own work. The growing legitimacy of themes such as sexual identity and AIDS within the Latin American communities of North America is addressed by artists who have the intellectual courage to tackle these topics. AIDS, of course, is a tragedy that hits not only gay men. In the Latino communities especially, AIDS is a problem for all and for straight women in the first place. The *AIDS Epidemic* series of the Cuban exile Luis Cruz Azaceta is to be seen against this context. But his work is inclusive of – and compassionate with – gay people as well, which is an indication of how rigid, simplistic representations of Latino homophobia are erroneous.

Criticism of surrounding heterosexism is expressed by Andres Serrano also, who, while positioning himself as a straight artist, calls for the embracing of most variant sexualities. His recent series *A History of Sex* presents crystal-clear and static, almost iconic and contemplative images of so-called taboo sexual experiences, some of these being homosexual. Serrano nevertheless 'banalizes' the realm of gay sex, simply by integrating these images in his larger series. The latter, while deconstructing public discourse on the borders of 'sexual normality', is a bold, if widely misunderstood call for critical self-reflection in the face of human imagination.

Serrano, born to a Honduran father and an Afro-Cuban mother, was raised in Brooklyn and identifies primarily as an American. But it is curious to see how the grid of his own Roman Catholic and syncretic heritage, when laid upon a North American reality, makes the artist into an avant-garde commentator upon social and cultural constructions of gender, sexuality, and – in many other works – ethnicity and race. He also commented upon religious discourse regarding sexuality, accusing both Roman Catholics and Protestants for not addressing the real needs of people with AIDS. His blood and semen pictures were set up deliberately to denounce the nefarious effect of rigid morality and sexual taboo.

Like González-Torres or René Santos, Ester Hernández or Maria Elena González, Serrano lays bare the mechanisms of stigmatization. Together, they show how the experience of stigmatization, whether sexual, gender or ethnic, compels the production of a critical art discourse that reaches beyond the ghetto and into the heart of contemporary society itself.

Conclusion

Perhaps it is no coincidence that the postmodern deconstruction of a Gay Liberation-inspired 'gay art' has been or is addressed by a fairly high number of artists of Latin American descent. Possibly, their awareness of the relative and culture-bound concept of gay identity has prompted them to subject the production of 'gay' imagery to a more critical gaze. At times reflecting a sort of universal celebration of same-sex eroticism, the images of *ambiente* have become increasingly ironic of such essentialist naïvety, and carry within themselves a more or less explicit criticism of the universalist claims of 'gay art'.

The alternative, 'queer' aesthetic surely is to be attributed in part to the artists, now living in North America or Europe, but involved in a process of negotiation between the sexual and gender systems of these societies' mainstream cultures, and their doubly marginalized status as gay men and lesbians of an ethnic minority. The conscious modification of an essentially Eurocentric, white middle-class gay (male) model is reflected in the dissemination of images that altogether present a far more diverse *ambiente* and enrich the more comprehensive agenda of 'queer' criticism. Inscribed in both a discourse of cultural and sexual diversity, such new, postmodern visions of the gay realm are destined to move beyond the provincial boundaries of community art and nurture society's actual reflection upon the self.

Evidently, such sophisticated guidelines are not equally shared by all and I have described earlier how straightforward legitimation of gay and lesbian imagery remains a popular trope of representation in view of ongoing sexism, heterosexism and homophobia. Witnessing the as yet limited achievements of Latino gays and lesbians in the face of their own community's moral standards, as of the mainstream gay and lesbian communities' racism, they are chronicling how, in Latino communities, an individual gay person's life is often marked by feelings of guilt and self-hatred, fear and hiding, a choice for the closet or even suicide. The inventive and creative work reviewed earlier has also revealed, however, how the visual arts are adopted by some as a weapon to claim justice towards gay people, or as a means of affirmation, a defiant posing to the outside world. AIDS, as a catalyser on the level of artistic debate and sensibilities, has contributed, in this context, both to images of vulnerability, sorrow and loss, and to visions of redemption, hope and assertiveness.

In close communication, finally, with artists who remain working in Latin America itself, these artists collectively break barriers as they emphasize cultural and sexual difference. Making the border between the USA and Mexico into an increasingly redundant category of description, the images of *ambiente* now reflect a coming of age of cultural diversity within the worldwide gay community itself. It has been the aim of this book, in fact, to stress that attention must be paid also to the rich visual imagination to be found in some of its segments that are wrongly defined as 'marginal'. Gay, or, at second instance, queer art thus positions itself as a prime and lively commentary upon the postcolonial centre/periphery debate.

Notes

1 During the 'Crossing Borders. Queer Sexualities in Latin/o America' conference at CUNY, New York, in October 1996, a paper was given by Rubén Ríos Ávila on the hidden sexual agenda of 'graduating' in the USA ('Desire builds more than one motherland in one's son's or daughter's heart'). His notion of de- and re-territorialization is instructive to a better

understanding of what 'coming out' in exile implies. Compare F. Negrón-Muntaner, who claims that liberation first comes in English and is only then translated in Spanish again. See D. E. Rodríguez, 'Un cine sospechoso: conversando con Frances Negrón-Muntaner', unpublished manuscript.

2 See S. M. Goldman and T. Ybarra-Frausto, *Arte Chicano: A Comprehensive Annotated Bibliography of Chicano Art, 1965–1981* (Berkeley, 1985), and *Dimensions of the Americas: Art and Social Change in Latin America and the United States* (Chicago and London, 1994), 'Women speaking' section.

3 See L. de la Graza's *Preliminary Chicano and Latino Lesbian and Gay Bibliography* (Berkeley, 1994).

4 It needs to be emphasized that 'marianismo' is not an indigenous concept, but was first used by social scientist Evelyn Stevens, 'Marianismo: the other face of machismo in Latin America', in A. Pescatello (ed.), *Female and Male in Latin America: Essays* (Pittsburgh, 1973), p. 91: 'the cult of feminine spiritual superiority, which teaches that women are semi-divine, morally superior to and spiritually stronger than men'.

5 H. Gamboa, Jr, 'In the City of Angels, Chameleons and Phantoms: ASCO, a case study of Chicano art in urban tones (or ASCO was a four-member word)', in *Chicano Art: Resistance and Affirmation, 1965–1985* (Los Angeles, 1990), pp. 121–30. Also, see S. Zaneta-Kosiba-Vargas, 'Harry Gamboa and ASCO: the emergence and development of a Chicano art group, 1971–1987', unpublished Ph.D. diss. University of Michigan, 1988.

6 Goldman and Ybarra-Frausto, *Arte Chicano*, p. 53. This rather large definition includes other 'performances', such as Brazilian carnival (itself an interesting stage of homosexual expression) or drag queen shows.

7 Gamboa, 'In the City of Angels', p. 124.

8 This, as well as the following paraphrases, are taken from Gamboa's account. See Gamboa, 'In the City of Angels', *passim*.

9 Personal communication by Biron, photographer and one-time acquaintance of Gronk and Sandoval, San Francisco, 27 June 1996. The flyer contains other names of artists, yet there is no certainty regarding their sexual identities.

10 Quoted in E. Carr, 'Just another painter from East L.A.', *LA Weekly*, 16, 16 (18–24 March 1994), p. 16.

11 *Ibid.* Also, see the interview in *Gronk: Fascinating Slippers/Pantuflas* (San José, CA, 1992), n.p. A survey of the artist's oeuvre can be seen in the catalogue *¡Gronk! A Living Survey, 1973–1993* (San Francisco, 1993).

12 M. Benavidez, in *Gronk: Hotel Senator. Paintings* (Los Angeles, 1990), n.p.

13 Personal communication by Biron.

14 Artist's statement. Thanks to Linda Vallejo.

15 See J. Alcina Franch, *Pre-Columbian Art* (New York, 1983), pp. 578, 580 and 586.

16 See M. Gregg Michaud, 'The passion of Miguel Angel Reyes', *Saludos Híspanos*, Summer 1996, pp. 106–11; Anon., 'Miguel Angel Reyes', *Hombres Latinos*, 2 (January 1996), pp. 22–9. The mural, now demolished for a new subway line, was located at the corner of Hollywood Blvd. and Western Avenue.

17 Letter from the artist, 23 June 1997.

18 Personal communication, Los Angeles, 1 August 1996.

19 For a more comprehensive study, see D. Román, 'Teatro Viva!: Latino performance and the politics of AIDS in Los Angeles', in E. L. Bergmann and P. J. Smith (eds), *¿Entiendes? Queer Readings, Hispanic Writings* (Durham and London, 1995), pp. 346–69.

20 Stellweg, *Uncommon Ground: 23 Latin American Artists*, p. 16.

21 This show, however, faced severe problems. The Mexican curator, José Maria Covarrubias, was denied entry into the USA due to 'lack of funds'. See K. Baca, 'INS denies visa to Mexican exhibit curator', *San Francisco Sentinel*, 7 June 1990, p. 14.

22 On Patiño, see Chapter 5.

23 *Queer Raza: el corazón me dio un salto* (San Francisco, 1995), curators' statement, n.p.

24 D. Contreras and D. Medina, in *Queer Raza*, n.p.

25 T. Avena, in T. Avena and Adam Klein, *Jerome: After the Pageant* (San Francisco, 1996), p. 83.

26 See A. Klein, 'Jerome! An incomparable pageant', *San Francisco Bay Times*, 16 November 1995, pp. 29–30.

27 Personal communication, 20 December 1996.

28 H. Cotter, 'Eclectic group new to the limelight', *New York Times*, 11 August 1995, p. C25.

29 F. Correa, in *Painters' Painters* (Norfolk, 1995), p. 8.

30 [Editor], '(Queer) art attack: the "virtually normal" vs. progressive queers of color organizing', *GCN*, 21, 2 (Fall 1995), pp. 6–7, 28–9. Also, see coverage of the issue in the centre's publication *La Voz*.

31 *Ibid.*

32 D. E. Hulick, 'Laura Aguilar', *Latin American Art*, 5, 3 (1993), p. 53.

33 Y. Yarbro-Bejarano, 'Laying it bare: the queer/colored body in photography by Laura Aguilar', in C. Trujillo (ed.), *Living Chicana Theory* (Berkeley, 1998), p. 286. Also, see L. Alfaro, 'Queer culture: "Exposing ourselves": photography expression workshops by Laura Aguilar', *Vanguard*, 7 August 1992, p. 17.

34 B. Sichel, in *El jo divers: Laura Aguilar* (Barcelona, 1998), p. 38.

35 See, in this respect, G.-N. Anderson, 'Eye-catching flesh and zone', *Northern Review*, 20 (April 1997), n.p.

36 Yarbro-Bejarano, 'Laying it bare', p. 284.

37 Y. Yarbro-Bejarano, 'The lesbian body in Latina cultural production', in Bergman and Smith (eds), *¿Entiendes? Queer readings, Hispanic writings*, p. 182.

38 *Ibid.*, p. 187.

39 *Ibid.*, p. 184.

40 G. Anzaldúa, *Borderlands/La frontera: The New Mestiza* (San Francisco, 1987), p. 84.

41 Quoted in Yarbro-Bejarano, 'The lesbian body', p. 192.

42 D. Deitcher, in *René Santos: Suspension of the Law* (New York, 1994), p. 43.

43 *Ibid.*, p. 13.

44 For a critical review, see E. García Gutiérrez, in *El Nuevo Día*, 23 July 1995. Also see previous chapter.

45 Personal communication by the artist, New York City, September–October 1996. Many thanks also to Mauricio Laffitte-Soler, New York City, September–October 1996.

46 L. D. Beghtol, in *HX Magazine*, 28 June 1996, pp. 40–1.

47 Personal communication, New York City, 16 October 1996.

48 *Ibid.*

49 *Ibid.*

50 See catalogue of the posthumous show 'Alberto Valderrama. My life is my art. Death is just a change of media', New York, 1997.

51 Personal communication by Andy Glasgow, Washington, DC, 1 February 1997.

52 Personal communication, 7 November 1997.

53 The full reference is: Miguel Ventura, *Die Notizbücher der Mademoiselle Heidi Schreber* [*The Notebooks of Mademoiselle Heidi Schreber*], edition in Spanish, English, German, Chinese, Arabic and Swahili (with translations in Spanish and English) (Mexico City: NILC (The New Interterritorial Language Committee), 1995).

54 R. Tejada, 'Miguel Ventura', *Sulfur*, 38 (Spring 1996), p. 35.

55 Most critics don't recognize this dimension, however. See C. Reid, 'Miguel Ventura and Jody Culkin', *Art in America* (November 1995), pp. 89–90, and N. Princenthal, 'Artist's book beat', *The Print Collector's Newsletter* (July–August 1995), p. 110.

56 Artist's statement, manuscript, 1999, n.p.

57 F. Negrón-Muntaner, 'Beyond the cinema of the Other or towards another cinema', unpublished manuscript, 1995, p. 1. Many thanks to the author.

58 See interview by D. E. Rodríguez, 'Un cine sospechoso', unpublished manuscript, p. 8.

59 'Brincar el charco' literally means 'to cross the puddle' and refers here to the intensive mobility between the island and New York.

60 For further information, see C. A. Rodríguez-Matos, 'Frances Negrón-Muntaner', in Foster, *Latin American Writers on Gay and Lesbian Themes*, pp. 288–90. Also, see her seminal article on contemporary Puerto Rican gay and lesbian history, 'Echoing Stonewall and other dilemmas: the organizational beginnings of a gay and lesbian agenda in Puerto Rico, 1972–1977', *Centro*, 4, 1 (Winter 1991–2), pp. 76–95; 4, 2 (Spring 1992), pp. 98–115.

61 On early Revolutionary Cuban policy towards homosexuality, see Lumsden, *Machos, Maricones and Gays*, chs. 3 and 4, and Leirner, *Sexual Politics in Cuba*, ch. 2.

62 See Lumsden, *Machos*, pp. 28–36, and J. Quiroga, 'Homosexual letters: the gender of correspondence', *passim*.

63 G. Pogolotti, *Angel Acosta León* (Havana, 1991).

64 Statement by Héctor Santiago, New York, 9 September 1996.

65 See *STET*, 1, 2 (Winter 1992), p. 26.

66 I. McManus, *Dreamscapes: The Art of Juan González* (New York, 1994), p. 13.

67 *Ibid.*, p. 11. Also, see D. Knaub, *Juan González: A Twentieth-century Baroque Painter* (Dallas, 1991), and R. H. Coen, 'The art of Juan González', *Arts Magazine* (May 1983), pp. 118–21.

68 Quoted in McManus, *Dreamscapes*, p. 92.

69 *Ibid.*, p. 120.

70 See *ibid.*, p. 178.

71 Interview with Héctor Santiago, New York City, 9 September 1996.

72 See I. Fuentes-Perez *et al.* (eds), *Outside Cuba/Fuera de Cuba* (New Brunswick, NJ, 1988), p. 206.

73 J. Boza, quoted in A. Lindsay (ed.), *Santería Aesthetics in Contemporary Latin American Art* (Washington, 1996), p. 185.

74 *Carlos Alfonzo: El triúnfo del espíritu. Muestra retrospectiva, 1975–1991* (Miami, 1998), pp. 23–4.

75 *Ibid.*, p. 29.

76 Quoted in *ibid.*, p. 42.

77 For more details, see N. Spector, *Felix González-Torres* (New York, 1995), pp. 4–10. Many thanks also to Andrea Rosen Gallery, New York City.

78 Spector, *Felix González-Torres*, p. 14.

79 Quoted in *ibid*.

80 Quoted by Ann Umland in *Projects #34* (New York: MOMA, 1992).

81 Felix González-Torres, quoted in Spector, *Felix González-Torres*, p. 73.

82 *Ibid.*, pp. 72–3.

83 Jo Ann Lewis, '"Traveling" light: installation artist Felix González-Torres shines at the Hirschhorn', *Washington Post*, 10 July 1994, G5.

84 Spector, *Felix González-Torres*, pp. 101, 106.

85 S. Watney, 'In Purgatory: the works of Felix González-Torres', *Parkett*, 39 (March 1994), p. 43.

86 N. Spector, 'Felix González-Torres: Travelogue', *Parkett*, 39 (March 1994), p. 26.

87 Watney, 'In Purgatory', p. 40. On this intricate process, also see R. Storr, 'Setting traps for the mind and heart', *Art in America* (January 1996), p. 72, and Spector, 'Felix Gonzáles-Torres', *passim*.

88 Personal communication, 16 January 1997. Also, see O. Zaya, 'La trilogía Cubana de Ernesto Pujol: el exilio, la memoria y el regreso', *Atlántica*, 15 (Winter 1996), p. 127.

89 G. Mosquera, 'Ernesto Pujol: Cuba visited once more', *Cuba Update*, 16, 4/5 (July–October 1995), p. 43.

90 Personal communication, 16 January 1997.

91 Y. Wood, 'Metaphors of a journey. The installations of Ernesto Pujol', *Third Text*, 31 (Summer 1995), p. 72.

92 Personal communication, 16 January 1997.

93 Solomon-Godeau, *Male Trouble*, p. 31.

94 L. R. Lippard, *Mixed Blessings* (New York, 1990), p. 223.

95 Interview with the artist, New York City, 17 October 1996.

96 Interview with the artist, Brooklyn, New York, 20 September 1996. Also, see Art in General, *Domestic Partnerships: New Impulses in Decorative Arts from the Americas* (New York, 1996), n.p.

97 Cf. a rather hostile critic in *Seattle Weekly*, 31 July 1996, p. 35: 'an unfortunate bristling-with-hair abstraction of the rubbing together of orifices'.

98 Artist's statement on brochure 'The persistence of sorrow', accompanying the installation, New York, 1996.

99 L. Kotz, 'Caged heat. New sculptures by Linda Matalón', *OUT*, 43 (May 1997), p. 52. I borrowed the phrase 'embodied abstraction' from the title of a show including work by Matalón at the Americas Society, New York, 1997.

100 L. Kotz, 'Small scale and personal: drawing, painting, "gay" aesthetics', in *Situation: Perspectives on Work by Lesbian and Gay Artists* (San Francisco, 1992), n.p.

101 A. Barclay Morgan, 'Linda Matalón: Wolfson Campus Galleries', *Sculpture* (October 1997), p. 58.

102 For a more comprehensive view of Ferro's oeuvre, see *Futuro/Anterior. Sérgio Ferro* (São Paulo, 1989).

103 See M. Maia, *Prometheus* (New York, 1997).

Epilogue

Today's images of *ambiente* in Latin American and Latino/a art are bold and striking testimonies of the cosmopolitan intellectual and artistic climate of Latin American metropolises. We have reviewed how, from the late 1970s onwards, an explicitly 'gay' trope of visual expression comes to the surface in Latin America's major cities, however belated in countries temporarily facing political dictatorship, such as Brazil. The new assertiveness was triggered in part by the rise of Gay Liberation movements that themselves were shaped after European and North American examples. New, 'modern' gay subcultures developed alongside persisting, more 'traditional' codes of sexual behaviour and identities.

Meanwhile, gay and lesbian artists of Latin American descent, who migrated to or were born in North America or Europe, equally produce refined and sophisticated visualizations of homotextuality. Living in forced or voluntary exile, they share in local gay and lesbian community life and contribute to these communities' cultural diversity. Often, they play a significant role in the development of a postmodern 'queer' critique of sexual, gender and cultural identity.

Indeed, the growing visibility of homosexuality in Latin American and Latino/a visual arts is accompanied by critical reflection by artists regarding cultural, gender or sexual identity, more particularly regarding the mutual relationship between discourses of Latin American identity and one's position as a gay or lesbian artist belonging to this cultural realm. How, they ask, does postcolonial 'deconstruction' of national and ethnic identity relate to the social and political struggle for sexual liberation? But also, how can an affirmation of homosexual desire be achieved that is not at the same time a product of cultural imperialism, but tuned instead to the distinct, often hybrid sexual cultures of Latin America? The physical realities of migration and exile, especially of the poorer classes, sharpens such awareness and operates as a catalyser for postcolonial reflection.

Resistance against the Eurocentric premises of North American and European gay and lesbian politics is accompanied also by criticism of the sexism, heterosexism and homophobia remaining endemic in Latino communities as in various countries of Latin America itself. The images of *ambiente* reviewed in this book recurrently reflect these issues, while they reveal equally that they cannot be fully resolved without subscribing to strategies of sexual and gender liberation adopted from countries in the Northern hemisphere.

The complexity as briefly summarized here has made this book into a story not so much of teleology, as of constant *bricolage* and 'negotiation' between various models of identity along the lines of culture, nation, class, gender or sexuality. We have been able to identify linear development towards more and more open visualizations of homotextuality, both by male and female artists, eventually even by artists who themselves are bisexual or straight. But such imagery is not unequivocally rooted in the Liberationist model of North American and European 'gay' identity, presumably applicable to the altogether different realities of Latin American society and culture. Artists, like others, question the very premises of a 'gay aesthetic' as they work in a distinct society and face an altogether different social and cultural construction of sexuality and gender. Images 'negotiate' between utopia – the expression of homoeroticism, of a gay *ambiente* – and dystopia – the adoption of models from the 'Northern hemisphere'.

Present most explicitly in the works of some contemporary artists, this moment of 'mediation' can nevertheless already be traced from the early days of academic drawing onwards. Negotiation surfaced repeatedly ever since the newly independent countries of Latin America adopted art as a medium for expressing national and cultural identity in the first place. It was the very fact of fluid or distinctly structured sexual boundaries in Latin America that, for many decades, provided space for images of homotextuality. Bisexuality, tolerated but not publicly embraced, made individual portrayal along the lines of reified sexual identities improbable, even, to a degree, until this very day.

In this context, I described how the peculiarly Latin American model of bisexual praxis allowed for images of male bonding, homosocial affinities and, recurrently, male-to-male intimacy. The continuous spectre of desire, inclusive at once of sexual relations between men as among men and women, explains why from the nineteenth century onwards, Latin American art is indeed rich, rather than poor, with homotextual imagery.

The modernization of sexual discourse has subsequently given rise to the model of 'gay identity' and, in its wake, to more or less explicit gay and lesbian communities.

A context of persistent and endemic homophobia made visual expression of homotextuality into a difficult task, however. Muralism and Modernism alike provoked an eclipse almost of the homoerotic, only for it to resurface from the 1950s onwards, even if only as coded images of same-sex friendship and *socialité*. It would take two more decades before Gay Liberation movements were initiated, but the newer images of *ambiente*, while apparently subscribing to dreams of sexual utopia, soon became critical of such naïvety in a Latin American context. Along with postmodern scepticism regarding reified and static sexual identities, came postcolonial objections to the imposition of Liberation models inadequately laid upon Latin America's reality. Postmodern images of *ambiente*, while historically inscribed in the emancipatory rhetoric of Gay Lib, thus carry traces of new, alternative and more diverse visions regarding sexual freedom and political emancipation for lesbians and gays.

The significance for a more general study of homosexuality in the arts is obvious as this book has clarified, I hope, how an interpretation of iconographic content is doomed to fail when it doesn't at once question and historicize its own vocabulary. Such implies a diachronic perspective, incorporating change through continuity, as well as attention to regional diversity – South American versus Caribbean, Mexican versus Brazilian, urban versus rural, communist Cuba versus Puerto Rico as affiliated with the USA. Simply emphasizing the 'hybridity' (Canclini) of homosexual subcultures as represented in the visual arts in Latin America therefore would be an inadequate descriptive mode, since hybridity itself is subjected to the processes of historical change. While brought about from the Colonial era already, but accelerated in the wake of modernization processes, hybridity has characterized Latin America through time. It has changed faces, however, and to a degree these processes can be described. In fact, the logics and rationale underlying the subsequent visualizations of homotextuality are proof of hybridity's very own roots in history.[1]

De-reifying what is peculiar about images of *ambiente* in Latin American art since approximately 1910 and re-inscribing it within the wider history of gay and lesbian experience there is what I have aimed to do in this book. Clearly, it remains a first attempt only that will be rewritten as additional studies in this field become available. Methodological refinement is required as well, since the method to uncover homotextuality often implies a 'critical hermeneutics [applied] to [images] not generally viewed as dealing with homosexuality'.[2] The art critic Charles Merewether has pointed out how the representation of stigmatized desire provokes a 'tension between place and displacement'[3] or, less abstractly, between its visualization at first and its cover-up through asexual narrative immediately afterwards. This makes the identification and interpretation of images of *ambiente* into a difficult, often even speculative ordeal.

Eventually also, a book like this one may contribute to a further 'deconstruction' of gay art in North America and Europe as well. For in these areas of the world too, the visual expression of homotextuality is more complex than some studies, recent or otherwise, seem to suggest. As historical research into the changing outlook of gay and lesbian experience proceeds, more studies will follow, no doubt, on the 'hybridity' of gay imagery there as well. A plea for such rewriting of the history of gay male and lesbian eroticism in the arts evidently is rooted in Queer Criticism, but this desperately requires historical evidence to further materialize and substantialize. Eventually, it will become clear that homotextuality reflects purity and hybridity, continuity and change, involvement and detachment also in countries presumably belonging to 'the centre'.

Notes

1 Relevant, in this context, is Ben Genocchio's critique of today's fetishization of Latin American hybridity. See B. Genocchio, 'The discourse of difference. Writing "Latin American" art', *Third Text*, 43 (Summer 1998), pp. 9–11.
2 Foster, *Gay and Lesbian Themes in Latin American Writing*, p. 131.
3 C. Merewether, 'Introducción/Introduction', in *Nuevos momentos del arte Mexicana/New Moments in Mexican Art*, p. 18.

Bibliography

ART HISTORY, FEMINISM, HOMOSEXUALITY, MULTICULTURALISM

Aliaga, J. V., *Bajo vientre. Representaciones de la sexualidad en la cultura y el arte contemporáneos*. Valencia: Generalitat Valenciana, 1997.

Anzaldúa, G., *Borderlands/La Frontera: The New Mestiza*. San Francisco: Spinster/Aunt Lute, 1987.

Art Journal, 50, 2 (Summer 1991): Feminist art criticism.

Art Journal, 55, 4 (Winter 1996): 'We're here: gay and lesbian presence in art', eds F. Rando and J. Weinberg.

Ashburn, E., *Lesbian Art: An Encounter with Power*. London: Craftsman House, 1996.

Atkins, R. and Sokolowski, T. (eds), *From Media to Metaphor: Art about AIDS*. New York: Grey Art Gallery, 1992.

Avena, T. (ed.), *Life Sentences: Writers, Artists and AIDS*. San Francisco: Mercury House, 1994.

Bad Object Choices (eds), *How Do I Look? Queer Film and Video*. Seattle: Bay Press, 1991.

Bal, M. and Bryson, N., 'Semiotics and art history: a discussion of context and senders', in D. Preziosi (ed.), *The Art of Art History: A Critical Anthology*. Oxford and New York: Oxford University Press, 1998, pp. 242–56.

Beurdeley, C., *L'amour bleu* (trans. from French). Bonn: Bild Kunst, 1994.

Biederbeck, R. and Kalusche, B., *Motivmann: Der männliche Körper in der Modernen Kunst*. Giessen: Anabas, 1987.

Blake, N. *et al.* (eds), *In a Different Light: Visual Culture, Sexual Identity, Queer Practice*. San Francisco: City Lights Books, 1995.

Blessing, J. *et al.*, *Rrose is a Rose is a Rrose: Gender Performance in Photography*. New York: Abrams, 1997.

Brand, D. *et al.*, *Sight Specific: Lesbians and Representation*. Toronto: A Space, 1988.

Bronski, M., *Culture Clash: The Making of Gay Sensibility*. Boston: South End Press, 1984.

Broude, N. and Garrard, M. D. (eds), *The Power of Feminist Art*. New York: Abrams, 1994.

Cameron, D. (ed.), *Extended Sensibilities: Homosexual Presence in Contemporary Art*. New York: New Museum of Contemporary Art, 1982.

Chadwick, W., *Women, Art and Society*. London: Thames and Hudson, 1990.

Chapman, R. *et al.* (eds), *Male Order: Unwrapping Masculinity*. London: Lawrence & Wishart, 1988.

Clair, J. *et al.* (eds), *Identity and Alterity: Figures of the Body, 1895–1995*. Venice: 46th Biennale of Venice, 1995.

Cooper, E., *The Sexual Perspective: Homosexuality in the Art of the Last One Hundred Years*, 2nd edn. London: Routledge, 1995.

Cooper, E., *Fully Exposed: The Male Nude in Photography*, 2nd edn. London: Unwin Hyman, 1995.

Crimp, D. (ed.), *AIDS: Cultural Analysis, Cultural Activism*. Cambridge, MA, and London, 1988.

Davis, M. D., *The Male Nude in Contemporary Photography*. Philadelphia: Temple University Press, 1991.

de Zegher, C. (ed.), *Inside the Visible: An Elliptical Traverse of 20th Century Art, in, of, and from the Feminine*. Boston-Kortrijk: ICA-Kanaal Art Foundation, 1996.

Difference: On Representation and Sexuality. New York: New Museum of Contemporary Art, 1985.

Doyle, J. *et al.* (eds), *Pop out Queer Warhol*. Durham, NC: Duke University Press, 1996.

Dynes, W. R. and Donaldson, S. (eds), *Homosexuality and Homosexuals in the Arts*. New York and London: Garland, 1992.

Ellenzweig, A., *The Homoerotic Photograph: Male Images from Durien/Delacroix to Mapplethorpe*. New York: Columbia University Press, 1992.

Féminin/masculin: le sexe dans l'art. Paris: Gallimard/Centre Culturel Georges Pompidou, 1995.

Ferguson R. *et al.* (eds), *Discourses: Conversations in Postmodern Art and Culture*. Cambridge, MA, and New York: MIT Press/New Museum of Contemporary Art, 1990.

Ferguson R. *et al.* (eds), *Out There: Marginalization and Contemporary Cultures*. Cambridge, MA, and London: MIT Press, 1990.

Fernandez, D., *Le rapt de Ganymède*. Paris: Grasset, 1989.

Foster, A., *Behold the Man: The Male Nude in Photography*. Edinburgh: Stills Gallery, 1988.

Gender, Fucked, curated by H. Hammond and C. Lord. Seattle: Center on Contemporary Art, 1996.

Goldstein, A. and Rorimer, A., *Reconsidering the Object of Art, 1965–1975*. Los Angeles and Cambridge, MA: MOCA/MIT Press, 1995/6.

Gott, T. (ed.), *Don't Leave Me This Way. Art in the Age of AIDS*. Canberra: National Gallery of Australia, 1994.

Goulma-Peterson, T. and Matthews, P., 'The feminist critique of art history', *Art Bulletin*, 69 (September 1987), pp. 326–57.

Great American Lesbian Art Show. Los Angeles: The Women's Building, 1980.

Gregg, P. and Blake, N., *Situation: Perspectives on Work by Lesbian and Gay Artists*. San Francisco: New Langton Arts, 1991.

Grover, J. Z. (ed.), *AIDS: The Artists' Response*. Kent, OH: Ohio State University Press, 1989.

Hunt, B. (ed.), *Art. AIDS. Action. Mapping no Boundaries*. New York: Visual Aids, 1997.

Ischar, D., 'Parallel oppressions: the ideal and the abject in gay representation', *AfterImage*, 16, 7 (February 1989), pp. 10–12.

Jones, A. (ed.), *Sexual Politics: Judy Chicago's Dinner Party in Feminist Art History*. Los Angeles: UCLA, Armand Hammer Museum, 1996.

Jullian, P., *Dreamers of Decadence: Symbolist Painters of the 1890s* (trans. from French). New York: Praeger, 1971.

Kosofsky-Sedgwick, E., *Epistemology of the Closet*. Berkeley and London: University of California Press, 1990.

Kotz, L., 'Guilty objects, unattainable desires', *Afterimage*, 17, 6 (January 1990), pp. 12–14.

Kotz, L. and Meyer, R., 'Situation', *Out/Look* (Fall 1991), p. 8.

L'art au corps: le corps exposé de Man Ray à nos jours. Paris and Marseille: Musées Nationaux, 1996.

Leddick, D., *The Male Nude*. Cologne, 1998.

Lewis, V., 'The world made flesh: AIDS and the visual arts', *Perversions*, 5 (Summer 1995), pp. 6–41.

Lippard, L. R., *Mixed Blessings: New Art in a Multicultural America*. New York: Pantheon Books, 1990.

Lord, C. (ed.), *All But the Obvious: Writing, Visual Art, Performance, Video by Lesbians*. Los Angeles: LACE, 1990.

Lucie-Smith, E., *Race, Sex and Gender in Contemporary Art*. London: Art Books International, 1994.

Lucie-Smith, E., *Adam: The Male Figure in Art*. London: Weidenfeld & Nicolson, 1998.

Lucie-Smith, E. and Boyd, S., *Life Class: The Academic Male Nude, 1820–1920*. London: Gay Men's Press, 1988.

Miller, J. (ed.), *Fluid Exchanges: Artists and Critics in the AIDS Crisis*. Toronto: University of Toronto Press, 1992.

Nairne, S., *State of the Art: Ideas & Images in the 1980s*. London: Chatto & Windus, 1987.

Nochlin, L., *Women, Art and Power and Other Essays*. New York: Harper & Row, 1988.

Novaes, A. (ed.), *O desejo*. São Paulo: Cia das Letras, 1990.

Novaes, A. (ed.), *Os sentidos da paixião*. Rio de Janeiro and São Paulo: FUNARTE/Cia das Letras, 1992.

Outrageous Desire: The Politics and Aesthetics of Representation in Recent Works by Lesbian and Gay Artists. New Brunswick, NJ: Mason Gross School of the Arts, Rutgers University, 1991.

Owens, C., *Beyond Recognition: Representation, Power, and Culture*. Berkeley: University of California Press, 1992.

Parker, A. *et al.* (eds), *Nationalisms and Sexualities*. London: Routledge, 1992.

Perchuk, A. and Posner, H. (eds), *The Masculine Masquerade: Masculinity and Representation*. Cambridge, MA, and London: MIT Press, 1995.

Pervert, curated by C. Lord, UC-Irvine, 11April– 6 May 1995.

Poliester, 3, 9 (Summer 1994): 'La abstracción del SIDA'.

Pollock, G., *Vision and Difference: Femininity, Feminism and the Histories of Art*. London and New York: Routledge, 1988.

Post-Boys & Girls. New York: Artists Space, 1990.

Raven, A. and Iskin, R., 'Through the poophole: towards a lesbian sensibility in art', *Chrysalis*, 4 (1977), pp. 19–31.

Rose, J., *Sexuality in the Field of Vision*. London: Verso, 1986.

Saslow, J., 'Closets in the museum: homophobia and art history', in K. Jay and A. Young (eds), *Lavender Culture*. New York: Jove/HBJ, 1979, pp. 215–27.

Saunders, G., *The Nude: A New Perspective*. London: Herbert Press, 1989.

Sillevis, J., 'Le beau idéal', *Maatstaf* (1984), pp. 73–84.

Smyth, C., *Damn Fine Art by New Lesbian Artists*. New York and London: Cassell, 1996.

Sontag, S., 'Notes on "Camp"', in *A Susan Sontag Reader*. New York: Farrar, Strauss & Giroux, 1982, pp. 105–19.

Sontag, S., *AIDS and Its Metaphors*, New York: Farrar, Strauss & Giroux, 1989.

Space of Time: Contemporary Art from the Americas/Espacio del Tiempo: arte contemporáneo de las Américas. New York: Americas Society, 1993.

Studies in Visual Communication, 9, 2 (Spring 1983): 'Gay art'.

Transgenéricas. Representaciones y experiencias sobre la sociedad, la sexualidad y los géneros en el arte español contemporáneo. San Sebastián: Koldo Mitxelena Kulturunea, 1998.

Wade-Salisbury, J. P., 'Homosexuality in art'. M.A. thesis, Eastern Illinois University, 1981.

Wagner, F. (ed.), *Les mondes du Sida: entre résignation et espoir*. Berne: Sida Info Doc Suisse, 1998.

Walters, M., *The Nude Male: A New Perspective*. New York and London: Paddington Press, 1978.

Weiermair, P. (ed.), *Il nudo maschile nella fotografia del XIX e del XX sec.* Ravenna: Essegi, 1984.

Weiermair, P., *Geschichte des männlichen Akts in der Fotografie des 19. und 20. Jahrhunderts*. Vienna: Ariadne, 1987.

Weinberg, J., 'Demuth and difference', *Art in America*, 76, 4 (April 1988), pp. 188–95.

Weinberg, J., 'It's in the can: Jasper Johns and the anal society', in W. R. Dynes and S. Donaldson (eds), *Homosexuality and Homosexuals in the Arts*. New York and London: Garland, 1992, pp. 160–76.

Weinberg, J., *Male Desire: Homoerotic Images in 20th-Century American Art*. New York: Mary Ryan Gallery, 1995.

Weinberg, J., *Speaking for Vice: Homosexuality in the Art of Charles Demuth, Marsden Hartley, and the First American Avant-Garde*. New Haven: Yale University Press, 1993.

West, C., 'The new cultural politics of difference', *October*, 53 (Summer 1990), pp. 93–109.

LATIN AMERICAN CULTURE AND THE VISUAL ARTS

General

Ades, D., *Art in Latin America: The Modern Era, 1820–1980*. New Haven and London: Yale University Press, 1989.

Art and Design, 37 (1994): 'New art from Latin America. Expanding the Continent', ed. O. Baddeley.

Art d'Amérique latine, 1911–1968. Paris: Centre Georges Pompidou, 1992.

Art Journal, 51, 4 (Winter 1992): 'Latin American art'.

Arte, história e identidad en América: Visiones comparativas (XVII Coloquio Internacional de Historia de Arte). Mexico: UNAM, IIE, 1994, 3 vols.

Artistas Latinoamericanas del siglo XX/Latin American Artists of the XXth Century, cur. W. Rasmussen. Sevilla, New York and Madrid: Comisaria de la Ciudad de Sevilla para 1992/MOMA/Taba Press, 1992.

Atlántica, 15 (Winter 1996): 'Latinoamérica'.

Baddeley, O. and Fraser, V., *Drawing the Line: Art and Cultural Identity in Contemporary Latin America*. London: Verso, 1989.

Bayón, D., *História del Arte Hispanoamericano*, vol. 3: *Siglos XIX y XX*. Madrid: Alhambra, 1988.

Bethell, L. (ed.), *Historia de América Latina, vol. 8: América Latina: cultura y sociedad, 1830–1930* (trans. from English). Barcelona: Crítica, 1991.

'Beyond loss: art in the era of AIDS', *Latin American Art*, 5, 2 (1993), pp. 69–70.

Biller, G. P. (ed.), *Latin American Women Artists, 1915–1995*. Milwaukee: Milwaukee Art Museum, 1995.

Billeter, E., *Canto a la realidad: Fotografía Latinoamericana 1860–1993*. Madrid and Barcelona: Casa de América/Lunwerg, 1993.

Brett, G., *Transcontinental: Nine Latin American Artists*. London and New York: Verso, 1990.

Brunner, J. J., *Un espejo trizado*. Santiago de Chile: FLASCO, 1988.

Buntinx, G. *et al.*, *El fulgor de lo obsceno*. Santiago de Chile: F. Zegers, n.d.

de Morais Belluzzo, A. M. (ed.), *Modernidade: vanguardas artisticas na América Latina*. São Paulo: Memorial da América Latina/UNESP, 1990.

Day, H. T. and Sturges, H., *Art of the Fantastic: Latin America 1920–1987*. Indianapolis: Indianapolis Museum of Art, 1987.

Foster, D. W., *Cultural Diversity in Latin American Literature*. Albuquerque: University of New Mexico Press, 1994.

Francis, M. and Martin, J.-H. (eds), *Magiciens de la terre*. Paris: Centre Georges Pompidou, 1989.

Franco, J., *The Modern Culture of Latin America: Society and the Artist*. London: Pall Mall, 1967.

Franco, J. and Yúdice, G. (eds), *On Edge: The Crisis of Contemporary Latin American Culture*. Minneapolis and London: University of Minnesota Press, 1992.

García Canclini, N. (ed.), *Cultura y pospolítica: el debate sobre la modernidad en América Latina*. Mexico: Centro Nacional de Arte, 1991.

García Canclini, N., *Hybrid Cultures: Strategies for Entering and Leaving Modernity*. Minneapolis: University of Minnesota Press, 1995.

Genocchi, B., 'The discourse of difference. Writing "Latin American art"', *Third Text*, 43 (Summer 1998), pp. 3–12.

Goldman, S. M., 'Latin visions and revisions', *Art in America*, 76, 5 (May 1988), pp. 138–47, 198–9.

Goldman, S. M., *Dimensions of the Americas: Art and Social Change in Latin America and the United States*. Chicago: University of Chicago Press, 1994.

Grynszstejn, M. (ed.), *About Place: Recent Art of the Americas*. Chicago: Art Institute, 1995.

La Duke, B., *Compañeras: Women, Art and Social Change in Latin America*. San Francisco: City Lights, 1991 (orig. 1985).

Leval, S. T. and Goldman, S. M., 'Latin American art and the search for identity', *Latin American Art*, 1, 1 (Spring 1989), pp. 41–2.

Lindsay, A. (ed.), *Santeria Aesthetics in Contemporary Latin America*. Washington: Smithsonian, 1996.

Lucie-Smith, E., *Latin American Art of the 20th Century*. London: Thames & Hudson, 1993.

Merewether, C., 'New world primitivism: ethnography, neo-colonialism and minority discourses', Ph.D. diss., University of Sydney, 1989.

Mesquita, I. (ed.), *Cartographies*. Winnipeg: Winnipeg Art Gallery, 1993.

Mito y magia en América: los ochenta. Monterrey: MARCO, 1991.

'Modernidad y pos-modernidad en América latina', 1 and 2, in *Nuevo texto crítico*, 6 and 7. San Francisco: Stanford University Press, 1990–1.

Morais, F., *Artes plásticas na América Latina: do transe ão transitório*. Rio de Janeiro: Civilização Brasileira, 1979.

Mosquera, G., '"Primitivismo" y "contemporaneidad" en nuestros artistas jóvenes', *Revista del Sur*, 11, 3/4 (Malmö, 1985), pp. 52–5.

Mosquera, G., 'Africa in the art of Latin America', *Art Journal*, 51, 4 (Winter 1992), pp. 30–8.

Mosquera, G. (ed.), *Beyond the Fantastic: Contemporary Art Criticism from Latin America*. London and Cambridge, MA: Institute of International Visual Arts/MIT Press, 1996.

Richard, N., 'Postmodern disalignments and realignments of the centre/periphery', *Art Journal*, 51, 4 (1992), pp. 57–9.

Rubiano Caballero, G., *La escultura en América Latina, siglo XX*. Bogotá: Universidad Nacional de Colombia, 1986.

Schwartz, J., *Las vanguardias latinoamericanas: textos programáticos y críticos*. Madrid: Catédra, 1991.

Stofflet, M. *et al.* (eds), *Latin American Drawing Today*. San Diego and London: San Diego Museum of Art/University of Washington Press, 1991.

Sullivan, E. J. (ed.), *Latin American Art in the Twentieth Century*. London: Phaidon, 1996.

The Decade Show: Frameworks of Identity in the 1980s. New York: Museum of Contemporary Hispanic Art/Studio Museum, 1990.

Tomassi, N. *et al.* (eds), *American Visions/Visiones de las América: Artistic and Cultural Identity in the Western Hemisphere*. New York: American Council for the Arts/Allworth Press, 1993.

Traba, M., *Dos décadas vulnerables en las artes plásticas latinoamericanas, 1950–1970*. Mexico: Siglo XX, 1973.

Traba, M., *Art of Latin America, 1900–1980*. Washington, DC: Inter-American Development Bank, 1994.

UABC. Uruguay-Argentina-Brazil-Chile. Amsterdam: Stedelijk Museum, 1989.

Uncommon Ground: 23 Latin American Artists, C. Stellweg (ed.). New Paltz: College Art Gallery, State University of New York, 1992.

Wood, Y. (ed.), *Las artes plásticas en el Caribe: pintura y grabado contemporáneo*. Havana, 1993.

Yúdice, G., 'No somos el mundo', *Cultura Norte*, 7, 31 (August–September 1994), pp. 14–24.

Brazil

Amaral, A., *Artes plásticas na semana de 22*. São Paulo: Perspectiva, 1992 (1971).

Amaral, A., *Arte para que? A preocupação social na arte brasileira, 1930–1970*. São Paulo: Nobel, 1984.

Araújo, E. (ed.), *A mão afrobrasileira: significado da contribuição artística e histórica*. São Paulo: Tenenge, 1988.

Boaventura, M. E., *O salão e a selva: uma biografia ilustrada de Oswald de Andrade*. Campinas: Ex Libris/Unicamp, 1995.

BR80: pintura Brasil década 80. São Paulo: Instituto Cultural Itaú, 1991.

Campofiorito, Q., *História da pintura brasileira no século XIX*. Rio de Janeiro: Pinacotheke, 1983.

Expresionismo no Brasil: heranças e afinidades (XVIII Bienal Internacional de São Paulo). São Paulo: Imprenta Oficial do Estado, 1985.

Fabris, A. T. (ed.), *Modernidade e modernismo no Brasil*. Campinas: Mercado de Letras, 1994.

Journal of Decorative and Propaganda Arts, 21 (1995): 'Brazil'.

Lemos, C. *et al.*, *The Art of Brazil*. New York: Harper & Row, 1983.

Lourenço, M. C. F., *Operários da Modernidade*. São Paulo: HUCITEC/EdUSP, 1995.

Melo Carvalho, M. L., *Novas Travessias: Contemporary Brazilian Photography*. London and New York: Verso, 1996.

Modernidade: l'art brésilien du 20ième siècle. Paris: Musée d'Art Moderne de la Ville de Paris, 1987.

Morais, F., *Núcleo Bernadelli: arte brasileira nos anos 30 e 40*. Rio de Janeiro: Pinakotheke, 1982.

Morais, F., *Cronologia das artes plásticas no Rio de Janeiro: da missão artística francesa à geração 90*. Rio de Janeiro: Topbooks, 1995.

Nova figuração: Rio/Buenos Aires. Rio de Janeiro and Buenos Aires: MAM/Instituto Cultural Brasil and Argentina, 1987.

Poliester, 2, 8 (Spring 1994): 'do Brasil'.

Pontual, R., *Entre dois séculos: arte brasileira do século XX na coleção Gilberto Chateaubriand*. Rio de Janeiro: JB, 1987.

Projeto arte brasileira: academismo. Rio de Janeiro: FUNARTE/Instituto Nacional de Artes Plásticas, 1986.

Sevcenko, N., *Orfeu extático no metrópolis*. São Paulo: Cia das Letras, 1992.

Universo acadêmico. Desenho brasileiro do século XIX da coleção do Museu Nacional de Belas Artes. Rio de Janeiro: MNBA, 1989.

Zannini, W. (ed.), *História geral do arte no Brasil*. São Paulo: Instituto Walter Moreira Salles, 1983, 2 vols.

Zannini, W., *A arte no Brasil das décadas de 1930–40: o Grupo Santa Helena*. São Paulo: USP, 1991.

Mexico

1910: el arte en un año decisivo. La exposición de artistas mexicanos. Mexico: MNA, 1991.

Bargellini, C. and Fuentes, E., *Guia que permite captar lo bello: yesos y dibujos de la Academia de San Carlos, 1778–1916*. Mexico: UNAM, 1989.

Bilder und Visionen: Mexikanische Kunst zwischen Avantgarde und Aktualität. Künselsau: Museum Würth, 1995.

Billeter, E., *Imagen de México*. Frankfurt: Schirn Kunsthalle, 1987–8.

Charlot, J., *Mexican Art and the Academy of San Carlos, 1785–1915*. Austin: University of Texas Press, 1962.

Charlot, J., *The Mexican Mural Renaissance*. New Haven and London: Yale University Press, 1963.

Covantes, H., *La pintura mexicana de la ingenuidad*. Mexico: Galería Maren, 1984.

Debroise, O., *Figuras en el trópico: plástica mexicana 1920–1940*. Barcelona: Ocáano, 1984.

Emmerich, L. C., *100 pintores mexicanos*. Monterrey: MARCO, 1993–4.

Fauchereau, S., *Les peintres révolutionnaires mexicains*. Paris: Messidor, 1985.

Fernandez, J., *Arte moderno y contemporáneo de México*. Mexico: UNAM, 1995 (1952), 2 vols.

Ferrer, E. and Sánchez, A. R., *Through the Path of Echoes: Contemporary Art in Mexico/Por el camino de ecos: arte contemporáneo en México*. New York: Independent Curators, 1990.

Goldman, S.M., *Contemporary Mexican Painting in a Time of Change*, 3rd edn. Austin and London: University of Texas Press, 1981.

Helm, MacKinley, *Modern Mexican Painters*. New York: Dover, 1989 (1941).

Merewether, C., *Mexico: Out of the Profane*. Adelaide: Contemporary Art Centre of South Australia, 1990.

Mexico: Figures of the Eighties. San Antonio and Washington, DC: Instituto Cultural Mexicano/Parallel Project, 1991.

Mexico: The New Generations. San Antonio: Museum of Art, 1985.

Nuevos momentos en el arte mexicano/New Moments in Mexican Art. New York and Madrid: Parallel Project/Turner, 1990.

O'Gorman, E. *et al.*, *Cuarenta siglos de plástica mexicana. Arte moderno y contemporáneo*. Mexico: Herrero, S.A., 1971.

Rochfort, D., *Mexican Muralists: Orozco – Rivera – Siqueiros*. Singapore: Lawrence King, 1993.

Ruptura 1952–1965. Mexico: Museo Carrillo Gil/Museo Biblioteca Pape, 1988.

Schávelzon, D., *La polémica del arte nacional en México, 1850–1910*. Mexico: Fondo de Cultura Económica, 1988.

Sullivan, E. J., '"Mexicanness" in Mexican painting in the 1980s', *Arts Magazine*, 63 (September 1988), pp. 54–7.

Sullivan, E. J., *Aspects of Contemporary Mexican Painting*. New York: Americas Society, 1990.

Sullivan, E. J. and Nochlin, L., *Women in Mexico/La mujer en México*. Mexico: Centro Cultural/Arte Contemporáneo, Fundación Cultural Televisa, 1990.

Tibol, R., *Arte mexicano: época moderna y contemporánea*. Mexico and Buenos Aires: Hermes, 1964.

Ziff, T. (ed.), *Between Worlds: Contemporary Mexican Photography*. London: Bellew/Impressions Gallery, 1990.

Cuba

Balderrama, Maria R. (ed.), *Wifredo Lam and His Contemporaries, 1938–1952*. New York: Studio Museum in Harlem, 1992.

Blanc, G. V., *Cuban Artists of the 20th Century*. Fort Lauderdale: Museum of Art, 1993.

Camnitzer, L., *The New Art of Cuba*. Austin: University of Texas Press, 1994.

Cuban Poster Art. A Retrospective 1961–1982. New York: Westbeth Gallery/Center for Cuban Studies, 1983.

CubaSigloXX. Modernidad y Sincretismo. Catálogo de exposición. Las Palmas, Palma and Barcelona: Centro Atlántico de Arte Moderno/Fundación La Caixa/Centre d'Art Santa Mónica, 1996.

Cuba–USA: The First Generation. Washington, DC: Fondo de Sol Visual Arts Center, 1991.

Fuentes-Perez, I. *et al.* (eds), *Outside Cuba: Contemporary Cuban Visual Artists/Fuera de Cuba. Artistas cubanos contemporáneos*. New Brunswick, NJ: Rutgers University Press, 1988.

Fusco, C., *Signs of Transition: 80s Art from Cuba*. New York: Museum of Contemporary Hispanic Art, 1988.

Gomez Sicre, J., *Art of Cuba in Exile*. Miami: Munder, 1987.

Kuba OK. Düsseldorf: Städtische Kunsthalle, 1990.

Made in Havana: Contemporary Art from Cuba. Sydney: Art Gallery of New South Wales, 1988.

Martínez, J. A., 'Afrocuban and national identity: modern Cuban art 1920s–1940s', *Athanos*, II (1992), pp. 70–3.

Martínez, J. A., *Cuban Art and National Identity: The Vanguardia Painters, 1927–1950*. Gainesville: University Press of Florida, 1994.

Mosquera, G., *Contemporary Art from Havana*. London and Sevilla: Riverside Studios/Museo de Arte Contemporáneo de Sevilla, 1989.

Poliester, 4 (Winter 1993): 'Dentro y fuera/Cuba/inside & out'.

Rigol, J., *Apuntes sobre la pintura y el grabado en Cuba (De los origenes a 1927)*. Havana: Letras Cubanas, 1982.

Weiss, R. and Mosquera, G., *The Nearest Edge of the World: Art and Cuba Now*. Brookline, MA: Polarities, Inc./New England Foundation for the Arts, 1990.

Wood, Y., *De la plástica cubana y caribeña*. Havana: Letras Cubanas, 1990.

Zuver, M. *et al.*, *Cuba–USA: The First Generation*. Washington, DC: Fondo del Sol Visual Arts Center, 1991.

Puerto Rico

Alegria, R. *et al.*, *The Art Heritage of Puerto Rico: Pre-Columbian to Present*. New York: Metropolitan Museum of Art/Museo del Barrio, 1974.

Campeche, Oller, Rodón: Tres siglos de pintura puertorriqueña/Three Centuries of Puerto Rican Painting. San Juan and Sevilla: Instituto de Cultura Puertorriqueña/Exposición Universal, 1992.

del Carmen Ramírez, M., *Puerto Rican Painting: Between Past and Present. Paintings from Puerto Rico*. Princeton: The Squibb Gallery, 1987.

De Oller a los Cuarenta: la pintura en Puerto Rico de 1898 a 1948. Rio Piedras: Museo de la Universidad de Puerto Rico, 1988.

Nuevas caras del arte puertorriqueño/New Faces of Puerto Rican Art. New York and San Juan, PR: Peter Madero Gallery/Ateneo Puertorriqueño, 1994.

Pérez Lizano, M., *Arte contemporáneo de Puerto Rico, 1950–1983: Cerámica, escultura, pintura*. Bayamón: Cruz Ansata, 1985.

Ramírez, M. C., *Puerto Rican Painting between Past and Present*. Princeton: Squibb Gallery, 1987.

Sturges, H., *New Art from Puerto Rico/Nuevo arte de Puerto Rico*. Springfield, MA: Museum of Fine Arts, 1985.

Tío, T., *El portafolio en la gráfica puertorriqueña*. San Juan: Museo de las Américas, 1995.

Venegas, H., *25 años de pintura puertorriqueña*. Ponce de Leon: Museo de Arte de Ponce, 1973.

Latinos/as and Latino/a artists abroad: General

Amaral, A. *et al.*, *Artistas Latino-Americanos de Paris*. São Paulo: MACUSP, 1985.

Art of the Other Mexico: Sources and Meanings. Chicago: Mexican Fine Arts Center Museum, 1993.

Barnitz, J. *et al.*, *Latin American Artists in New York since 1970*. Austin, TX: Archer M. Huntington Gallery, 1987.

Beardsley, J. and Livingston, J., *Hispanic Art in the United States: Thirty Contemporary Painters and Sculptors*. Houston and New York: Museum of Fine Arts/Abbeville, 1987.

Cancel, L. R. *et al.* (eds), *The Latin American Spirit: Art and Artists in the United States, 1920–1970*. New York: Bronx Museum for the Arts/Abrams, 1989.

Damian, C., 'Cuba–USA: la primera generación', *ArtNexus*, 3 (January 1992), pp. 92–6.

Flores, J. and Yúdice, G., 'Living borders/Buscando América: languages of Latino self-formation', *Social Text*, 24 (Spring 1990), pp. 58–84.

Goldman, S. M., 'Homogenizing Hispanic art', *New Art Examiner*, 15, 1 (September 1987), pp. 30–3.

Griswold del Castillo, R. *et al.*, *Chicano Art: Resistance and Affirmation, 1965–1985*. Los Angeles: Wight Gallery, UCLA, 1992.

Leenhardt, J. and Kalfon, P. (eds), *Les Amériques latines en France*. Paris: Gallimard, 1992.

Quirarte, J., *A History and Appreciation of Chicano Art*. San Antonio: Research Center for the Arts and Humanities, 1984.

Venegas, S., *Image & Identity: Recent Chicana Art from 'La Reina del pueblo de Los Angeles de la Porcincula'*. Los Angeles: Laband Art Gallery, 1990.

HOMOTEXTUALITY AND THE VISUAL ARTS IN LATIN AMERICA

Society and (homo)sexuality

Balderston, D. J. and Guy, D. J. (eds), *Sex and Sexuality in Latin America*. New York: New York University Press, 1997.

Bergmann, E. L. and Smith, P .J. (eds), *¿Entiendes? Queer Readings, Hispanic Writings*. Durham, NC, and London: Duke University Press, 1995.

Foster, D. W., *Gay and Lesbian Themes in Latin American Writing*. Austin, TX: University of Texas Press, 1991.

Foster, D. W. (ed.), *Latin American Writers on Gay and Lesbian Themes: A Bio-critical Sourcebook*. Westport, CT, and London: Greenwood Press, 1994.

Foster, D. W. and Reis R. (eds), *Bodies and Biases. Sexualities in Hispanic Cultures and Literatures*. Minneapolis and London: University of Minnesota Press, 1996.

Franco, J., 'The literature of outsiders: the literature of the gay community in Latin America', in *Latin American Masses and Minorities: Their Images and Realities. Papers of the Thirtieth Annual Meeting of the Seminar on the Acquisition of Latin American Library Materials*. Madison: SACALM, 1987, vol. 1, pp. 288–304; vol. 2, pp. 580–91.

Lacey, E. A., 'Latin America: myths and realities', *Gay Sunshine*, 40/41 (Summer/Fall 1979), pp. 22–31.

Melhuus, M. and Stølen, K. (eds), *Machos, Mistresses, Madonnas: Contesting the Power of Latin American Gender Imagery*. London and New York: Verso, 1996.

Murray, S. O. (ed.), *Male Homosexuality in Central and South America* (Gai Saber Monographs, 5). New York: Gay Academic Union, 1986.

Murray, S. O. (ed.), *Latin American Homosexualities*. Albuquerque: University of New Mexico Press, 1995.

Taylor, D. and Villegas, J. (eds), *Negotiating Performance: Gender, Sexuality and Theatricality in Latin/o America*. Durham, NC, and London: Duke University Press, 1994.

Brazil

Basualdo, C., 'Quelques annotations supplémentaires sur le Parangolé', in *L'art au corps: le corps exposé de Man Ray à nos jours*. Paris and Marseille, 1996, pp. 257–73.

Boletim de Belas Artes, special issue: 'O escultor Hugo Bertazzon', n.d.

Brett, G., 'Hélio Oiticica: rêverie and revolt', *Art in America*, 77, 1 (January 1989), pp. 163–5.

Brett, G., 'Fait sur le corps. Le *parangolé* de Hélio Oiticica', *Cahiers du Musée Nacional d'Art Moderne*, 51 (Spring 1995), pp. 33–45.

Edinger, C., 'Machismo and androgyny in mid-nineteenth-century Brazilian and American novels', *Comparative Literature Studies*, 27, 2 (1990), pp. 124–39.

Figueiredo, L. *et al.* (eds), *Aspiro ao grande labirinto: textos de Hélio Oiticica*. Rio de Janeiro: Rocco, 1986.

Fry, P., *Para Inglês ver: identidade e política na cultura Brasileira*. Rio de Janeiro: Zahar, 1982.

Green, J., 'Beyond carnival: Homosexuality in twentieth-century Brazil', Ph.D. diss., UCLA, Los Angeles, 1996.

Hélio Oiticica. Rotterdam: Witte de With Center for Contemporary Art, 1992.

Lagnado, L., *Leonilson: são tantos as verdades*. São Paulo: Galeria de Arte do SESI, 1996.

MacRae, E., *A construção da igualdade: identidade sexual e política no Brasil da 'Abertura'*. Campinas: Unicamp, 1990.

O desejo na Academia, 1847–1916. São Paulo: Pinacoteca do Estado, 1992.

Parker, R., *Bodies, Pleasures and Passions: Sexual Culture in Contemporary Brazil*. Boston: Beacon Press, 1991.

Paulo Sayeg: Paixão. n.l., 1993.

Salomao, W., *Hélio Mangueira Oiticica*. Rio de Janeiro: Galeria UERJ, 1990.

Trevisan, J. S., *Perverts in Paradise*. London: Gay Men's Press, 1986.

Vainfas, R. (ed.), *Historia e sexualidade no Brasil*. Rio de Janeiro: Graal, 1986.

Whitam, F. L., 'The *entendidos*: middle class gay life in São Paulo', *Gay Sunshine*, 38/39 (Winter 1979), pp. 16–17.

Young, A., 'Gay gringo in Brazil', in L. Richmond and G. Noguera (eds), *The Gay Liberation Book*. San Francisco: Rampart Press, 1973, pp. 60–7.

Mexico

Abraham Angel. Mexico: Talleres Gráficos La Nación, 1924.

Abraham Angel y su tiempo. Mexico: PBA, 1985.

Adams, B., 'Julio Galán's hothouse icons', *Art in America* (July 1994), pp. 65–9.

Angel Zárraga. Mexico: Museo Rufino Tamayo, 1985.

Angel Zárraga: Paris–México. Mexico: PBA, n.d.

Arturo Elizondo. Mexico: Galería OMR, 1995.

Baddeley, O., 'Her dress hangs there: de-frocking the Kahlo cult', *Oxford Art Journal*, 14, 1 (1991), pp. 10–17.

Blas Galindo, C., *Enrique Guzmán: transformador y víctima de su tiempo*. Mexico: CNCA, 1992.

Borsa, J., 'Frida Kahlo: marginalization and the critical female subject', *Third Text*, 12 (Autumn 1990), pp. 21–40.

Cameron, D., *Julio Galán*. New York: Annina Nosei Gallery, 1992.

Carrier, J., 'Family attitudes and Mexican male homosexuality', *Urban Life*, 5, 5 (1976), pp. 359–76.

Carrier, J., 'Mexican male bisexuality', in F. Klein and T. Wolf (eds), *Bisexualities: Theory and Research*. New York: Haworth Press, 1985, pp. 75–85.

Carrier, J., 'Gay liberation and coming out in Mexico', in G. Herdt (ed.), *Gay and Lesbian Youth*. New York: Haworth Press, 1989, pp. 225–53.

Carrier, J., *De los otros: Intimacy and Homosexuality among Mexican Men*. New York: Columbia University Press, 1995.

Cervantes, M. and MacKenzie, B. (eds), *Julio Galán: exposición retrospectiva*. Monterrey and Mexico: MARCO-MAM, September 1993–April 1994.

Cortázar: post-modernidad y romanticismo. Mexico City: INBA/PBA, 1995.

Covarrubias, J. M., 'Here and now: ten years, but also a century', *James White Review*, 48 (Summer 1996), p. 1.

Damian, C. E., 'Julio Galán', *Latin American Art*, 6, 1 (1994), pp. 58–9.

Debroise, O., *Alfonso Michel*. Mexico: CNCA, 1992.

Debroise, O., *Javier de la Garza: fusiones*. New York and Mexico: Calvin Morris, Inc./Galería OMR, 1992–3.

de la Torre, M. (ed.), *José Garcia Ocejo: su obra*. Veracruz, 1992.

Driben, L., *Julio Galán*. New York: Annina Nosei Gallery, 1990.

Drucker, M., *Frida Kahlo: Torment and Triumph in Her Life and Art*. New York: Bantam, 1991.

El mundo de Jesus Reyes Ferreira. Mexico: Museo de Arte Moderno, 1962.

Enrique Guzmán (1952–1986): precursor de su tiempo. Mexico: Galería Arvil, 1995.

Ex profeso: recuento de afinidades. Mexico: UNAM/Museo Nacional del Chopo/Circulo Gay Cultural, 1989.

Exposición homenaje a Angel Zárraga, 1886–1946. Mexico: Museo de Arte Moderno, 1969.

Exposición homenaje a Jesus Reyes Ferreira. Mexico: Palacio de Bellas Artes, 1979.

Exposición homenaje a Saturnino Herrán en los 60 años de su muerte 1887/1918. Mexico and Aguascalientes: INBA/Museo de Aguascalientes, 1978.

Flores Guerrero, R., *5 pintores mexicanos: Frida Kahlo – Guillermo Meza – Juan O'Gorman – Julio Castellanos – Jesus Reyes Ferreira*. Mexico: UNAM, 1957.

Franco, J., *Plotting Women: Gender and Representation in Mexico*. New York: Columbia University Press, 1989.

Garrido, F. (ed.), *Saturnino Herrán: accompañado por textos de Ramón López Velarde*. Mexico: Fondo Editorial de la Plastica Mexicana, 1988.

Garrido, L., *Saturnino Herrán*. Mexico: Fondo de Cultura Económica, 1971.

Gomez Arias, A. *et al.*, *Frida Kahlo: exposición homenaje*. Mexico: PBA, 1977.

Herencia y creación. Maria de la Soledad Baz de Wörnen – Ben-Hur Baz Viaud – Emilio Baz-Viaud – Juan Wörner Baz – Marysole Wörner Baz. Mexico: Museo de Arte Moderno, August–October 1991.

Herrera, H., *Frida: A Biography of Frida Kahlo*. New York: Harper & Row, 1983.

Herrera, H., *Frida Kahlo: The Paintings*. New York: HarperCollins, 1991.

Homenaje a Chucho Reyes, Jesus Reyes Ferreira. Mexico: Museo Rufino Tamayo, 1984.

Jesus Reyes Ferreira: pintor mexicano y universal. Mexico: Banco Serfin, 1987.

Julio Galán. Rotterdam: Witte de With, 1990.

Kozloff, M., 'Memories of the future', *Artforum*, (October 1991), pp. 106–11.

Lowe, S., *Frida Kahlo*. New York: Universe, 1991.

Lumsden, I., *Homosexuality, Society and the State in Mexico*. Toronto and Mexico: Canadian Gay Archives/Solediciones, 1991.

Luna Arroyo, A., *Zárraga*, 2nd edn. Mexico: Salvat, 1993.

Merewether, C. and del Conde, T., *The Art of Frida Kahlo*. Adelaide and Perth: Art Gallery of South Australia/Art Gallery of West Australia, 1990.

Mesa, J., 'Los cien años de Manuel Rodriguez Lozano', *Boys & Toys*, 14 (November 1995), pp. 66–8.

Monsiváis, C., 'Ortodoxia y heterodoxia en las alcobas. Hacia una crónica de costumbres y creencias sexuales en México', *Debate Feminista*, 6, 2 (April 1995), pp. 183–210.

Muñoz, V., 'Saturnino Herrán y la Escuela Nacional de Bellas Artes', *Revista ENAP–UNAM*, 2, 6 (December 1987), pp. 23–30.

Muñoz, V. (ed.), *Saturnino Herrán: la pasión y el principio*. Mexico: Banco BITAL, 1994.

Nahum B. Zenil: Witness to the Self/Testigo del ser. San Francisco: Mexican Museum, 1996.

Novo, S., *The War of the Fatties and Other Stories from Aztec History*. Austin, TX: Texas University Press, 1994.

Ortiz Gaitán, J., *Entre dos mundos: los murales de Roberto Montenegro*. Mexico: UNAM, IIE, 1994.

Paz, O., *The Labyrinth of Solitude: Life and Thought in Mexico*. Harmondsworth: Penguin, 1985.

Pellizzi, F., *Julio Galán*. New York: Annina Nosei Gallery, 1989.

Prignitz-Poda, H. *et al.*, *Frida Kahlo: Das Gesamtwerk*. Frankfurt: Neue Kritik, 1988.

Ramírez, F., *Saturnino Herrán*. Mexico: UNAM, 1976.

Ramírez, F., 'Notas para una nueva lectura de su obra', in *Saturnino Herrán: pintor mexicano (1887–1987)*. Mexico: INBA, 1987, pp. 7–32.

'Recuento de afinidades/Inventory of affinities', *Out/Look*, 12 (Spring 1991), pp. 61–5.

Rodolfo Morales: Games and Recollections. San Francisco: Mexican Museum, 1996.

Saturnino Herrán: Jornadas de homenaje (Cuadernos de historia de arte, 52). Mexico: UNAM, IIE, 1989.

Schaefer-Rodriguez, C., 'The power of subversive imagination: homosexual utopian discourse in contemporary Mexican literature', *Latin American Literary Review*, 33 (1989), pp. 29–41.

Schneider, M. *et al.* (eds), *Julio Galán*. Mexico: Banco Serfin, 1993.

Sims, L. S., *Julio Galán*. Monterrey: Museo de Monterrey, 1987.

Springer, J. M., 'Julio Galán. Nostalgia de lo inalcanzable', *ArtNexus*, 59 (July–September 1994), pp. 48–52.

Sullivan, E. J., 'Nahum Zenil's auto-iconography: Mexican-ness in Mexican painting of the eighties', *Arts Magazine* 63, 3 (1988), pp. 86–91.

Sullivan, E. J., 'Nahum B. Zenil y la política del alma', *Arte en Colombia*, 42 (December 1989), pp. 76–9.

Sullivan, E. J., *Nahum B. Zenil*. Mexico: Galería de Arte Mexicano, 1989.

Sullivan, E. J., 'Sacred and profane: the art of Julio Galán', *Arts Magazine*, (Summer 1990), pp. 51–5.

Sullivan, E. J., 'Frida Kahlo', *Latin American Art*, 3, 4 (December 1991), pp. 31–4.

Taylor, C. L., 'Mexican gay life in historical perspective', *Gay Sunshine*, 26/27 (1975–6), pp. 1–3.

Tendencies: New Art from Mexico City. San Francisco: Walter/McBean Gallery, San Francisco Art Institute, 1995.

Tibol, R., *Frida Kahlo: crónica, testimonios y aproximaciones*. Mexico: Ed. de Cultura Popular, 1977.

Toussaint, M., *Saturnino Herrán y su obra*. Mexico: 1990 (1920).

Valle-Castillo, J., 'El desnudo en Saturnino Herrán', *PLURAL: Revista cultural de Excelsior*, 103 (April 1980), pp. 33–7.

Cuba

Alonso, A. G., *Amelia Peláez*. Havana: Museo Nacional/PBA, 1988.

Amelia Peláez: exposición retrospectiva, 1924–1967. Caracas: Fundación Museo de Bellas Artes, 1991.

Blanc, G. V. *et al.*, *Amelia Peláez: A Retrospective, 1896–1968*. Miami: Cuban Museum of Arts and Culture, 1988.

de Vries, S., 'Thoughts in flight', *Cuba Update*, 14, 1–2 (February–March 1993), pp. 19–20.

Echevarría, G. C., *Antología de un artista: Raúl Martínez*. Havana, 1995.

Hernández, E., 'Cuadros móviles, filosofia y "mala rabia"', *Cartelera*, 252 (25–31 December 1986), p. 3.

Hernández, E., 'De donde se habla de René Peña, el cocinero, el ladrón, su mujer, su amante y el Quijote', *Atlántica*, 15 (Winter 1996), pp. 58–62.

Leirner, M., *Sexual Politics in Cuba: Machismo, Homosexuality, and AIDS*. Boulder: Westview, 1994.

Lumsden, I., *Machos, Maricones and Gays: Cuba and Homosexuality*. Philadelphia: Temple University Press, 1996.

Mosquera, G., 'Manuel Mendive y la evolución de su pintura', in *Exploraciones en la plástica Cubana*. Havana, 1983, pp. 232–310.

Mosquera, G., 'Ernesto Pujol: Cuba visited once more', *Cuba Update*, 16, 4–5 (October 1995), p. 43.

Pérez Vidal, A., 'Descubriendo a Alfredo Guevara (entrevista)', *Contrapunto* (n.d.), pp. 51–4.

René Portocarrero: 25 años de color de Cuba. Havana: Museo Nacional/PBA, 1988.

Smith, L. M. and Pedula, A., *Sex and Sexual Revolution in Socialist Cuba*. New York and Oxford: Oxford University Press, 1996.

Valdés Jr, G., 'El color de la palabra: 32 artistas cubanos', *STET*, 1, 2 (Winter 1992).

van den Boogaard, H., *Cuba. Homoseksualiteit: ideologie en politiek*. Amsterdam: SUA, 1982.

Viso, O. M. (ed.), *Carlos Alfonzo; Triumph of the Spirit. A Survey 1975–1991*. Miami: Miami Art Museum, 1998.

Puerto Rico

Arnaldo Roche Rabell: los primeros diez años. Monterrey: MARCO, 1993.

del Conde, T. and Sullivan, E. J., *Arnaldo Roche Rabell*. Mexico: MAM, 1995.

Entre cortinas: el gran desnudo caribeño. Pinturas y dibujos de Myrna Baez. San Juan: Galería Botello, 1994.

Expresiones: un grito visual. San Juan: O.P.Art/Instituto de Cultura Puertorriqueña, 1995.

García Gutiérrez, E., 'Arnaldo Roche, agonista: la lucha por la identidad', *Plástica*, 17, 2 (September 1987), pp. 18–28.

García Gutiérrez, E., 'Arnaldo Roche Rabell: New Expressionism', *Latin American Art*, 2, 1 (Winter 1990), pp. 40–4.

García Gutiérrez, E., 'Eros y Zilia Sánchez', *El Nuevo Día*, 6 October 1991, pp. 12–15.

García Gutiérrez, E., 'Néstor Millán. El espectador como intérprete', *El Nuevo Día*, 19 May 1996, pp. 10–13.

García Gutiérrez, E. and Bonesteel, M., *Arnaldo Roche Rabell: eventos, milagros y visiones*. Rio Piedras: Museo de la Universidad de Puerto Rico, 1986.

García Gutiérrez, E. and Knight, G. G., *Arnaldo Roche Rabell: actos compulsivos*. Ponce de Leon: Museo de Arte de Ponce, 1984.

López, I., 'Néstor Millán: en otros cuerpos', *Imágen* (June 1996), p. 28.

Myrna Baez: pinturas. San Juan: Galería Botello, 1992.

Niurka, N., 'Zilia sublimiza el cuerpo feminino', *El Miami Herald*, 24 January 1982, n.p.

Pintura, escultura, grabado, dibujo. San Juan: Galería Francisco Oller, Universidad de Puerto Rico, 1984.

Pintura y gráfica de Myrna Baez. San Juan: Museo de Bellas Artes, Instituto de Cultura Puertorriqueña, 1985.

Prida, D., 'El erotismo espacial en la pintura de Zilia Sánchez', *Revista La Nueva Sangre*, 3, 9 (1970), n.p.

[Roche Rabell, A.], *In the Hands of the Beholder*. Chicago: Chicago Cultural Center, 1987.

Sarduy, S., 'Las topologías eróticas de Zilia Sánchez', in *Estructuras en secuencia*. San Juan: Universidad de Puerto Rico, 1970.

Tres décadas gráficas de Myrna Baez. San Juan: Museo de Arte de Puerto Rico, 1988.

Zilia Sánchez: tres decadas. Humacao: Museo Casa Roig, 1991.

Latino/a 'gay art' abroad

AIDS/Arts/Communities Realizing the Archive Project. Boston: Cyclorama, Boston Center for the Arts, 1996.

Almaguer, T., 'The cartography of homosexual identity and behavior', *differences*, 3, 2 (1991), pp. 75–100.

Alonso, A. M. and Koreck, M. T., 'Silences: Hispanics, AIDS, and sexual practices', *differences*, 1, 1 (1989), pp. 101–24.

Angeline, J., 'Maria Elena Gonzalez', *Art Nexus*, 20 (April–June 1996), p. 123.

Atkins, R., 'Art = Life', *Seven Days*, 24 May 1989.

Avena, T. and Klein, A., *Jerome: After the Pageant*. San Francisco: Bastard Books, 1996.

Avgikos, J., 'This is my body', *Artforum* (February 1991), pp. 79–83.

'"Brincando el charco" challenges homophobia and racism within Puertorican communities', *Au Courant*, 28 November 1994, p. 7.

Bruve-Novoa, J., 'Homosexuality and the Chicano novel', *Confluencia: Revista Hispanica de Cultura y Literatura*, 2, 1 (1986), pp. 69–77.

Cameron, D., 'Sweet thing', *Artforum* (December 1992), pp. 58–9.

Carr, E., 'Just another painter from East L.A.', *LA Weekly*, 16, 16 (18–24 March 1994), pp. 16–21.

Cooper, D. and Yancy, C. 'Lari Pittman: the August vigilante', *Artforum* (December 1990), pp. 54–7.

de Castro Mori, X., 'Félix Gonzalez-Torres: boyfriend in the sky', *Ars*, 4 (Spring/Summer 1996), pp. 28–9.

Domestic Partnerships: New Impulses in Decorative Arts from the Americas. New York: Art in General, 1996.

Elger D. *et al.* (eds), *Felix Gonzalez-Torres: catalogue raisonné.* Stuttgart, 1997.

El arte sana. Fourth Annual Latina/o Lesbian, Gay, Bisexual Visual Arts Show and Commemorative Archives Exhibit. San Francisco: Mission Cultural Center, 1994.

El jo divers: Laura Aguilar. Barcelona: Fundació 'La Caixa', 1998.

Felix Gonzalez-Torres. New York: Intar Gallery, 1988.

Fox, H. N., *Lari Pittman.* Los Angeles: LA County Museum of Art, 1996.

Give Life to Art: The First Step. New York and Fire Island Pines: Gallery (+) Positive/Visual AIDS, 1996.

¡Gronk! A Living Survey, 1973–1993. San Francisco: Mexican Museum, 1994.

Hulick, D. E., 'Laura Aguilar', *Latin American Art*, 5, 3 (1993), pp. 52–4.

Lugo, D., 'Brincando el charco: raza, preferencia sexual y nación', *Diálogo* (February 1996), p. 28.

McManus, I., *Dreamscapes: The Art of Juan González.* New York: Hudson Hills Press, 1994.

Miguel Ventura. Mexico: MAM, 1979.

Miguel Ventura. Mexico: Galería Arte Contemporáneo, 1990.

Miguel Ventura. Mexico: Galería Arte Contemporáneo, 1991.

Mooney, J., 'Queer pickings: the art of Lari Pittman', *Third Text*, 44 (Autumn 1998), pp. 79–86.

Moraga, C. and Anzaldúa, G., *This Bridge Called My Back: Writings by Radical Women of Color.* New York: Kitchen Table/Women of Color Press, 1981.

Morgada, M., 'Felix Gonzalez-Torres', *Ars*, 4 (Spring/Summer 1996), pp. 26–7.

Negrón-Muntaner, F., 'Echoing Stonewall and other dilemmas: the organizational beginnings of a gay and lesbian agenda in Puerto Rico, 1972–77', *Centro*, 4, 1 (Winter 1991–2), pp. 76–95; 4, 2 (Spring 1992), pp. 98–115.

Negrón-Muntaner, F., 'Beyond the cinema of the Other or towards another cinema', unpublished manuscript, 1995.

Nickas, R., 'Felix Gonzalez-Torres: all the time in the world', *Flash Art*, 161 (November–December 1991), pp. 86–8.

Ochoa, M., *La Ofrenda.* Ann Arbor: [self-published], 1991.

Palacios, M., 'Latin lesbo comic', unpublished manuscript, n.d.

Pogolotti, G., *Angel Acosta León.* Havana: Museo Nacional/Palacio de Bellas Artes, 1991.

Queer Raza: el corazón me dio un salto. San Francisco: Galería de la Raza, 1995.

Relya, L., 'What's love got to do with it?', *Frieze* (September–October 1994), pp. 46–51.

René Santos: Suspension of the Law. A Retrospective. New York: Grey Art Gallery and Study Center, 1994.

Román, D., 'Teatro Viva! Latino performance and the politics of AIDS in Los Angeles', in E. L. Bergman and P. J. Smith (eds), *¿Entiendes?* Durham, NC, and London: Duke University Press, 1995, pp. 346–69.

Schjeldahl, P., 'Tender sentience', *Village Voice*, 21 March 1995, p. 76.

Spector, N., 'Felix Gonzalez-Torres: travelogue', *Parkett* (1994), p. 24–37.

Spector, N., *Felix Gonzalez-Torres.* New York: Guggenheim, 1995.

Storr, R., 'Felix Gonzalez-Torres. Être un espion', *Art Press* (January 1995), pp. 24–32.

Storr, R., 'Setting traps for the mind and heart', *Art in America* (January 1996), pp. 70–7.

Tejada, R., 'Miguel Ventura', *Sulfur* (Spring 1996). Ypsilanti, MI: Eastern Michigan University, pp. 33–6.

The First Ten. New York: Archive Project, PS122 Gallery, 1995.

Trujillo, M., 'The dilemma of the modern Chicana artist and critic', *Heresies*, 2, 4 (1979), pp. 5–10.

Watney, S., 'In purgatory: the work of Felix González-Torres', *Parkett* (1994), pp. 38–63.

Windhousen, R., 'La naturaleza sensual de Maria Elena González', *El Nuevo Herald*, 23 November 1992, p. 3D.

Yarbro-Bejarano, Y., 'Laying it bare: the queer/colored body in photography by Laura Aguilar', in C. Trujillo (ed.), *Living Chicana Theory.* Berkeley: Third Women Press, 1998, pp. 277–305.

Zaya, O., 'La trilogía Cubana de Ernesto Pujol: el exilio, la memoria y el regreso', *Atlántica*, 15 (Winter 1996), pp. 119–33.

Index